CW01670059

JOHN WHITE ALEXANDER

AN AMERICAN ARTIST IN THE GILDED AGE

Mary Anne Goley

PWP

Published by Philip Wilson Publishers
an imprint of I.B.Tauris & Co. Ltd
London • New York
www.philip-wilson.co.uk

Copyright © 2018 Mary Anne Goley

The right of Mary Anne Goley to be identified as the author of this work has been asserted by the author in accordance with the Copyright, Designs and Patents Act 1988.

All rights reserved. Except for brief quotations in a review, this book, or any part thereof, may not be reproduced, stored in or introduced into a retrieval system, or transmitted, in any form or by any means, electronic, mechanical, photocopying, recording or otherwise, without the prior written permission of the publisher.

Every attempt has been made to gain permission for the use of the images in this book. Any omissions will be rectified in future editions.

ISBN: 978 1 78130 060 2

A full CIP record for this book is available from the British Library
A full CIP record is available from the Library of Congress

Library of Congress Catalog Card Number: available

Designed by Oliver Keen
Printed and bound in China by 1010 Printing

FSC www.fsc.org MIX Paper from responsible sources FSC® C016973

CONTENTS

This publication is generously supported by:

JOHN D. HODDER

NATALIE REED ADAMS

DONALD W. KREUZER

THELMA AND MELVIN LENKIN FAMILY CHARITABLE FOUNDATION, INC.

PETER AND PAULA LUNDER

THE HONORABLE MARILYN LOGSDON MENNELLO AND
MICHAEL MENNELLO,
FOUNDERS OF THE MENNELLO MUSEUM OF AMERICAN ART

RONALD D. ABRAMSON

HERSH D. COHEN

RISA MANN (in memory)

SAMUEL H. VICKERS

FOREWORD

MARY ANNE GOLEY HAS STOOD TO HER POST as the champion of the American artist John White Alexander, scholar of his work, curator of his exhibitions and now his biographer, for more than forty years. Artists need such champions if their work is to be held in public esteem and appreciated by coming generations, especially if, like Alexander, they have fallen below the radar. Those of his works that have commanded attention in recent times have been his *fin de siècle* pictures of femmes fatales, ancient and modern. What the present biography does so well is to present an artist who is altogether more complicated and rounded, portraitist as well as landscapist, decorative painter and muralist. Add to that his statesmanship as a leader of the arts, president of the National Academy of Design and other prominent bodies, and you end, as one contemporary put it, with "a man for all seasons".

Like many another would-be painter, the young Alexander crossed the Atlantic to complete his artistic education. Interestingly, this led him to Munich rather than Paris, where he joined a group of realists around the charismatic Frank Duveneck. The lure of Paris claimed him in the end, and it was there, during the 1890s, that he painted some of his most original and challenging compositions: those sinuous, undulating studies of women in distended poses and enormous dresses that seem on the point of flight. The model for many of these works was a lithe Parisian, Juliette Very, whose ability to strike a pose and assume a dramatic persona inspired the artist. Little is known of her, though she does appear to have modelled for the sculptor Auguste Rodin, one of Alexander's heroes. The symbolist pictures by Alexander made his reputation in Paris as an artist of rare originality, earning him in due course the award of the Légion d'honneur. Much of his income, however, derived from American portrait commissions, and his native country eventually reclaimed him.

Alexander's move to America was probably inevitable, given his reliance on American patronage and the responsibility of a wife and child. However, without the stimulus of the French art world and of his model Juliette, some of the electricity of his earlier work does seem to diminish. There were to be many triumphs, as his works earned plaudits in exhibitions across America, and you can trace innovations in the use of colour and light in his decorative studies of women. He was also much in demand as a portraitist, of men as well as women and children. In the theatre he designed sets and costumes, and he masterminded large-scale *tableaux vivants*, so popular at the time. Finally there are the murals, in the Library of Congress and the main entrance hall of the Carnegie Institute in Pittsburgh, the artist's home town, which combine allegory with scenes of labour. All this was achieved against a background of public involvement in the arts, as organizer, campaigner, lecturer and perpetual chairman. His hopes of creating a national exhibition center in New York to unite conservatives and radicals never materialized but it was not for lack of trying. The International Exhibition of Modern Art in 1913 at the Armory, New York and elsewhere, introduced American audiences to the latest avant-garde art in Europe, including Matisse, Picasso and the cubists, and opened up an unbridgeable gap between right and left in the American art world. That Alexander was seen to be on the wrong side of the line may explain his fall from grace to relative obscurity in the years following his early death in 1915, the result of fragile health and years of overexertion.

The present biography charts the story of an artist who deserves his place in the pantheon of American art. It is thoroughly researched, comprehensive in its coverage and insightful about the art and the engaging personality of its subject. Let us hope it leads to wider appreciation of Alexander's genius and contribution, not least a retrospective exhibition of his work that is long overdue.

Richard Ormond, CBE
Highgate, London, September 2016

PREFACE

MUCH WAS WRITTEN OF JOHN WHITE ALEXANDER at the time of his death (1865–1915), none of it more poignant than the tribute by his confidant, Harrison S. Morris, former director of the Pennsylvania Academy of the Fine Arts. Morris positioned the painter and distinguished head of the National Academy of Design in the Valhalla of American genius.[1] High praise indeed, for a man for whom Morris had unbridled admiration as the soul of chivalry, the essence of noble-heartedness, and having an uplifting radiance, and a warm grip of friendship. That was 1916.

Today, if you ask a specialist in American Art for a favourite painting by John White Alexander, the response most likely would be *Isabella and the Pot of Basil* (Boston Museum of Fine Arts) or *Repos* (Metropolitan Museum of Art); if you poll museum visitors, most likely nothing immediately comes to their mind. The purpose of this biography, the only one since Alexander's death just over 100 years ago, is to reclaim his rightful place in that Valhalla of American genius. Painter, illustrator, stage set and costume designer, and leader of men – this book makes a case for a revised narrative of the career of a man far less widely recognized than his contemporaries, John Singer Sargent and William Merritt Chase. Fresh observations are drawn, particularly about the modernity of his pictures of women – setting these apart and distinct from commissioned male and female portraits, where the artist is working for hire. Methodologically, the biography encourages a sustained and close examination of the pictures in order to decipher their true meaning. Organized chronologically, it tracks his evolution from mere portrait painter to a figure painter, while upending clichés about what it meant to be a modern painter at the end of the nineteenth century.

Endorsements in his lifetime as to his character and leadership were unwavering in their consistency. As a student at the Munich Royal Academy in the late 1870s, he earned a medal not only for first place in drawing but also for conduct and attendance. In the words of Oliver Dennett Grover, one of the

Duveneck boys, as quoted by Norbert Heermann, "Alexander of course was the born favorite and leader which he continued to be throughout his life."[2] On his election for the first time to the Presidency of the National Academy of Design during a time of dissension, Leon Dabo gave the ultimate vote of confidence: "most important of all, you, your personality, your great talent, should impress the art world of our country that there is no need for a 'secession' for a rival institution in our midst – but that the academy will admit that there are many expressions of beauty – that 'art' is not in the keeping of a few gentlemen no matter how refined their taste nor how profound their learning."[3]

The accolades accorded Alexander at the time of his death were uniform in their praise: "World Famous Painter," "One of America's Prominent Artists," "Great American Painter," and "Art World Mourns." The *New York Globe* of June 2, 1915 touched upon the salient points of his being: "Few men of his generation had a better sense of the beautiful. His spirit turned toward the bright and joyous things of life rather than toward its tragedies … But Mr. Alexander was more than [an] artist – he was a useful citizen, a friend highly prized, a man of most engaging personality." The strength of his character that sustained him in life was not unlike the resilience of a Huckleberry Finn: "Mark Twain once declared that many of the most important incidents in his story of Huckleberry Finn were told to him by Mr. Alexander who actually witnessed them on that river trip," the one down the Ohio with Robert Burns Wilson on an open boat in December 1874.[4] Like Huck, Alexander did not confront those in authority, but rather accepted them on their own terms, keeping his thoughts to himself.

There should be no surprise that in March 1916, eight months after his death, the Carnegie Institute mounted a large memorial exhibition of 76 pictures. This was followed by a smaller exhibit (46 pictures) under the auspices of the American Federation of the Arts at the Corcoran Gallery of Art in May 1916. In turn, a still significantly reduced exhibit (26–32 pictures) toured eleven museums beginning in Detroit in November 1916, circulating as far west as Colorado Springs, and continuing until November 1917 in Rhode Island.

Alexander made and sustained friendships for a lifetime, the deepest being those with ties to Pittsburgh. Colonel Edward J. Allen recognized the talents of this orphaned boy when he aided in identifying an unnamed customer of the Pacific & Atlantic Telegraph Co. by making a sketch. Soon thereafter Allen brought him into his household and became his guardian, mentor and confidant for life. Edward Elisha Phelps was the son of a trunk dealer and a high-school classmate; later, as an employee in the controller's office of the city of Pittsburgh, Phelps was well positioned to advise Alexander about investments. John W.

Beatty, a friend from the days of the Scalp Level School of landscape painters, who preceded Alexander at the Munich Royal Academy, relied heavily on the advice of his friend as the director of the Carnegie Institute and the Carnegie International. Charles and Albert G. Reinhart treated him like a third brother, Charles while at Harper's and Ab as his companion in Munich and Polling. Thomas Shields Clarke, another Pittsburgher and a Princetonian, was a lifelong friend whose grandfather was brother-in-law to the railroad baron, philanthropist and patron of the arts William Thaw. Though not a Pittsburgher, Harrison S. Morris was a confidant of Alexander during and after Morris's time serving as Director of the Pennsylvania Academy of the Fine Arts.

Individuals central to his development included Richard Watson Gilder, editor of *The Century* and founder of the Fellowcraft Club, whom Alexander succeeded as its President. Robert Abbe, whose family was an early patron, was a renowned surgeon and pioneer in radiology, and was best man at Alexander's wedding. Alexander knew Mark Twain from the early days when they both worked for *Harper's*; he attended his birthday celebrations and painted his portrait and that of his daughter. Whistler, whom Alexander first met on a canal in Venice in the summer of 1880, was very grateful to Mr. and Mrs. Alexander who, unlike others, were at his side during the second hearing of the Eden trial in Paris in 1897.

He found a partner for life in Elizabeth Swan Williamson Alexander; the old-fashioned way. They knew each other first as friends, then a long engagement followed, beginning in late December 1884, with their union in marriage taking place in November 1887. Not of the same social class as his wife, the painter benefited from the privileges and connections of her family to Princeton and the Equitable Life Assurance Company (now AXA). Her great-grandfather, Archibald Alexander, was the first professor and principal of the Princeton Theological Seminary from its foundation in 1812 until his death in 1851. Alexander Road and two separate Alexander Halls on the Princeton campus are named after him. Archibald's eldest son, Dr. James Waddell Alexander, was a leading clergyman of the Presbyterian Church. As rector of the Fifth Avenue Church in New York City from 1849 until his death ten years later, he served a congregation of great wealth and influence. His brother, William Cowper Alexander served as the first President of the Equitable Life Assurance Company from 1859 until his death in 1874. Various members of the Alexander family came to hold high-ranking positions in the firm. Elizabeth's brother Henry Martyn Alexander was a director. Her father, nephew to Archibald and father-in-law to the painter, James Waddell Alexander, Sr., was the third President of Equitable, with his brother William serving as Secretary. As President of Equitable, James was a formidable presence, and an influential one. His social connections created many opportunities for his son-in-law to gain portrait commissions, particularly from those associated with the insurance company.

My study of Alexander began in 1973 as a graduate student at Case Western Reserve University and the Cleveland Museum of Art. In anticipation of writing a dissertation, I chose Alexander as my subject and gained an introduction to his granddaughter, Irina Reed. Her father, James Waddell Alexander II, a Princeton mathematician with a specialty in algebraic topology and one of the first members of the Institute of Advanced Study (along with Einstein), had died in 1971 leaving an estate of his father's paintings, letters and ephemera. The trove of letters reveals the journey of an orphaned youth rising with resourcefulness and resilience above the station into which he was born. The size of the estate was a shock to Irina, particularly as her father displayed very little of her grandfather's work in his home. I was permitted unfettered access to the estate, cataloguing and photographing works of art, taking notes, and documenting labels and inscriptions on the paintings prior to the estate being placed on the market in 1980. My inventory of slides documents the estate paintings in their original condition. Unfortunately, a portion of the estate pictures was lost when a cargo ship went down at sea in 1997. Irina's daughters enthusiastically continue their mother's legacy and remain supportive of my research, including the publication of this book.

In reconstructing the details of another person's life from the recent past, one can be blessed by an abundance of archival material, and cursed by the lack, or defectiveness, thereof. The worry for the scholar is always that something may be overlooked; but in the case of Alexander another worry is the inaccuracy of his wife's well-intended recollections, including the lists she made for the 1916 memorial exhibition catalogue. The cache of papers from the estate was deposited with the Archives of American Art; because of my early access to the estate, my records include documentation of items that for an unexplained reason were not transferred to the Archives. For example, the whereabouts of a concept drawing for *Isabella and the Pot of Basil* is unknown,[5] as is a photo album of postcards of old master paintings kept by the artist.

These postcards of reproductions of paintings and prints, mounted in an album, are of importance as an insight into what influenced Alexander. In particular, Peter Paul Rubens was well represented by *Rubens and Isabella Brant in the Honeysuckle Arbor* (Figure 5), *Portrait of Maria de' Medici*, and *Portrait of Jan Gaspar Gevartius*. From the Prado collection were postcards of

Velázquez's *Mariana of Austria, Queen of Spain* and *The Infanta Margarita de Austria* (considered to be by Velázquez at the time). Of great relevance to Alexander's scheme for the Carnegie murals was a reproduction of a painting by his French contemporary Henri Martin, of the *Apparition of Clemence Isaure* from the mural series in the Salle des Illustres in the Capitole in Toulouse (Figure 72). Other images mounted in the album included Albert Besnard's *Mme. Réjane* and prints by Durer.

Piecing together information from a myriad of sources other than the Reed cache had the excitement of discovery and has richly enhanced this study. The papers of Charles Mills (a "Duveneck Boy") in the library of William H. Gerdts served as a primary source for the life of Duveneck's followers in Munich, Polling, Florence, and Venice. To Roy Pederson I am grateful for sharing with me the unfinished autobiography of Albert G. Reinhart by his widow that sheds light on his and Alexander's departure together to Europe in 1877, their final destination being the Munich Royal Academy. The papers of Harrison S. Morris are invaluable in understanding the politics behind the Harrisburg Capitol mural commission and shed much light on the deteriorating and debilitating state of Alexander's health, to the extent that the question becomes: how was Alexander able to continue? The Carnegie Institute papers reveal the unconditional support of Alexander for his friend John Wesley Beatty as the latter inaugurated the Carnegie International and continuing until Alexander's death. Several letters in the Mark Twain Papers & Project, University of California, Berkeley, confirm business ties in the mid 1880s between Twain and Elizabeth Alexander's uncle, Henry Martyn Alexander, Sr., a principal of Alexander & Green. Elizabeth Cahill shared with me a December 1894 letter from Elizabeth Alexander to Edna Allen, Cahill's adoptive great-aunt, a daughter of Colonel Allen and Alexander's favorite among the Allen children. In it, Elizabeth Alexander confides that her husband has discovered the perfect model (that is, the Parisian Juliette Very). Finally, the Alexander Autograph Collection in the Department of Rare Books and Special Collections, Firestone Library, Princeton University, was compiled by Alexander's nephew DeForest, and consists of letters written by historically prominent figures. The collection includes several letters given to him by Alexander, among them six sent to Alexander by Whistler. The Phyllis Harrington Papers, at the Mark Twain Birthplace, verify that Elizabeth Alexander designed costumes to her husband's specification to be worn by his models. The Malvina Hoffman papers at the Getty Research Institute contain sketchbooks with class studies made by Hoffman when a student of Alexander (Figure 58).

The curatorial process by which certain late nineteenth-century American paintings disappear from museum walls and museum collections, relegated to storage or deaccessioned, and eventually forgotten, is a matter of the vagaries of taste – even of the lack of curiosity and the thirst for discovery. At the time of Alexander's death, two years following the Armory Show, the notion of beauty and the reputation of the conveyors thereof, such as Robert Blum, William M. Chase, Thomas Dewing, Arthur W. Dow, Alexander Harrison, Childe Hassam, J. Alden Weir, and others began gradually to be relegated to obscurity in favor of the practitioners of fragmented forms, sharp angles and the elusive fourth dimension. By the late 1950s and 60s many museums chose to deaccession their work and replace it with examples of contemporary art. Such was the fate of Alexander's *A Ray of Sunlight* (Figure 53, deaccessioned by Minneapolis Institute of Arts), *Auguste Rodin* (Figure 54, deaccessioned by the Cincinnati Art Museum), and *A Meadow Flower* (Figure 86, deaccessioned by the Corcoran Gallery of Art).

A renewed interest in Alexander in our time has been gradual, beginning with *Revealed Masters*, a prescient 1974 exhibition by William Gerdts that anointed artists "equally obscure but of equal merit" and ripe for discovery. On the cover of the exhibition catalogue was Alexander's most symbolist work, *Isabella and the Pot of Basil*. Two other exhibitions followed in 1976 and 1979 that pursued the symbolist line of investigation, placing Alexander in the context of *fin-de-siècle* decadence: *The Pre-Raphaelite Era 1848–1914* (Rowland and Betty Elzea) and *American Imagination and Symbolist Painting* (Charles Eldredge). Working with Alexander's granddaughter, Irina Reed, I was able to organize a small survey for the National Collection of Fine Arts (now Smithsonian American Art Museum) in 1976. Meanwhile *Munich & American Realism in the 19th Century* (Michael Quick, 1978) examined the student years of the Duveneck Boys of which Alexander was one at the Munich Royal Academy and later in Polling, Bavaria. Then came the excitement of a fresh cache of pictures from the estate of James W. Alexander II that generated two exhibitions at James Graham & Sons Gallery, New York, in 1980 and 1985. An atypical two-figure composition on a divan (Figure 40) acquired by the Detroit Institute of Arts from Graham Gallery was included in the Institute's exhibition *The Quest for Unity* in 1983. I drew on pictures remaining in the family to mount an exhibit of still-life paintings at the Federal Reserve Board in 1995. In 1996 there was interest abroad in his Munich period with the exhibition *Vice/Versa 1813–1913* (Deutsches Historisches Museum, Berlin), for which the family lent *Bavarian Peasant*. Works by Alexander frequently appear in exhibitions organized on the themes of Symbolism and the influence of Whistler. Such was the case with *Lost Paradise* (Museum of Fine Arts, Montreal), *Art Nouveau, 1890–1914* (National Gallery of Art, Washington, DC) and *Americans in Paris, 1860–1900* (Boston Museum of Fine Arts) which highlighted *Isabella and the Pot of Basil*, a grand symbolist statement, yet nevertheless an aberration in his oeuvre. Other exhibitions, such as *After Whistler* (High Museum of Art, 2003), *Like Breath on Glass* (The Clark, 2008) and *Rodin and America* (Iris & B. Gerald Cantor Center for Visual Arts, Stanford University, 2011), explored Whistlerian aspects of Alexander's technique and style. In recent developments, Alexander's work will be considered in terms of pictorialism in *American Art in Clarence H. White and His World: The Art and Craft of Photography, 1895–1925* (Princeton University Art Museum, Princeton, New Jersey, (October 7, 2017–January 7, 2018).

This investigation aims to become the standard by which all further Alexander research will be based, correcting misstatements and misperceptions and establishing new details of his biography as well as his artistic career. It places him stylistically and aesthetically within the formal and thematic innovations of his time, while acknowledging the assimilation of a myriad of aesthetics with their commonalities and differences. It is imperative to the understanding of his oeuvre to take a prolonged look at his figure painting to fully grasp his unique contribution, transforming what he learned from others into his own. Tonal harmonies with an accent of color are lessons learned from Whistler. The use of coarse-weave canvas is the application of a technique practiced by the Nabis. So too, are compositions with sharp angles that cut off the edges of figures and corners of rooms. But what is uniquely his own is the movement of the figure, manipulated into twists and turns that are frankly unnatural, if not anatomically impossible. As will be noted, Alexander had developed an expertise on the Delsarte system of gesture and movement. With his understanding of Delsarte's tenets and with the perfect model for his purposes in Juliette Very, he produced a body of work, primarily in France, that is startlingly original and like no other. The genius of the figure pictures of the 1890s in Paris – a compressed state of sentiment and movement – was unlocked by what Juliette Very brought to the creative process. One of the finest examples of Alexander's modern tendencies is *The Blue Bowl* (Figure 50, Museum of Art, Rhode Island School of Design), which sees the figure of Juliette Very manipulated in a flat space that defies the allusion of gravity and perspective.

The challenge in studying Alexander, however, remains to redefine the place held by this genius of American imagination. The purpose of this biography is to meet that challenge, addressing the critical remarks made by John Richardson, the pre-eminent scholar of Picasso. In an interview with the author for his column in the July 2006 issue of *Vanity Fair* about the exhibition *Americans in Paris, 1860–1900*, Richardson observed that Alexander's pictures were the standout in an otherwise all too familiar ensemble of pictures by Cassatt, Chase, Eakins, Hassam, Homer, Prendergast, Robinson, Sargent, and Twachtman, among others. He concluded by equating Alexander's *Repos* to Sargent's *Madame X* and suggesting Alexander was overdue for an exhibit of his own.

As the reader turns the pages of this book, unfamiliar images will reveal themselves, some known only by black and white reproductions, or otherwise on the margins of Alexander studies. They enable fresh discoveries as to how Alexander conceived of a composition, how he devised a concept and his tendency to think and create serially. For instance, he often explored a particular theme repeatedly – a black cat, a divan or a mirror, or most notably of all, the effects of sunlight. If this biography succeeds in the telling of the Alexander story, the reader will put it down having discovered clues to reading his pictures and with many mischaracterizations and facts of omission corrected.

There are a few special people who deserve applause for their shared passion for an under-recognized painter. All labored in the trenches of research to aid and abet my efforts to elucidate the life of John White Alexander and to attempt to answer the question, "who was this useful citizen?" Stalwarts in my repeated entreaties for help were Jane Curley, Randall Gabrielan, David Grinnell, and Susanne Scharf. Jane Curley, who occupies a family cottage in Onteora, Tannersville, New York, is the closest thing to being Onteora's historian; my understanding of Alexander's time in Onteora and gaining sense of place, along with the surprise discovery of several pictures in private hands specific to the way of life in Onteora, is thanks to her. Randall Gabrielan, Monmouth County Historian and author of *Rumson: Shaping a Superlative Suburb* (in *The Making of America Series*), was key to understanding the part played by Seabright, N.J. in Alexander's history. The world of scholarship is a better place thanks to reference librarians such as David Grinnell and his colleagues Jennifer Needham, Archivist, Special Collections, and Zach Brodt, University Archivist, University of Pittsburgh. Grinnell's knowledge of the holdings of the special collections of the University of Pittsburgh Library System, and in particular, those concerning the history of Pittsburgh, allowed me to correct certain important assumptions. One was the timing of Alexander's return to America and his first assignment for *Harper's* in Pittsburgh in late 1880, and another was unraveling the confusion over two art events in the new Carnegie Music Hall and Art Galleries at the end of 1895, the second being a forerunner of the Carnegie International.

Thank goodness for Susanne Scharf and her understanding of German, particularly her ability to decipher old German typeface. W. Barry Thomason was the linchpin to researching the Blair family, their estate in New Jersey, Blairsden, the portrait of Mrs. C. Ledyard Blair, and Alexander's former studio on 123 East 63rd Street in New York City paid for by C. Ledyard Blair. Eric Denker, Senior Lecturer, National Gallery of Art, and his encyclopedic knowledge of Venice, identified sites depicted by Alexander. Thanks to Jan Reeder, Consulting Curator of the Brooklyn Museum Costume Collection at the Metropolitan Museum of Art, this study benefited from her encyclopedic knowledge of costume, that validated the individualism of Alexander's costumes. To Richard Ormond, whom I consider a friend, but who is widely known as the pre-eminent scholar on John S. Sargent, a contemporary of Alexander, I am grateful for his enduring intellectual and moral support. To Marc Simpson and to Ilene Fort, Senior Curator and the Gail and John Liebes Curator of American Art, Los Angeles County Museum of Art, two colleagues and distinguished scholars and curators, I am indebted for their time in critiquing a draft manuscript in need of polish. And I am grateful to Sophie Lynford for her generous offer to carry out research during her summer in Paris in 2012.

This biography is all the more satisfying because of two grand moments of discovery enabled by colleagues. The first was when Hélène Pinet, archivist of the Rodin Museum, Paris, put together two pieces of a puzzle. I asked her, as the author of a book on Rodin's models, if the name Juliette Very was familiar. It was not, but at the same moment she realized the significance of a receipt in the Rodin Museum Archives. Written on a brown scrap of paper that had lain heretofore unidentified in the museum archives for decades was a receipt for services signed by "J. Very," the one and the same Juliette Very who modeled for Alexander and subsequently for Rodin. A second triumph of discovery was when Rosella Mamoli personally examined Katherine de Kay Bronson's Birthday Book. She found that Alexander signed and illustrated the page for those born on October 7, thus confirming that Alexander partook of the Bronson hospitality in Venice along with other international guests in the summer of 1880.

There are two couples who bear the weight of history with pride of place and whose ongoing communications greatly informed this biography. Elizabeth and Lawrence Cahill are keepers of the Colonel Edward J. Allen family history and of Allen's relations with John White Alexander; Elizabeth provides the direct link to Colonel Allen, as the adopted daughter of Edna Allen (Rickmers). Marieanne von König, former director of the Museum Polling (Bavaria) and her husband Dominik are keepers of the legacy of Polling, which is particularly important for the study of the American students who colonized the village. These two couples are an example of a practiced devotion to history, with each of the couples complementing their partner and enthusiastically sharing their knowledge with others.

In one way or another, the efforts of many have been brought to bear on the project's ultimate form. In addition to those already mentioned, I extend my gratitude to the following who responded beyond the norms of a simple inquiry or appeal for help: Garrett Barmore, Museum Curator, W.M. Keck Earth Science and Mineral Engineering Museum, University of Nevada, Reno; Elizabeth Beaman, Christie's; Chantal Beauvalot; Kevin Bolling, Natural Resource Manager, Mark Twain State Park and Historic Site; Sue Canterbury, The Pauline Gill Sullivan Associate Curator of American Art, Dallas Museum of Art; Johan Cederlund, Zorn Museum; Connie Choi, Assistant Curator of American Art, Brooklyn Museum; Julie Edwards, Childs Gallery, Boston; Barbara Briggs Folger; Debra Force, Debra Force Fine Art; Deborah Hatch, San Francisco; Joan Hendricks, The Taft Museum; Michael Hendych; Sherry Hollingsworth; John Huffman, formerly Historic Site Administrator, Mark Twain Birthplace SHS; Karl E. Kusserow, Curator of American Art, Princeton University Art Museum; Mallorie Livingston, Taylor/Graham; Sabine Maggiani, Musée de Cahors Henri-Martin; Nancy Malloy, American Academy of Arts and Letters; Akemi May, Assistant Curator, Fine Arts, Carnegie Museum of Art; Judy Metro, Editor, National Gallery of Art; Dorothy Moss, Associate Curator of Painting and Sculpture, National Portrait Gallery; Tamera Lenz Muente, Assistant Curator, Taft Museum of Art; Ken Myers, Chief Curator, Detroit Institute of Arts; David Nissinson; Maureen O'Brien, Curator of Painting and Sculpture, Museum of Art, Rhode Island School of Design; Keely Orgeman, Assistant Curator, American Paintings and Sculpture, Yale University Art Gallery; Derek Ostergard; Michael Quick; The Pennsylvania Academy of the Fine Arts, Registrar's Office: Jennifer Johns, Mary Claire Ramirez and Gale Rawson; Lisa Peters; Diana Thompson, National Academy Museum; Stephanie Thompson, Jean and Graham Devoe Williford Charitable Trust; Joy A. Thornton; Steve Naifeh; Raymond Wemmlinger, The Players Club; Timothy J. De Werff, Century Association Archives Foundation; Elizabeth Wood, Stonington Historical Society; Sylvia Yount, Lawrence A. Fleischman Curator in Charge, American Wing, the Metropolitan Museum of Art; and Laura Vookles, Chair, Curatorial Department, Hudson River Museum.

Mary Anne Goley

1

A HUCKLEBERRY ORIGINAL

HAVING BEEN BROUGHT INTO THE WORLD with few advantages and leaving it with great privilege, John White Alexander, in a lifespan of only 59 years (1856–1915), personified the American dream. His upbringing was a matter of making the most of circumstances, both good and bad, much like Huckleberry Finn, to whom Mark Twain himself once compared him.[1] Harrison S. Morris, former director of the Pennsylvania Academy of the Fine Arts, predicted his place "in the Valhalla of our American genius" while mourning the loss of this "soul of chivalry" and the "warm grip of his loyalty," attributes that made Alexander the leader of men, and that only improved with age.[2] By 1909 he had risen to the pinnacle of the official art world as President of the National Academy of Design, favored guest at gilded age fêtes, popular public speaker by night and a painter in demand by day. Product of the Gilded Age as he was, none other than Charles Dana Gibson chose his tall slender frame as the consummate male counterpart to his Gibson Girl in illustrations. At the time of his death he was ranked with Whistler, Abbey and Sargent as one of "the big four."[3]

The timeline of Alexander's early years is sketchy. He was born on October 7, 1856, in Allegheny City, the impoverished section of what became Pittsburgh, to Scottish Presbyterians who had emigrated from Northern Ireland. His father, John Alexander, died about six months before his birth, a sister before then, and his mother (née Smith) when he was about five.[4] He was given a lesson in the vicissitudes of life, being prevailed upon by both his mother, Frances, and his grandfather, to witness her death. He continued to be raised by his god-fearing maternal grandfather, a bank cashier, who maintained discipline with a switch at the ready. Grandfather Smith and his second wife adhered to the strict religious tenets of the Covenanters, a Scottish Presbyterian movement. Sunday was for worship, beginning with prayers at home followed by church services.

Alexander was blessed with a resilient nature and positive outlook that served him all his life. Enrolled in Pittsburgh's Second Ward School, he took matters into his own hands against his grandfather's wishes and quit school to

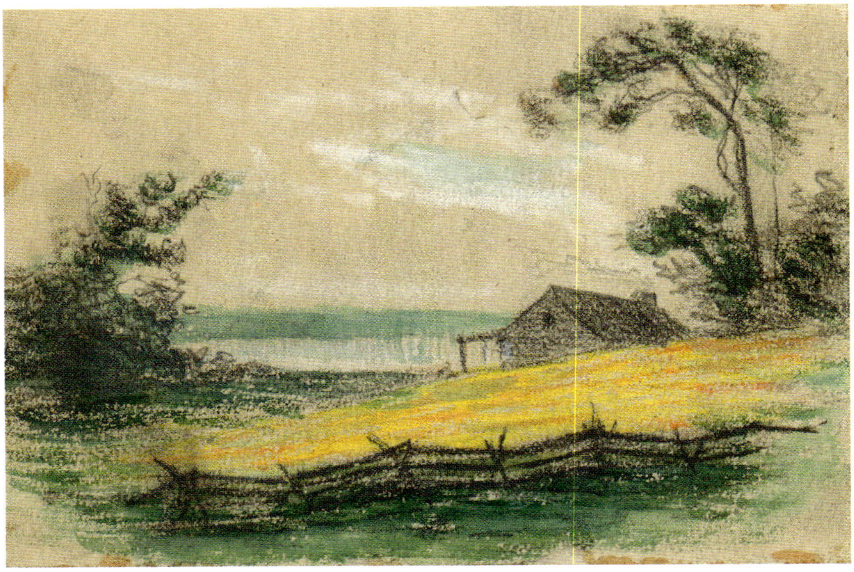

1
Wedding Album, Golden Anniversary, Edward Jay Allen and Elizabeth Allen. *c.* 1871, pastel, 3¼ × 4¾ in. (8.3 × 12.1 cm.), Hervey Allen Papers, 1831–1965, SC.1952.01, Special Collections Department, University of Pittsburgh

take a job at the Pacific & Atlantic Telegraph as a messenger boy (*c.*1868). From then on everything he did was to prepare for what he wanted most, to become an artist, specifically an illustrator and cartoonist in the tradition of Thomas Nast. He showed his quick-wittedness in making a sketch so as to identify a customer of the Pacific & Atlantic Telegraph Co. who left without leaving his name. Colonel Edward Jay Allen (1830–1915), secretary/treasurer of the company, recognized the boy's talent and took an interest in him. With the consent of Grandfather Smith, Allen assumed guardianship and brought Alexander into his household with his wife, Elizabeth Robeson Allen, her mother and brother, and four children, William, Edna, Mary and Edward. No doubt Allen regaled the boy with stories of past exploits, one of which was a trip west over the Oregon Trial claiming land near the village of Olympia on the shores of Puget Sound; another, fighting at Fredericksburg and Gettysburg during the Civil War as the Colonel in charge of the 155th Regiment Pennsylvania Infantry.

Aware of the value of education, Allen urged Alexander to return to school, which he did at the Fourth Ward School. It is also possible that he may have attended the School of Design in the 1870–1 academic year. However in the spring of 1871, at age 14, with an eye fixed on the future, he set up a studio in Pittsburgh with Robert Burns Wilson from Kentucky, another orphan who had toured with a circus before becoming an itinerant painter.[5] It may have been about this time that Allen entrusted Alexander with a commission to illustrate a Golden Wedding anniversary album for his parents with 18 pastels (Figure 1).[6] By September Wilson had moved on and Alexander entered Pittsburgh Central High School, no doubt at the behest of his guardian. Edward Elisha Phelps, son of a trunk dealer who though one year older became a friend for life, also entered Central High School and together they were placed in the academic department.[7] Students of the 1871 fall term reported to a new high school building on Fulton Street that was a state-of-the-art facility. It was built thanks to the vision of Principal Philotus Dean, who personally oversaw the design and construction of offices, laboratories, library, furniture, and a modern system of ventilation.[8] Dean did not live to witness the dedication on October 13. Instead, the duties fell to his successor Dr. Benjamin Cutler Jillson. Alexander attended this school for a year and a half, showing a proclivity for math, but he really did not like school.

Wanderlust got the better of him. He quit school without graduating and joined up with Wilson again. On board a skiff powered by oars or sail, to which they attached a Conestoga wagon, they navigated the Ohio River, heading for New Orleans. After two or three days' start they were already out of money, so they hatched a plan to provide for themselves by making sketches of farmhouses. This required stops at various river towns along their route where they would broadcast their services at private homes or local gathering places. The venture was not as lucrative as they had hoped, so they switched to copying portraits "from miserable originals, for miserable prices."[9] Better yet was the greater financial return they earned by repairing daguerreotypes, particularly those showing husbands and sons who had gone off to fight in the Civil War and did not return. Daguerreotypes are sealed with paper tape behind glass. It tarnishes and becomes blotchy once the seal is broken or deteriorates, thus exposing the daguerreotype to air. Wilson and Alexander repaired them by coating the back with black ink.[10]

From Caseyville, Kentucky, two days after Christmas, Alexander wrote the Allen family with news of his adventures. He complained about how slowly the skiff moved when they were rowing. The river was plentiful with fish and was probably the source of many a free meal, and they walked miles to the nearest post office to collect mail from home. They had been boarding in a cabin for several weeks, which Alexander described as follows: "It is built of logs, without any plastering, except mud between the logs, and there is not a single door in the house that is high enough for me to get through … The fire place is about six feet wide, and three deep. The chimney is made of wood and mud …"[11] In this rustic cabin Alexander and Wilson partook of a turkey feast for their

Christmas meal. It is probably this trip that Mark Twain was referring to when he declared that many of the most important incidents – murders, kidnappings, drunkenness, debauchery, and confidence scams – in his famous *Huckleberry Finn* were told to him by Mr. Alexander who actually witnessed them on that river trip.[12]

Alexander did not lose sight of his goal to go to New York City once he came of age and had saved enough money. Given his determination and his talent in drawing, he possessed the overconfidence of youth, mistakenly thinking he could readily land a job in the big city as an illustrator. He also knew that he would need academic training, either at the Cooper Institute or the National Academy of Design, but first he needed a job. Having arrived in New York in late February 1875, he set out to the big four publishing houses, *The Graphic*, *Frank Leslie's*, *Free Lance*, and *Harper's* with his only introduction being his presentation sketchbook, probably the ledger-size soft leather-covered book with " Drawings & Sketches" on the cover (Figure 2).[13] The title page is a masterful pyramid design with a classical head atop the center of an arch supported by columns. At the apex of an easel a jester bows. The easel is flanked by an anthropomorphic caricature of a quill pen on the left and an inkwell, partially full, on the right, the head of which is as grotesque as any drawing by the celebrated political cartoonist of the day, Thomas Nast. The response from the various editors was positive with several giving heartfelt advice. Only the editor of *The Graphic* dismissed him outright. At *Harper's*, Charles Parsons, head of the art department and an illustrator himself, cautiously held out the very slight possibility of a position for an office boy currently occupied by the son of an employee. Out of respect for the father, Parsons wanted to wait for the boy to realize he was ill-suited to the position and resign.[14]

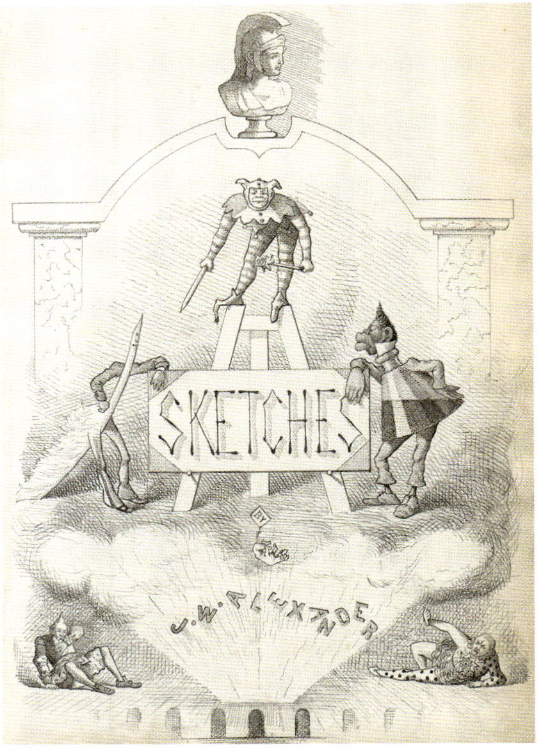

2
Title page, sketchbook sold by Stationers' Hall, New York, leather covered, *c.*1875, 15¾ × 10¼ in. (40 × 26 cm.), John White Alexander papers, Archives of American Art, Smithsonian Institution

The one personal letter of introduction that Alexander carried was from Colonel Allen to Dr. Marion Sims, a surgeon whom Allen had befriended during the Civil War. Sims, in turn, introduced Alexander to a Mr. Stewart who took the boy under his wing. He personally escorted Alexander back to *Frank Leslie's* where Leslie himself critiqued his book. As Leslie saw it, the problem was that Alexander was not yet skilled enough to draw on wood, but he was sure that with some instruction he could learn how to transfer a sketch into something the engraver could use. Toward this end he gave Alexander a plaster foot to make drawings from and advised him to attend the Academy for one month, after which he thought he could take him on.[15]

In the meantime Mr. Stewart had left the sketchbook with Francis Bicknell Carpenter who, eleven years before, had completed his best-known work, *First Reading of the Emancipation Proclamation of President Lincoln* (United States Senate collection) and was working on his portrait of Horace Greeley when Alexander visited the studio. After complimenting Alexander, saying he had four times as much talent as he had possessed at his age, Carpenter tasked him to make a drawing from the cast of the foot given to him by Mr. Leslie. After several tries Alexander became discouraged but Carpenter admonished him, saying he was too sensitive, and guaranteed that the second drawing would qualify him for admission to the Academy. Carpenter personally accompanied him to the Academy to meet Professor Lemuel Wilmarth.[16] Meanwhile, Mr. Soteldo, editor for a new magazine, *Free Lance*, held a similar opinion of Alexander's style and offered to introduce him to a Matt Morgan who would teach him how to work up a drawing for the engraver.[17] The extent to which these seasoned professionals went out of their way to help Alexander clearly suggests that he came to New York with more talent than most.

The search for a job took about three months. There apparently was no follow-up with Wilmarth, Matt Morgan or Leslie. Convinced that the best chance for advancement as an illustrator was to accept the position of office boy with the House of Harper, Alexander began what would become a lifetime association with the firm on May 19, 1875 with a beginner's wage of $3 per week.[18] He thrived as a member of the community of artists employed in the illustration department under Charles Parsons. Edwin A. Abbey, Arthur B. Frost, Ivan Pranishnikoff, and Charles Stanley Reinhart became lifelong friends, some more dear than others. Pranishnikoff was particularly fond of him, which proved invaluable a decade later in Paris. Once an illustrator, Alexander became part of a team of figure specialists along with Frost, Reinhart and Pranishnikoff, whose job was to work up a drawing on wood for the engraver. Granville Perkins was the landscape specialist and there was another for architecture. Alexander's first piece, which he described as "a little house," was published shortly after May 26, 1875.[19] The first illustration bearing his initials and those of a Mr. Bisbee who conceived the image, appeared on October 24, 1875.[20] His work was featured in both *Harper's Weekly* and *Monthly* but most of his early illustrations cannot be positively attributed to him, one exception being *The Centennial – Washington's Relics* (1876, Figure 3), executed while on assignment at the Centennial Exposition in Philadelphia.

It was Reinhart whom Alexander called an "intimate" friend, meaning his best friend while at *Harper's*.[21] After all they were two Pittsburghers living in the big city. After work they would walk home together. Reinhart often invited him in for dinner with his family. They shared a studio for which Alexander's form of payment was to model for Reinhart. It was to Reinhart that Alexander turned for advice about studying art abroad once what he called his "indenturship" with *Harper's* was over.[22] They shared mutual friends back home including those who frequented Scalp Level, a regional school led by George Hetzel (1826–99) named for its locale near Johnstown, Pennsylvania.[23] This is likely where Alexander first painted landscapes.[24]

When it came time to plan for Europe, Alexander did so in consultation with Colonel Allen during the Christmas of 1875, with added help from Reinhart.[25] He and the Colonel agreed that he would leave *Harper's* at the beginning of the summer of 1877 rather than October 7, the end of his indentureship. The plan was for Alexander to return to Pittsburgh where Colonel Allen had arranged sufficient commissions to help finance his trip abroad.[26] He would only take leave of *Harper's* once he knew how many commissions there were. Until his departure for Europe in August he would occupy himself with crayon portrait commissions, allowing two weeks for each portrait.[27]

Coincidentally, Charles Reinhart's younger brother, Albert (Ab) Grantley Reinhart, was equally determined to study abroad, turning down an invitation from his closest Pittsburgh friend to join him in a new business venture.[28] Charles introduced his best friend from New York to his brother in Pittsburgh and together they made their plans. The twenty-one-year-old Alexander, in the company of his new friend, twenty-two-year-old Ab Reinhart, departed from Philadelphia on the SS Indiana on August 18, 1877.[29] This was days after Alexander's most important assignment to date: "The Great Strike" in Pittsburgh, with at least three densely rendered illustrations, appeared in the August 11 issue of *Harper's Weekly*.

As aspiring artists, there was no doubt that to better themselves a European art education was superior to what was available in their native country. Their initial destination was Paris, but not for long. Arriving at the beginning of the school term, Alexander and Reinhart stayed with Charles Stanley Reinhart and his family for several days.[30] In short order the two formed a harsh assessment of the École des Beaux-Arts. They considered it run down. Professors were mostly

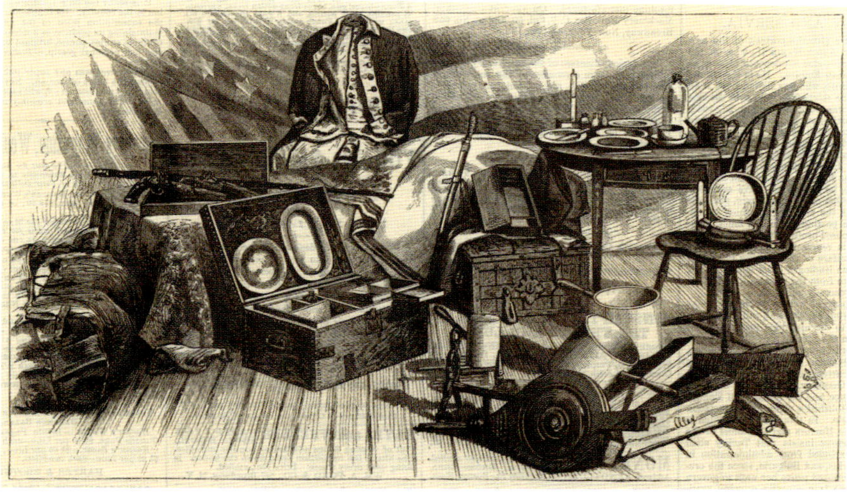

3
"The Centennial – Washington's Relics," *Harper's Weekly*, September 23, 1876. New York Public Library Digital Collections

absent, infrequently showing up in an otherwise unruly classroom. There was not a single picture that they liked. In a word, Alexander was "disgusted."[31] The fact that Munich was also cheaper made their decision to leave easier.

Munich, the self-proclaimed "city of the arts," culturally rich in historic and modern art and music, was enjoying an artistic renaissance under King Ludwig II of Bavaria. The Academy ranked above London, Paris and Brussels in popularity among American artists. Of 2,000 painters in Munich in 1875 about 40 were American students.[32] By the Ohio-born painter and etcher, Otto Bacher's calculations, the peak years for American enrollment in the Munich Royal Academy were 1878, 1883 and 1884 with 42, 44 and 43 students respectively.[33] The academy had earned a reputation as a bastion of the realist tradition promulgated by the appointment of Karol von Piloty to the directorship in 1874. He had appointed faculty who subscribed to his teachings that abrogated so-called "objective realism" for a realism of a different sort. Painters like Wilhelm von Diez, Wilhelm Lindenschmit, Alexander von Wagner, and Hungarian-born Gyula Benczúr practiced a brand of realism that sought to express the authenticity of the sitter – a real person with character. Their technique called for the robust application of paint, a practice that defined the singular look of the Munich school.

Arriving in Munich on September 8, Alexander and Reinhart had immediately to prepare for admission to the Academy.[34] The fall term began on October 10 and to qualify, a drawing made from life had to pass scrutiny. Having gained enrollment, a typical school day was from 7 am to noon and 1 to 6 pm in the summer, starting one hour later and finishing one hour earlier in the winter.[35] The professor came every second day to review an assignment, which in the case of the Antique class was to complete an outline drawing. Alexander's sketch of a face of a dead woman with large bones and sunken eyes so pleased the professor that he found no fault with it.[36] Though we have only a written description of this "faultless" sketch, there is a schoolboy's sketchbook in the Alexander papers in the Archives of American Art that holds a clue to the quality of his work at the time.[37] Inside the sketchbook are outline drawings, with a minimum of shading, of biblical and religious personages. They are types such as those that appeared in operatic history paintings by Gyula Benczúr (*Baptism of Vajk*, 1875) and Karol von Piloty (*Thusnelda in the Triumphal Procession of Germanicus*, 1873). The former was Alexander's drawing instructor and the latter taught both Benczúr and William M. Chase. Alexander would have been aware of these paintings as he practiced his drawing. The head of a bishop wearing his mitre, for example, could suit for one of the aforementioned history paintings.

Alexander's second term, where he advanced to the life class that began April 28, did not begin well. The professor, Ludwig von Löfftz, who Alexander did not name in his letters home, did not tolerate individuality but rather wanted the students "to do everything as he says."[38] Alexander suffered through a miserable first week in May 1878 with the professor so critical during two

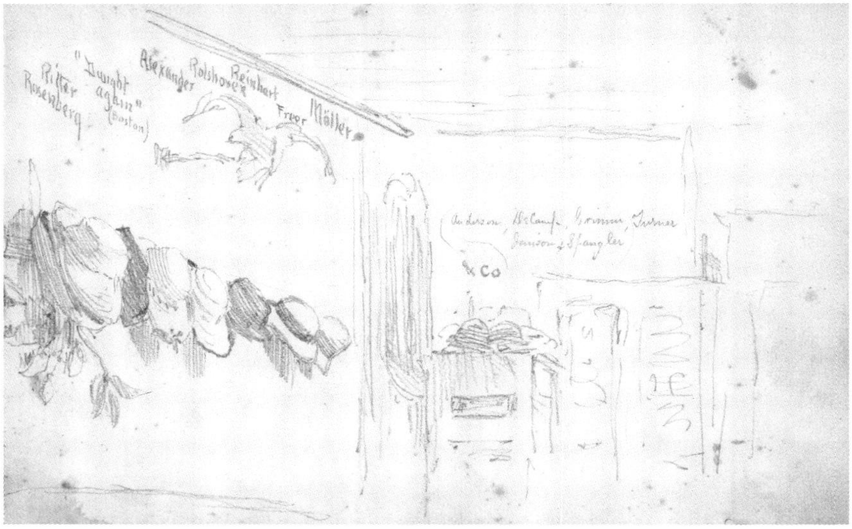

4
The American Club Polling, Summer –79, 1879, sketchbook page, graphite on paper, 6½ × 9¾ in. (16.5 × 24.8 cm.) (page), collection of Mr. and Mrs. Michael Quick

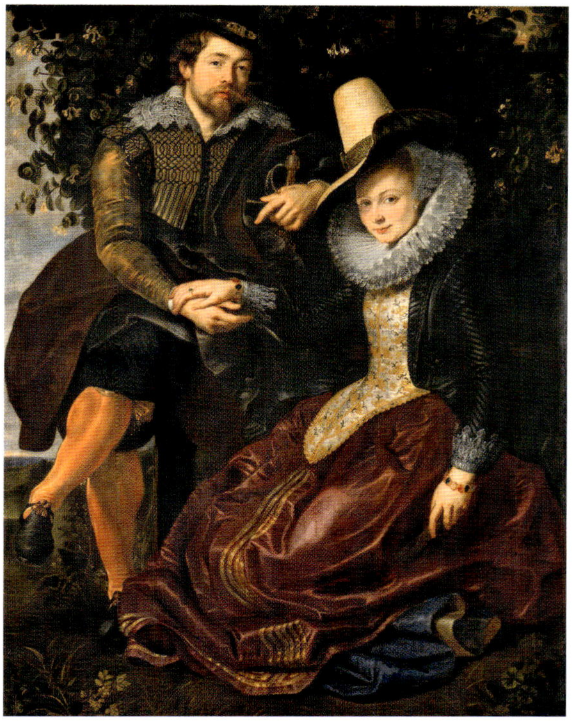

5
Peter Paul Rubens (1577–1640), *Rubens and His Wife, Isabella Brant, in the honeysuckle*, 1609–10, oil on canvas, 70 × 53½ in. (178 × 136 cm.), Alte Pinakothek, Munich. Photo: Erich Lessing/ Art Resource, New York

successive visits that he rubbed out Alexander's drawing.[39] This was enough for Alexander to make plans to sever ties with the academy. The lack of freedom to be original, the large size of the classes and the cost of living in Munich were reasons to alter his circumstances.

During term break Ab had visited the village of Polling, southwest of Munich. In the retelling, Alexander described Polling as "full of artists, who have studios … a gay, jolly and easy going set … they live at the hotel, and grow fat" (Figure 4).[40] To Americans, Polling, with its pronounced steeple, a cluster of buildings dominated by a former monastery and a flowing brook through the center, was a quintessential picturesque European village. German artists had been going there since 1830, but Americans began to frequent it in the 1870s. Students either registered at the hotel or rented a room in a private home. Frank Duveneck was the very first American to sign the hotel register on March 30, 1872.[41] Alexander chose to rent a room in the home of Herr and Frau Josef Seitz, residing at Haus 38 (today Propst-Hartl-Strasse 10) in June 1878.[42] Other boarders at Haus 38 were the Americans Charles Mills, Louis Ritter and the two Turners, Ross and Walter, but it is not clear if they were there at exactly the same time as Alexander.[43] Polling's main attraction for artists perpetually in search of affordable studios and housing was the former monastery building. The lower floors had been converted into a stable for cattle and one wing was a brewery. This left the small rooms where the monks had slept available for rent as studios at a cost of 8 marks per month.

Camaraderie was warmly described in Alexander's letters. It was indeed a life among a group of friends filled with shared ambitions and experiences. When Alexander and Reinhart arrived in Polling, the American, J. Frank Currier (1843–1909) was the "old man whose opinions carry the most weight."[44] His strength as a painter was for portrait heads and figure painting. Alexander was in awe of how explosive Currier could get with the handling of the brush: "In some places the paint is loaded up fully a quarter of an inch – and so rough that one can hardly tell whether they are upside down or not unless he gets away about six or eight feet."[45] The younger men took enormous satisfaction in

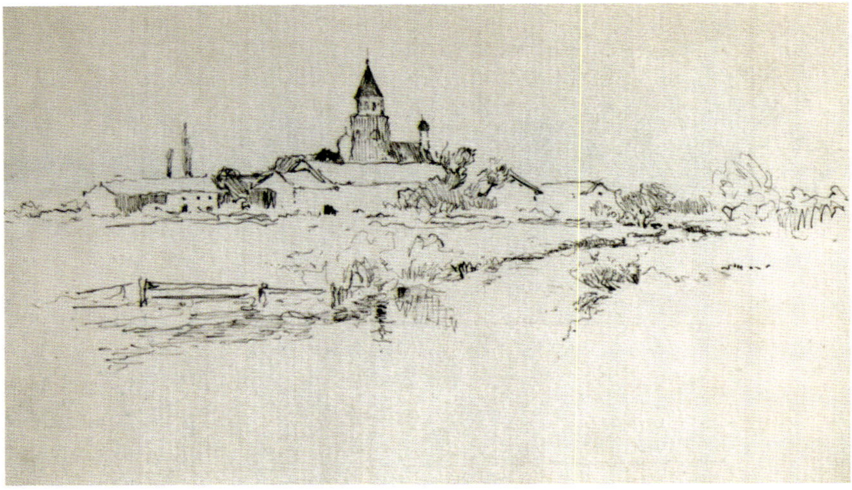

6
Polling skyline, sketchbook manufactured by Adrian Brugger, 1878–9, pencil, 6¾ × 4 in. (17.1 × 10.2 cm.), American Academy of Arts and Letters, New York, gift of Mrs. John White Alexander

joining Currier on sketching excursions to the nearby mountains in the direction of Dessein and Murnau, and to Munich to study the Old Masters.[46] Evidence of visits to the Alte Pinakothek and a favored painting, Peter Paul Rubens' self-portrait with his wife in the honeysuckle arbor, notable for its undulating line (Figure 5), are found among the postcards Alexander mounted in an album.[47] There is no evidence that Alexander painted landscapes while in Polling, yet there does exist a sketch of the village skyline in a sketchbook (Figure 6), which, if it had been a painting, would merit comparison to Duveneck's Polling landscapes.[48] Alexander concentrated his efforts on portrait heads instead. One that he was particularly proud of was a drawing of Currier that he boasted of rendering in 20 minutes (unlocated).[49]

In the summer of 1878 Frank Duveneck would once again stop in Polling. By this time Duveneck, who was eight years Alexander's senior, had already earned acclaim at home and abroad. Before leaving New York, Alexander would have certainly been aware of the sensation Duveneck's Munich pictures were making at the Boston Art Club in the spring of 1875. Henry James wrote favorably of the pictures (as did the New York press): *Lady with a Fan* (Metropolitan Museum of Art), *Portrait of Professor Ludwig Löfftz* (Cincinnati Art Museum), *The Old Professor* (Museum of Fine Arts, Boston) and what would be one of his most famous works, *The Whistling Boy* (Cincinnati Art Museum). What these pictures had in common was the conspicuous brushwork of a robustly modeled head revealed by a strong light with the torso emerging from darkness. It is likely that Alexander saw Duveneck's *Turkish Page* (Cincinnati Art Museum) when it was exhibited at the National Academy of Design in 1877. The signature Munich style and technique that favored bravura brushwork in contrast to the academic style of the French who preferred a finish achieved by a tightly controlled brush, held the promise of a bright future. The younger men in Polling in the summer of 1878 willingly followed Duveneck's lead.

The renegade group of American art students did not have the patience to remain at the Academy for four years encumbered by a strict program of instruction, as did the older William M. Chase. The short-timers abandoned the academy for the camaraderie, easy-going informality, and lower cost of living of Polling. As for Chase, he was returning to the United States to teach at the new Art Students League in New York after six years at the Royal Munich Academy as a talented student and studio assistant. He went down to Polling from Munich to say his goodbyes to the American colony. The highlight of his visit was the "Abschied," or farewell party, staged in his honor on August 17. He was given a raucous farewell that began at the Weilheim train station. He was greeted by a mob and placed on a decorated throne which itself was set high on an ox-drawn cart and then led into Polling.[50] Charles Mills recalls a keg of beer as well as the flag pallet of wood and a broomstick at the front of the wagon, and when Chase appeared – fireworks.[51] Two or three days later Mills and Alexander delivered to Chase, who had already returned to Munich, a diploma signed by all the participants of the Abschied.[52] With Chase going home to teach a new generation of Americans, Alexander repeated a prediction ascribed to Piloty, "that in a few years German students will go to America" instead of the other way around.[53]

It so happens that a true American celebrity was visiting Munich at the time. With his family in tow, Mark Twain was writing *A Tramp Abroad* while in the city from about November 15, 1878 to February 29, 1879. He was honored by his fellow Americans at Thanksgiving dinner.[54] This may be the party Charles Mills recalled as, "a great party given by the Americans for Mark Twain at the Rathskeller in Munich," though there may have been others.[55] It is not likely that Alexander would have missed this dinner and the opportunity to deepen ties with Twain, whose friendship began when Alexander was first employed by *Harper's*.

Polling was appealing not just for the low cost of food and rent. For the smallest of fees, the local population – men, women and children – provided a steady stream of models. Even cheaper were artists modeling for artists or sharing models. One example is a head of a young girl by Alexander, perhaps unfinished, floating on an ill-defined background.[56] The head, positioned at a

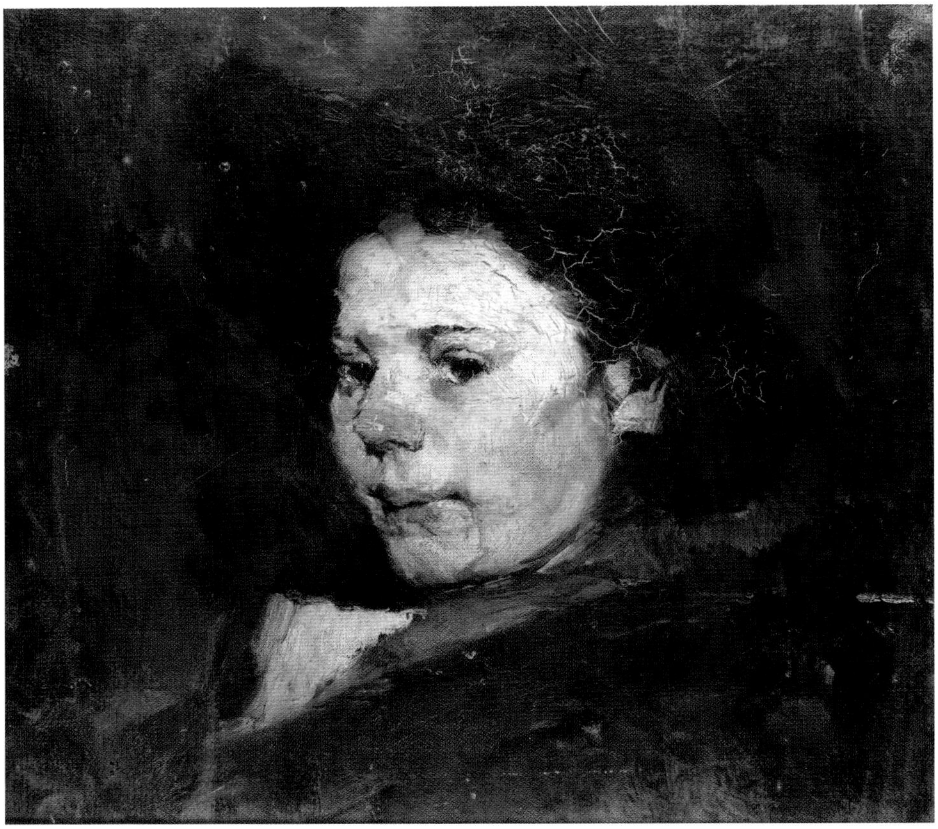

7
Munich Portrait (head of a child), *c.*1878–9, unlocated. Photograph, J0019552, © Peter A. Juley & Sons Collection, Smithsonian American Art Museum

slight angle, is of a child with large dark eyes and a sweet countenance. It invites comparison to Duveneck's *Girl in Black Hood*, *c.*1878 (Cincinnati Art Museum). Another example is Alexander's Munich portrait known only through a photograph (Figure 7).[57] The young boy's features: the eyes, the eyelids, the eyebrows, the nose, the pudgy face, and the cap, merit comparison to Duveneck's *He Lives by His Wits* (private collection, Cincinnati) of 1878 or, better yet, to Currier's *Head of a Boy* (Brooklyn Museum) that at one time belonged to Alexander. The most accomplished of Alexander's Munich pictures is *Profile of a Girl* (Figure 8). The robustly modeled head is in profile leaving the viewer to deduce the personality of the sitter from the restlessness in the turning of the shoulders. White pigment, sketchily applied, suggests a frilly bodice. The introduction of touches of red on the lips, on the diaphanous cap that covers the left ear, and in the underlying tone of the canvas make for an accomplished picture.

8
*Profile of a Girl (Study Head of a Munich Peasant), c.*1879, oil on canvas, 20⅛ × 17¼ in. (51.1 × 44.5 cm.), Taft Museum of Art, Bequest of Charles Phelps and Anna Sinton Taft, Cincinnati, Ohio, 1931.471. Photo: Mark Rohling, Cincinnati, Ohio

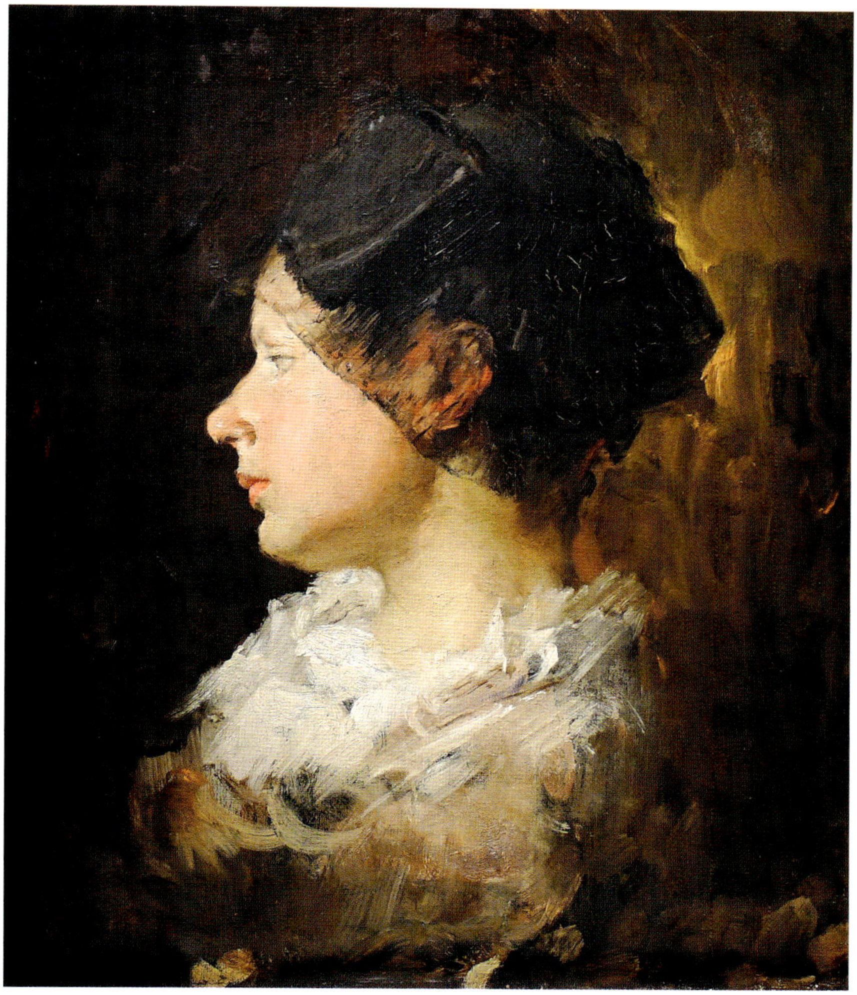

By August 1879 Alexander reached a decision that it was no longer worth his while to remain in Polling. The simple fact is that what he learned of Munich realism was from observation and from his own circle under the leadership of J. Frank Currier and Frank Duveneck, rather than the result of instruction at the Academy where he did not matriculate as far as the painting class. His plan was to return to Munich, but not the Academy, take a studio and "pitch in" for the winter.[58] His plans were short-lived, however, as his relationship with Duveneck developed into a more mutually beneficial one. Duveneck was moving to Florence to set up a school and he wanted the "boys" to join him, particularly

Alexander. On October 5, 1879, Alexander, Louis Ritter, and possibly two others accompanied Duveneck to Florence.[59]

"A little treasure-city, she sat in the sunshine beside the yellow river," wrote Henry James, describing the attraction of Florence in *Italian Hours* (1909). There is no better testimonial to its alluring appeal for artists. Yet the search for the picturesque was not the reason Duveneck chose Florence to set up a school. It had been years since its heyday as an art center for the American neoclassical sculptors; to be sure it had its American ghosts, the painters John La Farge, George Inness, and Elihu Vedder, and sculptors Horatio Greenough, Hiram Powers, and William Wetmore Story, and outliving them all Larkin Goldsmith Mead, the brother-in-law of William Dean Howells.

The credit for the move, rather, goes to Elizabeth "Lizzie" Boott, who while in Munich to study with Duveneck was transformed from a great admirer of his talents into the object of his affection. She succeeded in luring him and his school to Florence. The move was a matter of convenience for Lizzie and her father, wealthy Boston Brahmins, who wanted to return to their permanent residence in Florence at the Villa Castellani, a property owned by Louisa Greenough, a sister of the sculptor. A welcomed guest was Henry James who, in addition to his literary charms, functioned as a mediator with Mr. Boott when it came to matters of the heart between Lizzie and Duveneck. Alexander and Duveneck roomed together at Palazzo Russo, Via Lungo il Mugnone 11, and shared a studio along the Arno. The rest of the "boys" resided in the region of the Piazza della Indipendenza.[60] They frequented a trattoria on the Via Guelfa that over time they decorated with caricatures that became a feature in William Dean Howells' novel *Indian Summer*.

Even before the remainder of the "boys" arrived from Munich in the third week of October, the Duveneck school was taking form. It was attracting a lot of attention, with students coming from America, Munich and Paris.[61] Of the men coming from Munich, there were Alexander, Otto Bacher, John Twachtman, Joseph Decamp, Julius Rolshoven, Olivier Dennett Grover, Theodore Wendel, Louis Ritter, either Ross or Walter Turner, Harper Pennington, Charles Forbes, George Hopkins, Julian Story, Charles Mills, Albert Reinhart, Charles Freeman, Henry Rosenberg, John O. Anderson, and Charles A. Corwin.[62] Three studios had been set up, each offering the choice of different models, but the school was getting so large that more studios were needed. Duveneck also needed to lighten his teaching load. To Alexander, the "head of all the boys," he gave responsibility for a private watercolor class of four privileged ladies, Lizzie Boott and her three friends, Gertrude Elizabeth Blood (later

Lady Colin Campbell), Miss Wagniere from France and Miss Gordon from England.[63] Privately, the four ladies and four men, Duveneck, Alexander, Ritter and the sculptor Edward R. Smith, also formed a Monday evening Charcoal Club that may have been as much social in its purpose as professional.[64]

Lizzie Boott not only facilitated finding students for Duveneck's school but was the center of his social life and that of his favored student, Alexander. The four ladies of the watercolor class particularly enjoyed fawning over Alexander and bestowing gifts on him; for example, they purchased supplies for him when his own had not yet arrived from Munich. The ladies did not hesitate to shower him with sweets and cakes and even writing paper.[65] They built up Alexander's confidence to the point that he uncharacteristically boasted of it in letters home. One letter closed with a sketch of the boy from behind in a top hat and swallow-tail coat just like the one that he posed in for Duveneck's portrait painted in Venice in the summer of 1880 (Cincinnati Art Museum).

Of the network of acquaintances cultivated by Alexander while in Florence were several women known only by their surnames. From Boston, there were a Mrs. Jackson, a Mrs. Huntington and a Miss Sturgis. The latter was a writer of articles for which she proposed that Alexander make the illustrations. Mrs. Jackson commissioned several watercolors, one of a negro sentinel holding a gun. He gave lessons to an old lady, a Mrs. Coale, who also became a patron, placing an order for two watercolors. Regarding another lady, Alexander noted a certain discomfort in what he described as getting "almost confidential" with a Mrs. Whitcombe.[66] Then there were the Samuel Tiltons of Boston whose friendship would result in the commissioning of a portrait of Mrs. Tilton the summer after Alexander returned home.[67]

Recasting Duveneck's Boys as Inglehart's Boys, in the novel *Indian Summer*, Howells lauded them as the sensation of Florence. Their presence was felt wherever they went, be it singing in the streets, boisterous behavior at the local trattoria which bore permanent scars of their visits in the form of caricatures on the walls, sketching trips to the surrounding countryside, or standouts in artistic dress in the salons of the Florentine aristocracy or the homes of the expatriate community. "They made the greatest excitement everywhere, and had the greatest fun."[68] Florence, the little treasure-city set in the sunshine, lured the most fascinating people of all of Europe to make their homes there. For their own amusement, these most fascinating people welcomed into their salons the antics of an unsophisticated group of young American artists. Otto Bacher recalled their intense and concentrated youthful days led by the genius Duveneck, "the usual student experiences of work and play, elation and

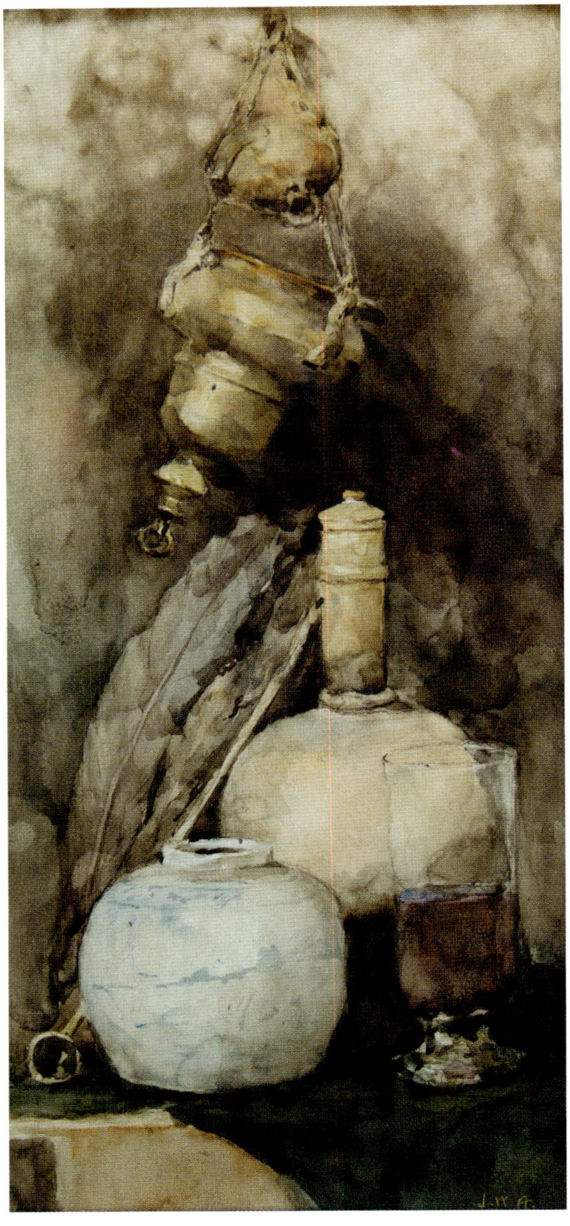

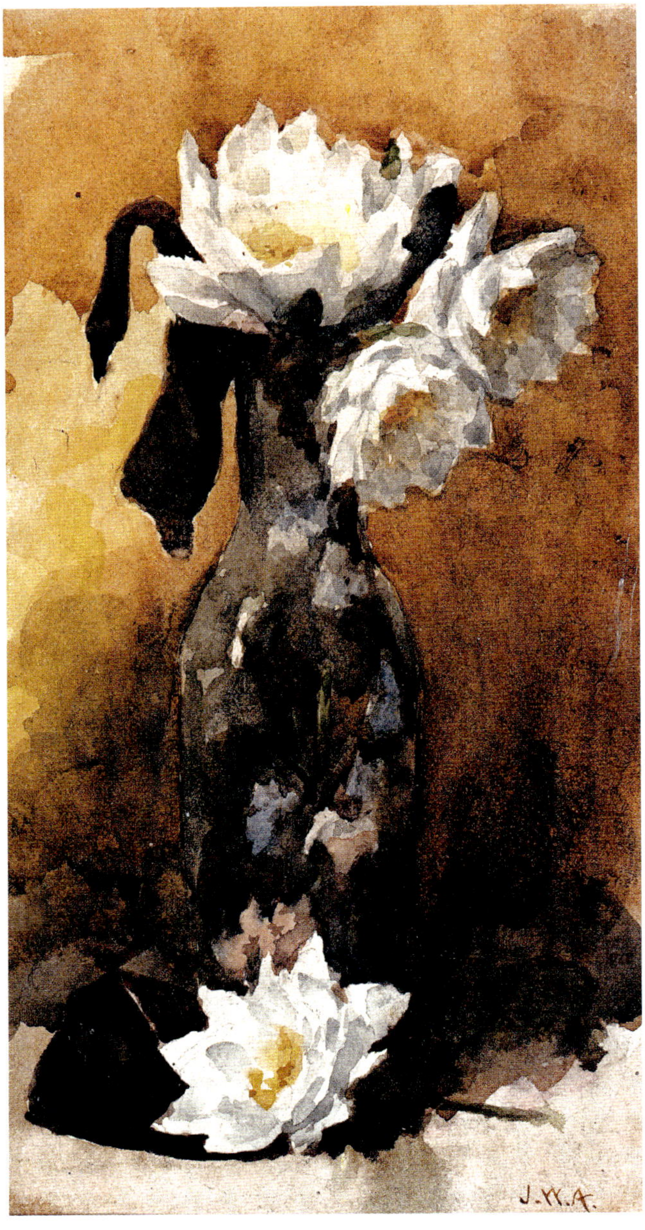

9 *Still Life* (glass, ginger jar, quill pen and wick, incense burner), *c*.1879, watercolor, 14 3⁄16 × 6 5⁄8 in. (36 × 16.8 cm.), collection of Mr. and Mrs. Joel Leitner

10 *Still Life* (vase with four white flowers), *c*.1880, watercolor, 9 × 4½ in. (22.9 × 11.4 cm.), Hodder Family Collection

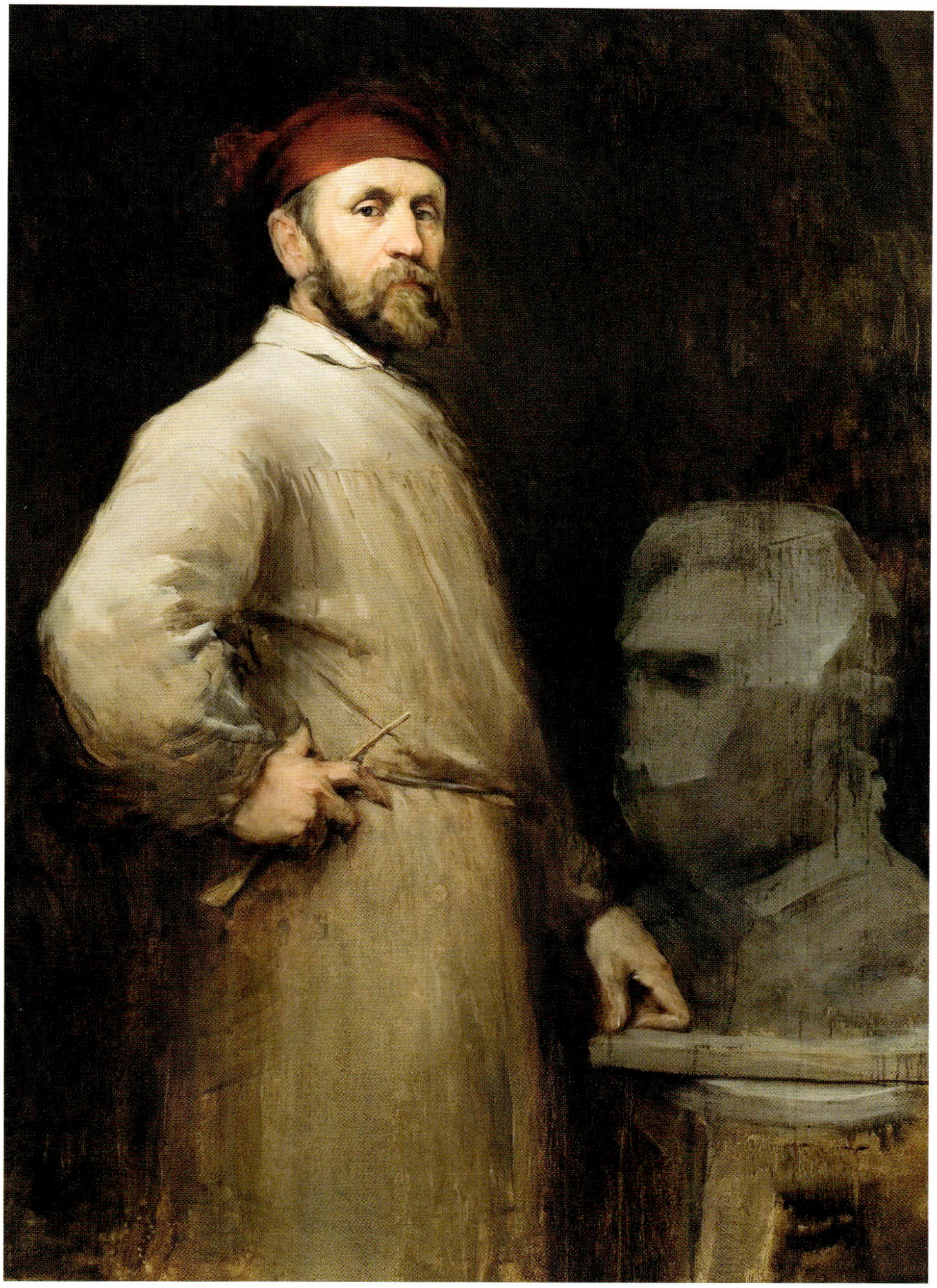

11 *Portrait of Larkin Goldsmith Mead*, March 1880, oil on canvas, 51 × 36½ in. (129.5 × 92.7 cm.), private collection. Image courtesy of James Graham & Sons

dejection, feast and famine, were ours ... and owing to peculiar circumstances and conditions, the advantage of the intimate association and constant companionship we enjoyed not only with our leader but also with his acquaintances and fellow artists, men and women from many lands ..."[69]

With the move from Munich to Florence in late 1879, Alexander showed signs of a transition to a lighter palette, one perhaps infused by the warm Tuscan sun. Evidence of this appears more so in the watercolor medium than in paintings. One example, with German accoutrements such as a glass goblet, ginger jar, quill pen, and incense burner dates from Munich or Polling (Figure 9). Its somber, brownish tones contrast with a still life of a vase with white flowers and yellow pistils that shows a brightening of the tonal variation in the background (Figure 10). Alexander's grand accomplishment for the year, however, a portrait of Larkin Goldsmith Mead, was still in the Munich style (Figure 11). The dean of the American expatriate artistic community stands before a very dark warm green background, his gaze directed at the viewer. He wears a deep red cap and is dressed in a grayish yellow jacket. He holds a tool for modeling the unfinished head of President Lincoln that sits on the pedestal, a head that Alexander could have seen at the Centennial Exhibition.[70] It is a sign of respect that Frank Duveneck, the teacher, generously made his studio available to his student for the inaugural showing of the Mead portrait during the first two weekends of March 1880 where it generated considerable interest.[71] Alexander considered it his first real attempt at portraiture and held out high expectations that it would generate commissions from peripatetic Americans passing through Florence on the grand tour.

Though Alexander was part of the initial "invasion" of Venice by a younger generation of American artists, his stay was limited to the summer of 1880. Some of his best pictures, though few in number, were produced there. As he relocated with Duveneck from Munich to Florence to Venice, his attention turned to views of the canals made *en plein air* which, by their nature, called for less somber colors. The intimate nooks and crannies of a city defined by lagoons and quays were his subjects, not the grand vistas or *vedute* that interested artists of an earlier time. This city, with a promising motif around every corner, with the presence of James A. M. Whistler, and with a truly international mix of artists, both visual and literary, who socialized in private salons including that of Katherine de Kay Bronson, enriched Alexander's final months abroad and prepared him for what he must do upon his return to the United States.

The center of activities was the Casa Jankowitz, where most of the "boys" lived, not far from the public gardens and near the intersection of the Via

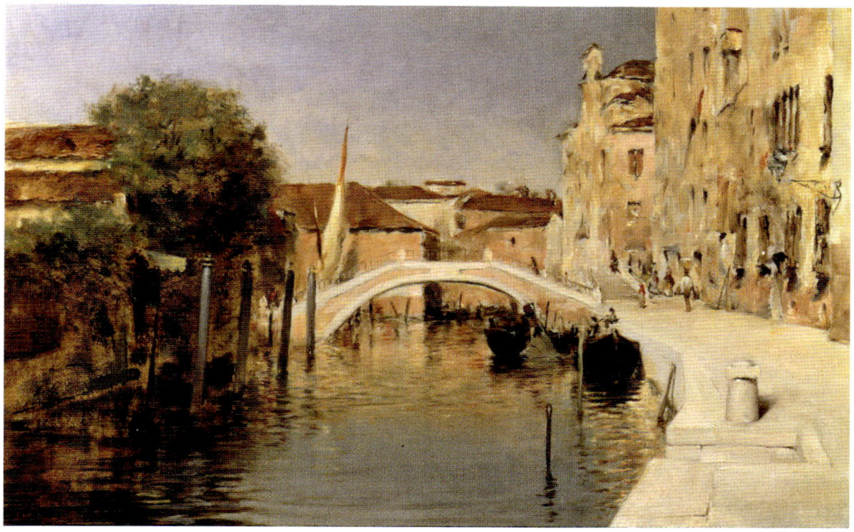

12
Venice Sketch, 1880,
oil on canvas, 21 × 33 in.
(53.3 × 83.8 cm.),
Barbara Reale

Garibaldi and the Riva degli Schiavoni. Duveneck resided at the Casa Kirsch sharing accommodation with Alexander. It is a mark of Alexander's character that his favored status did not result in jealousy or recriminations. According to Bacher's reminiscences of their student days, Alexander was universally accepted as a "born favorite and leader."[72] Alexander was particularly close to a new addition to the group in Venice, Robert Blum, a student of Duveneck's from the Mechanics Institute in Cincinnati. As for the ladies, while there appears no record that they continued their classes in Venice, the Irish beauty, Miss Blood, was there at least while Duveneck, now free of teaching, painted a masterful portrait of her.

The boys were enthused by the presence of Whistler, who had been in Venice since September 1879. One can easily imagine how eager Whistler was, both starving and starved for attention, to be indulged by a younger set of admirers. As Bacher tells it, the American Consul John Harris introduced him to Whistler and, in turn, he introduced Whistler to Duveneck.[73] In short order Whistler changed residences to Casa Jankowitz. The full impact of this move was remembered by Otto Bacher who wrote that the "boys" who "lived in adjoining rooms, dined in the same restaurant, frequented the same cafes, worked and played together with an intimacy" could count among their intimates none other than Whistler.[74] Such circumstances and constant companionship was to everyone's advantage. None more so than Whistler, not just for the sake of art, but also for sustenance. At this time and in this place, the "boys" proved to be a source of financial aide for Whistler.[75] With unabashed solicitousness Whistler sought financial help from them, as recalled by Alexander. Whistler, who was just downstairs, was "dry – Has not a single cent and is making the rounds of the boys. Living on them in fact. Of course all the boys knew that he was hard up."[76]

Alexander's recollection of first meeting Whistler is one of happenstance, with Whistler coming upon him at his easel by a canal, surrounded by onlookers. Whistler sat down and began to critique Alexander's work, speaking "only in the kindliest manner, suggesting where the composition might be improved, and where a bit of color needed a higher tone. He knew that I knew that the picture was crude ... I was much surprised at his manner for I had heard of his being always brutally frank."[77] This story lends credence to the supposition that the painting *Venice Sketch* (Figure 12) is most likely the work in question. The left side is sketchy and the right side thicker with pigment applied with a palette knife. Compositionally, Whistler would have approved of the choice of a near view of a less trafficked waterway, and he would have particularly liked how the viewer is invited to step into the picture on the path at the right edge, which meanders back and across to the left. The view is of the Rio dei Ognissanti, Ponte Trevisan, in the Dorsoduro.[78] At a time when Whistler espoused painting thinly like breath on glass, *Venice Sketch* shows Alexander's inclination toward the Duveneck manner of love of paint: "It was the brushwork instead of the carefully finished charcoal or crayon drawing that he insisted upon with his pupils as the real foundation of a picture."[79] An apt comparison is Duveneck's *Harbor, Chioggia* (Addison Gallery of American Art, *c.*1880).

Venice Sketch is the only recognized major work from Alexander's Venetian summer, but there are other minor pieces. Two small oils depict typical Venetian boats with orange sails furled, seen from the water's edge and under a sunny Venetian sky (John White Alexander great-granddaughters, and private collection, Chicago). Two watercolors merit high praise for the skillful rendering of the architecture, the framing of the image and the coloration. *Ca d'Oro* (Hodder Family Collection) invites comparison to Whistler's pastel of the same subject, *The Palace*. Alexander has framed the sun-scorched fifteenth-century Gothic palace facing the Grand Canal more closely and taken fewer liberties than Whistler with the orchestration of arches and niches of the façade. A second watercolor (Figure 13), a view in the Cannaregio district of a canal flanked by buildings, is of the historic late Gothic doorway of the Palazzo Sanudo van Axel at a right angle to the Rio de la Panada. The ornate doorway is the focus of Alexander's attention, unlike that of Whistler's etching of the same subject, *Quiet*

13
A Venetian Palazzo (Palazzo Sanudo on the Rio de la Panada), 1880, watercolor, 9 9/16 × 5 7/16 in. (24.2 × 13.8 cm.), Los Angeles County Museum of Art, gift of John David Hodder in memory of his grandparents, Renato Federio Violi Gallo and Rachel Veissid-Sidelio Gallo

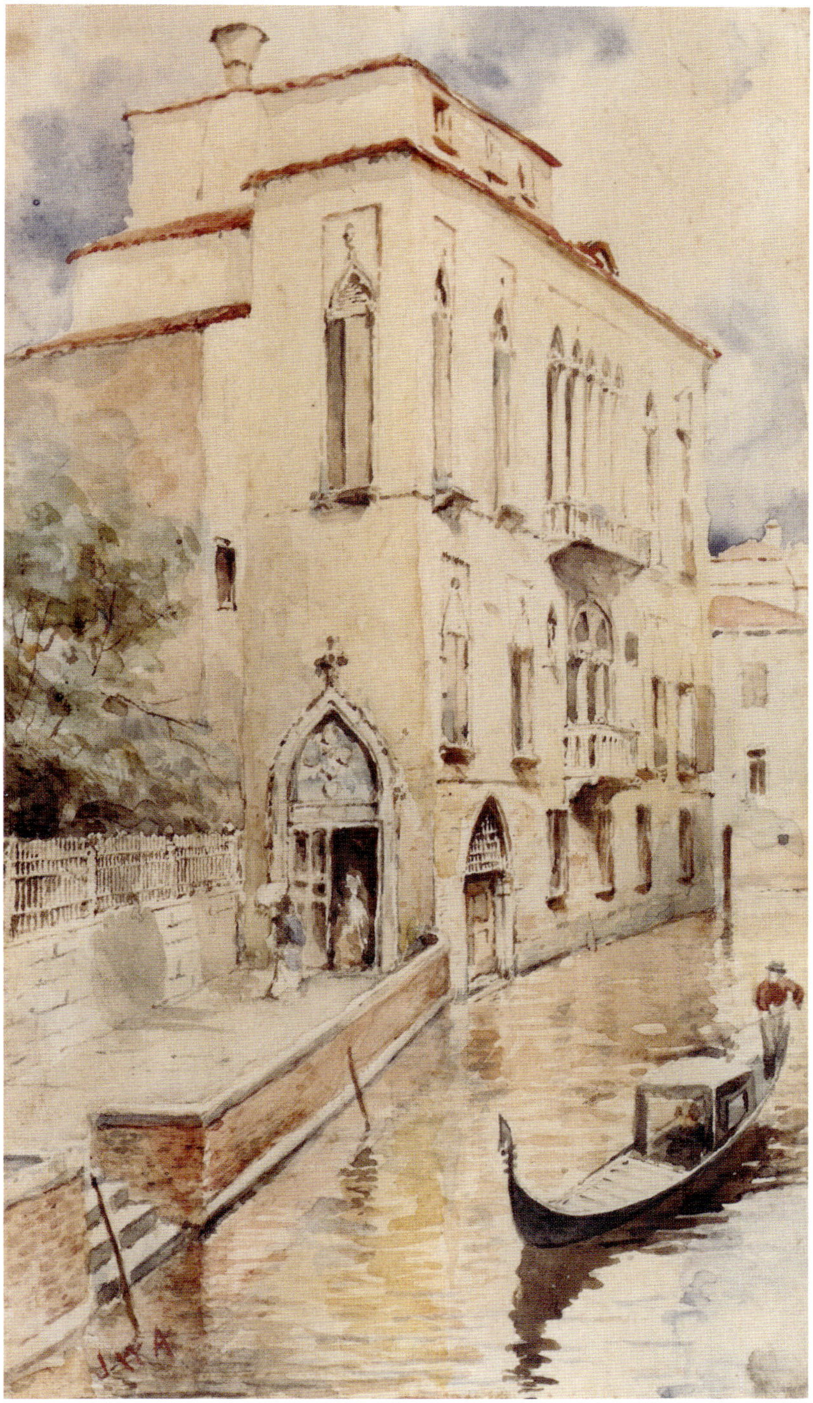

Canal (*c.*1879/80), with its summary rendition of the doorway and a restricted view of the narrow canal.[80]

Experimenting with printmaking not only by the "boys" but also by the senior men, Whistler and Duveneck, became a group preoccupation enabled by Otto Bacher's German press which he had transported from Munich to Venice. It was on Bacher's press that Duveneck's etchings of the Riva were pulled, and then those of Whistler. Prints by Bacher, Charles Corwin, George Hopkins, Theodore Wendel, and Blum are known. None are known by Alexander, though he was the beneficiary of their printmaking in other ways. He owned two etchings by Blum, *Ca' da Mosto* (gift of Alexander's granddaughter to the author) and another, *Men and Donkeys, Rome* (National Gallery of Art, Washington, DC) and a Duveneck etching of the *The Riva Looking toward the Caserna*. All were most likely gifts. Alexander also sat for his etched portrait by Duveneck in a broad brim hat on July 8, 1880. If there was ever a moment for Alexander to try printmaking this would have been it, yet there is no evidence of etchings by his hand.

A central figure of the international set in Venice since 1876 was Katherine de Kay Bronson, sister to Charles de Kay and sister-in-law to Richard Watson Gilder. She opened her door to the rich and poor, the famous and the not-so-famous at the Casa Alvisi. Just to name a few, in the summer of 1880 at the Bronson salon, one could cross paths with the French painter Ernest Meissonier who would go on to help found the Société Nationale des Beaux-Arts; two leading English literary figures, George Eliot and Robert Browning; expatriate painters Martín Rico y Ortega and Cecil van Haanen from Spain and Austria respectively, and two Italian painters Eugene de Blaas, and native Venetian, Guglielmo Ciardi.[81] Though Alexander makes no mention in his correspondence of her salon or of these public figures, he did indeed visit the Casa Alvisi. As was her wont, Bronson requested guests to enter their name and a sketch in her Birthday Book, and so his name and a sketch appears on the page for those born on October 7.[82]

With hindsight, Alexander's student days in Munich, Polling, Florence, and Venice between August 1877 and August 1880, seemed all too short. For impressionable twenty-year-olds, this time was significant not only for the opportunity to study with and be mentored by a talented teacher and to build friendships, but also for the lessons of life. To Duveneck goes the credit for creating "the peculiar circumstances and conditions" from which came "intimate associations and constant companionship." The "Duveneck Boys" lived next to each other or shared rooms, took meals together, lent each other money, shared

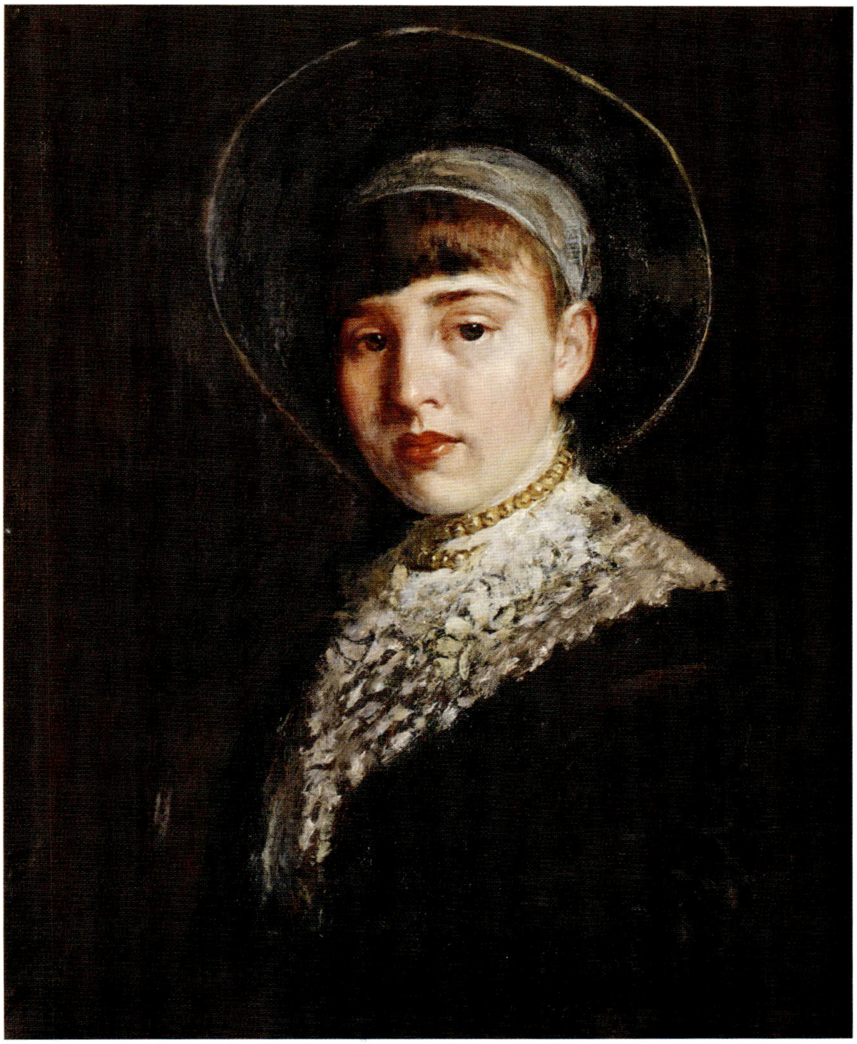

14
Edna J. Allen, 1880,
oil on canvas, 25½ × 20 in.
(64.1 × 50.8 cm.),
Lawrence and Elizabeth
Cahill, Florida

models, and critiqued each others' work. Art, politics and anything else that came to mind were discussed over a meal at the local trattoria. Newspapers and magazines sent from home and passed around one to the other were a source of current events. Letters between students and parents were exchanged regularly, usually containing a stipend from home. The trick was to make the stipend stretch between letters. Some were more successful than others. Those who were careless looked for handouts. After three years abroad, all this constant companionship was left behind, but not forgotten, by Alexander. Friendships formed here would be renewed as the boys blossomed into men, building careers based on a shared foundation.

When it came time to leave Venice in August, it is easy to imagine Alexander's acquaintances participating in or witnessing the frivolity of his farewell. He was accorded a rousing send-off with festivities along the canal aboard a barge festooned with fireworks. "Music and hilarity were the order of the night and the Venetians looked on applauding at the scene."[83] Coincidentally, there was a rumor about Whistler departing in August that turned out to be premature, but nevertheless, the "boys" organized a second fête. The description of the parade up and down the Grand Canal sounds almost identical to the one for Alexander: "Bacher transformed a coal barge into a fairy-like floating bower festooned with the wealth of autumn."[84]

Alexander departed Venice in mid to late August, destination Pittsburgh, to settle a severe case of homesickness which had permeated his letters ever since his arrival in Munich.[85] To pay for his trip home he planned to "send over a box of sketches" (work which remains unaccounted for) to be sold.[86] On his way home he may have stopped in New York, because when he arrived in Pittsburgh in early October he had an assignment from *Harper's*. It was probably to cover the dispute between Waverly Coal & Coke Co. and the miners' union.[87] While staying with the Allens into the new year his brush was kept busy with the completion of six family portraits. Only Edna Allen's portrait is known, and it is fully in the tenebrist Munich style and technique (1880, Figure 14).[88] Showing her dressed in rich contrasts of materials, a gold necklace, a white bib-like collar and a broad-brimmed hat, this could very well have been for a birthday celebrated on November 22.

2

NEW FRIENDS, NEW PATRONS, A NEW WIFE

NEW YORK, NOT PITTSBURGH, would become the base for this promising artist with his newly minted European credentials. The early eighties was a time of finding his footing among the community of artists, developing a network of patrons and exhibiting. Commissioned portraits were exhibited in venues in New York, Philadelphia and Boston. The sun-filled work of Venice seemed to be an interlude, unsuitable for patrons commissioning portraits. A friendship with Thomas Shields Clarke, a Pittsburgher and a Princetonian, was essential for making advantageous social connections.

Alexander was fortunate that being an illustrator for *Harper's* was a reliable source of income while allowing him to pursue his painting career. Coming home again, it was as if he picked up where he left off with the House of Harper. An October 1880 assignment to document a union dispute in Pittsburgh was not realized because the strike never took place, but the following March another assignment was like a reprisal of his Ohio River trip with Robert Burns Wilson, but this time *Harper's* was paying. Traveling with C. Fred Muller, he prepared sixteen illustrations to accompany Muller's story of "King Coal's Highway" which appeared in the forthcoming January issue of *Harper's New Monthly Magazine*. It was the story of the kingpin of the fuel industry, dirty coal, transported by boat down the Ohio and the Mississippi to New Orleans. To paraphrase Muller's description of this gritty industry, from a black void in western Pennsylvania within the sight of Pittsburgh's perpetual cloud of smoke, they traveled 2,100 miles to the carbon heap of Port Eads. Alexander would conjure up images from this trip decades later when planning for the Harrisburg and Carnegie murals. This assignment was so lucrative that he was able to lease what was probably his first New York studio in the German Savings Bank Building (14th & 4th Avenue), where he found remnants of its previous occupant, Augustus Saint-Gaudens's death mask of Lincoln.[1] In Alexander *Harper's* had their man for coverage of Pittsburgh-related events, sending him again to cover the

Pittsburgh flood for July and August issues of *Harper's Weekly*.

Once settled in a studio, he commenced with his first commission, probably that of Rev. Charles Bridgman (unlocated) of the Madison Avenue Baptist Church. The summer took him to Newport to paint Mrs. Samuel Tilton (Boston Museum of Fine Arts), a patron whom he had met in Florence. The wife of a wealthy milliner from Boston, she is somberly, but richly clothed in satin and fur with a matronly white cap. Her compelling physiognomy is achieved with a more refined handling of the brush than the bravura manner of the Munich peasant painted some two years earlier. Alexander had to travel to Newport to meet with his client because the Tiltons were overseeing the young, progressive architectural firm of McKim, Mead and White in the construction of their summer residence.

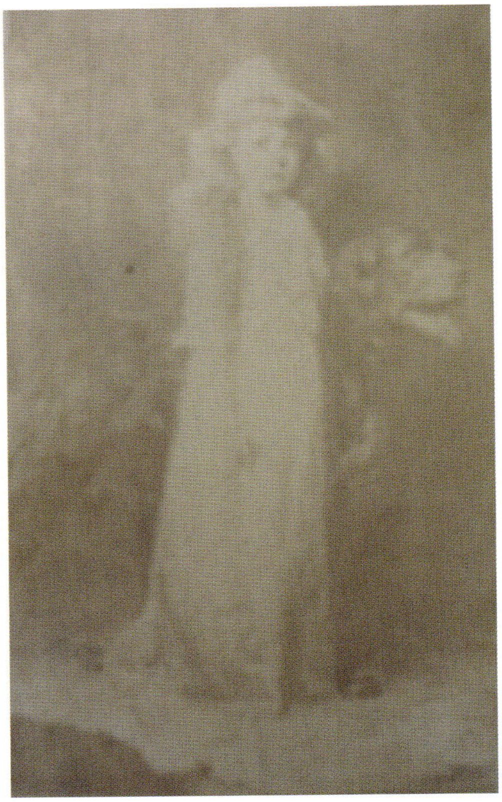

15
May Harper, 1881,
unlocated. Photograph,
John White Alexander papers,
Archives of American Art,
Smithsonian Institution

In 1881, a close association, if not favoritism, had a part to play in the commissioning of Alexander to paint the portrait of May Harper, daughter of Joseph Henry Harper. The "nineish" year-old May was dressed in a "costume that her mother had made, a very quaint little gown" with ruffles and a cap standing next to a black dog almost her equal in size (Figure 15).[2] Alexander thought well enough of it to present it at his New York debut in March 1882 at the 57th Annual Exhibition at the National Academy of Design. The overall tone for the dress and the color of the rug was white, but it was not to the liking of one reviewer who faulted the tones as not being "thought out."[3] No doubt Whistler's *White Girl* on view at the Metropolitan Museum the previous May to October was the reason for a proliferation of pictures of women in white dresses at the academy annual, of which this was one.[4]

Alexander submitted a second portrait for his academy debut, that of Thurlow Weed, a political operative and "boss" of New York's Whig Party, but it was no more liked by the critics than that of May Harper. They found it "more striking than original," an "uncompromisingly white" face, "lacking the right tone," and an expression "somewhat staring." Allowing for overcrowding and poor lighting as a consolation, one critic continued, "Both the portraits are hung worse than not at all, and appear, therefore, to greater disadvantage."[5]

Weed's portrait started out as a drawing assignment for *Harper's*.[6] However, intrigued by his face, "certainly the most interesting sitter imaginable," Alexander turned it into an oil.[7] Criticism of the way Alexander built up the face with thick impasto, as he had learned to do in Munich, followed the portrait to the Boston Art Club in late January. There, too, a review by the *Boston Daily Evening Transcript* (January 27, 1883) faulted the "bluff manner of the artist be [it] hearty frankness or ostentatious contempt."[8]

Either by the fall of 1881 or at the beginning of 1882, Alexander had secured an appointment as a drawing instructor in the School of Science at Princeton.[9] Enrolled at Princeton was another Pittsburgher, Thomas Shields Clarke, whose pedigree, unlike Alexander's, was socially prominent. Clarke's grandfather, his namesake, was a founder of the Pittsburgh and Cincinnati Packet Line in partnership with William Thaw. The elder Clarke married Eliza Thaw, his partner's sister. (Despite Thaw's business success the family name would forever be associated with the scandals that beset his son Harry Thaw, rather than the business acumen of the father.) Since there are no records of Clarke having attending Pittsburgh's Central High School, it is unclear how, or if, Clarke and Alexander met in Pittsburgh.[10] It was not until Princeton, with Clarke in his senior year, that the two Pittsburghers began what would become a close friendship.

Clarke was one of Alexander's best friends, seemingly always looking after his interests. He arranged for Alexander to illustrate the inaugural issue of *The Princeton Tiger* (March 7, 1882), a satirical student newspaper that he founded.[11] After he graduated in 1882, the two of them, along with the second generation of the brothers Moran, Edward and John, spent the first week of August in Port Jefferson, Long Island.[12] A sketchbook of that trip (John White Alexander papers, Archives of American Art, Smithsonian Institution) consists of gouaches of views of harbors, boats beached and boats with masts down, rendered with a generous use of Chinese white on tan paper. In the fall Alexander continued to journey to Princeton at irregular intervals to conduct classes for a student Sketching Club while in the meantime finishing a portrait of the New York journalist Parke Godwin for the 58th Annual Exhibition at the National Academy.[13] Clarke continued to look out for Alexander's interests. He arranged an invitation home to Pittsburgh so that Alexander could paint a portrait of his sister Mabel.[14] Alexander stayed with the Clarkes, not the Allens, and most likely at this time was introduced to Mrs. William Thaw, Sr. who would become a patron of his after the turn of the century.

Joe Jefferson (Figure 16), a legend of the theater, was the subject of a so-called commission around 1883. Alexander was a theater aficionado all his

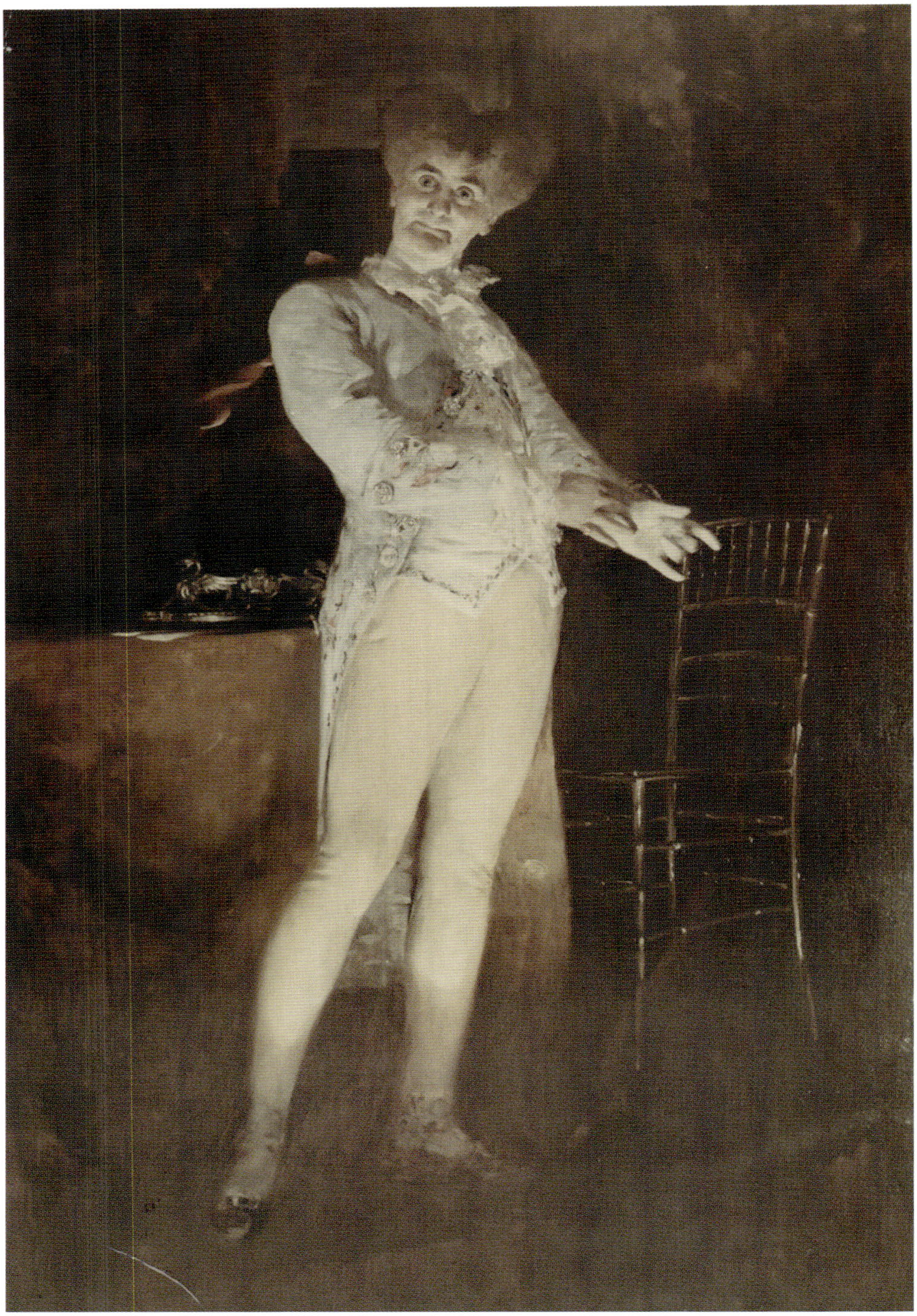

adult life and knew Jefferson's name as early as 1875.[15] Jefferson's reputation and fortune were based on his dramatization of the story of Rip Van Winkle and subsequently a new role in 1880 as Bob Acres in Richard Sheridan's eighteenth-century romantic comedy, *The Rivals*. It opened in Philadelphia and moved to New York on September 12, 1881.

By this time Jefferson was a practitioner of a new form of acting introduced to the American stage by playwright, actor, and theater manager, Steele MacKaye. In the painting, Alexander's effective use of footlighting mitigates the stiffness of the gesturing and dramatizes sentiment expressed through realism and the new naturalistic method of acting. At the Academy's Spring Annual the Jefferson portrait was unequivocally acclaimed. One admirer was the Hudson River School painter Jervis McEntee who noted in his diary, "ignoring all grace and beauty seems to be the idea in most of the pictures," with the exception of Alexander's.[16] The dynamic figure is set in an austere and undefined space, tonally modulated from floor to wall, not unlike Velázquez's figure of *Juan Calabazas*. Alexander was no Velázquez, but Manet's acclaim of *Calabazas* is worth invoking when describing the Jefferson portrait: "The background vanishes and atmosphere envelops the good man." While Elizabeth Alexander recalled the circumstances of the portrait as being a commission, it was in fact one of those unrequited commissions, taken possession of by the sitter, used liberally for years in the lobbies of theaters wherever he performed, and then returned to the painter with a note saying he did not like it.[17] Some years later, John S. Sargent's 1890 bust-length portrait of Jefferson was commissioned specifically for The Players Club, unlike Alexander's full-length portrait which was donated by the artist's widow.

Though not listed among the exhibited works in the National Academy Spring Annual, *An Empty Canvas* (Figure 17) was also on view.[18] While it did not receive the same attention that the Jefferson portrait did, it nonetheless caught the attention of one reviewer, "a studio interior with easel and canvas, which as we can see by the light falling through it, is untouched: beyond sits a pleasing woman artist gazing fixedly. She is absorbed ..." seated in her chair, right arm bent supporting her head with palette and brush in her left hand.[19] The studio is aesthetically and tastefully furnished as was the fashion for artists: work hanging on the walls in stages of completion; a vase on the floor; a settee behind which is a shelf with a glass and bottle. On the wall hangs a surprising choice, a funereal mask looking every bit like Auguste Préault's *Le Silence* (1842–3). As a viewer, one shares the woman's frustration at being stumped and unable to put brush to canvas. Her dilemma is enhanced by the light that penetrates the blank canvas

16
Joe Jefferson, as Bob Acres in Richard Brinsley Sheridan's "The Rivals", 1883,
oil on canvas, 83½ × 53¼ in. (212 × 136.5 cm.),
The Players Club, New York

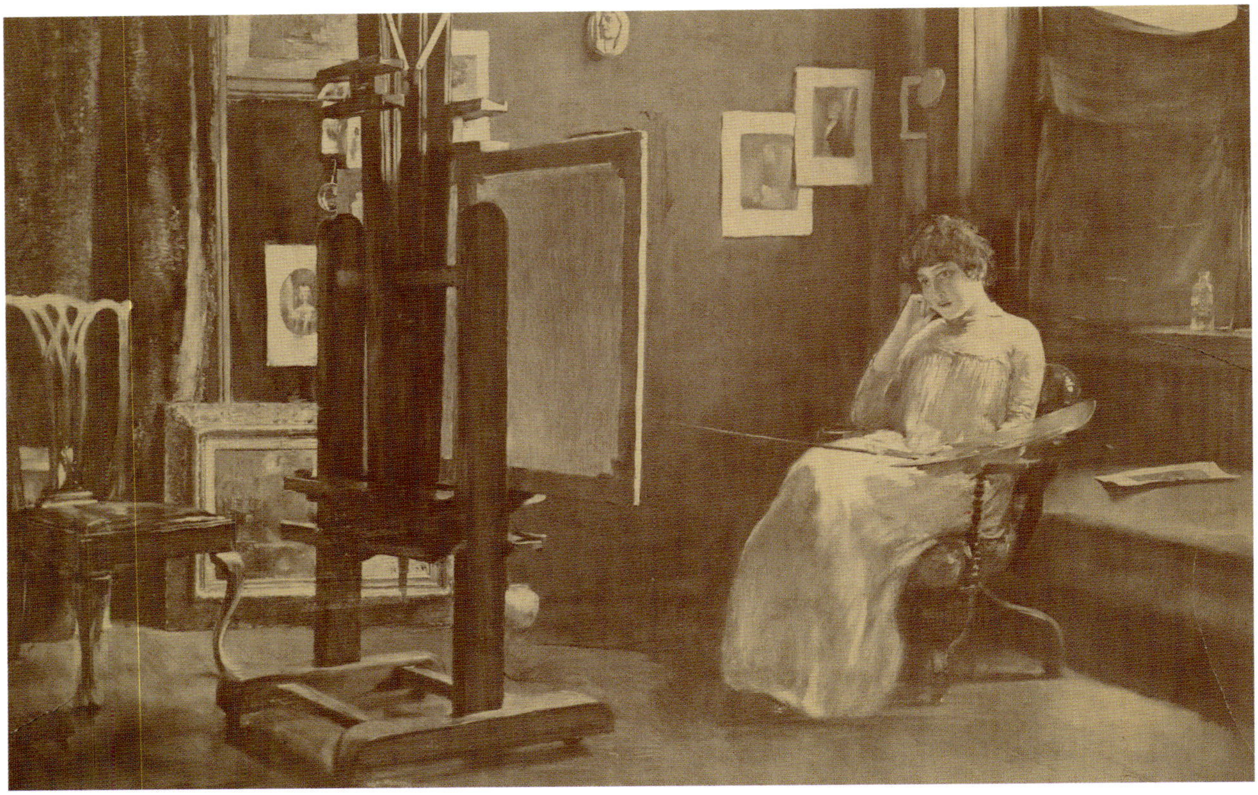

17
An Empty Canvas, c.1884, unlocated. Photograph, John White Alexander papers, Archives of American Art, Smithsonian Institution

from the reverse. This composition, one of a kind at this time in Alexander's career, is emblematic of change that would come in the foreseeable future.

Change came on a trip abroad in the summer of 1884. Before the Academy Annual closed, Alexander and Clarke, along with a third friend, crossed the ocean, destined for Madrid via Gibraltar and Tangier, then for Paris and finally Holland.[20] For someone who had previously been only in Western Europe, the exotic Morocco put Alexander's head in a "whirl" to the point that he couldn't "get his mind down to painting." Pages of his sketchbook show Moorish architecture, images of domestic animals and the locals, even though he knew better than to sketch them.[21] In Madrid the awe of standing before a Velázquez brought him back to the Prado day after day. Unlike his peers, he did not register to make copies, instead purchasing postcards of Velázquez's women, *Infanta Margarita* and *Mariana of Austria* (Figure 18).[22] He took time to attend a bullfight that filled him with disgust for what he called a cowardly and brutal sport, more so for the horses whose bodies were punctured and ripped apart.

The three young men were on schedule to arrive in Paris before June 18 to see the Salon that would close on the 20th. There they would have viewed Puvis de Chavannes's *Bois Sacré* (*The Sacred Wood*) with its levitating angels, a painting that would have bearing on Alexander's future work. They may have visited Siegfried (Samuel) Bing's L'Art Japonais. There was talk of painting landscapes with Charles S. Reinhart in an artist colony outside Paris (probably Grez-sur-Loing). After Paris, there followed a stay in Holland, where they took studios for a month, most probably in Dordrecht. A sketchbook view of the Dordrecht countryside, with its *de rigueur* windmill, raises the question of what Alexander was painting.[23] Whereas upon his arrival in Morocco he had been overwhelmed by the heady sights that country had to offer, in Holland, settled in one place for a month, there is no evidence of his producing any paintings. If he did make any, they most probably would have interpreted natural light in the Hague School manner. The trip came to a close on or about August 16, with Alexander leaving from Liverpool to return to New York while Clarke remained behind to enroll at the Académie Julien.[24]

18
Diego Rodríguez de Silva y Velázquez (1599–1660), *Mariana of Austria, Queen of Spain*, c.1652, oil on canvas, 92 3/16 × 52 in. (234.2 × 132 cm.), Museo del Prado, Madrid. Image © Museo Nacional del Prado/Art Resource, New York

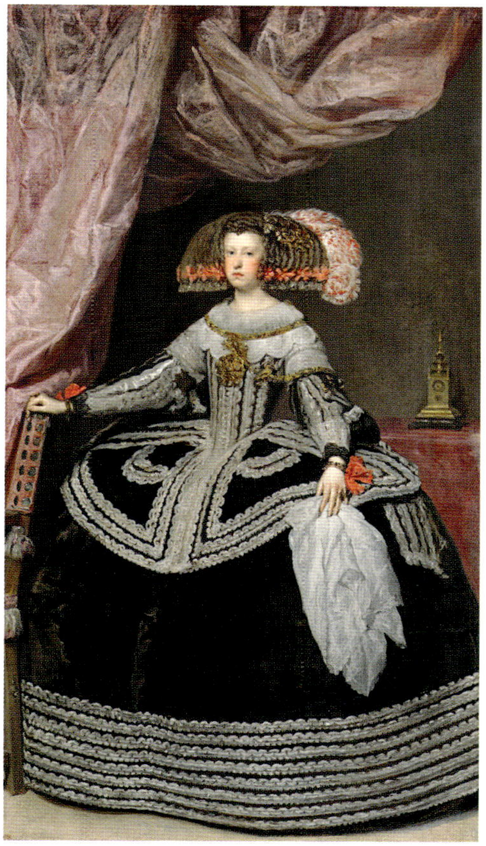

Traveling and the chance for new experiences gave Alexander time and opportunity to reflect upon his aspirations as a painter. His finest moment, two-thirds of the way into his trip, came when he resolved the direction he wanted to pursue as a painter. He had thought carefully about his aspiration, and he described it in a letter to Colonel Allen from Dordrecht: "I hope to have a picture in this Ex[hibition] – a subject and not a simple portrait. It will be my first serious attempt and I have been working hard at it for some months all through this trip. It is very simple – only one figure but in it I want to express a sentiment – and I think it will either be a hit or a grand slip up."[25] By "working hard at it" we should understand him to mean in his imagination, because there is no evidence of subject pictures being made on his trip.

When he left New York he had a solid body of work. He was in the front ranks of American portraiture, working in the Munich style, annually exhibiting portraits such as Thurlow Weed in 1882, Park Godwin in 1883, and Mrs. Samuel Tilton and Mrs. Charlotte Colgate Abbe in 1884. The exceptions to the Munich style were the theatrical

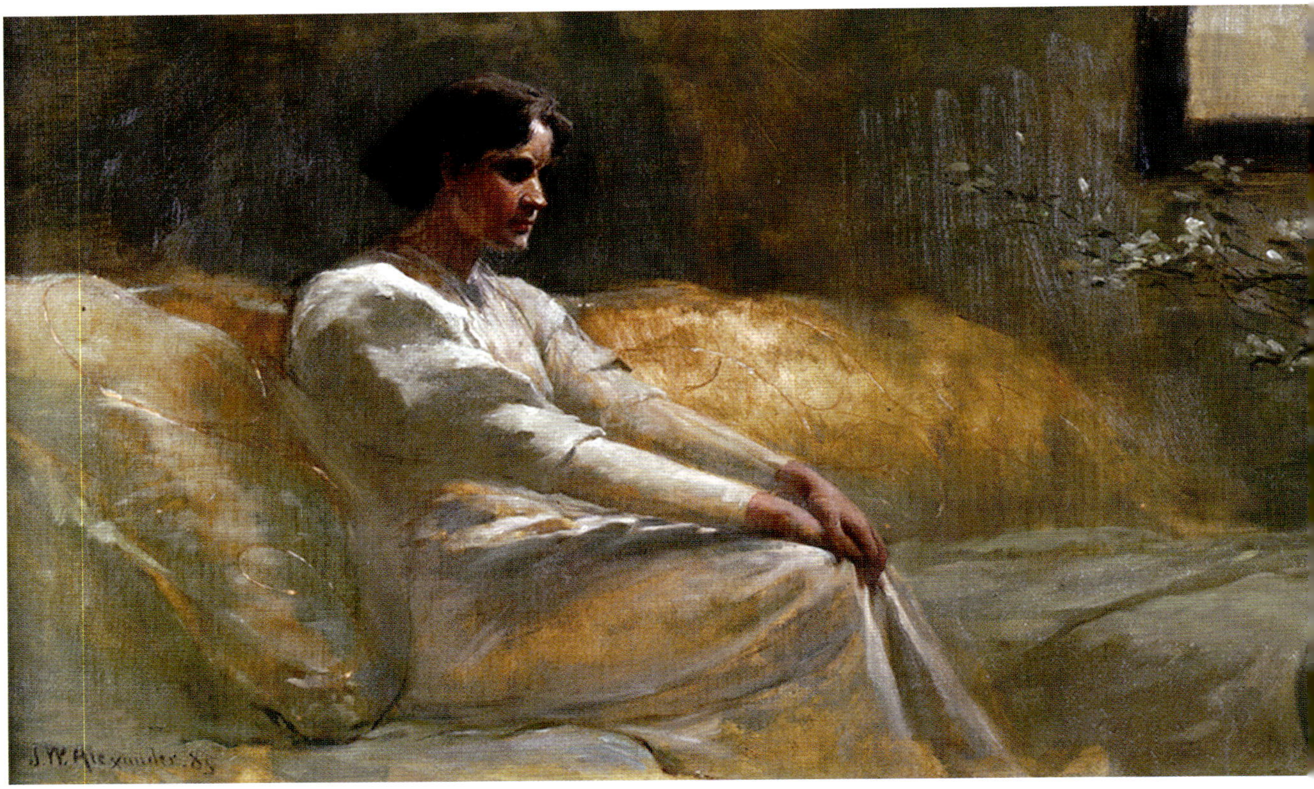

19
Azalea (*Portrait of Helen Abbe Howson*), 1885, oil on canvas, 19¼ × 44¼ in. (46.4 × 110.5 cm.), The Hudson River Museum, Yonkers, New York, gift of Mrs. Gertrude Farmham Howson, 74.16.6

portrait of Joe Jefferson and *An Empty Canvas*, and possibly another, *A Prize* (unlocated).[26] He had also made a prodigious number of illustrations of distinguished men of letters and politics, this time for *Harper's*, beginning with his portrait of U.S. President Arthur in *Harper's Weekly* of October 1, 1881 followed by the likes of Alexander H. Stephens, Daniel Webster, Longfellow, Emerson, and Peter Cooper. Add to this his two sizable assignments, illustrations for "King Coal's Highway," and illustrations of Yellowstone, and he had in his sights the elusive goal, for an artist, of financial security. The Yellowstone trip, also for *Harper's*, took place in the summer of 1883, and the result was a composite of some thirteen illustrations published in *Harper's Weekly* on November 10, 1883.

Alexander had left for Europe without seeing the portrait of Charlotte Colgate Abbe (unlocated) on exhibit. By his own account it was the hit of the exhibition.[27] In his signature Munich style, the matriarch is posed facing forward in front of a dark background with the light revealing her face.[28] Most likely Alexander first met the Colgates around 1881 in connection with his

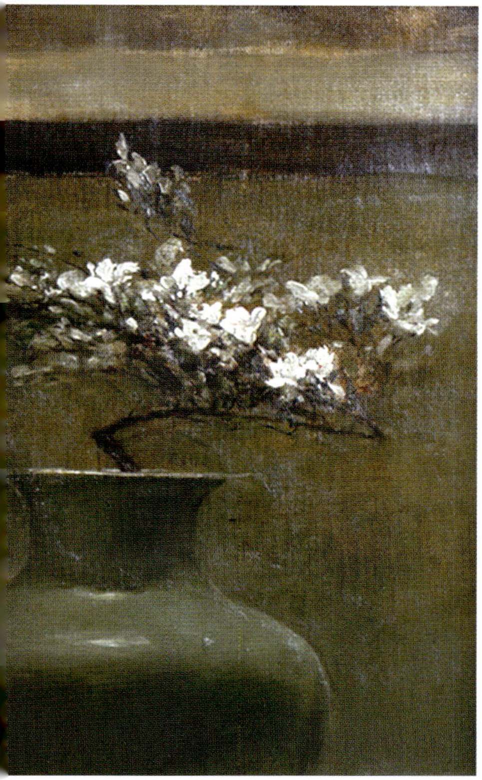

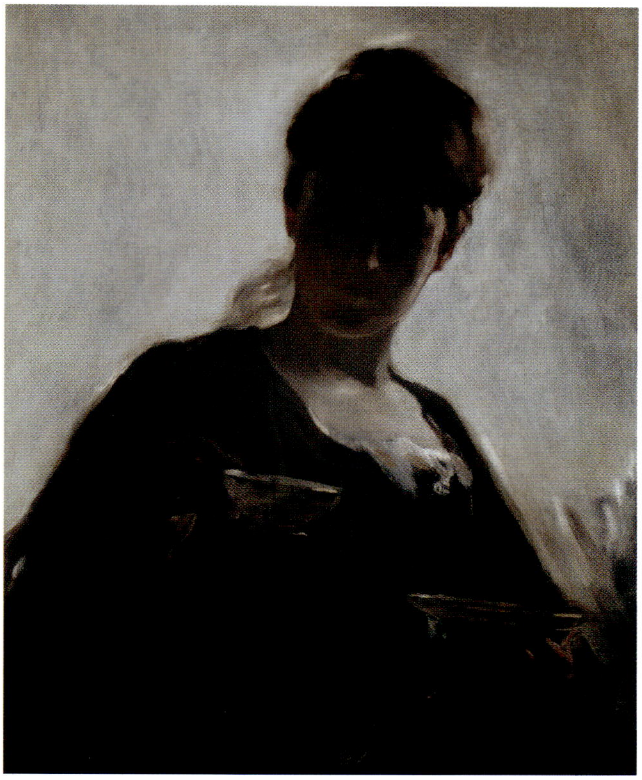

20
Girl with Teacup, *c.*1884, oil on canvas, 27 × 22½ in. (68.6 × 56.5 cm.), private collection, image courtesy of David Nisinson

commission to paint the Rev. Charles Bridgman; George Waldo Abbe was a deacon at Bridgman's church. Now, in search of an artist to paint a portrait of their daughter, the Abbes turned to someone they knew, commissioning Alexander for what was possibly a celebration of their daughter's engagement.[29] Fortuitously, the timing of the portrait coincided with Alexander's new aspiration, formulated during his several months abroad, to paint a subject picture and not simply a portrait. *Azalea* (*Portrait of Helen Abbe Howson*) would represent a step up for all the right reasons (Figure 19).

Azalea is a harbinger of what Alexander's style would ultimately become. Yet another single figure wearing white is posed in a spare interior and shallow space. She is seated on a divan to the left of center. The composition is balanced on the right by a large celadon vase with an azalea branch. Behind it hangs a picture in its frame, cropped so that only one corner is visible. What is unusual about this canvas is the elongated format in which a figure is positioned among an overscaled divan, vase and frame, intimating that the artist is struggling with his compositon. Exhibited in November of the following year at the American Art Galleries, one critic described it as "what Mr. Whistler would probably call a nocturne. It looks as if it was painted in green moonlight."[30] It contained all the hallmarks of Alexander's mature work – harmony of tone, a decorative female, a symbolic flower, a divan, and the visual extension of space suggested by a framed picture. His debt to Whistler is obvious, no doubt inspired by the portrait of the artist's mother on view in New York in 1882.

At the end of 1884 a private motivation complicated the course of his burgeoning career. Alexander began an engagement with Elizabeth Swan Williamson Alexander that would culminate in marriage not quite three years later. Though she shared the same family name with her fiancé, they were not directly related. Like many young men whose fancy turns to love, he began paying particular attention to finances. For advice Alexander turned to his trusted high-school friend, Edward Phelps, now in the Pittsburgh Controller's Office, who invested and managed his money. There is most likely a correlation between wanting to improve his financial situation and accepting as many portrait commissions as he could, two of which were from members of his fiancée's family, Henry M. Alexander, a great-uncle (private collection, Maryland) and James L. Cabell (unlocated). Female portraits include the socialite Eliza Colt (before 1887, unlocated) and Charlotte Houston or Heuston (1884, unlocated). Wearing white, Colt's three-quarter-length portrait could very well have been in celebration of her debut. She posed again in a white gown in the John Singer Sargent portrait (1898, Cleveland Museum of Art), this time for her marriage to Ralph Curtis.[31] Taking on more commissions meant less time for more "aesthetic" pictures of women such as *Girl with Teacup* (*c.*1884, Figure 20), *Azalea* (1885), and *An Idle Moment* (*c.*1885, Gabriel and Jane Auerbach, Florida). Despite the focus on portraits, he also found time to dabble in still lifes (*Pink Roses*, 1885, Federal Reserve Board, Washington, DC).

The year 1886 began with the completion of his portrait of the President of Princeton University, James McCosh (Princeton University), after which the remainder of the year was monopolized by work for Richard Watson Gilder's magazine *The Century*. The specifics of how the two met are not clear, but their paths would have crossed often enough in New York where Gilder was known as a magazine publisher and advocate for the profession of journalism, with an association with the Society of American Artists. Their shared interests would have earned Alexander an invitation to the home of Gilder and his wife Helena de Kay, a nexus of intellectual discourse and artistic life in New York City from the mid 1880s; the Bronsons in Venice may also have been instrumental in

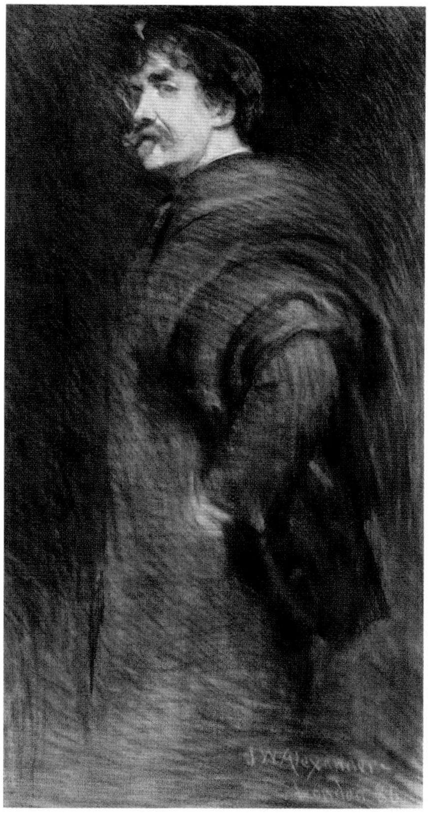

21
Whistler in London,
1886, charcoal on paper,
32½ × 17 in (83 × 43.2 cm.),
The Metropolitan Museum of Art, New York, gift of A.E. Gallatin, 23.230.2

making an introduction: as we have seen, the young painter had visited Helena's sister Katherine in the summer of 1880. Frequent guests at the Gilder salon included the likes of Joe Jefferson, Wyatt Eaton, John La Farge, Augustus Saint-Gaudens, Stanford White, Candace Wheeler, and art historian Charles Eliot Norton.

In February Alexander began an assignment for *The Century* with a round of portrait drawings of distinguished authors. On the thirteenth he sketched John Burroughs (American Academy of Arts and Letters, New York City). On the twenty-second through the twenty-fourth he was in Camden to sketch a portrait of Walt Whitman, which he ultimately turned into a painting. The very next day, back in New York, he sketched Frank Stockton (Carnegie Museum of Art, Pittsburgh). After sketching Milton Hay (American Academy of Arts and Letters) in March there was a pause until June when the assignment took him abroad through about mid November.

This 1886 trip provided opportunities to make new acquaintances and renew old ones. The assignment called for travel within the British Isles and a side trip to Paris where he sketched Alphonse Daudet (formerly collection of Graham Williford). In London he sketched Austin Dobson (American Academy of Arts & Letters, New York City), Robert Browning (American Academy of Arts & Letters, New York City), Henry James (unlocated) and Whistler (Figure 21). Years later Alexander repeated an amusing story about Lady Colin Campbell (the former Miss Blood from his Florence days) who was present for the session with Whistler. Having tried literally to take over Alexander's drawing, Whistler was scolded by Lady Colin: "Jimmy leave it alone. Mr. Alexander was beginning to make a real likeness of you, and now it doesn't look any more like you than it does like me."[32] Alexander traveled to Dorchester to sketch Thomas

Hardy, and also to Bournemouth to sketch Robert Louis Stevenson (unlocated). The latter came about as a result of an introduction by Edmund Gosse, writer, critic and member of the Broadway set, a group of artists and writers who fraternized in the Cotswold town of that name. It cannot be said with certainty that Alexander socialized with Francis D. Millet, John Singer Sargent or Edwin Austin Abbey of the Broadway set at this time, but it is likely, as Abbey was a colleague from his days at *Harper's*.

While at the Stevenson home Alexander had a grim experience that was one of the earliest manifestations of a persistent indelicate constitution. Over lunch he felt quite ill and had a headache. After describing his symptoms to Mrs. Stevenson, she professed to have a remedy. He took the proffered pills immediately, but his condition grew worse. "He grew faint, and blue, and then his eyes … seemed to leave his head and stand out before him in space. Then he lost consciousness."[33] After he recovered it was determined that he had a "spell of indigestion," but his symptoms continued to go unsatisfactorily diagnosed for the remainder of his life. From this episode Stevenson was inspired to write *The Wrong Box*, a black comedy about a coffin intended for a reluctant victim.

In London Alexander renewed friendships not only with Lady Colin Campbell, but also another former Florentine student, Miss Gordon. At a dinner party at the home of the latter's mother, guests included Albert Ludovici and John O'Connor, principal scene painter at the Haymarket Theatre.[34] Further afield, travel to Ireland took him west, north and south, including County Cork, along with a traveling companion, Charles de Kay, brother of Katherine Bronson.[35] (It is not clear whether de Kay traveled to London and Paris with the artist.) Alexander's illustrations from this trip would appear in *The Century* as late as 1890 in stories written by de Kay.[36] According to one account, as a result of this trip, "Alexander handed over fifteen portraits in oil and sixty pencil sketches."[37] Not all of them can be accounted for; not all of them were reproduced in *The Century*; some were reproduced later. On the trip home a fortuitous opportunity occurred. Having just completed a sizable assignment for *The Century*, he met James Gordon Bennett, Jr., a rival publisher and owner of the New York Herald Co. Within weeks of his return one of Alexander's political cartoons, "Harry Watterson's Petits Chevaux" (November 13, 1886), appeared in Bennett's *New York Evening Telegram* with more to come in early 1887.[38]

Alexander's good fortune persisted through the year with a large number of portrait commissions that would grow his bank account, financing a studio in the city and another on the Jersey shore, and positioning him for marriage.

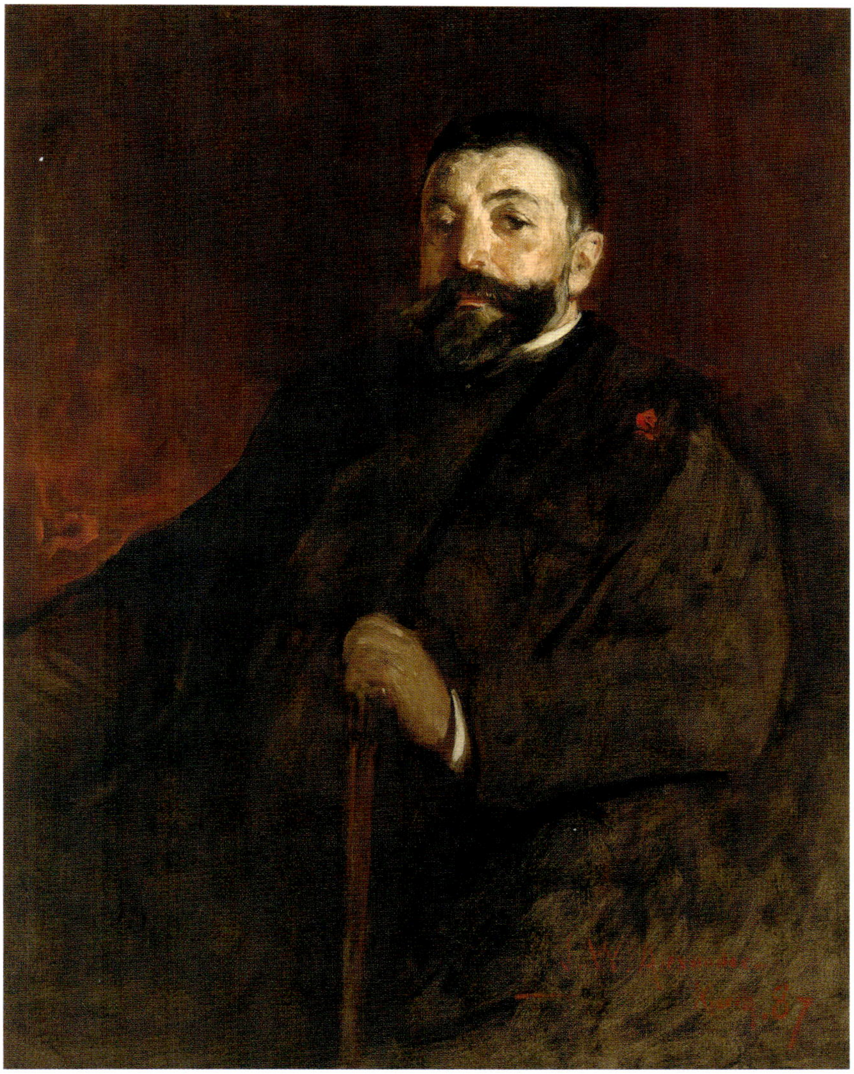

22 *Thomas Nast*, March 1887, oil on canvas, 40 × 30¼ in. (101.6 × 76.8 cm.), National Portrait Gallery, Smithsonian Institution, NPG.66.40

The year began with a portrait of a man to whom Alexander owed his choice of a career as an illustrator, the political cartoonist Thomas Nast (Figure 22). Nast quit *Harper's Weekly* on a career high with his popular new image of Santa Claus appearing on the cover of the 1886 Christmas issue. Five weeks into 1887 he posed for Alexander. Nattily dressed with a red rose in the lapel, he sat with his left hand resting on a cane, his "fine head" luminous in the painting's otherwise dark palette.[39] Having no doubt thought about this fine head for months, if not years, Alexander worked quickly, completing the portrait in no more than seven weeks.

Meanwhile plans for a November wedding that necessitated 4,000 invitations and the building of a studio were sure to raise his adrenalin.[40] Alexander explained to Ed Phelps, "you have not heard from me ... because I have been more than busy – It has been impossible for me to leave the studio during banking hours."[41] And again, "Hardly a minute to myself – Am out every evening till late. Have not been to bed before 12 for some weeks."[42] By May 21, after James Waddell Alexander, Sr. publicly sanctioned the engagement, Elizabeth (a.k.a. Bess) and John, and probably her parents, retreated to Seabright, N.J., where her extended family owned second homes.[43] There in Seabright Alexander made plans to build a studio, bearing in mind that he would likely be spending a considerable amount of time there. Five days after his arrival he requested funds from Phelps, writing that he expected to close with a builder that afternoon on what was to be one of the largest studios in America, at a cost of up to $2,000.[44] He was drawing down funds of sizable amounts – $1,000 to $2,000 or more – which he had entrusted to Phelps for investment.[45] Because there are no records of the artist being a property owner, the exact location of the studio is unknown but there is speculation that it was on his father-in-law's property. A few years after Alexander, Sr. sold the property at 17 North Ward Avenue in 1897 there is record of a building being destroyed by fire. This may have been what was once the artist's studio.[46]

Originally known as Greater Seabright, New Jersey, encompassing Rumson Road and Monmouth Beach, it had been ripe for major development beginning in 1870. What was once a community of farms, fishing huts and shanties was about to be transformed by the construction of new residences for society's elite from New York, Philadelphia, and as far away as Pittsburgh. Previously, that "sand-spit which ends in Sandy Hook was a desert ... nothing but a long beach stretching ten or fifteen miles, with here and there an acre of salt-grass, where the Jersey mosquito took his origin."[47] The development of the coastline was driven by its proximity to New York City. Samuel H. Hartshorn, a local merchant and property owner, sold parcels of his riverfront property in 1870 to three individuals, one of whom was Henry Martyn Alexander (1822–99), a principal of the New York City law firm Alexander & Green.[48] The following year his nephew, James Waddell Alexander, Sr., a Princeton-educated lawyer, purchased property at 17 Ward Avenue, the year he became Second Vice President of Equitable Life Assurance Society. With other members of the family acquiring waterfront property on Ward Avenue in the late 1880s, Seabright offered respite for the extended Alexander family. For the artist, now with a second studio in a familial environment, he, too, had a private retreat.[49]

Attending the nuptials on November 2, 1887 at Zion Episcopal Church on Madison Avenue and 38th Street were many who were not strangers to the groom, having been the subject of portraits or having facilitated commissions. Parke Godwin had been painted in 1883 (The Century Association). The mother (portrait unlocated) and sister of Dr. Robert Abbe, the best man, had already posed. Abbe, the son of Charlotte and George, was a pioneering plastic surgeon and radiologist. The father of bridesmaid Carrie Hoe would be painted in 1889 (The Grolier Club). Mrs. Jeremiah Milbank's husband also sat for his portrait in 1889 (New York State Museum, Albany), and she was the donor of Alexander's portrait of Walt Whitman to the Metropolitan Museum two years later. Henry Baldwin Hyde, founder of Equitable Life Assurance Society would be painted in 1899 (unlocated).

23
Courtlandt Palmer, 1888,
oil on canvas, 56 × 36 in.
(142.2 × 91.4 cm.),
Stonington Historical Society,
Stonington, Connecticut

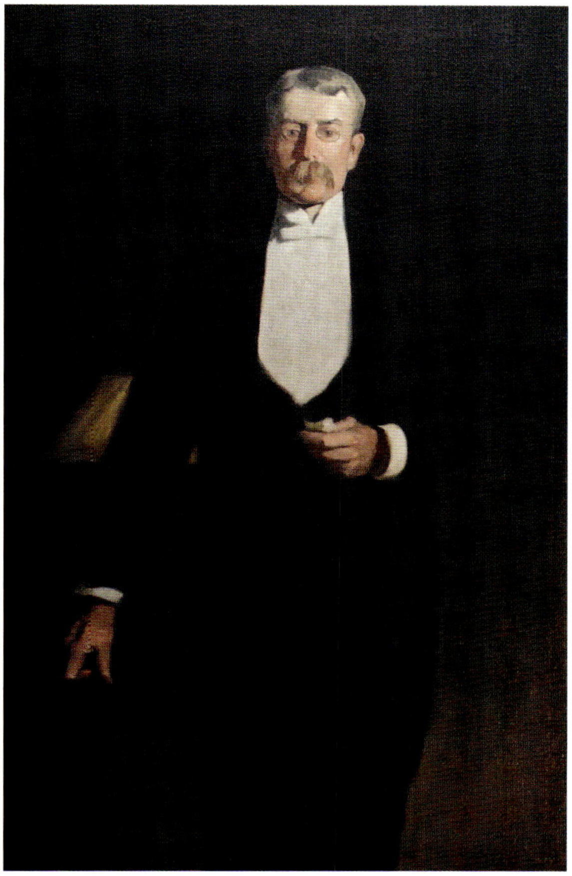

Numerous portrait commissions kept Alexander more than busy in the first half of 1887. Those who may have sat for him before the wedding include the opera star, Clara Louise Kellogg, who had retired from the stage the previous year (unlocated).[50] She first met Alexander at the Gilder home. Also painted was James Gordon Bennett, Jr. (unlocated). Annie Russell posed in her costume as Lady Vavir in W. S. Gilbert's *Broken Hearts*, a three-act play that premiered at Madison Square Theater on April 12, 1886 (Rollins College, Winter Park). Russell stands next to a large vase filled with blossoming branches forming a balanced composition somewhat like in *Azalea*. The following April, Russell took the title role in Lathrop and Edwards's *Elaine* and sometime thereafter posed for Alexander again (unlocated).

A flattering article in the *New York World* of July 1888 cited several portraits that had been worked on during the winter after the wedding.[51] Among them were Benjamin Franklin Manierre, ex-police commissioner (unlocated) and Miss Percy Breese (unlocated). Courtlandt Palmer (Figure 23), heir to a splendid fortune and founder of the Nineteenth Century Club, a liberal debating society that advocated for universal tolerance, posed for his portrait suited in white tie, reviewing his notes for a speech before the club. The three Palmer children, including Mary Ann (or May) who had been a bridesmaid, were arranged on one canvas in an unusual horizontal composition (unlocated).[52] Palmer's widowed sister, Mary Anna Palmer Draper also sat for her portrait (Michael Altman, New York). In a carefully calculated design, the sleek undulating bodies of her whippet dogs lean into the seated figure of their mistress. Not mentioned in the article but probably painted around this time were portraits of Eva Palmer and Manierre's two young sons (unlocated).[53] Eva Palmer, age 13 or 14, posed alone, in profile with her hair up like a Gibson Girl (unlocated).[54]

The family of the bride proved to be generous patrons of their talented new in-law. Several portraits cited in the article as being worked on or completed after the wedding were of members of the Virginia branch of the family. There were portraits of Mr. John Stewart and his wife (Stewart Trust, Virginia) and Dean James Lawrence Cabell of the University of Virginia (unlocated).[55] From New York there were portraits of Henry M. Alexander of Alexander & Green and Frederick Beasley Alexander, the bride's eight-year-old brother, richly dressed in black velvet, a dog at his feet and holding a pointing stick, posed as would Velázquez (John White Alexander great-granddaughters).

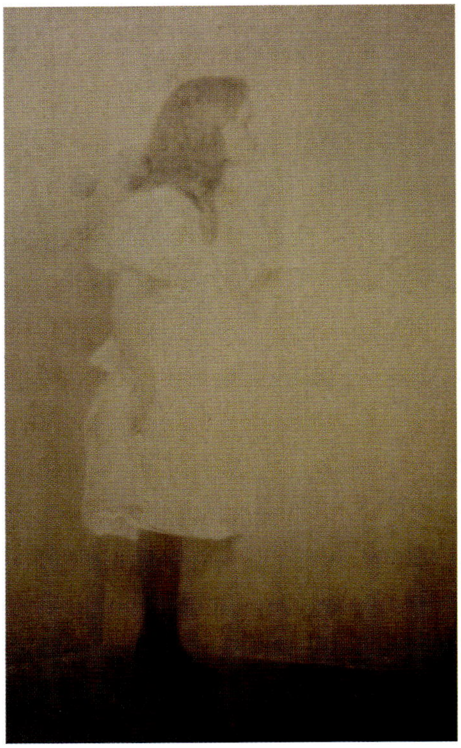

24
Dorothea Gilder, 1887, unlocated. Photograph, Archives of American Art, Smithsonian Institution

While there is no record of the Gilders attending the wedding, they were aware of it. Fifteen days after the wedding Alexander acknowledges a wedding present in a letter to Helena de Kay Gilder. The intended purpose of the letter was to propose a date to paint her daughter Dorothea.[56] In the portrait, the five-year-old, wearing a white dress, is posed standing forward and facing right (Figure 24).[57]

It may have been Alexander's private life that kept him from exhibiting in 1887 – but neither did he in 1888. A plausible explanation attributed to the artist appeared in a local newspaper in the late summer of 1888. "None of the artist's portraits have been seen in the galleries this year, as it has been his intention to exhibit the larger number of his recent works next season at one time and in one place."[58] There is, however, no evidence of such an exhibition ever taking place.

Paintings that Alexander was working on, two of which are known only through the printed word, show that his imagination was occupied with new types of composition. One was described as, "A likeness of a well known gardener in the vienage, who is represented in the act of pruning two immense hydrangea plants in pots."[59] A second was a sea picture inspired by his time in Seabright. It was an idea for a painting that endeared Alexander to the local fishermen, who overwhelmingly responded to his invitation to bring him the "queer fishes" they sometimes found in their nets.[60] Then there was a caricature of a destitute old man with white hair, *Brudder Bones*, that captured the attention of the writer for *Town Topics*.[61] While strolling up Sixth Avenue the previous winter (i.e. 1887–8), the artist "encountered Brudder Bones and at once recognized him as a character worthy of his pencil. Brudder Bones' hat was in the last stages of decomposition. His long coat was tattooed with patches, perforated with rents, and rivaled anything short of a scarecrow's business suit. His boots were of different patterns and thoroughly ventilated at the toes." Despite the indignities of Brudder Bones' circumstances, neither the artist nor the critic overlooked the nobleness of the man.

Though one can speculate as to the extent to which Alexander's career may have been hampered by not exhibiting in 1887 and 1888, it surely would have been advanced by his inclusion in Alfred Trumble's *Representative Works of Contemporary American Artists* (*c.*1887). This influential book was a testament to the historical divide in American art that had evolved since the Civil War. Trumble asserted that, "The past decade … has brought forward a little army of young and fresh talents … The present is a remarkable period in American Art, and every contribution to its history will assume, in the future, an importance which it is not now easy to comprehend."[62] The remarkable period to which Trumble was referring witnessed the "liberation of American art from the rule of subject matter." A work of art was no longer expected "to tell a story or communicate a moral."[63] Truth to nature was usurped by art for art's sake. Instead of a literal imitation of nature as it appeared, for example, in Frederic Church's *Heart of the Andes* (1859, Metropolitan Museum of Art), the new art expressed an artist's subjective observation of nature while at the same time evoking sentiment, as for example in Whistler's *The Falling Rocket* (1875, Detroit Institute of Arts). In 1877 Whistler took John Ruskin to court for the accusation that Whistler slung "a pot of paint in the public's face" by exhibiting *The Falling Rocket*. For Ruskin, who faulted its lack of truth to nature, the visual sensation of a fireworks display was made disreputable by the absence of detail. But for the post-Civil War generation, the viewer, when stepping back from the canvas, could read the cascade of dots of paint as fireworks lighting up the night sky. Whistler's painting was the antithesis of Church's.

There were others who wrote of this divide between the older generation and the new men of which Alexander was one. In a series for *Scribner's* (1880–1), William C. Brownell elucidated the delineation between the old and the new, the painters of the literal versus the painters of the ideal, as the "Renaissance of 1877," otherwise termed the American Renaissance. There was also Mariana Griswold Van Rensselaer's *Book of American Figure Painters*. The premise of the book concerned the way that figure painting had overtaken the dominance of portraiture and landscape since the Centennial. She credited the Centennial for playing "what seems an almost 'providential' part in opening a path."[64] Identifying a group of forty figure painters, she announced that such a compilation "could not well have been … even a very few years ago." As recently as 1983, the art historian David Huntington raised the schism to the level of a revolution, likening the circumstances of the annual exhibition at the National Academy of Design in 1877 to the Boston Tea Party.[65] The so-called army of young and fresh talents boycotted the Academy where the old guard held sway and founded an alternative group, the Society of American Artists. When Alexander returned from Munich, he, too, joined the army of young talent – but not at the expense of forsaking the Academy.

Trumble's book memorialized the triumph of art for art's sake in the years since the Centennial. One work each by thirty top contemporary American painters was illustrated with a single page devoted to a discussion of the painting and a short biography.[66] Some of Trumble's predictions have stood the test of time: Eastman Johnson, Edwin A. Abbey, J. C. Beckwith, Edwin Blashfield, Francis D. Millet, Thomas Moran, and Elihu Vedder. Others, for example William Bliss Baker, Gilbert Gaul, Constant Mayer, Leon Moran, and C. D. Welden have not fared so well. By including Alexander in his book, Trumble places him squarely within the chronicles of change. Illustrating *Azalea* couldn't have been a better choice. Perhaps this is the picture Alexander had in mind when he wrote in July 1884, "Next spring I hope to have a picture in the Exhibition, a subject and not a simple portrait … It is very simple – only one figure but in it I want to express a sentiment." Given the recognition the Trumble book was sure to engender, perhaps the decision to illustrate *Azalea* validates it as a signifier – if not *the* signifier – of Alexander's new direction.

Alexander's new direction evolved gradually. Between 1884 and 1887 there appear to be only two other examples of Alexander's intent to express a sentiment in a single figure, *An Idle Moment* and *Girl with Teacup*. In the former, a woman is posed in profile in a shallow space, contemplating a fish bowl. In the latter (Figure 20), the tonal treatment of light that leaves the girl's face in dark shadow, emotes sentiment as she elegantly handles a cup and saucer as if participating in a Japanese tea ceremony. It is all about movement and gesture, and not about reading the facial expression. These figures represent a new breed of thinking woman, but at the same time they are made decorative. By illustrating *Azalea*, Trumble chose one of three pictures that represented Alexander's new aesthetic direction, rather than one of his many commissioned portraits in the Munich style that monopolized his time in the months preceding and following his wedding.

Alexander's subject for the January 1888 issue of *The Century* was of another man of the theater, the actor John Gilbert. The issue opened with a reproduction of the artist's 1886 full-length portrait of Gilbert in character as Sir Peter Teazle from Sheridan's *The School for Scandal* that Gilbert revived for the Wallach Stock Theater in New York (unlocated). For the playgoers of New York, Gilbert's Sir Peter Teazle was the standard, and Alexander captured the old man's full-bodied and well-rounded vigor – in contrast, for example, to the static figure in Edwin Austin Abbey's earlier illustration. The remainder of the article contained five illustrations of Gilbert in various starring roles. It may or may not have been coincidental that the article appeared shortly before the February 12 announcement of the final season for the company, featuring a series of revivals scheduled from the company's repertoire through May 5. Charles Burnham, the new manager for the 1888/9 season, acquired and displayed the portrait in the Wallach Theater, though Gilbert was no longer performing there.[67]

Remaining in Seabright from May to the end of October 1888 for the birth of his one and only child James on September 19, the family returned to the city and Alexander "rejoined the artistic colony."[68] Other than his family, the one constant in his life was Richard Watson Gilder. *The Century* followed up on Alexander's portraits of John Gilbert by publishing a sequence of illustrations in the first six months of 1889. They accompanied articles on Irish themes, and must have been drawn from the sixty sketches he reportedly made on his 1886 trip to Ireland. Then there were the Gilder family portraits. Having begun with Dorothea, Alexander made portraits of Richard, his brother Joseph and niece Jeannette Cholmeley-Jones in 1889. The latter portrait (The Ackerman Family Collection) was in oil, while that of Joseph, editor of *The Critic*, was only a sketch (unlocated). The shoulder-length portrait of Richard (unlocated) captures him looking the part of an aesthete with longish hair, a mustache and deep-set eyes.[69]

Richard Gilder's portrait was presented to the Fellowcraft Club, which he had founded two years earlier for journalists, artists, and illustrators.[70] The presentation on February 20, 1890 was marked by speeches by Alexander and Mark Twain. Gilder was re-elected President and Alexander elected Vice President.

There was some unfinished business left from Gilder's 1886 commission of likenesses of distinguished authors – that of Walt Whitman. It remained unfinished at the time of Whitman's 70th birthday party on May 31, 1889. Why it took so long must be pure speculation, but the painter was not helped by Whitman's own expectations concerning the portrayal of his physical self. Alexander's nearly creaseless face and the lines of the body and of the chair (not the poet's rocking chair) were too elegant for Whitman's liking. It lacked the "shagginess" of the man himself.[71] The poet could not be persuaded otherwise, despite assurances from a friend, John Burroughs, on April 3, 1886, who apparently had been in contact with the artist days after the sitting at the poet's home in Camden.[72] Whitman was holding it up in contrast to another of his portraits, an oil painted by Thomas Eakins in 1887, which in his own words was more "brutally natural."[73] Yet Alexander was capable of all the honesty Whitman craved. He described as well as sketched his visceral initial impressions of the poet in a letter to Harold Allen the day after the original sitting in Camden, and they are evident in two heads drawn in a sketchbook – yet regrettably, they did not find their way into the final likeness.[74] Whitman himself refers to more sketches by Alexander that did not impress him, but how many and which ones cannot be verified.[75] As for the protracted nature of the affair, Whitman himself speculated that it was because he let it be known to others what he thought of it, and this had possibly got back to Gilder.

Whitman may have sat again for Alexander following his Lincoln lecture on April 14, 1887.[76] But the event that most likely determined the fate of the lingering portrait was the poet's 70th birthday party in 1889, where as it happened Gilder was seated at the poet's right.[77] Months after, a writer for *The Critic* (September 28, 1889) called for a "finished portrait." Alexander must have felt the pressure as the writer complained that though Whitman had sat for Alexander, he had done nothing with it. "What I want to see is a finished portrait, giving the fine contrasts of coloring in the old poet's face and head." Alexander "owes it to posterity to do his best." A short four months later the finished portrait was exhibited in the annual exhibition at the Pennsylvania Academy of the Fine Arts on January 30, 1890. The dignified formal pose and elegant presentation of the poet was not of the ilk of the preliminary sketches, and the portrait was never illustrated by *The Century*. Nevertheless a little more than a year later, five days before the artist departed for Europe, it ended up in its final resting place, the Metropolitan Museum of Art, gifted by Mrs. Jeremiah Milbank.

Probably for health reasons and the need to separate himself from the maddening din of the city, Alexander chose a different venue for the summer of 1890: Cornish, New Hampshire. Sometime in 1889 he was diagnosed by his physician, Dr. Robert Abbe, with grippe, that is understood today to be a severe form of influenza with symptoms such as chills, fever, runny nose, sore throat, muscle pains, headache, coughing, and fatigue as well as the discomfort associated with stomach flu. Abbe advised him "to pack up and go off and have a change of scene for a year."[78] Having been encouraged by fellow artists Charles Platt and Henry Oliver Walker of the merits of Cornish – its camaraderie and domesticity – he substituted the largest studio in America in Seabright for a New England-style farmhouse belonging to one Stephen Alden Tracy and a nearby studio.[79] Alexander and Platt would have crossed paths in the city both socially and professionally. Socially, both had connections to the Hoe family. Charles Platt's first wife was a Hoe, daughter of Colonel Richard Hoe; Alexander had painted Colonel Hoe's nephew Robert, whose daughter, Carrie had been a bridesmaid at Alexander's wedding.

Cornish, New Hampshire had become a destination for artists around 1885 when Augustus Saint-Gaudens began to summer there, having been encouraged by his lawyer Charles C. Beaman who owned property in the town. Others followed and in the summer of 1890, along with Saint-Gaudens, Alexander found himself in the company of Thomas Dewing, Platt, Walker, Henry and Edith Prellwitz, and, for a few unhappy weeks, Dennis Miller Bunker. Walker and his wife tipped off Alexander about boarding at the Tracy farmhouse on Platt Road.[80] It had become common practice among local families like the Tracys to take in boarders for the summer and send their children off to work on other farms.[81]

The artists' colony in Cornish had a reputation for hard work uninterrupted by unwelcome visitors, and punctuated by gatherings for holidays and special occasions. Cornish provided a haven that was quiet, pastoral and nurturing for the creative spirits who visited or chose to remain. Housing and land were easily available at reasonable prices and children were welcomed. The Alexanders arrived around May 20 and stayed probably into October.[82] They participated in the social activities of the season such as the July 4th party at the home of Charles Platt to which all of the artists were invited. His presence at the Beamans' picnic on August 9 is documented in a group photograph in which Alexander appears in the top row, fourth from the left.[83] Other artists

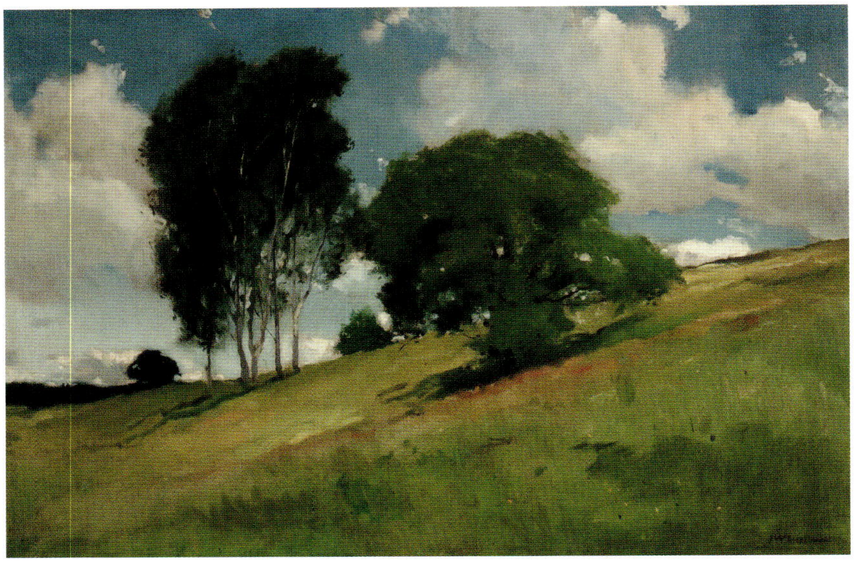

25
Landscape, Cornish, 1890, oil on canvas, 24 × 36 in. (61 × 91.4 cm.), Jean and Graham Devoe Williford Charitable Trust

in the photograph were Platt, Henry Prellwitz, Saint-Gaudens, and Walker. Around Labor Day on September 11, there was a celebration marking the placing of the cornerstone of Annie Lazarus's villa High Court, designed by Platt, followed by a dinner at Platt's home.

Alexander's output in 1890 was nothing like it had been in 1888 and 1889. This may have been exactly what the doctor ordered – but that did not stop him from working, albeit at a less frenzied pace. While in Cornish he started a new body of work purely in landscape, a genre Alexander had pursued intermittently and infrequently while occupied with portrait commissions. But the Cornish landscapes represent a bold leap forward in terms of composition and quality of light. He avoided the clichéd panoramic view with Mount Ascutney in the background. Instead he used high horizons to close off the distant views, painting rolling hills dotted with beech trees swaying in the wind under a bold light (Figure 25). Each canvas is an arrangement of azure-blue sky, fluffy white clouds and undulating green pastures painted in a higher key than was normal for Alexander. Two compositions are quite modern for their time, with high horizon lines broken by beech trees silhouetted against the sky.[84]

Alexander's limited output, and his turning to the landscape genre that freed him from the expectations of demanding patrons, suggests his diminishing capacity to work. He made the occasional watercolor of lush white roses (Figure 26).[85] Intimate in scale, they would serve as source material for

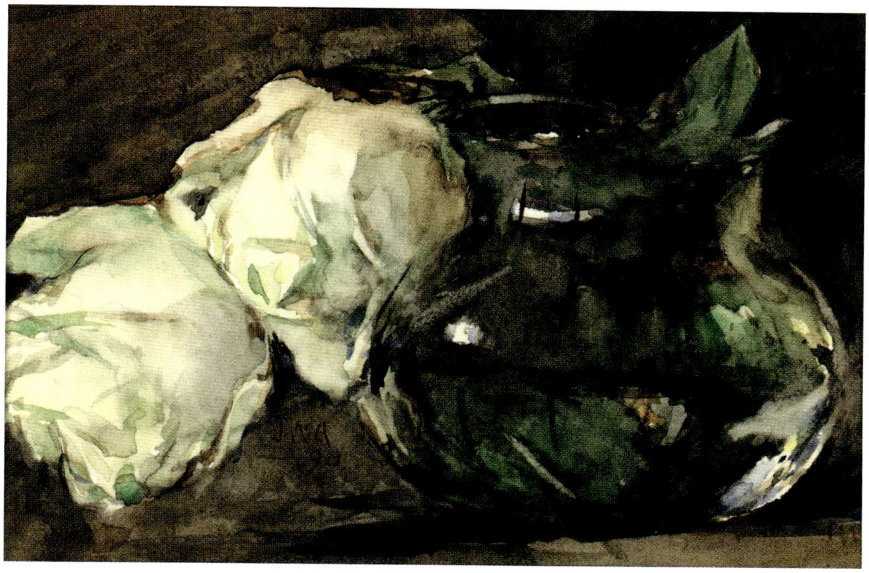

26
Still Life, Vase of Flowers, 1890, watercolor, approx. 4 × 6 in. (10.6 × 15.2 cm.), Bennington Museum, Bennington, Vermont, 2004.60

inclusion in the figure paintings of the 1890s. There is a reference in the Tracy correspondence to a possible portrait of a Mr. Bryant (probably a member of one of the oldest Cornish families), but there is no evidence of a portrait being painted.[86] Also at this time more of his illustrations from his 1886 trip to Ireland appeared in print, with several illustrating Charles de Kay's article "The Old Poetic Guild in Ireland" for the April 1890 issue of *The Century*.

The end of the year saw a reprise of the *Brudder Bones* type in *Ole Hanover* (unlocated), both a portrait and a caricature. The character of Ole Hanover is the subject of Thomas Nelson Page's novelette, "Plaski's Tunaments." A reproduction of Alexander's painting accompanied the publication of the story in the 1890 Christmas issue of *Harper's Magazine*. In the American southern negro dialect Page tells the story of a negro protagonist from Hanover County, Virginia (the author's birthplace). He leaves nothing to chance for Alexander who faithfully depicted Page's subject. Of an indeterminate age, Ole Hanover could be mistaken for clergy, wearing a "very long and baggy coat which had once been black, but was now tanned by exposure … a vest which looked as if it had been velvet." His freshly washed shirt had a "high clean collar" that amply covered a white cloth at the neck. "His skin was of that lustrous black which shines as if freshly oiled …" There were two tuffs of short white hair … which shone like snow against his black cheeks." His silver rimmed spectacles gave him "an air of portentous dignity" as if he were a head of state brandishing, in this case, a long hickory stick.[87] Just like Brudder Bones, Alexander discovered his model for Ole Hanover on the streets of New York.

The likeness of Ole Hanover was the outlier, hanging in the Fellowcraft Club along with notaries of the journalist profession.[88] Two conventional portraits by Alexander hung in the club, the one of Gilder and a second of George William Childs (unlocated), publisher of the *Philadelphia Ledger*, philanthropist, public-minded citizen and successful businessman. At a meeting on the night of April 29 the Childs portrait was presented along with a portrait of Alexander by Benoni Irwin (Graphics Arts Collection, Princeton University Library). Alexander appears pensive in the portrait, as well he should. He was about to uproot his family and relocate to Paris. Highly regarded more than just for his skills as a portrait painter, but also as a leader, Alexander had been elected to succeed Gilder as President in late February.[89] The April meeting was his last appearance in that post, which explains the reason for the portrait.

3

THE FIRST SOJOURN IN PARIS

WITH ALEXANDER'S HEALTH NOT FULLY RESTORED after a few months in Cornish – instead of the full year the doctor had prescribed – a more drastic and distant change of scenery was called for. This time it would be Paris. Setting sail on May 2, 1891, the family was welcomed on the European side by Elizabeth's mother and younger brother. On May 21 Whitelaw Reid, envoy extraordinary and minister plenipotentiary, issued a protective order from the Legation of the United States for Mr. and Mrs. Alexander, child and nurse. Alexander, age thirty-four, stood five foot eleven, with blue eyes, straight nose, brown hair, fair complexion and long face.[1]

Shortly after arrival in Paris Alexander was well enough to take his family to Bavaria for a short visit to Polling.[2] But as for the painter's well-being, "He was absolutely sure that he would never be able to do any more work."[3] He confessed to his high school friend Ed Phelps in November the extent of his debilitation. Having arrived in Paris a wreck and taken all summer to improve, he wrote, "I had to take such a thorough rest that letter writing was not allowed … Now – however I have fully recovered."[4] Only three years into a marriage, and with Alexander already showing signs of a weakened condition that would sap his strength, his wife took on the role of protector, one that she would resume frequently for the rest of his life, whenever there was a recurring debilitation.

Given this bleak forecast, once again Alexander showed an inordinate capacity to find the good and to excel amidst uncertainty. He had made the best of tragic circumstances as an orphan. He prevailed in getting a position as an illustrator in a major New York publishing house despite the odds. He did everything possible to stretch his financial resources to be able to study in Europe long enough to improve his prospects for earning a living as a painter. All the while his inherent ability to lead was recognized by his peers. Now in Paris, far from home, instead of succumbing to doubts as to his fitness ever to work again, he was uplifted by a perpetual spirit of optimism, sustained by what was going on around him. Though he was facing a "discouraging time" personally, the city that welcomed him was an exhilarating place to be professionally. It "was a big moment for art in Paris. Nearly all the well known painters of all the different nationalities were living there, because they were taking an interest in forming this new society, which had broken from the old salon under the direction [i.e. leadership] of Puvis de Chavannes and Meissonnier [*sic*]."[5] If Alexander, strong in spirit, but weak in body, needed motivation, all he had to do was look around him.

Alexander saw a great deal of all the painters in Paris as he began making a place for himself in this exciting artistic milieu that was a nexus for change. The new direction was adumbrated in Joris–Karl Huysmans' *À Rebours* (1884) which predicted the modern taste for the artistically beautiful. With hindsight it was more than apt that the controversy surrounding the publication of Huysmans's book occurred in the very summer of 1884 when Alexander passed through Paris and determined to change the direction of his painting from standard portraiture towards the representation of a single figure to express a sentiment. And in 1896, as a witness to change, the art historian Richard Muther observed that "the over-refined society" of the *fin de siècle* had come to loathe all that was banal and commonplace and thus retreated into an ideal artistic world of its own making.[6] Zola's naturalism was passé, replaced by the symbolist writings of Stéphane Mallarmé, Paul Verlaine and others. The future, according to Muther, lay in the minds of men of intelligence, "the chosen people, the small band comprising the elite of the intellect, those whose pleasure is in pure beauty [i.e. art for art's sake]." He called this new type "l'homme libre."[7]

The wheels of change amongst the art establishment were propelled by Pierre Puvis de Chavannes, Ernest Meissonier, Auguste Rodin, Carolus-Duran, Félix Bracquemond, Albert-Ernest Carrier-Belleuse, Jules Dalou, and Alfred Roll – two of whom were Alexander's neighbors – who founded the Société Nationale des Beaux-Arts in 1890. At the apogee of the anti-establishment movement, the new society seceded from an official salon riddled with self-perpetuating favoritism and control over matters of style. Its founding members did the nearly impossible: they brokered the structural change of "the" dominant nineteenth-century French art institution. Their new society welcomed all who sought a fair opportunity to exhibit their work free of favoritism from jurors and academy professors, and the interminable battles over who voted for jurors, who served on juries and the protocol for medal winners and *hors concours* status.

The old regime no longer had a monopoly. The new salon welcomed foreign artists and artists who worked in other media such as the decorative arts, mural decoration and architecture. The result was two salons that looked nothing alike. In the new salon, the walls were no longer covered with scenes from the working life and religious practices of peasants and artisans. Instead, as Richard Muther described it, "a fragrant archaism has taken the place of Naturalism; singularity, that of everyday life; mystical dusk or a light blue, fine grey, or rosy, faded Gobelin tone, that of glaring daylight."[8] The spiritual ancestors of the younger generation were the visionary Gustave Moreau and the ascetic Puvis, who were considered too solitary and mystical in their own time.

The Paris that greeted Alexander offered multiple opportunities to advance his career. In addition to the two main salons there were independent salons, group exhibitions, and even opportunities to exhibit elsewhere on the Continent as new secessionist groups emerged. Exhibitions were constantly opening and "the finest of modern pictures are at all times to be seen."[9] There was a vibrant press, with coverage by increasing numbers of art journals and critics. Alexander found the art community to be more agreeable than in New York: "everything here is on a higher plane." When Alexander's neighbor, Puvis, then vice president, assumed the presidency of the Société Nationale in February 1891 upon the death of Meissonier, only one Salon exhibition had as yet been sponsored by the new society. Being in Paris at this time of change would make a marked difference in Alexander's work. His handmaiden was his "remarkably quick" wife about whom he said, "I never travel an inch from the studio without her."

To help him ease into his new circumstances Alexander did not lack for contacts, both in the art community and among the American expatriates. The Russian Ivan Pranishnikoff (1841–1909), a dear friend from his days at *Harper's*, was a fount of information and influence. With his advice, the couple located an apartment on the corner of Boulevard Berthier and Rue Alphonse de Neuville. It was "superb" and the light "simply magnificent", with an adjoining salon and studio separated by a door and bedrooms in the back on the mezzanine.[10] It was not, however, located in the Latin Quarter, but on the Right Bank in a neighborhood that included artists such as Alfred Roll (Puvis' successor as Vice President of the Société Nationale des Beaux-Arts), Paul-Albert Besnard, Giovanni Boldini, Ernest Duez, Walter Gay, Jean-François Raffaëlli, Alfred Stevens, and Puvis himself.

With his long beard, Pranishnikoff "wore" his Russianness with great aplomb. He held a ceremonial title of "art attaché to the Russian Ministry of War." This required him to return once a year to the country of his birth where he fulfilled his obligation to the crown by depicting military maneuvers. When he returned to Paris he came bearing Russian luxury goods, from furs to gastronomic delicacies. He was a favorite of the Russian embassy and his soirées and studio were very popular destinations. In turn, he was a frequenter of one of the premier Parisian salons, that of Princess Matilda Bonaparte, daughter of Napoleon's brother Jérôme.[11] Her wealth came from her marriage to a boorish Russian with a title not recognized even in his home country, whom she abandoned. It was Pranishnikoff who introduced Alexander to Rodin, Jean-Charles Cazin and Puvis at the very first Salon he attended, probably in 1892, though it could have been 1891.[12] It should not come as a surprise that Alexander chose to paint Pranishnikoff and exhibit the portrait in the Salon of 1894.

Introductions to two American expatriates provided the necessary social entrées for a new man in Paris. Mrs. Philip Van Rensselaer, a widow friend of Henry James residing in London, extended him an introduction to Henrietta Reubell, a bohemian hostess since the 1870s.[13] Reubell functioned as "keeper of erotic secrets and illicit information … that allows her to facilitate liaisons."[14] On making the introduction Rensselaer warned, "If she does not [like you] she will pay no attention to you whatever and perhaps be rude."[15] She "permitted anything but dullness and ill manners, delighting in wit and paradox and adventurous conversation," as the English artist William Rothenstein reminisced.[16] The most interesting people would come to her residence in the heart of the American colony near the Champs-Élysées on Sunday afternoons, particularly writers and artists and others passing through. Among them were Henry James, John Singer Sargent, Robert de Montesquieu, Oscar Wilde, Mr. and Mrs. Edward Darley Boit, Edmond de Polignac – and, indeed, Alexander, whom Rothenstein much admired.[17]

Henry James was an intimate of Reubell and had been much more so in the 1870s. Her character is written into *The Ambassadors* (1903) as Miss Barrace, of whom James wrote, she "doesn't live all [she] can – so much as approve of those who do."[18] By the time Alexander knew her, the onetime marital prospect for James (who showed no mercy when he described her in 1876: "If I wanted to desire to marry an ugly Parisian-American, with money and *toutes les elegances* Miss R would be a very good objective, but I don't.") was past her prime.[19] Around 1895 she was described rather differently by a dispassionate female friend, Elizabeth Alexander: "She was not beautiful, but had a tremendous amount of character and style … She always reminded us of one of those witty 18th century French miniatures and she still wore her grey hair in a series of large puffs, forming a chignon which style of hair dressing had been fashionable during her youth."[20]

Whistler was in Paris on and off in 1891, and settled there in April 1892. Alexander attempted to re-establish contact with him by offering to paint his portrait. Instead of approaching Whistler directly he turned to Henrietta Reubell who brought the subject up with Beatrix Whistler. She rebuffed the idea in the most polite of terms, adding that Jimmie "will be delighted to meet Mr. Alexander again, but says he has a horror of sitting or standing to any one."[21] Within days, "Jimmie" invited John to 33 Rue de Tournon, where the Whistlers were staying temporarily in a little hotel over the Foyot restaurant, to meet Mrs. Alexander for the first time.[22] It is notable that at a time when Alexander was thinking about when to commence painting again and what to paint, his thoughts were of a portrait of Whistler.

In any foreign city the American embassy is a haven for its citizens, whether settling in as expatriates or simply passing through. It frequently happened that Americans came to Paris for a short stay and, once ensnared by the city's charms, remained instead of returning home. The American quarter as described by Alexander was "always the best part of the city and the society always amusing."[23] His access to the embassy was personal, eased by the arrival of Henry Addison Alexander, a first cousin to Bess, who would serve as legal counsel from 1892 to 1899. When Whitelaw Reid resigned as ambassador on March 25, 1892, he was not replaced until June by Thomas Jefferson Coolidge; he in turn was replaced by James Biddle Eustis in May 1893. Ambassador Eustis earned a reputation as a man about town, often accompanied by one of his cronies, the artist and illustrator Charles Dana Gibson.[24] As embassy regulars under each of these ambassadors, the Alexanders took great amusement in the antics of guests who had trouble disguising their social ambitions.

Supposedly restored to health, Alexander was ready to partake of all that Paris had to offer. Pranishnikoff shepherded Alexander's entrée into the art community, Reubell the literati group and Henry Alexander the American expatriate group. A sign that he had "arrived" came in the form of a missive from Armand Dayot, Inspector General of the Ministry of Public Instruction and Fine Arts, who extended his sentiments and invited him for a chat.[25]

Taking it all in during his first full year in Paris, Alexander attended the inaugural exhibit of the independent Salon de la Rose Croix. Founded in August 1890 by Joséphin Péladan, its manifesto published in *Le Figaro* in September 1891 welcomed "Catholic Subjects, Oriental religious themes, decorative allegories, Renaissance nudes, and 'expressive' portraits." Unacceptable subjects were "historical, military, humorous, illustrative, contemporaneous, landscapes, seascapes, and still-life."[26] Decorating the walls of the Galerie Durand-Ruel for the inaugural Salon were works in this spirit by Émile Bernard, Fernand Khnopff,

Ferdinand Hodler, Jan Toorop, Félix Vallotton, Carlos Schwabe, and Charles Filiger. Immense crowds were entertained by a piano performance composed for the occasion by Erik Satie.[27] A modern score in three parts, neither dissonant nor atonal, it had an elegant, austere chorale-style metric structure. While the exhibit was on view Albert Aurier published an important article on the Symbolists in *La Revue Encyclopédique* with illustrations by the Nabis, in which he singled out Gauguin as the motivator behind the movement, among them Paul Sérusier, Meyer de Haan and Charles Filiger. The Nabis's synthesis of natural forms by means of strongly outlined and simplified shapes with solid patches of vivid color would have bearing on Alexander's art, beginning in the summer of 1892 in the Breton village of Le Pouldu. Finding Filiger there, he surely could not have forgotten three of Filiger's works from the Salon de la Rose Croix exhibition – *Holy Family* (formerly Arthur Altschul collection), *La prière* (Musée Départemental Maurice Denis) and *Sainte en prière*.

Then there was Puvis. Having debuted in the old Salon of 1851, he lived long enough to enjoy admiration by an entirely different generation. He painted classical subjects with a simplification and reduction of form, color and line – techniques inspired by the plastic arts, particularly suited to reinforce images that had to be seen from afar, such as his murals for the Panthéon, which for Alexander exemplified Puvis's tenets. For the generation of the 1890s, the future of modern painting was beholden to Puvis's simplified structural framework. Given Alexander's opinion that Puvis was "undoubtedly the greatest painter of the century," he probably made an effort to view Puvis's *L'été* in the new Salon of 1891 before going off to Polling, and in the following year to take note of *L'hiver*. The future American muralist understood fully the merits of Puvis's technique: "simplifying the line detracts as little as possible from the line & colour scheme of his work as a complete whole."[28]

Alexander's understanding of color is indebted to Whistler, from whom he learned the subtlety of color harmony. Most easily available for him to see in Paris would have been Whistler's submission of older work to the Salon of 1891: *Arrangement in Brown and Black: Portrait of Miss Rosa Corder* (1876–8, Frick Collection) and *Crepuscule in Flesh Colour and Green: Valparaiso* (1866, Tate Gallery). At the end of the year there was news of Whistler's portrait of his mother being purchased by the Musée du Luxembourg. The following year, Whistler was working on his portrait of Comte Robert de Montesquiou (1891–2, Frick Collection) at the time he and Alexander resumed their friendship. While at the 1892 Salon, Alexander could have admired Whistler's portrait of Lady Meux (1881–2, Frick Collection) and five *Nocturnes*. The two portraits, of Montesquiou as a study in black and of Lady Meux as a study in gray would resonate with Alexander as he prepared to make his Salon debut the following spring.

Assimilating Whistler, Puvis, and the Nabis, as well as all that Paris had to offer, Alexander pursued his own individual style in earnest in the summer of 1892, his health permitting. To Reubell may go the credit for facilitating the choice of the Breton hamlet of Le Pouldu. William Rothenstein, a frequenter of her salon, made the introduction to fellow Englishman Arthur Studd, who convinced Alexander to go.[29] The family spent about five months in this tiny provincial hamlet, beginning in May. It was a choice that afforded "economy, comfort and surroundings conducive to slowly taking up his painting again."[30] Despite fits and starts Alexander had not been actively painting since before he left the United States. Now it was time.

Le Pouldu was cheaper, less congested and offered a disparate topography for picture-making compared to the neighboring village of Pont-Aven. It is situated on the south coast of Brittany, west-south-west of Paris, in the département of Finistère. The picturesque location was imbued with the weight of its history, from the time of the Druids, through Roman occupation, the Middle Ages, the Vikings, to the Bourbon kings. Unchanged over centuries, its isolation and crude and hard way of life were celebrated in the romantic novels of Pierre Loti, Henry Blackburn and Blanche Willis Howard; through the studies of Anatole Le Braz at the University of Rennes; and of course in grandiose paintings of Breton life by the likes of Pascal Dagnan-Bouveret, Lucien Simon and others exhibited at the annual Salons. Fishing and farming were fundamental to its way of life. The romance of the sea, lives lost and the solitariness of the women and children left to the farming for extended periods of time were commemorated in words and in pictures.

The youthful Arthur Studd, a British painter from a titled family and of independent means, had already spent two summers in Le Pouldu, where he met Paul Gauguin. In the summer of 1891, he had taken a house at the top of the *falaise* (cliff) with a tennis court below.[31] The following summer this became the hub of activity for a group of English-speaking artists, among them Americans William Sergeant Kendall, J. Humphreys Johnston and Walter Nettleton, and, in addition to Studd, another Englishman, Alfred Thornton. Thornton and Kendall boarded with Studd; Johnston and Nettleton at a neighboring farm.[32] Around the corner from the tennis court, Alexander and a fellow American, Guy Maynard boarded at the Goulven Inn. On occasion Alexandre Harrison, an American artist known for his paintings of the Breton shoreline, ferried over from nearby Pont-Aven; Alexander would sometimes take the ferry in the other direction.

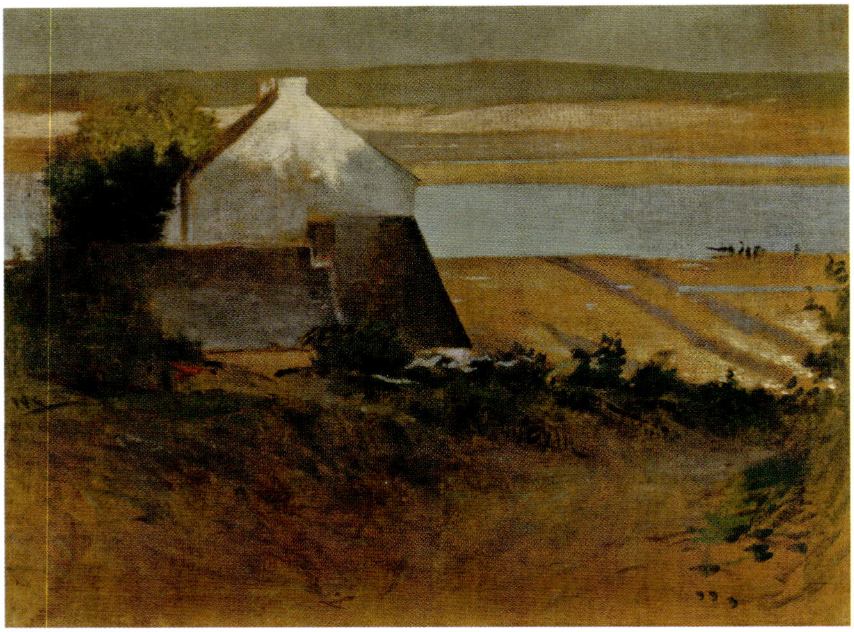

27
Landscape, Le Pouldu, 1892, oil on canvas, 35½ × 47¾ in. (90.2 × 121.3 cm.), John White Alexander great-granddaughters

Within a five-minute walk, beginning at the quiet Laïta River and ending on the tumultuous Atlantic coastline, could be found a mélange of motifs to appeal to an artist's imagination. There is something of a metaphor in the location chosen by the two groups of artists: the English-speakers resided down by the placid river, while the French-speaking group – Charles Filiger, Meyer de Haan and Paul Sérusier – boarded at Marie Henry's inn up the hill not far from the ocean. Nearby was Gauguin's former studio and the Plage des Grands Sables. Stretching away from the rugged coastline, the farmland is dotted with distinctive two-chimney farmhouses. Down by the river, the Goulven Inn, owned by the Portier and Goulven families, was essentially a local gathering place with rooms upstairs for guests to sleep off their inebriation. Next to it is the Jacob building, named for the family of the boat pilot. Facing the two buildings, a steep set of stairs to the right ascends the side of the *falaise*. At the top, a tree-lined path with a stone wall on the river side forks to the right. The left leads to the villa that Studd occupied, overlooking the tennis court behind the inn.

Alexander ventured to all these sites, as is evidenced by his work. On the wooded path at the top of steps from the Jacob building he painted two Breton maidens resting on the stone wall with the slightest of pink-dappled sunlight piercing through the trees (Eldridge and Erika Blanton, Virginia). A rather conventionally conceived picture of figures in a landscape, it contrasts with two others that are far from conventional. *Landscape, Le Pouldu* (Figure 27) depicts a farmhouse just beyond the tree-lined path whose vantage point has been manipulated to give a distant view of the Laïta. Executed in broad horizontal swaths of subdued color, it is just as Alfred Thornton described the actual scene, "a misty blue, of the little estuary of the Laita, at low tide striped with yellowish sandbanks."[33] That Alexander had learnt Gauguin's lessons in the simplification of nature cannot be denied when comparing this landscape to the latter's *The Loss of Virginity* (1890–1). Allowing for Alexander's spatial manipulation, both views are painted from the same vantage point.

Another painting, *Pouldu, The Deep Curl* (Figure 28) shows that Alexander also made his way to the coast and the neighborhood of the Nabis. He frames the composition tightly and dramatically, looking directly down from the cliffs onto black rocks over which waves break. The flattening of both depth and distance begs a comparison with Gauguin's *Seascape with Cow on the Edge of a Cliff*, a scene painted in Le Pouldu in 1888. Both artists feature the wet "black rocks" created by "encrustations of blackish mussels."[34] The forces of nature captured in these two canvases do not occur by the side of the calm Laïta. In Alexander's case, the painting's ambiguous orientation and breeching of the rules of perspective was unlike anything he had previously attempted. While much has been made of the Nabis group, little has been written about the English-speakers down by the river, and even less regard has been paid to the effect of the one upon the art of the other; but in the case of Alexander these two examples clearly demonstrate a shared visual experience.

28
Pouldu, The Deep Curl, 1892, oil on canvas, 48 × 35¾ in. (121.9 × 90.8 cm), Gregory White Smith and Steven Naifeh, South Carolina. Photo: Brent Cline

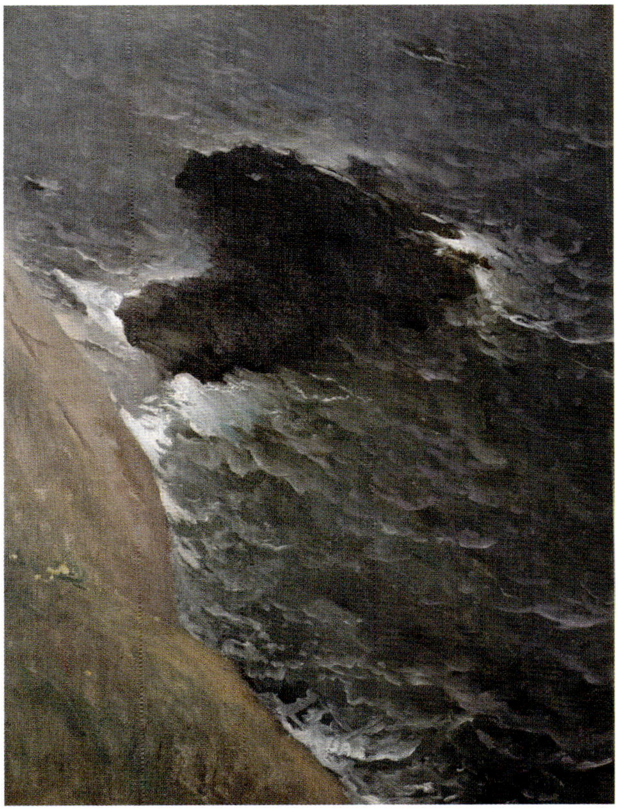

While Alexander's Le Pouldu landscapes display a high level of experimentation with regard to compression of space, the same cannot be said of his figure painting. In a full-length portrait of Josephine, the housekeeper at the Goulven inn, as a *Bretonne peasant* (Figure 29), Alexander was guided

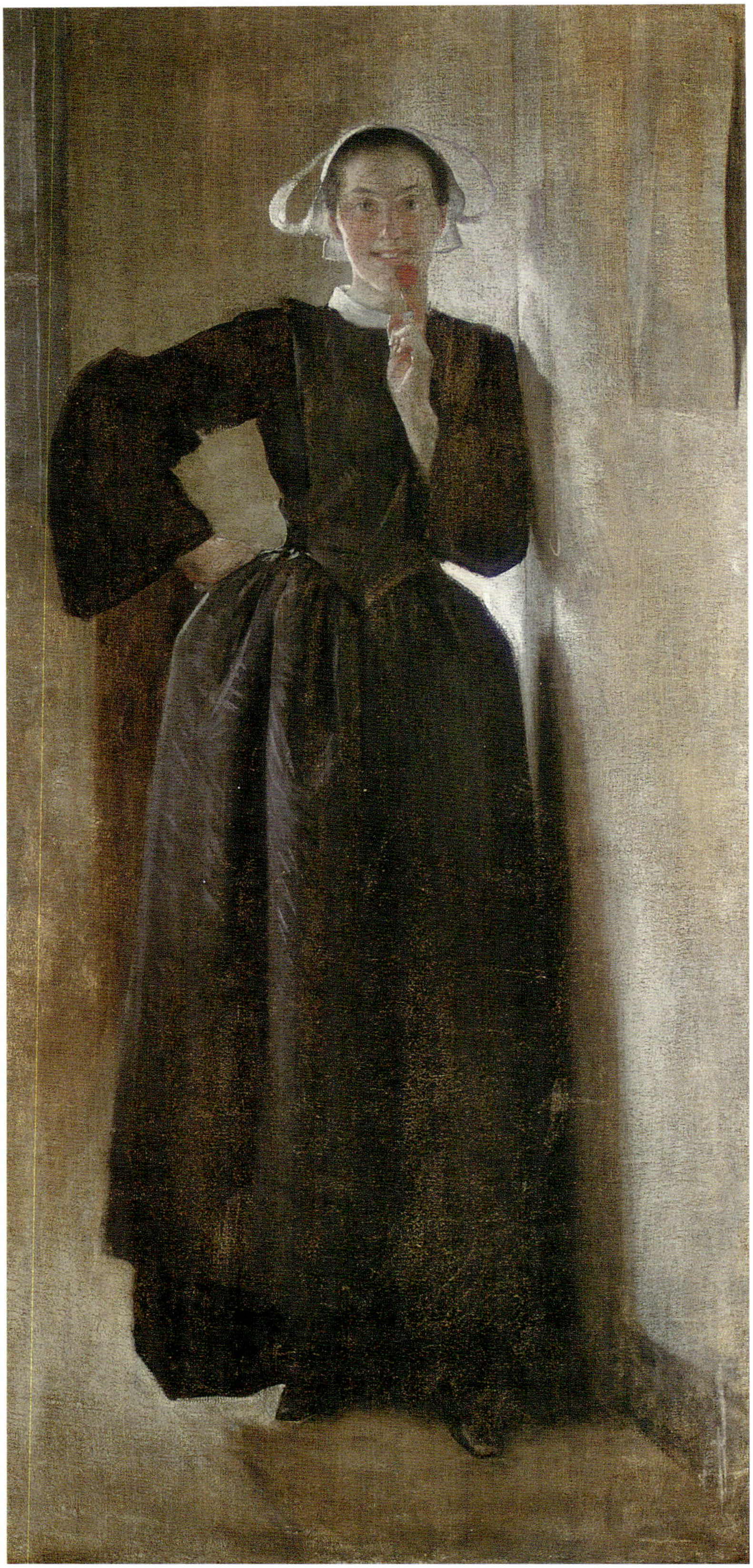

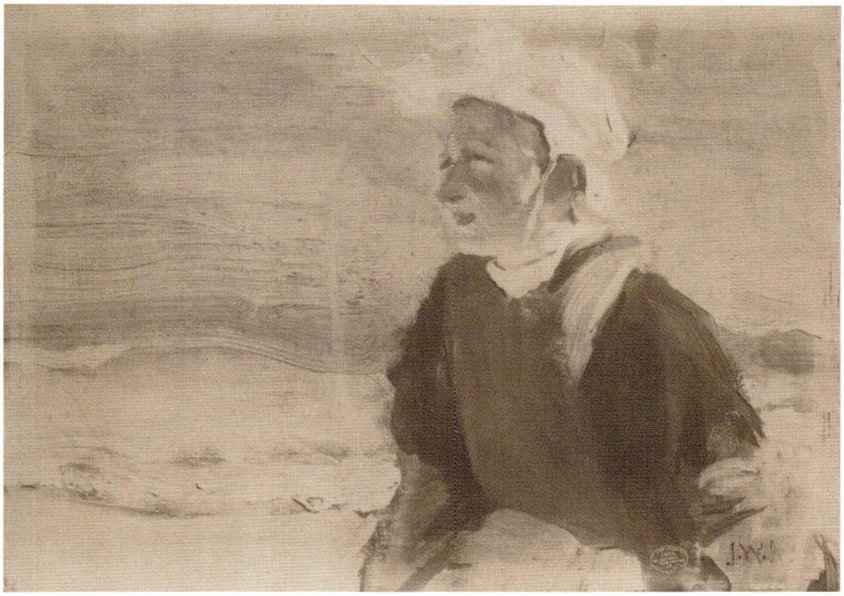

30
Brittany Sketch, 1892, unlocated. Photograph, John White Alexander papers, Archives of American Art, Smithsonian Institution

by the somber colors of the regional dress, black with a long deep-blue apron and white coif. The rosy, smiling face of the good-natured Josephine is framed by her snugly fitting coif, with wings in the style of Moëlan-sur-Mer, a village in the département on the other side of the Laïta.[35] The spare interior space in which she is standing is defined by an earthen color with only the slightest variation of tone, indicating how closely Alexander looked at Velázquez, and more immediately, Whistler's portrait of Montesquiou. Bess, who did a considerable amount of writing while in Le Pouldu, brings Josephine to life: "Perched over the dirtiest face they had ever seen on any human being was a spotless white coif – starched, immaculate and with the bright ribbon that bound its under cap carefully and neatly adjusted. This was their first introduction to 'Phine' (short for Josephine), the maid of all work of the Inn who for the next five months … presided over their domestic machinery."[36] At seventy-five inches high the portrait was a major work suitable for exhibiting at the Salon, but it was not shown in Paris.

In addition to these three significant works from his time in Le Pouldu, there are others that are not finished or unaccounted for. In an unfinished canvas of a Breton maid standing in a doorway, she wears the same type of dress as Josephine.[37] Two other peasant subjects that appear to have been major works are known only from black-and-white reproductions. One is of a Breton

29
Bretonne Peasant (Josephine), 1892, oil on canvas, 75 ⅝ × 35 ⅝ in. (190.5 × 91.4 cm.), private collection, New York. © 1996 Christie's Images Limited

maid seated with her hand on her left hip clearly posing for the artist.[38] The grand coif and the addition of the collerette at the neckline differ from those depicted in other Le Pouldu canvases.[39] The ample starched coif sits in all its fullness on her head like a halo. The collerette looks like a bib with additional pieces over the shoulders. The costumes are of the type depicted in Gauguin's Pont-Aven painting *Four Breton Maidens* (1886). *Brittany Sketch* (Figure 30), another example of a figure in a landscape, displays a remarkable freedom of execution, with a horizontal swath of the brush capturing a shimmering impression of the shore meeting the water behind, a female figure in close-up in three-quarters view, her eyes squinting in the scorching sunlight.[40] The expediency of the brushwork belies the fact that it is a finished work, signed and subsequently copyrighted by the Detroit Publishing Company in 1906. While none of these Le Pouldu pictures seem to have been exhibited in Paris, in subsequent years Alexander thought enough of them to include some in exhibits in America in 1909 and 1913. Another medium that he took up while in Le Pouldu, was the silhouette. Profiles of Studd and Guy Ferris Maynard are annotated "Pouldu" and "1891" as if intended as a record of their summer together (John White Alexander great-granddaughters).

The most demonstrable and sustained influence of the Nabis is unquestionably one of technique – that of painting on coarsely woven jute canvas. There must be a correlation between Alexander's expressed disappointment with the canvas he initially purchased in Paris and his adoption of a rougher coarse-weave canvas while in Le Pouldu; "coarse" meaning seven per inch as opposed to twenty in fine-woven canvas.[41] All of the aforementioned canvases, *Landscape, Le Pouldu, Pouldu, The Deep Curl*, *Breton Girls in a Landscape,* and *Bretonne Peasant* are on coarsely woven canvas and bear the stamp of the canvas supplier on the back: Collardeau, 4 Rue Victor Massé. In choosing a coarse canvas Alexander's purpose was the same as that of the Nabis, one of aesthetics. An unprimed coarse weave sucks up pigment from the brush, yet the finish appears thin and matte and when not varnished the canvas takes on a primitive look. Alexander had help from Sanford B. Pomeroy to develop a coarse canvas that came to be called *Alexandre toile*.[42] Pomeroy was an American of independent means who spent time on both sides of the Atlantic and exhibited in the French Salons as a craft artist. He was listed as a new member of the Société Francaise d'Archéologie in 1928; otherwise little is known about him.

In the winter of 1892–3, Alexander presumably chose not to exhibit at the Chicago World's Fair, instead spending his time preparing for the French Salon in the spring. When the time came for his debut, the positive reception of his three studies of female figures benefited from the enthusiasm of some influential artists and critics. Whistler had already introduced Alexander as someone to watch, as a result of which the press was favorably predisposed.[43] Alfred Roll spoke highly of him to the *New York Herald* (May 9, 1893) the day before the Salon opened. The excitement of the moment reverberates in Elizabeth Alexander's account of two Salon regulars fawning over her husband. Pranishnikoff, who served on the jury, promised to tell her husband of their decision once it was made. To his disappointment when he arrived, he discovered Giovanni Boldini had already told the artist that Alexander's pictures had been "received with enthusiasm."[44] The critic Octave Mirbeau wrote in admiration of the pose, style and solidity of Alexander's three canvases.[45] Arsène Alexandre echoed his sentiments, commenting that Alexander carried off a startling success even though he was new to the public.[46]

As for the entries themselves, *Portrait Gris* (Figure 32) is a study of a female figure in shades of gray, a color closely associated with Whistler. Silvery grays in the dress and pearly grays in the curtain are offset by the black hair and the touch of red in the rosette and artist's signature. The posing of the subject from behind, with her arm by her side, mimics Whistler's *Mother of Pearl and Silver: The Andalusian*, which Alexander could have seen in Whistler's studio. Velázquez is also invoked, never more so than in this painting: the unfettered space, the Spanish profile and the exaggerated bouffant skirt to which is added banding like the detailing in the skirts worn by royalty in the portraits of the *Infanta Margarita* and *Mariana of Austria*.[47] Cleverly, the horizontality of the stripes of the curtain and the bands of the skirt counter the vertical lines of the curtain and the folds of the skirt, animating an otherwise static figure. In the more conventional *Portrait Noir* (Figure 31), Elizabeth Alexander faces her audience with all the nobility of her being. She is dressed in black velvet with black brocade trim; a partially open door to the far right is a convention adopted to allow some variation of tones in an otherwise dark study. In a brighter key is *Portrait Jaune* (unlocated, Figure 33) with the figure dressed in yellow with green velvet trim. Of the three, this is the most ambitious not only in terms of color but also of movement, with an unnatural twist to the torso.[48] One of his Paris sketchbooks demonstrates how Alexander imagined his canvases: independent, but also interdependent and complementary. A sketchbook page shows *Portrait Gris* and *Portrait Noir* side by side.[49] Another drawing in the same sketchbook shows three unidentified pictures of women in long dresses as a triptych.[50] The three Salon entries were hung side by side in the same spirit.

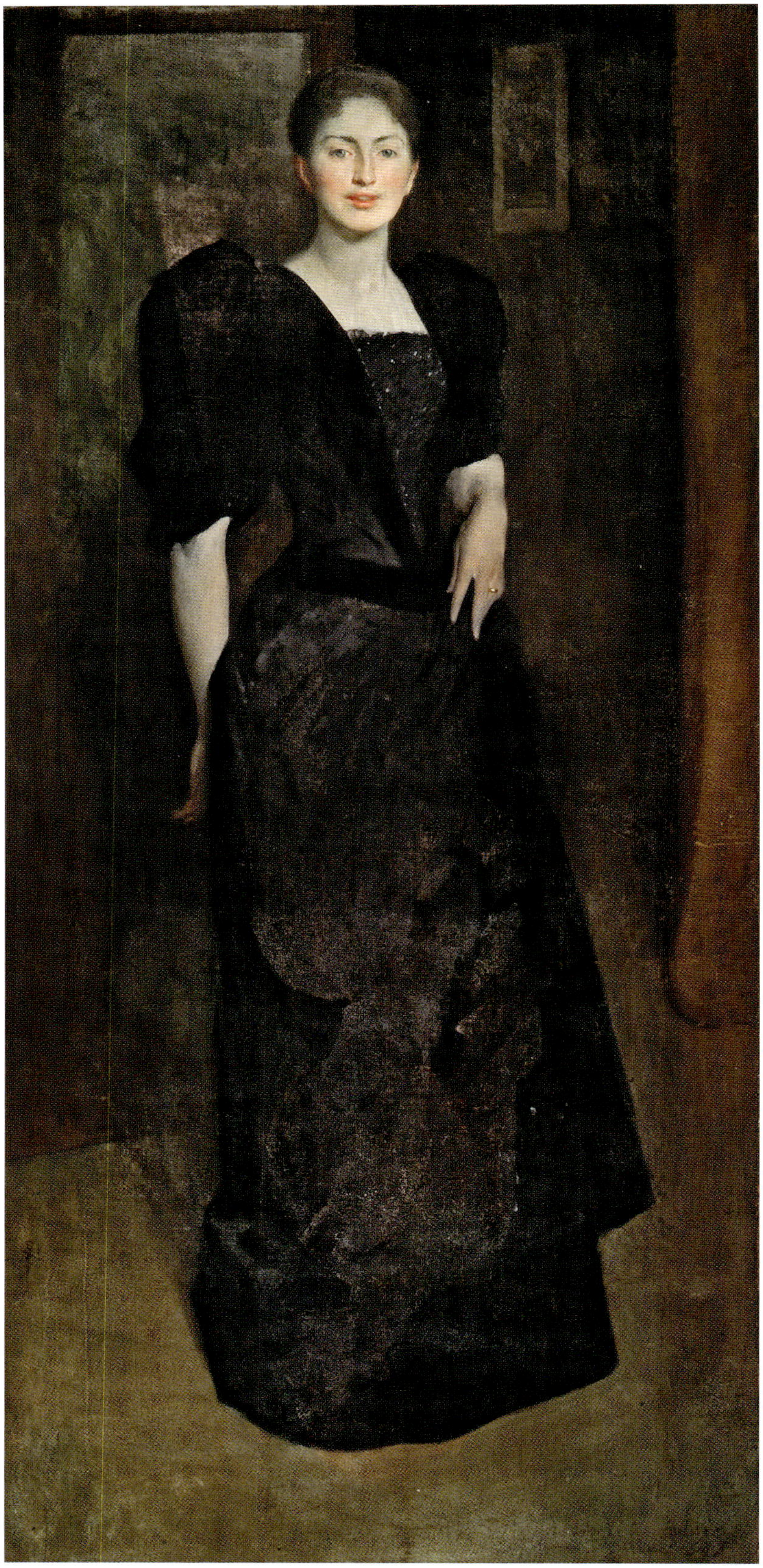

31
Portrait Noir, 1892,
oil on canvas,
74½ × 35½ in.
(188 × 88.9 cm.),
John White Alexander
great-granddaughters

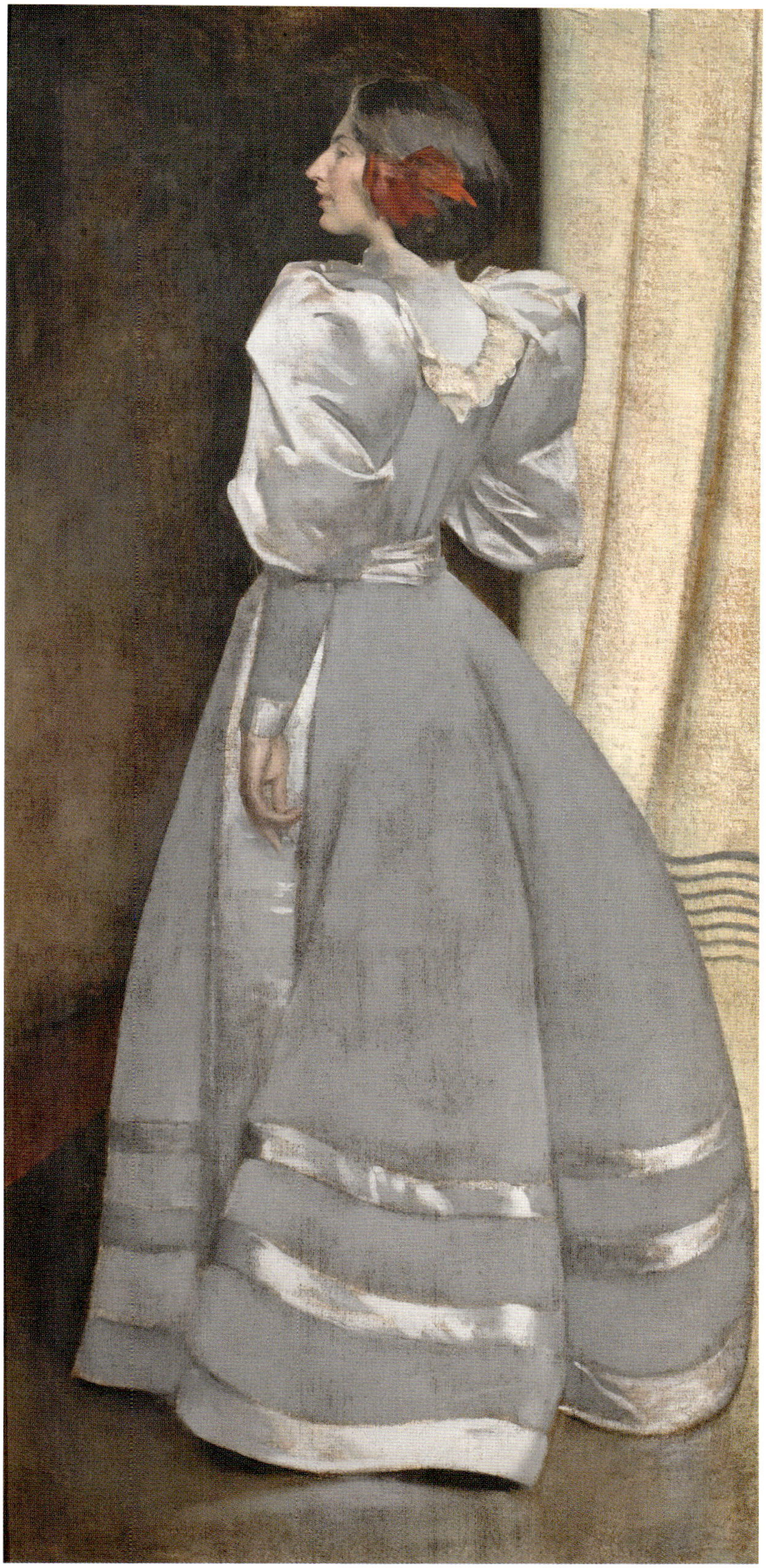

32
Portrait Gris, 1892, oil on canvas, 72 ⅛ × 35 ⁷⁄₁₆ in. (190 × 90 cm.), Musée d'Orsay, FR 1151. Photo: Patrice Schmidt, © RMN-Grand Palais/ Art Resource, NY

Though absent from the Salon, Whistler's name was invoked by the critics when discussing his disciples. There was a proliferation of pictures by artists who adhered to his principles of harmonious variation of color and tone, such as Sir James Guthrie's *Portrait Heliotrope*, and Antonio de La Gándara's *La Petite Fille en Jaune*. So, too, for Alexander, as announced by the titles, *Portrait Gris*, *Portrait Noir* and *Portrait Jaune (Etude in Yellow and Green)*. These three canvases charted his future in pursuit of a new decorative style that – unlike conventional portraiture – was not concerned with the subject's identity, and that would be refined in one Salon exhibition after another. For Alexander "decorative" meant pictorial rather than illustrative, with flat areas of color bound by an elegantly turned line. When discussing technique by the likes of Alexander, Edmond Aman-Jean, de La Gándara, and Ary Renan, the French critic Louis de Fourcaud coined the phrase "les portraitistes-tapisseurs."[51] Invoking Whistler again, Fourcaud meant that by following his example (as in Whistler's portrait of his mother by now in the Musée de Luxembourg collection), these artists' coarsely woven canvases had the look of a woven tapestry. Though one cannot take issue with de Fourcaud's critique of Alexander's work (his "[d]ecorative portraiture is based on the formula of 'harmonies' … there is no search for personality"), his assessment is too limiting.[52] The singularity of Alexander's achievement, that elevated him to the rank of Associate of the Société Nationale des Beaux-Arts within weeks of his debut, can be attributed to more than mere "harmonies": Alexander's concept of serialization is indeed based on harmony of color, but also on the movement of the figure.

Meanwhile, the Paris experiment was over, but only briefly. Back in New York, his success at the Salon was followed up with news that he had been invited to send pictures to the Grafton Gallery and to the Munich Secession.[53] Summering in Seabright, he found his ability to attract commissions was noticeably improved by his success abroad. Alexander had never intended to stay in Paris for more than two years, but one reason for returning home may have been financial. None of his pictures sold from the

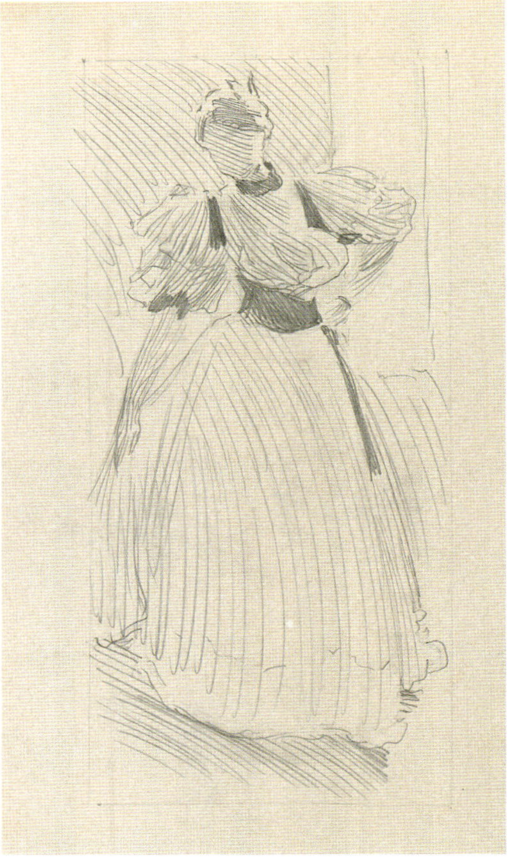

33
Sketchbook page for *Portrait Jaune*, 1893, pencil, 8¼ × 12 in. (20.96 × 30.48 cm.), Sketchbook circa 1905–8, box 3, folder 6, frame 6, John White Alexander papers, Archives of American Art, Smithsonian Institution

Salon, whereas in New York he was asking $1,000 for a portrait. In the summer of 1893 he took four commissions for at least seven paintings, which means he earned in the neighborhood of $7,000. All but perhaps one of these could be attributed to extended family and business associates of his father-in-law who were now seeking him out. Understandably, the decorative Parisian figure style was the stylistic opposite of these portraits of American businessmen, for which the artist reverted to the Munich style.

The plum assignment for at least three portraits came from Marcellus Hartley, a financier, millionaire, philanthropist, arms strategist during the Civil War, and business associate of Alexander, Sr. Marcellus's head (Nicholas W. Platt, Hartley House, Morristown, N.J.) is robustly modeled with an alert and noble expression, raised eyebrows, deep-set eyes, and full head of white hair framed by a lush fur collar or stole. On the other hand, the three-quarter-length portrait in profile of Marcellus' father Robert (Hartley House, N.Y,) is a spiritless rendering, probably due to the fact that the artist had to work from a photograph. A third Hartley portrait was a full-length picture of a child in a white dress (unlocated).

Additionally, there were two portraits of Chief Justice Beasley, a relative (private collection, Connecticut, and New Jersey State House Collection, Trenton); one very elegant portrait of Alexander, Sr. (University Club, New York); and a commission from the Mendelssohn Glee Club of Joseph Mosenthal (National Academy Museum). Mercer Beasley was the Chief Justice of New Jersey from 1863 until his death in 1895. His reputation was that of a judicial mind of the highest order of intellectual and legal acumen. One sees the restlessness of his mind echoed in the movement of the seated body, listing to one side with legs crossed in the other direction. The portrait of the artist's father-in-law has the air of an urbane and cultured man with business sagacity. Nonchalantly seated while holding a newspaper, he is elegantly attired in white tie, accessorized with a top hat and gloves. The portrait of Joseph Mosenthal may have been the result of a personal recommendation, or the Club may have directly approached the artist who was riding a wave of success. A German-born and trained musician, Mosenthal was the founding director of the foremost male choir in the United States. With these commissions of prominent citizens, Alexander established a pattern of work by which portraits painted in America supported his freedom to paint as he pleased when in Paris.

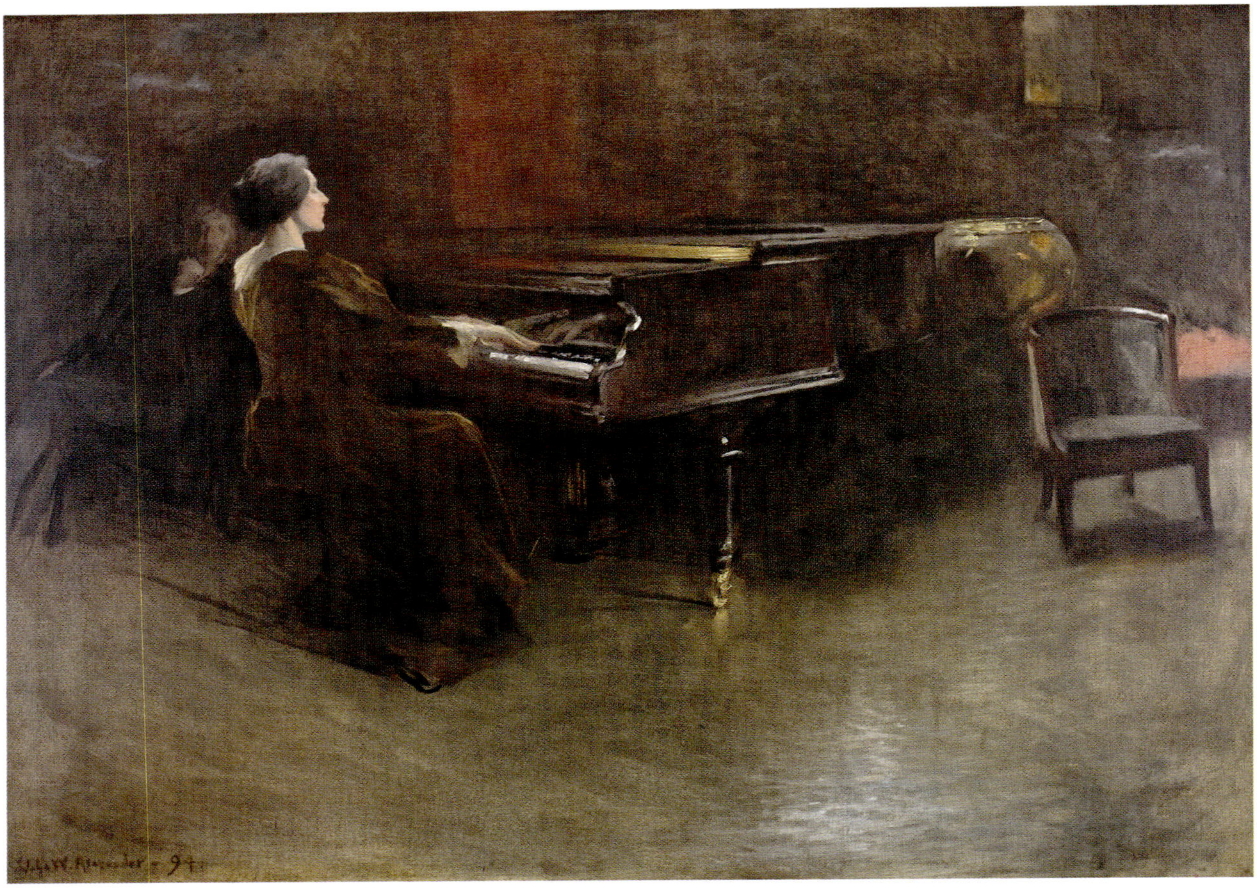

34 *Le Piano* (*At the Piano*), 1894, oil on canvas, 31½ × 43 in. (80 × 110.5 cm.), Ann and Gordon Getty, San Francisco

4

PARIS–NEW YORK–PARIS–NEW YORK

PARIS BECKONED, and Alexander made a decision to return for an indeterminate number of years, in his words "burning all his bridges."[1] He was flattered by the accolades garnered from his Salon debut as "the new man and the new sensation," but he also realized that all "may fall flat." Either way the "intimate companionship of the first artists of the world which money cannot buy" lured him back. There were new bridges to be built in Paris and he was well positioned to follow up with contacts he had made during his first sojourn in the "city of lights". He had already passed the litmus test of acceptability by Henrietta Reubell and her intoxicating milieu. He could always count on his dear friend Pranishnikoff. His entrée to society at the American embassy was secure thanks to his wife's cousin. Having established their own Saturday salon in their combination home-and-studio, lorded over by a mad black cat, the Alexanders were not above fueling rumor or being the subject of gossip.[2] Unlike in New York where men found companionship in clubs, in Paris it was done in the studio. Men and women alike were welcomed on the spur of the moment or at an open house.

Now that Whistler, too, was back in Paris amusing friends and foes alike, there was an abundance of stories to go around the various private salons to keep the American expatriates amused. Some of the oft-repeated stories were of Whistler's ribbing William Dannat for his overuse of the color blue; the repartee with Lady Eden who wanted Whistler to authenticate an original J. M. W. Turner painting discovered by her husband; and a "call to arms" to the most distinguished literary figures in all of Paris (Mallarmé, Mirbeau, Arsène Alexandre, André Gide, and others) to gather at Whistler's home and hand-write press releases about his victory at the Eden trial. Meeting him on the street, Howard Cushing, another American portrait painter, warned Alexander that he "better not go near Whistler, he is very angry at you … he thought of course you would come down and be with him at the hearing" (that is, the Eden trial). Wisely, the Alexanders did attend the second hearing.[3] But despite all that Paris had to offer, Alexander was wise not to abandon New York entirely, returning annually for an extended stay of several months. The reasons were practical: to avoid the tariffs on art for those who had completely expatriated and did not return home with any regularity, and to fulfill the portrait commissions which were his single most important source of income.

With more energy than in the years leading up to and following his wedding (1887–8), and with greater confidence, he completed seven new paintings between his return to Paris in early October and the March 18 deadline for Salon submissions. Collectively, they represented a primer of the artist's breadth of ideas as well as the company he kept. The Scandinavian painters were very much in the public eye, and apparently Alexander's. His portrait of the Norwegian artist Frits Thaulow (Figure 35), with an elegant line from the profile to the jacket that can hardly contain the bulging torso of an outsize personality, is the male version of a decorative picture. Of particular interest in American and Scandinavian circles would be the portrait of Mrs. Paul W. Bartlett (private collection, New York); a beauty among the American expatriates, she was the object of Zorn's affection while both were married to other people. The present-day condition of the canvas, darkened due to aging pigments, does not live up to the 1894 description: "This woman, who is one of the fairest beauties of the American colony, is wearing a black lace dress, trimmed with jet. A purple sash, extending to the floor, is seen through the lace, and forms a striknote against the green background, which harmonizes with the brilliant golden hair."[4] Though Zorn never sat for Alexander, their friendship is memorialized in Zorn's 1893 etching of Alexander, that given Zorn's extended stay in the United States, must have been completed prior to his trip. Zorn's arrival in New York became a burdensome affair due to a quarantine restriction. He would be forever indebted to Alexander and to Bess's father who arranged for Zorn and his wife to be released, housed, provided a carriage, and entertained before continuing on to the Chicago World's Fair.[5]

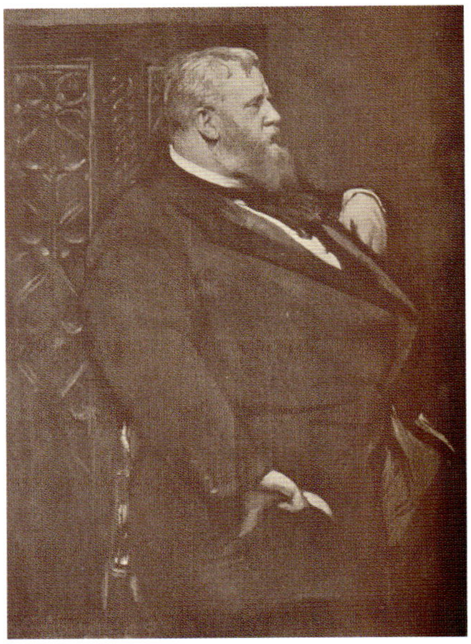

35
Frits Thaulow, 1894,
oil on canvas, 47½ × 35 in.
(120.7 × 88.9 cm.), unlocated.
Reproduction from
catalogue of the W. P.
Wilstach Collection, 1910

Another 1894 Salon entry, *Le Piano* (Figure 34), was a tone painting in brown that critics compared to Eugene Carrière. The empty sweep of the foreground, the deft sketchiness of the brush and the closely held range of color is a triumph of charm and sentiment embodying the melodious sound of music. Seated at the piano is Helen Hopekirk Wilson with her husband fading into near-obscurity to her left. She was in Paris to rehearse and teach. Her student Clara Clemens – daughter of Mark Twain – was painted by Alexander the following year (Figure 36). Of two paintings at the Salon for which Elizabeth Alexander modeled, the Salon critics ranked one as the most admirable of his seven submissions; in it, Bess stands turned to the viewer with a wide-eyed expression wearing an opalescent taffeta dress with a voluminous skirt à la Velázquez (unknown private collection). In the other, *Femme en Rose* (John White Alexander great-granddaughters), she is in profile, seated, leaning forward. It is the epitome of a portrait of a personality, animated and determined. Alexander continues to mine Velázquez in another canvas, *La Glace* (lost at sea in 1997), of a woman standing, seen from behind but reflected in a mirror, arranging her cape in preparation for going out. The dominant color is determined by the black ensemble – cape, dress and hat – with the hat accented by a red bow; the Spanish master is also recalled in the zigzag banding at the dress's hem and a mirror that extends the visual space. The last of the seven Salon entries was a salute to a mentor of long standing, a likeness of Ivan Pranishnikoff seated before his easel (unlocated).

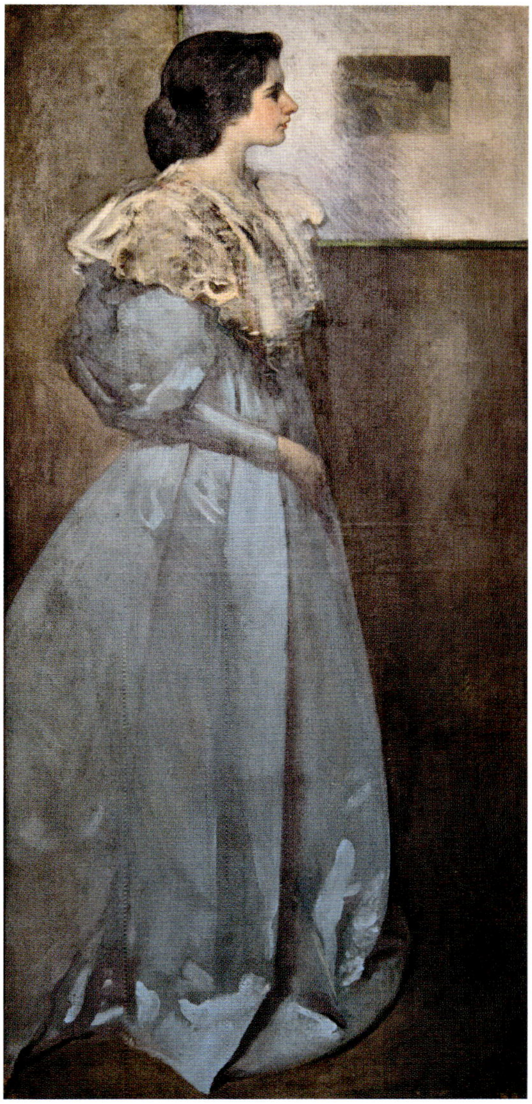

36
Clara Clemens,
January–February 1895,
oil on canvas, 74 × 34½ in.
(189.2 × 87.6 cm.), Mark
Twain Birthplace State
Historic Site, Missouri
State Parks, Jefferson City,
Missouri, 40.1966.025

The critics seemed well disposed to Alexander's solid performance. One, Arsène Alexandre in *Éclair* (April 25, 1894), commented favorably upon the sensation of the group of strong silhouettes and the harmonies of color and tone.[6] Charles Yriarte in *Le Figaro* (April 26, 1894) praised Alexander's ability to execute compositions of the first order.[7] Having now successfully completed a second appearance at the Salon, Alexander could retreat knowing that the French press had embraced him as an accomplished disciple of Whistler, yet still his own man. No sooner was the salon season over than thoughts turned to recharging for the next Salon in twelve months' time, at which much would be expected of Alexander.

Remaining in France instead of returning to America for the summer, he was nonetheless not without commissions. He painted Mrs. J. Randolph

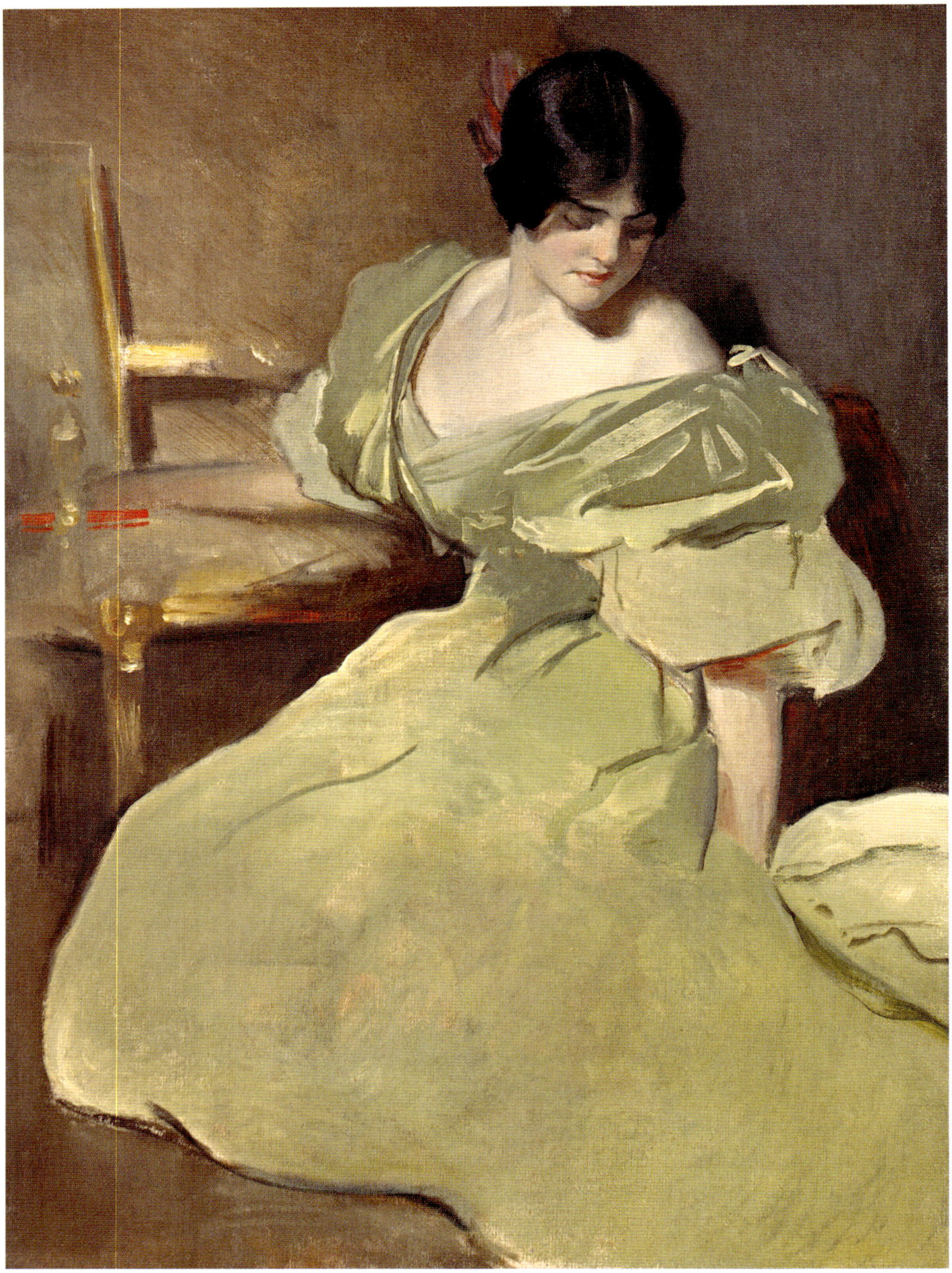

Coolidge, Jr. (Boston Museum of Fine Arts) whose brother-in-law had recently resigned the U.S. ambassadorship, and the opera singer Sybil Sanderson (unlocated). The aristocratic Mrs. Coolidge wears a dress with a pronounced bouffant skirt and banding similar to the dress worn by the Infanta Margarita, a signifier of her social class as American aristocracy. The real work, however, for the 1894–5 season began with a productive summer in Étretat, near Honfleur on the Normandy coast. It was here in this former fishing village, forever identified with the French Impressionists but now a tourist destination, that he found a cohesiveness of form and content not seen in the previous season. It would be likely that his path crossed with other residents such as the French painter Eugène Boudin and the Americans, Mark Twain and Henry Bacon, who was writing *Etretat, Hamlet of the Setting Sun*.

After two years as an initiate, Alexander's third year at the Paris Salon revealed exceptional maturity of vision and technique. On loose-weave canvas he mastered form through simplification and narrative restraint rather than striving for finely modeled features. As the vaunted master of the sensuous line framing broad, unmodulated areas of paint, he earned praise as the "painter of the flowing line." This body of work is also unified by intimate lighting and a shallow visual space that functions like a cocoon, not only enveloping the subject, but imprisoning it. Like Whistler, Alexander limited the range and softened the intensity of color, achieving uniformity by the harmony of its parts. So different was the 1894–5 palette compared to the previous Salon that Yriarte of *Le Figaro* (April 24, 1895) lamented, "Where are the beautiful reds and deep black brightened up by the delicate grays of last year?"[8]

For the 1895 season fourteen new pictures were destined for exhibition either at the Salon or at his first showing with the Société Internationale de Peinture et Sculpture at the Galerie Georges Petit. Two of the fourteen were exhibited at both; none were portraits. Most are characterized by soft atmospheric light that envelops in a shallow space a figure seen in profile or from an oblique angle, caught in a private moment and weighted down by her dress (Figure 37). A prop is introduced – a book, a mirror and/or a divan – that is an instrument of gesture and movement. A consummate example, with all of the recurring leitmotifs, the floral-pattern dress, the divan and the mirror, is *Devant la Glace* (Figure 38). Modeling a tea gown in a Liberty-like floral pattern with a fichu at the neckline, fitted bodice and cinched waist with folds cascading to the ground, the figure is placed in a closed space before a mirror hanging over a divan. In such a context, the mirror alludes to an opening up of a tightly controlled space, that could be read as a metaphor for the role of the woman in

37
Juliette, *c.*1895,
oil on canvas, 48 × 35½ in.
(121.9 × 90.2 cm.),
Joan and Bernard Carl,
Washington DC

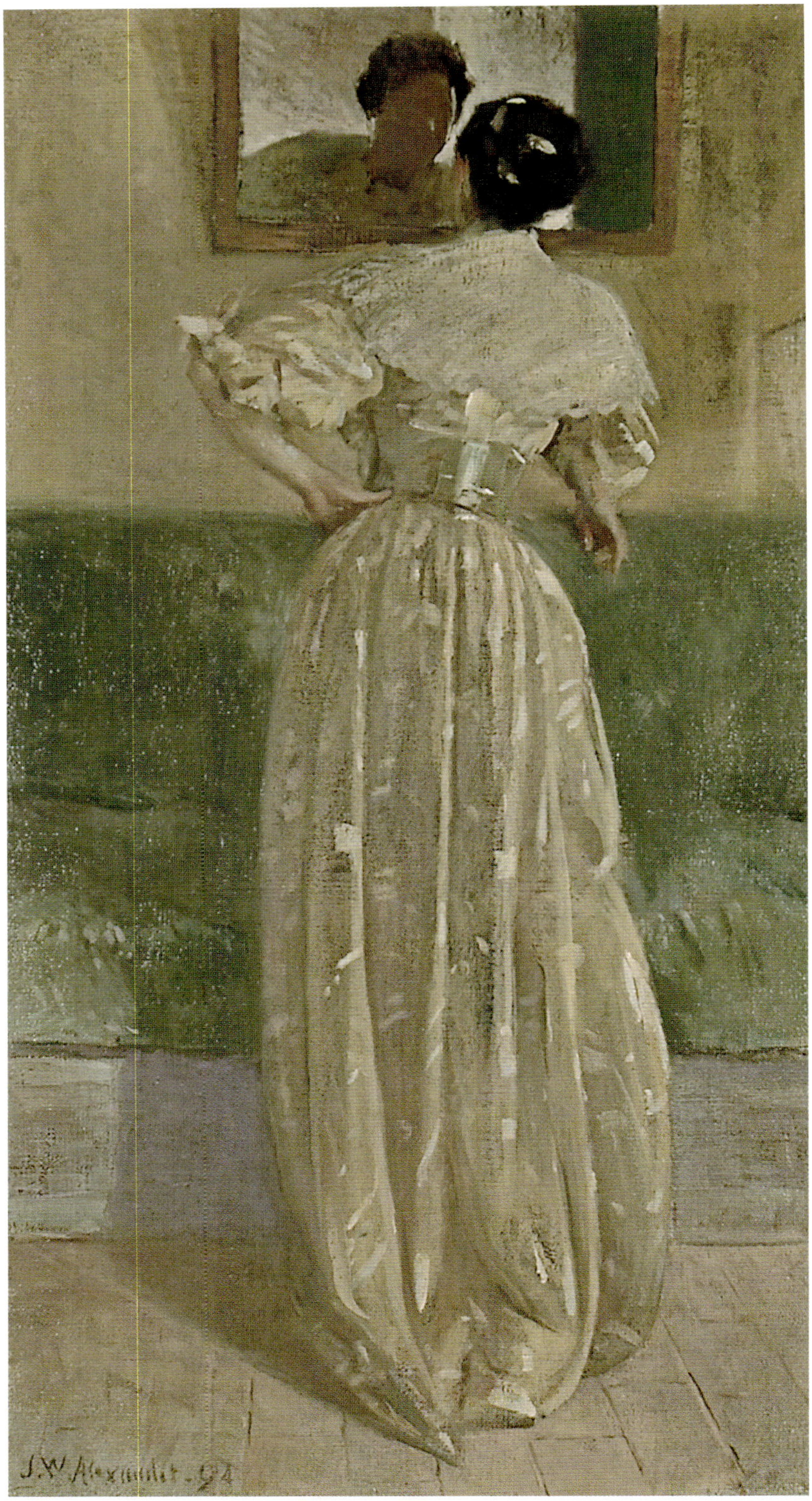

38
Devant la Glace, 1894,
oil on canvas,
39¾ × 22 in.
(101 × 55.9 cm.),
unknown private
collection

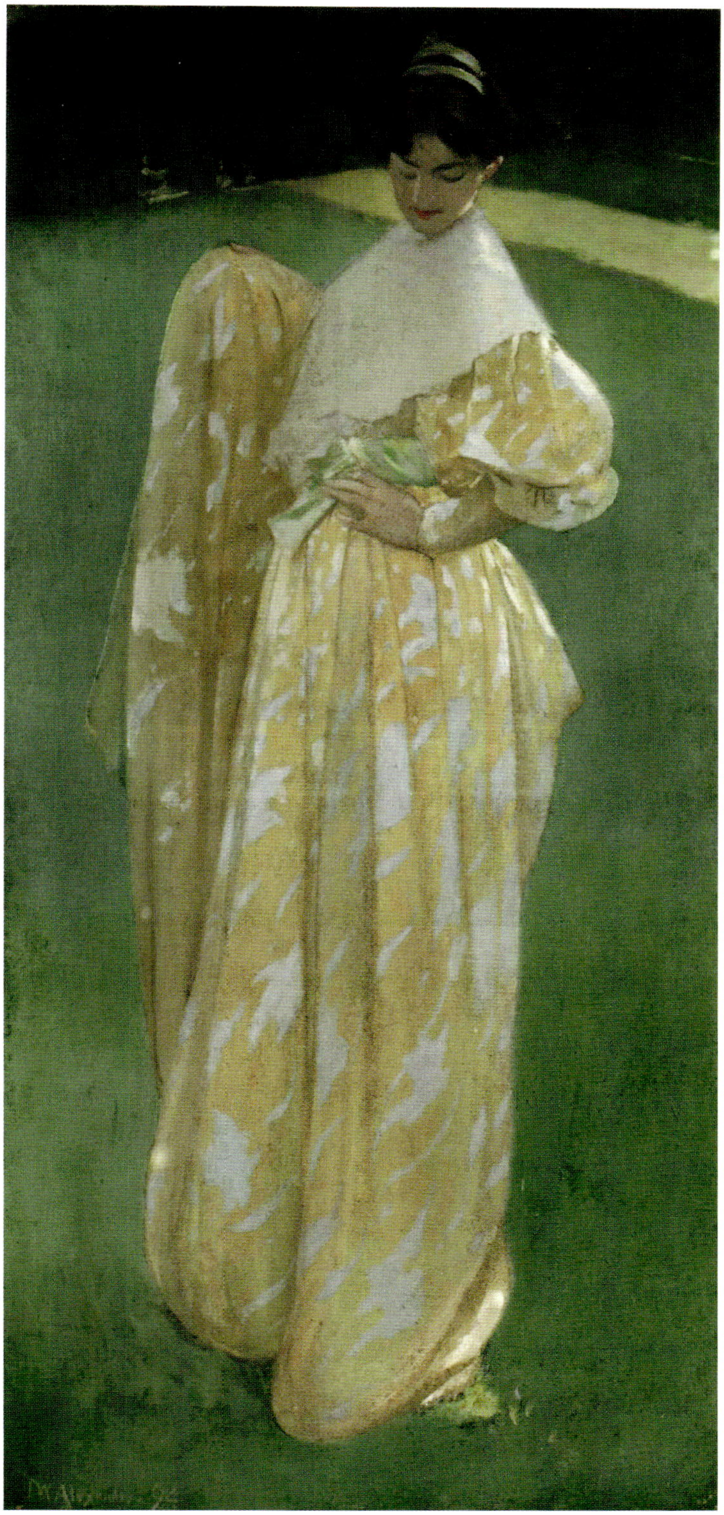

39
In the Orchard, 1894,
oil on canvas, 72 × 36 in.
(182.9 × 91.4 cm.), American
Academy of Arts and Letters,
gift of Mrs. John White
Alexander, 1923

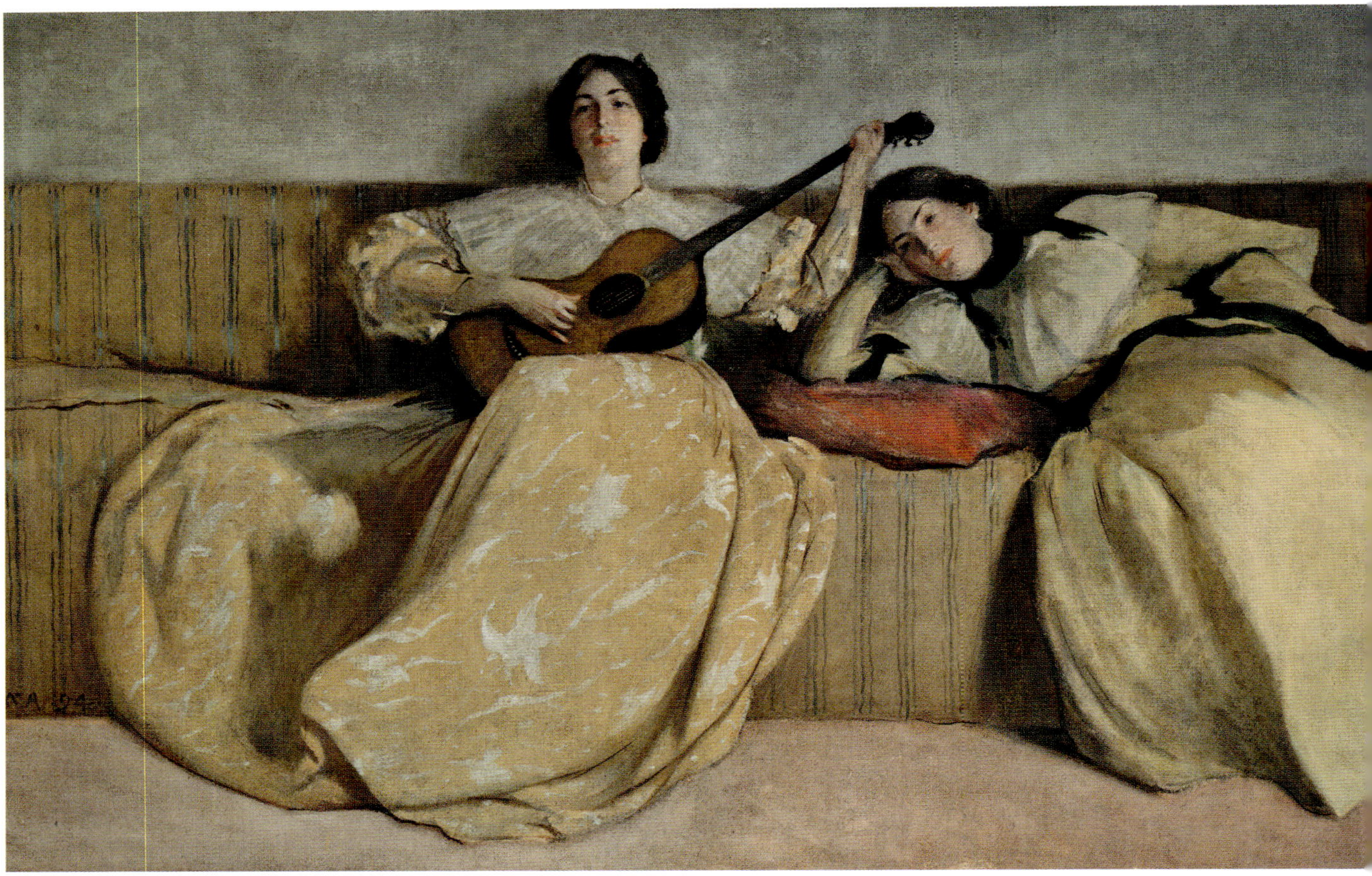

society.[9] The painting sold directly from the Salon to a Scottish businessman, John James Cowan, who was in Paris sitting for his portrait by Whistler.

Two costumes of Alexander's own design added to the uniformity of the group.[10] The style is uncorseted as befitting a lady of the house at home. The patterned dress of *Devant la Glace* appears in several other pictures, one being *In the Orchard* (Figure 39). In a creative rearrangement of the dress, it is wrapped around the figure like a Japanese kimono and the fichu is wrapped like a stole. The pattern reappears in *Girl in Black with Red Bows* (Ruth Bell, Maryland) and *The Divan* (unlocated), both exhibited at Galerie Georges Petit, and a much smaller painting, *Reflections* (unlocated), that is a detail of *Devant la Glace*. The patterned dress is paired with a second costume in the unusual two-figure horizontal panel that was intended not for show but for Alexander's

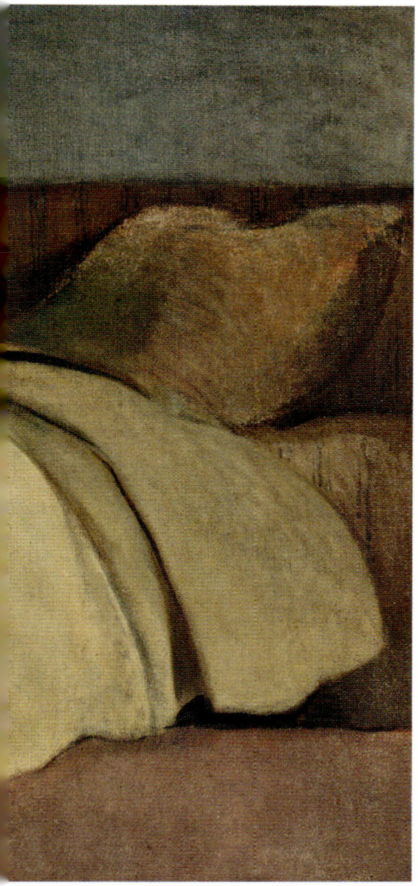

40
Panel for Music Room, 1894, oil on canvas, 37 × 77¾ in. (94 × 197.5 cm.), Detroit Institute of Arts, Founders Society Purchase, Beatrice W. Rogers Fund, Dexter M. Ferry, Jr. Fund, Merrill Fund, and Eleanor and Edsel Ford Exhibition and Acquisition Fund, 82.86

in-laws, *Panel for Music Room* (Figure 40).[11] The face is that of Bess, in two positions, each leaning toward the center on a divan while listening to the sound of the guitar. The familiar figured dress and fichu is coupled with a white dress with undulating black ribbons that reappears in *The Guitar* (John White Alexander descendant), *Repos* (Figure 41), and *Girl in Pale Green with Sash Ends* that was sold to the politician and collector of Picasso, Olivier Sainsère (unlocated). A clue to one of Alexander's sources for the complex two-figure composition of *Panel for Music Room* lies in a clipping the artist kept of the east pediment of the Parthenon, with three headless women in flowing classical robes nestled next to each other.[12] Another was Whistler.

The two most talked-about paintings, *Repos* and *Alethea* (Figure 42), were painted once Alexander was back in Paris after the summer interlude. The figure in *Repos* is positioned somnolently on a divan, wearing a billowy white dress with long black ribbons that accentuate the curve of the body. The weight of the woman's body sinks into the pillows, creating a sense of counterbalance. Conjuring up images of Loie Fuller performing her signature serpentine dance, the painting was ripe for lampooning in the French paper *La Lanterne*.[13] Once again in a shallow space, the bouffant blue dress in *Alethea* fills almost the entire canvas, arranged in an exaggerated circle to great effect, imprisoning and suspending the body within. The figure vanishes under a dress that feels as weighty as the clerical garments of Jean d'Aire in Rodin's *Burghers of Calais* or the robes in Rodin's studies for *Balzac*.[14] The same model in both paintings exudes "*décadisme*" in the drowsiness of a sensuous face, the showing of skin in the decolleté neckline, and the tension of the pointed fingers. In these two paintings Alexander has expressed a level of the erotic not heretofore seen in his work. In the mind of the critic Frantz Jourdain, these examples heralded Alexander's separation from "the platitude of the self-absorbing terrible master, Whistler" and had returned to his true self.[15] Another critic, Arsène Alexandre, seemed to suggest that Alexander had overreached himself, "spoiled by his early success; that he wanted to be a genius this year and his genius consisted of engulfing woman with their dresses."[16]

In addition to the "engulfing" dresses, the other unifying motif that appears in the majority of the salon paintings as well as in *Panel for Music Room* is the divan, a long low horizontal sofa backed up to a wall. For a painter composing his canvas, it is a convenient instrument for a horizontal orientation on or against which a figure or figures can be placed sitting, standing or reclining. For a device to flaunt his originality, Alexander had to look no further than the divan in his studio, piled high with cushions as a backdrop for his novel

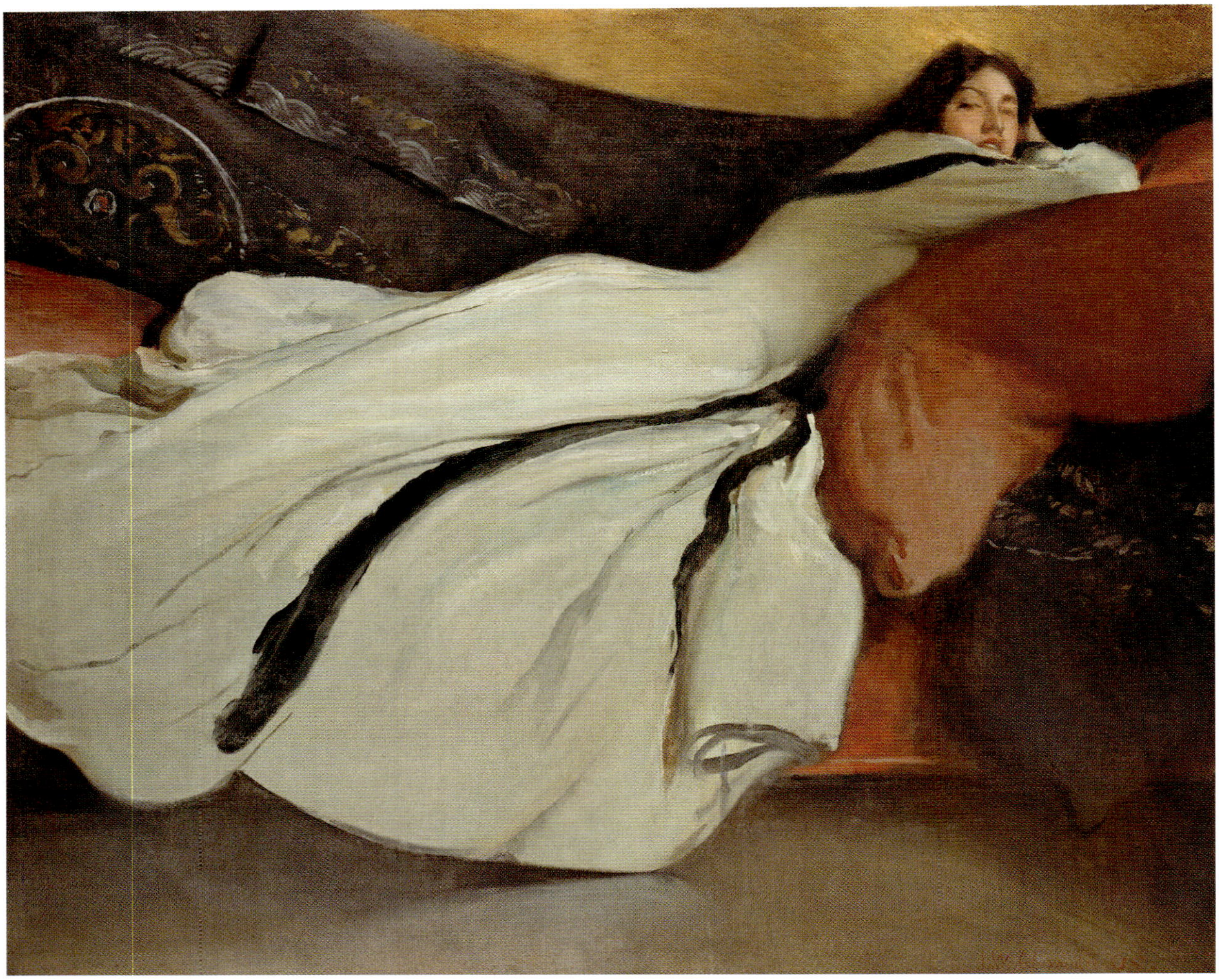

41
Repos, March 1895,
oil on canvas,
52¼ × 63⅝ in.
(132.7 × 161.6 cm.),
The Metropolitan
Museum of Art,
anonymous gift, 1980.224

arrangements of the female form.[17] The use of a divan as a popular motif for painters in the late nineteenth century can be traced to Albert Moore's *The Marble Seat* (1865, unlocated), his iteration of the east pediment figures of the Parthenon. The three classically robed women seated on a marble bench in an arbor prompted one critic to draw a comparison with the antique model that was on permanent exhibit in the British Museum.[18] Many artists chose to reinterpret the antique precedent in contemporary terms, Whistler's *Symphony in White, No. 3* (1865–7, Barber Institute of Fine Arts, University of Birmingham,

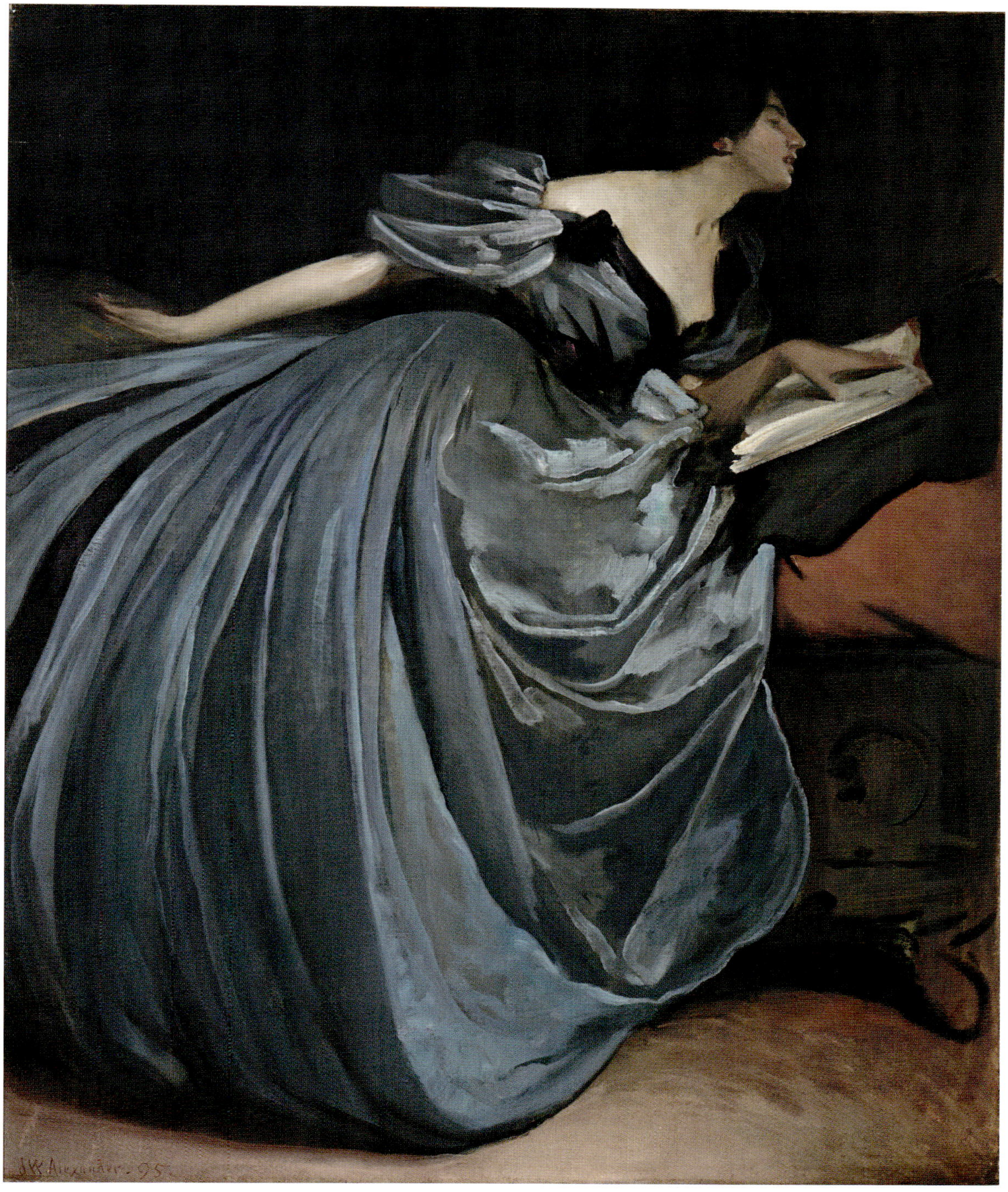

42 *Alethea*, 1895, oil on canvas, 63½ × 52½ in. (161.3 × 133.4 cm.), private collection, New York

England) being an important contemporary version. A proliferation of figures in various states of repose on a divan were perpetuated in paintings by Chase, Degas, Dewing, Manet, Morisot, and Alfred Stevens. Yet unlike his peers', Alexander's work differs in its modernity. He is not interested in composing interiors with figures placed according to the rules of perspective. Rather, the figure, as the *Glasgow Herald* astutely observed in 1893, is a caryatid carrying its frame; tightly framed within the limits of the canvas, occupying a flat space close to the surface, the figure interrupts or nearly obscures the horizontal element of the composition, the divan.

Alexander's search for effect by which he masks the body with voluminous skirts and the serpentine movement of the fabric is precisely what made his genius unique. His originality was honed in tandem with his finding his muse and model – someone other than his wife – Juliette Very. Her malleable, short-waisted torso, her mass of black hair, and strong profile find their place thereafter in the spring-loaded poses that fill the frames of so many of Alexander's canvases, beginning with these two paintings from the 1895 Salon, *Repos* and *Alethea*. Biographical details about Very are piecemeal at best. An early mention of her can be found in the press as a model for the French painter Picard (probably Louis).[19] He apparently monopolized her until she started modeling for Alexander, at the latest by the fall of 1894. She worked for Rodin eighteen years later, presumably as a model, and for all we know may have done so earlier than that.[20] Bess thought Very the "almost perfect model ... not only good looking but ... bright & knows how to pose. As a rule the handsomer they are the more stupid they are & one can do little with them."[21] With the discovery of Very, Bess, who modeled for the Étretat paintings, was now free to turn her attention to writing for *Harper's New Monthly Magazine*. Until his permanent return to the U.S., Very would be his muse, inspiring one composition after another in which the female figure is contorted beyond reason.

It was surely on the strength of Alexander's growing international reputation that he was invited to decorate the Library of Congress in Washington, DC. The invitation to decorate six lunettes in the entrance hall to the main reading room must have come as a surprise, particularly so as he had no prior experience as a mural painter. The federally funded project was extensive, calling for nineteen artists to design 112 mural decorations. The campaign for a new and larger building to house the nation's library was first proposed by the Librarian of Congress, Ainsworth Rand Spofford, in 1871. He argued simply that "In every country where civilization has attained a high rank, there should be at least one great library" with "a complete representation of the intellectual product of the country in every field of science and literature."[22] The new building was realized at a time when the democratic experiment called America was coming of age, a time of political and cultural alignment in articulating the American experience, both nationally and internationally. By the close of the century, none other than President Theodore Roosevelt lauded the value of cultural diplomacy as America sought its rightful place among the great and enlightened civilizations of the world.

Much has been made of the parallels between America's coming of age and the Italian Renaissance: concentrated wealth in the hands of a few combined with the unfolding drama of the democratic experience and the promise of individual liberty enabling a middle class. In the world of culture, comparisons to the Italian Renaissance became the apt paradigm for America's enhanced sense of national identity. The benchmark for the ensuing invigoration of art and culture was the World's Columbian Exposition of 1893, held in Chicago, with buildings modeled after classical architecture and the requisite domes, arches, columns, colonnades, and pediments all in need of decoration. Painters decorated the World's Fair buildings according to classical and allegorical pictorial conventions to express America's new world image that projected clarity of purpose, order and authority. Though built as temporary buildings, the art and architecture of the 1893 Fair was a harbinger of what was to follow. Together with the Boston Public Library (1895) and the Library of Congress (1896), these monuments to a civilized society marked the beginning of a building boom that gave rise to the mural movement in America. Well over four hundred new buildings between 1895 and 1927 were decorated with murals.[23]

Upon authorization by Congress in 1886, the design and construction of a building to house the nation's library was placed under the supervision of Thomas L. Casey, Chief of the Army Corps of Engineers, and his Superintendent of Construction, Bernard R. Green. Casey's son, Edward Pearce Casey, was entrusted with the orchestration of the mural embellishments for the dome, the grand staircase and the second floor. Without a formal committee, Casey junior and his advisors sought out the leading muralists of the day, awarding the decoration of the dome to Edwin Blashfield and making offers to others, several of whom declined – most notably Abbey and Sargent, who were otherwise engaged, Whistler, and La Farge, who was denied a request for an alternative site. The alumni of the World's Columbian Exposition who accepted the invitation included Blashfield, Dodge, Maynard, MacEwen, Melchers, Reid, and Shirlaw. It could be said that Casey was taking a chance with Alexander.

From Paris, Alexander responded in twenty-one days with a proposal on the theme of the evolution of the book to be painted in one of three styles: ideal, historical or realistic.[24] Having no experience in mural decoration, knowing how to proceed was at least mitigated by the lessons of one master, Puvis de Chavannes. When it came to producing large decorative effects, Alexander adhered to Puvis's warnings to avoid unnecessary detail. Puvis worked with decorative simplicity and narrative restraint – unlike Cabanel, Bonnat, Laurens, and other French muralists whom Alexander faulted for "confusing canvases full of undesirable detail."[25] Having settled on an historical approach for the library, Alexander created a narrative that begins with The Cairn and progresses through Oral Tradition, Egyptian Hieroglyphics, Picture Writing, The Manuscript Book, and concludes with the Printing Press (Figure 43). The compositions, forced by the lunette shape, are unexpectedly modern. Here, Alexander applied the lessons of the Nabis by using sharply receding perspective, foreshortening, and cropped forms; one example is the figure of Gutenberg's apprentice, tucked into the structural arc of the lunette. The critic Royal Cortissoz complimented Alexander, the decorative figure painter turned muralist, finding, instead of facileness in Alexander's work, "solid merits of composition and style."[26]

The sheer size of Alexander's obligations on the mural project foreclosed any possibility of a new body of work for the remainder of the year. Settling in Seabright from about June 9, 1895 through late March 1896, he did, however, manage one new painting modeled by his wife, *Portrait Study in Pink* (unlocated), for the Salon of 1896.[27] During this time he probably also made illustrations for six of seven articles written by Bess, the first of which was published in the *Harper's New Monthly Magazine* April 1896 issue and the last in July 1897. Of their combined efforts Bess wrote, "They got so well paid, that it makes us feel quite independent."[28] Alexander attended the dedication of the Carnegie Library in Pittsburgh on November 5, 1895 with remarks given by several dignitaries including Andrew Carnegie. The highlight was a loan exhibition initiated by the Pittsburgh Art Society of 325 historical and contemporary paintings, among them two by Alexander, *Harmony* (unlocated) and a portrait. He rounded out the year by returning to Pittsburgh for the opening of the Two Hundred and Fourteenth Reception of the Art Society in the new Carnegie Music Hall and Art Galleries on December 9, for which he was the featured artist represented by a selection of twenty-two pictures. A local paper called it "a fitting recognition of the esteem in which this famous artist is held by Pittsburg."[29]

This new building, dedicated to learning, music and art, of which Andrew Carnegie was the benefactor, was a celebration of the creative talents of the city

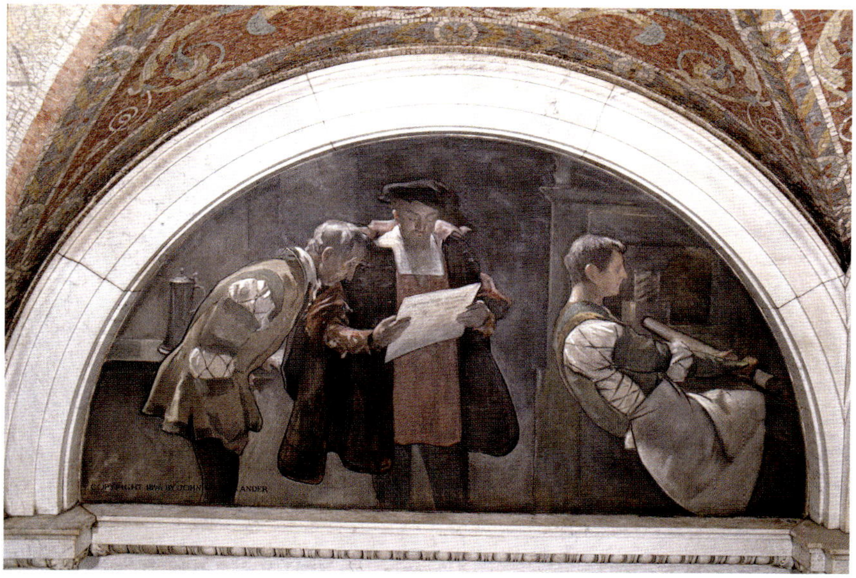

43
The Evolution of the Book: Printing Press, Library of Congress, Thomas Jefferson Building, Washington, DC, 1896, image courtesy of the Architect of the Capitol

of Pittsburgh, and it was to a Pittsburgher, Alexander, that the Art Society of Pittsburgh turned for a one-person show in the new galleries – rather than say Abbey, Harrison or Violet Oakley who were associated more with the eastern part of Pennsylvania. This was a matter of local pride, lauding native talent that had gone on to achieve international success. The exhibit of twenty-two paintings was sizable, with several, *Alethea*, *Repos*, *In the Orchard*, *Devant la Glace*, and *Reflections*, fresh from the spring Paris Salon of 1895. Two others, the portrait of Frits Thaulow and *Le Piano*, had been shown in the previous Salon and one, *Portrait Jaune*, in the Salon of 1893. Two recent male portraits were included, that of James W. Alexander, Sr. and Marcellus Hartley. Regarding this group of pictures, an astute critic drew an apt distinction between portraiture as a picture and portraiture as a near-photographic likeness. According to the critic, Alexander's work was made along the lines of the former, being pictures "to be enjoyed in no ordinary degree."[30] Another critic admired the costumes in the portrait of Mrs. J. Randolph Coolidge and another unnamed painting for their extraordinary radiance. Indeed, Mrs. Coolidge's opalescent dress was described as being "of changing green and purplish hues, with the sheen intermingling of tints seen in bird plumage."[31]

There was something about these remarkably attractive pictures that caught the eye of Harrison S. Morris, Director of the Pennsylvania Academy of the

Fine Arts. Having the utmost esteem for Alexander, he requested on short notice from Carnegie all twenty-two pictures for the 65th Annual Exhibition opening on December 23.[32] The shipment was delayed, forcing Morris to reserve a small room to hang them together, in effect creating a one-man show within a larger exhibition. The tactic was noted with consternation by some. Morris's overt favoritism may have been the reason why John C. Van Dyke, the critic for the *New York Evening Post*, was particularly critical. He found fault with *Repos* and the portraits of Mrs. Coolidge and Marcellus Hartley, while reserving compliments for the portrait of Thaulow.[33] On the other hand, John V. Sears described the group as "unquestionably the most important and most distinguished portrait exhibition ever made by one artist in America."[34]

The Pittsburgh Art Society's 1895 Loan Exhibition gave rise to the idea of an annual international exhibition. This was the beginning of what came to be known as the Carnegie International, under the 26-year leadership of the founding director John Wesley Beatty. For his friend Beatty, who had just favored him as the featured artist at the new Carnegie Library and Art Gallery, Alexander assumed an unofficial role representing the interests of the International in Paris. The demands of this role required his warm grip in negotiating matters such as vetting the pictures to be submitted, delivering the pictures to the shipper, and the added complications arising when the artist was out of town. Some artists were more difficult than others and all had high expectations as Alexander cajoled the likes of Abbey, Giovanni Boldini, William Dannat, Thomas Alexandre Harrison, Gari Melchers, Sargent, Thaulow, Whistler, and others, to send their best pictures.

Much of the summer of 1896 in Paris was devoted to organizing the Carnegie International and finishing the canvases for the Library of Congress murals. For part of July and August Alexander was back in America without the family, traveling to Washington before returning to Paris. No doubt Bess remained in Paris to prepare for what would be the highlight of the social season for the two of them and for the French nation as a whole. From October 5 to 9, the Czar and Czarina of Russia were welcomed in Paris on a state visit. The pageantry of the visit marked a renewed Franco-Russian alliance, showing to the rest of Europe that France was emerging from a period of isolationism. In turn Russia was seeking a financial loan from the French government. When Ambassador James Biddle Eustis welcomed the imperial couple to the American embassy, it fell to Elizabeth Alexander to serve as hostess, probably at the behest of her cousin, Henry Addison Alexander. Five weeks later Alexander was back in America, primarily to install the murals that he had brought with him but also with stops in New York and Pittsburgh, having missed the opening of the First Carnegie International.

As Frantz Jourdain had rightly observed, it was in 1895 that Alexander eased out from under the shadow of Whistler. It had been eleven years since Alexander declared his intent to find ways to express sentiment. In doing so, he realigned his artistic instincts with that of Rodin and with François Delsarte, while still adhering to the color code of a Whistlerian.[35] His friendship with Rodin dated from Alexander's Salon debut, if not earlier.[36] Since Rodin's breakthrough exhibit at the Galerie Georges Petit in 1886, influential critics including Gustave Geffroy and Octave Mirbeau lauded the "extraordinary life given to the female figures," citing specifically the crude *Crouching Woman*.[37] Rodin's intent was not to be descriptive but rather to be suggestive, inventing surprising, unconventional orientations; placing or hanging the figures in a different way, alienating them and depriving them of their gravity. This "atopia", or placelessness, is one of the essential characteristics of Rodin's sculpture, with emotion being the second.[38]

It is little recognized that in Paris in the 1890s Alexander was known for a certain expertise in Delsarte's system of expression through movement.[39] Alexander could have been aware of Delsarte's method as early as the 1880s when he was painting the stars of the New York stage, Joe Jefferson, Annie Russell and John Gilbert. Delsarte, a Frenchman, introduced in 1839 a program of oratorical gestures that had applications across disciplines. Ministers, politicians, and performers in theater and dance adopted his system of gestures to communicate effectively with their audiences. In the 1880s American theater was undergoing a transition away from the stiff method of pointing to a more natural system of gesture championed by the playwright, actor, and theater manager Steele MacKaye, who happened to be an American disciple of Delsarte.

Very was the key that unlocked Alexander's individuality and the unconventional orientations of the figure, hinted at in *Portrait Jaune*, *Alethea*, and *Repos*, now spewed forth in *Peonies* (Figure 44), *Le Chat Noir* (Figure 45) and *La Robe Jaune* (Figure 46). Of the eight pictures Alexander sent to the Thirteenth Annual St. Louis Exposition in late 1896 there were two that represented Alexander's evolving interest in figures in motion, *Le Chat Noir* and *The Bronze Bowl* (Figure 47), for which Very was the model. Following St. Louis came the inaugural Carnegie International at which Alexander's principal picture was the graceful and chic *The Mirror* (Odessa Museum of Western and Oriental Art), made specifically for the exhibition, and shown with the more daring *Peonies, Red and Black* and *La Robe Jaune*.[40] A reviewer for the Carnegie singled out

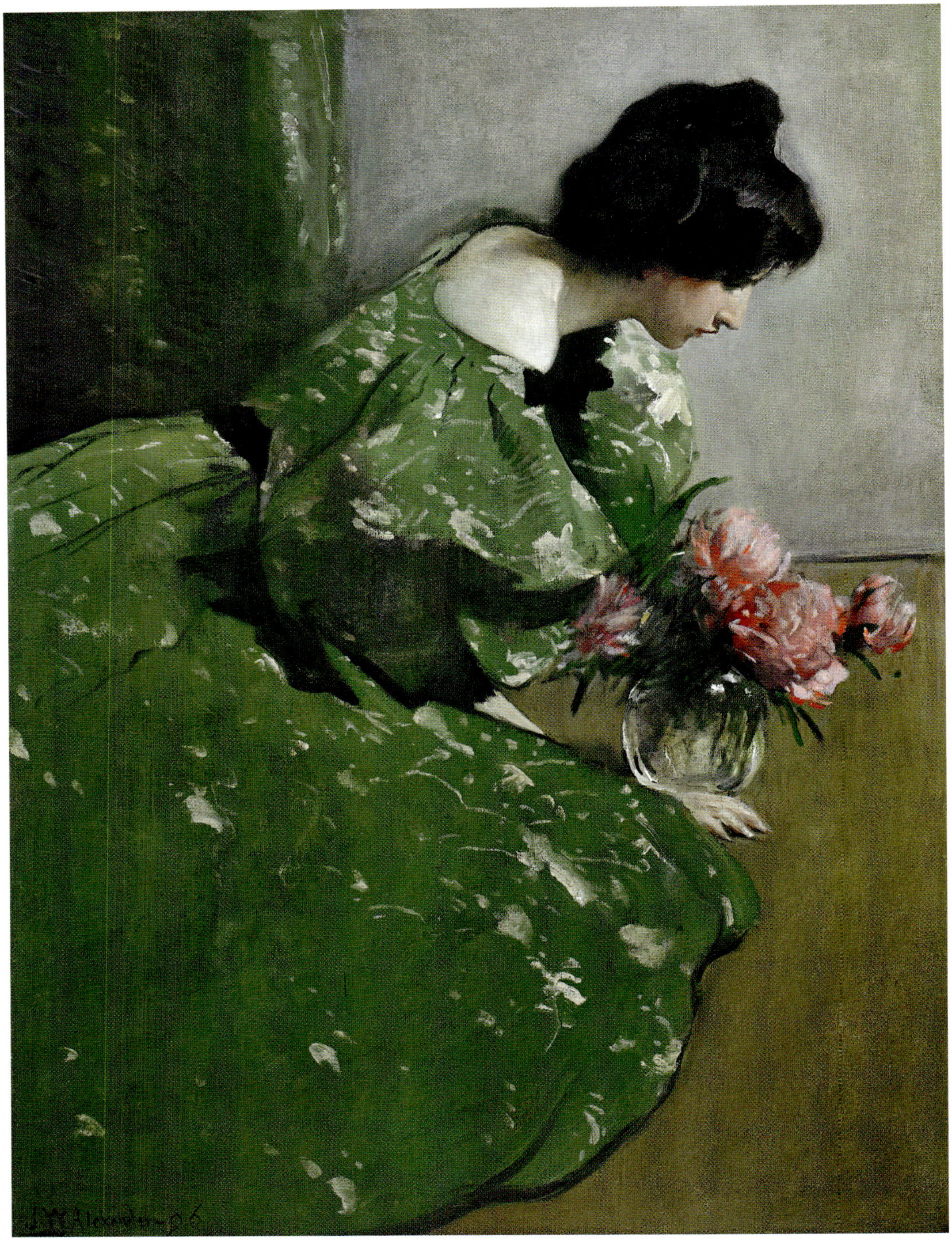

44 *Les Pivoines* (*Peonies*), 1896, oil on canvas, 48 × 36½ in. (121.9 × 92.7 cm.), private collection, Pennsylvania

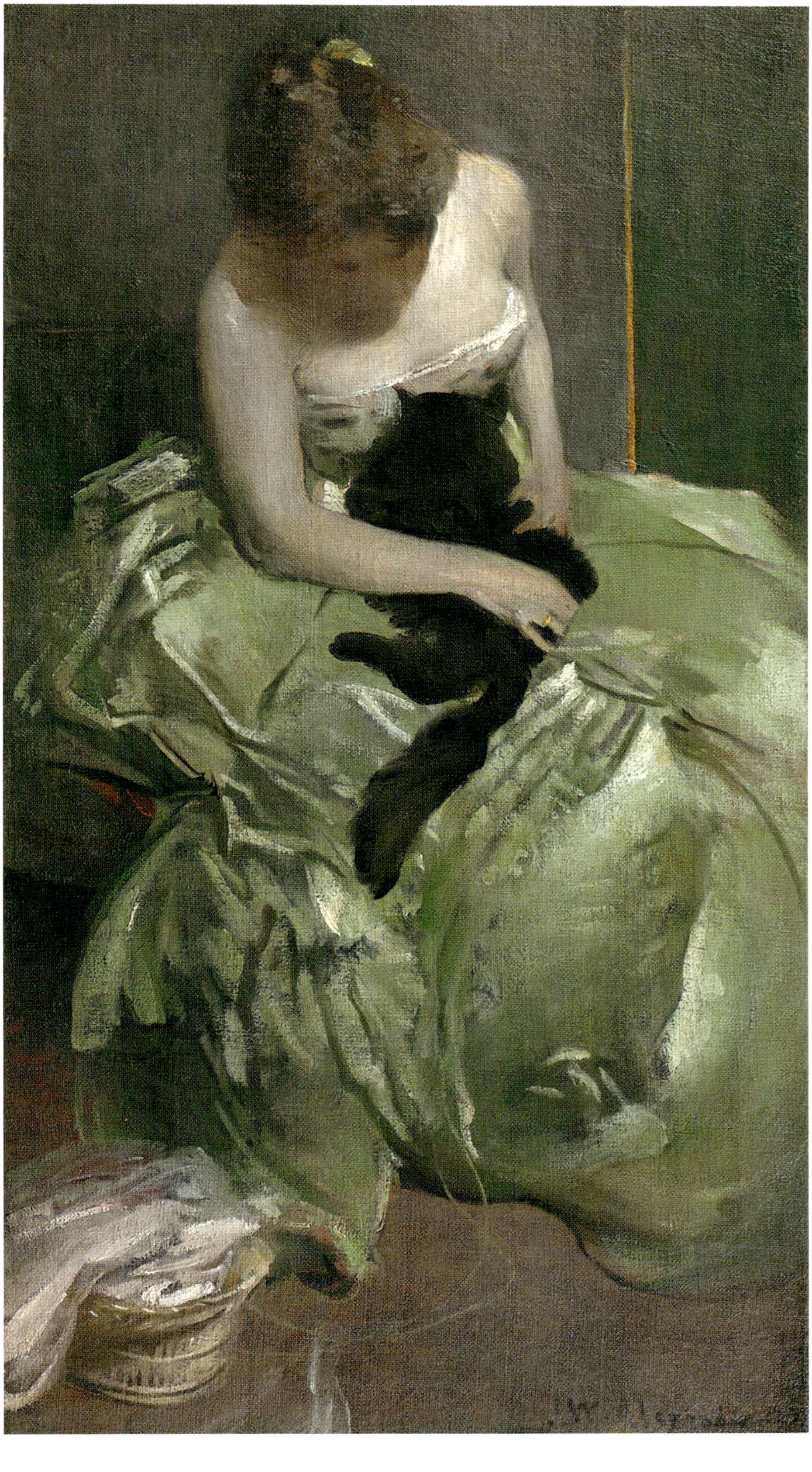

45
Le Chat Noir (*The Black Cat*), 1896, oil on canvas, 39 × 21 in. (99 × 53 cm.), unknown private collection

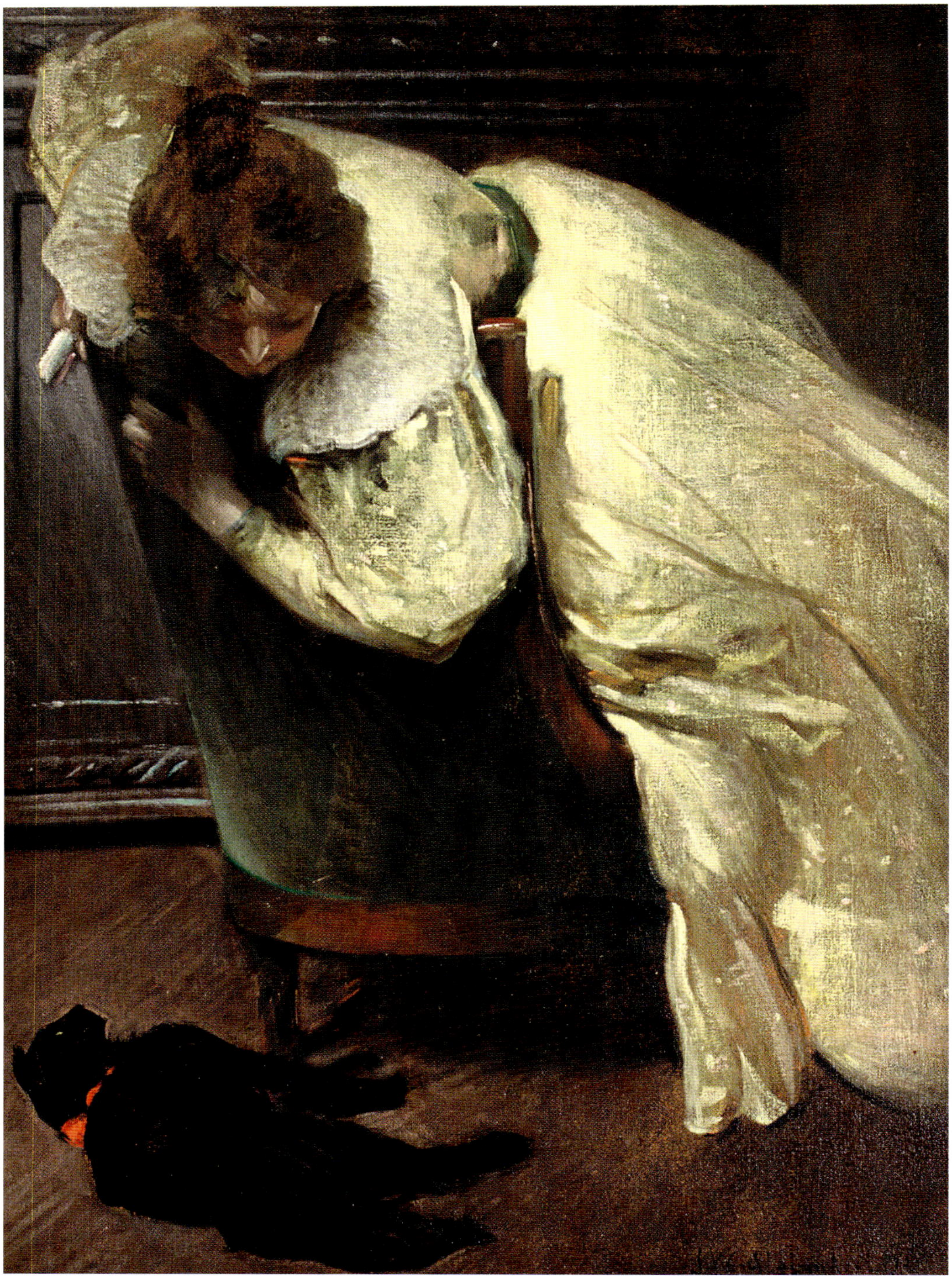

46 *La Robe Jaune*, 1896, oil on canvas, 47 × 35 in. (119.4 × 88.9 cm.), Elizabeth Alexander descendant

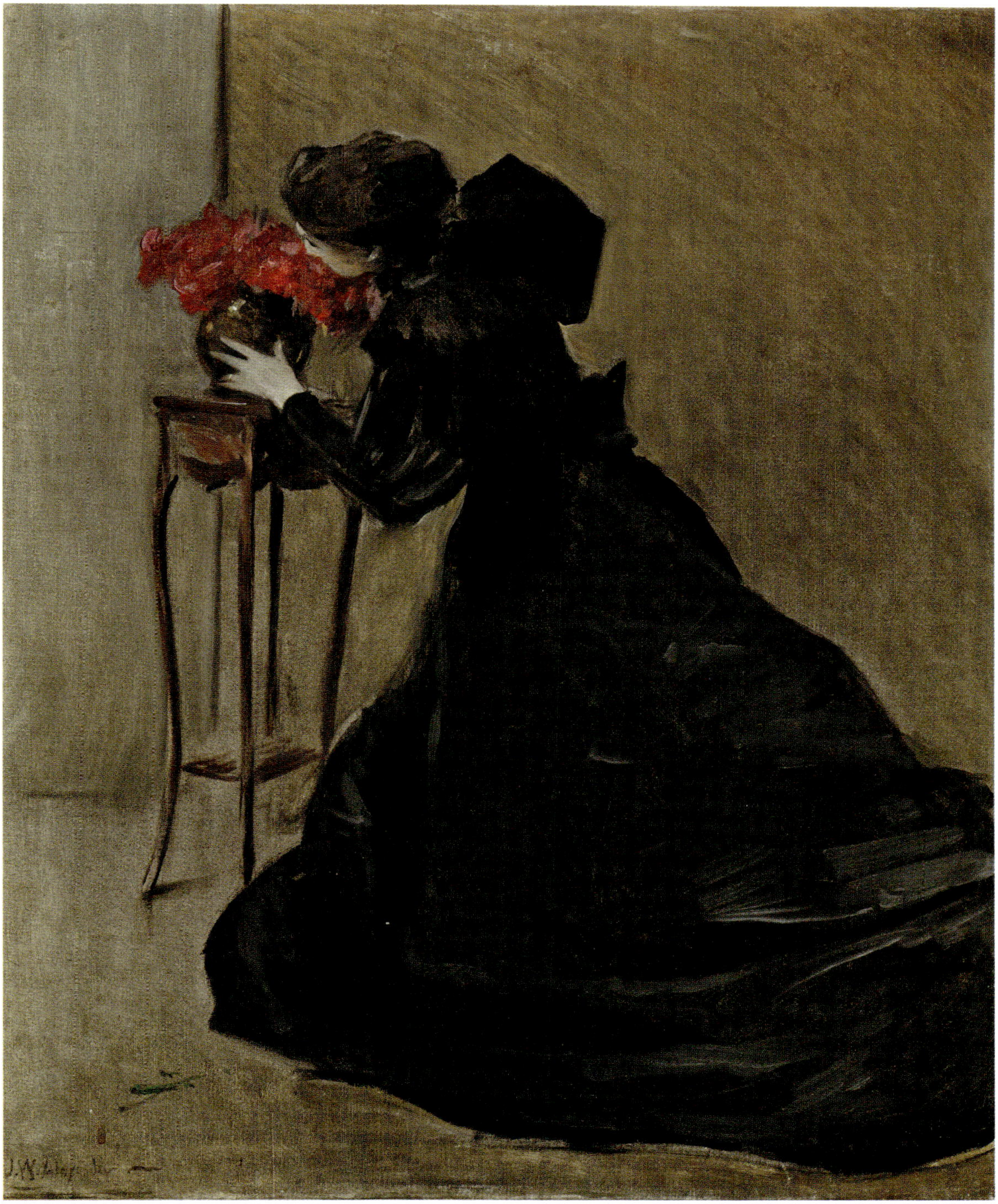

47 *The Bronze Bowl*, *c.*1896, oil on canvas, 24¼ × 19¾ in. (61 × 49.5 cm.), Los Angeles County Museum of Art, gift of The Cecile Citron Bartman Trust, M.2016.12.5

the artist for "a wonderful palette" with the scarlet and yellow being "the gayest of colors." *La Robe Jaune*, with Juliette Very nearly propelling herself over the back of a chair, merited the comment, "one is not quite sure whether the position is a comfortable one or not."[41] The reviewer for the *Pittsburgh Dispatch* focused on the surprising placement of figures "squatting in a corner of the frame or twisting themselves."[42]

Alexander's single-figure compositions attain a highly developed sense of placelessness to the point of defying the illusion of gravity – not unlike what Rodin was doing in sculpture or Loie Fuller in dance. The figure in *Les Pivoines (Peonies)*, seen from above crouching down over a bowl of peonies, suggests a dressed version of Rodin's *Crouching Woman*. In a trilogy of canvases, two of which were first shown in America, Alexander used the family pet, a black cat, as a prop to invent surprising orientations for Very in varying degrees of placelessness, the most extreme being the nearly upside-down figure in *La Robe Jaune*. It compares nicely with Rodin's drawing *Nude Woman in a Running Motion* (after 1896, Musée Rodin, Paris).

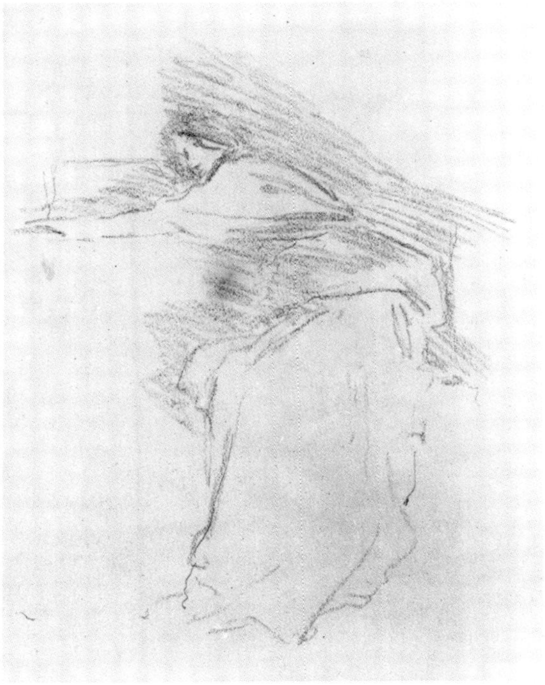

48
Sketch (female turning), *c.*1898, sepia drawing, 17³/₈ × 10½ in. (44.1 × 26.7 cm.), (sheet), John White Alexander great-granddaughters

Rarely did Alexander make preparatory studies for paintings, but there was an exception between 1896 and 1898. He produced a group of sepia-colored Conté crayon drawings (Figure 48), many, but not all, of which were for *Pandora* (1898, unlocated), of a single figure in motion placed in an unfettered space.[43] He employed hatched parallel lines to render the atmosphere around the figure, a technique used by Rodin to enhance movement and give spatial clarity. Alexander's drawings coincided with Rodin's new practice of rendering swift and spontaneous drawings of female nudes in crude and uninhibited poses that continued into the new century. There is every reason to speculate that Juliette Very, who was Alexander's model when Rodin started drawing nudes in the mid 1890s could have been introduced to Rodin by Alexander and modeled for the sculptor at that time, seeing as she did so in 1912.[44] The malleability of her body, allowing her to assume difficult poses, would have appealed to Rodin, as it had to Alexander.

Meanwhile Alexander was represented internationally in exhibitions in New York, Venice, Nashville, Copenhagen, and Stockholm, all opening within

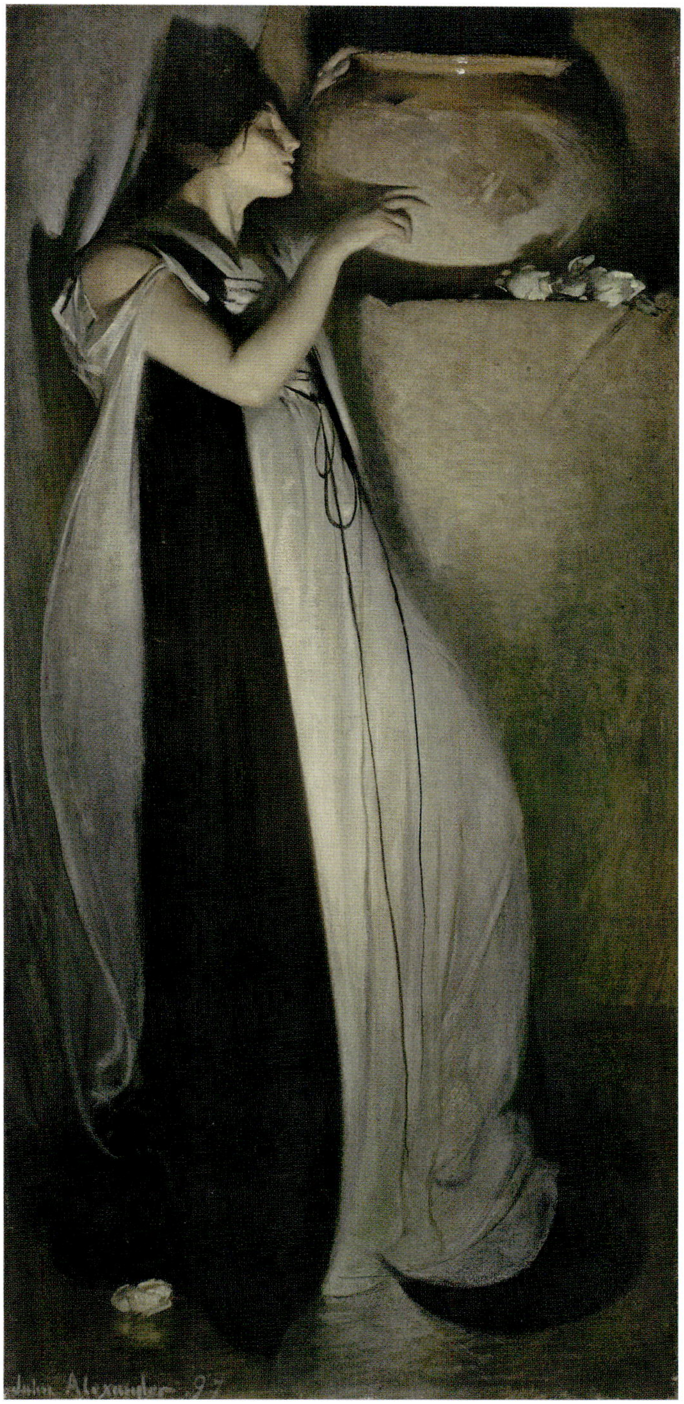

49
Isabella and the Pot of Basil, 1897,
oil on canvas,
75⅝ × 36⅛ in.
(191.8 × 88.6 cm.)
Museum of Fine Arts, Boston, gift of Ernest Wadsworth Longfellow, 98.181. Photograph © 2017, Museum of Fine Arts, Boston

weeks of each other in the spring of 1897. In a reversal of his practice of showing pictures first in Paris, all but one entry for the 1897 Paris Salon had been premiered in America. The fresh picture, his principal painting for the 1897 Salon, was an atypical choice based on a narrative poem, *Isabella and the Pot of Basil* (Figure 49). It was grouped with *Peonies* and three paintings with Whistlerian titles, *Le Chat Noir*, *La Robe Jaune* and *La Robe Noir* (Charles & Emma Frye Museum, Seattle).[45] For the most part reviewers of the salon referred to the entries collectively. Frantz Jourdain likened the women as "adorably strange flowers," "painfully broken," and "modestly concealed."[46] Fourcaud allowed that they were extreme yet deserving of consideration.[47] When singled out for comment, descriptions of Isabella ranged from amusing, magnificent, sorrowful, and having charm, rather than any new-found tendency toward decadence. Based purely on iconography, the viewer would not know that Isabella is the subject. The key is in the title taken from the poet John Keats who revived the theme of unhappy women in love in his poem *Isabella, or the Pot of Basil* (1818) from Boccaccio's *Decameron* (*c.*1350).

Circumstances were such that it is likely that Alexander's *Isabella* turned into a tribute to the British painter Frederic, Lord Leighton, who died that January. Leighton was very much on Alexander's mind while painting the portrait of Henry Marquand, and while his wife was writing an article on Marquand as a collector. Marquand was a private patron of Leighton (the President of the British Royal Academy), as well as a patron and President of the Metropolitan Museum. Leighton had decorated the ceiling of Marquand's New York music room, and the shipping of Leighton's *Lachrymae* to the Metropolitan Museum was finalized while Alexander was painting Marquand's portrait.[48]

Juliette Very appears in the title role, wearing an uncorsetted, loose-fitting Grecian-inspired white gown layered with a black stole and with the undulating lines of black lacing following the contour of the body as it falls to the hem. The ubiquitous stiff bouffant skirt is no more. Isabella stands erect in a dark space with black, deep blue and violet overtones. In profile, she stands face to face with the severed head that Keats tells us is contained within the vessel. She fondles the "embowled" head with an outstretched arm. There are no sprouting basil shoots. Instead, placed in front of the jardinière, similar in shape to the vase in *Lachrymae* and resting on a niche, is a still life of white roses, a subject Alexander had dabbled with since the mid 1880s. While Alexander sustains his tendency for sparseness, the composition is an appropriation and simplification of the formal properties of *Lachrymae*. Alexander's debt to the latter is most obvious in a rare instance of a preparatory drawing for a painting, showing Isabella's right arm fully extended.[49] Alexander achieves a tour de force in conveying the sentiment of the bereaved while abstaining from an unnatural twisting or turning of the figure. The canvas did not escape branding as degenerate by the critics Max Nordau and Sadakichi Hartmann. But their tone of criticism tended to be more ominous than that of the Salon critics, and the fact remains that Alexander painted the "dark side" rarely. When he did, it tended towards harmless hints of *décadisme*, more dreamy than demonic.

So impressed was Ernest Longfellow, artist and trustee of the Boston Museum, who sublet Alexander's New York studio in 1891, that he acted on his own to purchase *Isabella* on behalf of the museum. The understanding was that if the museum did not want the painting, Longfellow would buy it for himself. To complicate matters, Léonce Bénédite, Director of the Luxembourg Museum, also asked to acquire the painting.[50] His offer was tendered as a member of the consultative committee of the Ministry of Public Instruction and Fine Arts charged with acquiring art for the national collection. Longfellow did not waver, forcing Bénédite to wait until the next Salon. Out of the eight entries in the 1898 Salon, he chose *Femme au Noeud Vert* (private collection, courtesy of Hirschl & Adler Galleries) with the understanding that he would exchange it for a more important painting. The three-quarter-length figure stands at a slight angle, arms raised to secure a bow in her hair. All the movement is on the surface of the dress, flattened almost like a Japanese screen and decorated with serpentine whirls. The figure is static rather than exaggerated as in another choice available to Bénédite, the more daring *Le Bol Bleu* (Figure 50). Then in December the French government paid 1,000F (equating at the time to $200) for *Portrait Gris*.[51] Bénédite's choices are interesting for their inconsistency, ranging from decorative to daring with the final choice being one of Alexander's earliest explorations of the figure in motion.

Now in a position of influence, rumored to be a candidate for the Légion d'honneur, having been a juror for the 1897 Salon, and with discussions underway for the purchase of a painting for the French national collection, Alexander was particularly well positioned to wield his "manly sweetness," as Harrison Morris put it, on behalf of the Carnegie International.[52] With a new Department of Fine Arts headed by John Wesley Beatty, the trustees voted for an annual exhibition that would feature the finest recent work by Americans and Europeans. A donation from Andrew Carnegie to fund two purchase prizes made headline news: "More Cash for Art Fund" and "Prize Offers."[53] Given the perhaps predictable shortcomings of a new arts organization with an

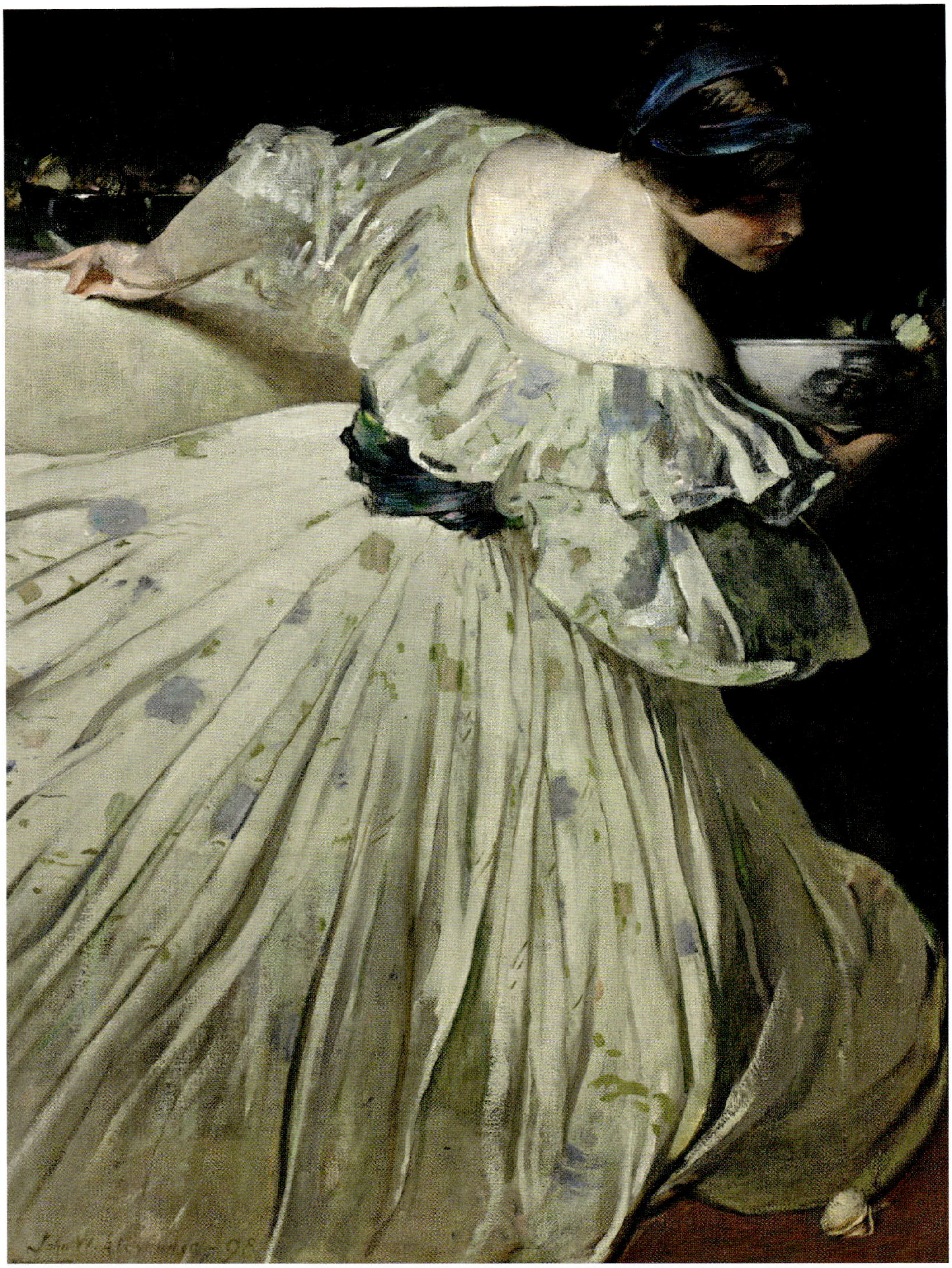

international reach, expectations were raised and then dashed. As a result of the first International in 1896, artists objected to an award committee of businessmen rather than a jury of their peers; artists were also not happy that so many pictures were accepted that they could not be displayed all at once. Thomas Dewing was a casualty of poor placement after "a dainty exquisite little portrait" was skied.[54] Gari Melchers was awarded a prize for an ineligible picture that had to be rescinded. Worst of all, not a single purchase was made.

To their credit, the Carnegie administration reorganized the process for the Second Annual in 1897. The major change was the replacement of a jury of businessmen with the appointment of foreign advisory committees of artists based in London, Munich and Paris who determined submissions from which a jury of peers in Pittsburgh, including two European jurors, would decide the awards. This improved arrangement put an added burden on Alexander, who became an indispensible handmaiden to Beatty, particularly in the first years of the International, but continuing until the end of his life. As chairman of the Paris jury committee, he was the one who ameliorated contentious issues, always giving his best and candid advice to Beatty. Alexander knew the power of persuasion and he wielded it with a warm grip, be it in a letter, a conversation, or a social occasion.

One of several issues that arose was the meaning of "invitation." To an invitee it meant all expenses paid and the presumption that the picture would be hung, but that was not the case. In this regard, the 1897 Paris jury considered the question, "had we the right to refuse any that had been invited – We decided that we had not," and then proceeded to mark the number 1 on the back of any picture that should have "choice of place."[55] Then there was the meaning of an "eligible" picture: it had to be less than three years old and never exhibited, and the artist had to own the painting to be eligible for a prize. Sometimes this was complicated by the timing of a sale. For example, Alexander submitted a painting that at the time of shipment had just been purchased from his Paris studio. Under such a circumstance, the picture became ineligible for a prize because the artist no longer owned it, and in turn, it gave the hanging committee license to sky it. This gave the impression that the painting was a lesser picture, which certainly was not the case.[56] This was too much even for Alexander who informed Beatty that he would never again send a picture for consideration for a prize, but cleverly left open the possibility of sending a picture for display only.[57] Giovanni Boldini, Italian-born but living in Paris, was insulted by the fact that one of his pictures was skied after he had been "raked over" by Alexander to send a good representation.[58] He, too, announced to

50
Le Bol Bleu, 1898,
oil on canvas, 46 × 36 in.
(116.8 × 91.4 cm.), Rhode
Island School of Design,
Jesse H. Metcalf Fund. 04.141.
Photography by Erik Gould,
courtesy of the Museum of
Art, Rhode Island School
of Design, Providence

Beatty that he would never bother again.[59] For some, the amount of the prize money was an issue. If an artist priced his pictures higher than the $5,000 prize, there was little incentive to send his best picture.[60] As for Americans living abroad, they were convinced that they would never be awarded a prize, leaving it to Alexander to persuade them otherwise.[61]

In his private letters advising Beatty, Alexander showed both his realistic and compassionate side. He urged Beatty to keep Ferdinand Roybet and Jean-Jacques Henner on the list despite his own misgivings.[62] With regard to Edmond Aman-Jean, Alexander urged, "I do hope someone will take a shine to the Aman-Jean. It is a good thing and he needs the money."[63] Alexander did not hesitate to offer favorable opinions about the entries by Jacques-Émile Blanche, Eugène Burnand and Émile-René Ménard. Having a high opinion of Henri Martin in general, he considered the current entry insulting, but still advised Beatty to keep his name on the list.[64] Alexander was genuinely accomplished at handling a myriad of issues like these with finesse and he did so generously for the sake of the Carnegie International. On more than one occasion he assured his good friend Beatty that he would do all he could.[65]

Now with a revised process, and as head of the Paris committee, Alexander convened a luncheon meeting once everyone had returned from their summer break – himself included, having rented a house in Saas-Fee in the Valais, Switzerland. As wide-ranging as the make-up of the 1897 committee of Paris advisors was in theory, in terms of styles and points of view, the list did not in practice represent the actual decision-makers. Puvis accepted but then changed his mind, as he was "off on his wedding tour."[66] Cassatt and Whistler declined.[67] Whistler was probably distracted by the Eden trial and his need to defend himself over the price of a portrait commission. Léon Lhermitte was expected but failed to show. Pascal Dagnan-Bouveret never responded to the original invitation. This left J. J. Benjamin-Constant, Walter Gay and Charles Sprague Pearce, in addition to Alexander, to vet the pictures.[68]

After the Paris Salon, *Isabella*, now owned by the Boston Museum, represented Alexander in the Second Annual Carnegie International in November, where according to the rules it was ineligible for a prize. It was then shown at the Pennsylvania Academy of the Fine Arts and the Society of American Artists in New York. At all venues the painting garnered similar praise. In Pittsburgh it was the "exquisitely simple" line.[69] In Philadelphia it was the "astonishing sweeping lines.[70] At the Society of American Artists it was "grace of line and color sense."[71] But the real measure of success is ridicule. Since 1891, pictures featured at the Society of American Artists annuals could suffer the fate of being parodied by students at the Art Students League who exhibited their fresh interpretations at the Annual Exhibition of the Society of American Fakirs. Their purpose was a serious one, to support scholarships, but for a few days the student fakirs had fun. Their quest was "searching out the weak points of the original picture and bringing them forward with remorseless logic."[72] In 1898 *Isabella* was parodied, not once, but twice. Miss Alice Sargent was awarded second prize for her "independent looking young woman ... tipping up a beer-can the better to drain its contents and below are the words: 'the Pot of Bass Ale; with humble apologies to Mr. Alexander.'"[73] Another student, James Montgomery Flagg, interpreted Isabella as a spinster holding a pot of baked beans, the deference being to Boston's love of baked beans and the fact that the painting belonged to a Boston museum.[74]

Across Europe in the 1890s there was a multinational movement to secede from state-sponsored exhibitions. There was shared dissatisfaction with the control wielded by the traditionalists who were not in favor of the new progressive and experimental aesthetic. Les Vingt, the earliest of these artist-based organizations, was formed in Brussels by Octave Maus in 1884. The Société Nationale des Beaux-Arts, founded in 1890, was the French version of a secession. Three secession groups in German-speaking Europe were founded in quick succession, at Munich in 1892, Vienna in 1897, and Berlin in 1898. Alexander participated in the inaugural show in Munich in 1893 and then again in 1896 and 1898, and in the inaugural exhibit in Berlin. In Vienna there were two exhibits in 1898 in which he participated, and he exhibited again in 1900. While visiting the First Vienna Secession, the emperor made a perceptive observation in front of Alexander's canvases – *Portrait Gris*, *A Study in Pink*, *Le Chat Noir*, *The Mirror*, and *Girl in Green (Sketch)* (location unknown) – asking his escorts Gustav Klimt and Carl Moll if the canvases were finished or whether they still needed to be varnished.[75] At the end of the First Vienna Secession in mid June, *The Mirror* was reportedly sold to the Imperial Gallery in St. Petersburg.[76]

Another new picture for 1897 was *Green Girl* (Figure 51). Juliette Very is seated in a low empire chair, a frequent studio prop, and wears a now familiar floral-pattern dress (*Peonies*, *La Robe Noir*, and *Girl in Black with Red Bows*). Its reception in Paris at Galerie Georges Petit was quiet compared to the attention it received the following February in Brussels in the La Libre Esthétique exhibition. The merits of the painting were extolled in the Belgian press at least nine times. For example, it was called "une vision bien moderne" in the *Gazette* (March 8) and it was admired for "la simplicité et l'aisance de la pose" in *L'Art Moderne* (March 27).[77] A detail that received little notice is the tension caused by the expressive gesture of the hand resting in the woman's lap. The upstretched fingers and the bowed head harbor the quintessential sentiment that characterizes the best of Alexander.

Forming the largest group that he had sent to a Salon since 1895, though less thematically cohesive, were the eight paintings for the Salon of 1898. In addition to five figure paintings for which Juliette Very modeled, there was a still life, a *Sketch of Old Ladd* (unlocated), and *Child with Doll*.[78] The most daringly modern work of the group was *Le Bol Bleu* (Figure 50). Very is modeling a Liberty-style floral-pattern dress. The blue of the bowl is echoed in the pattern of the dress and the headband. The most remarkable element of the painting is the figure's context. There is a lack of a sense of gravity; the boundaries of the room and the place where her feet meet the floor are merely alluded to. The only hint of depth of field in the otherwise compressed space is the gap between her chin and the delft bowl nestled in her bent arm. Movement is both frozen and dynamic as she is flattened and splayed like a butterfly.

Alexander is deft at reducing the anecdotal to a minimum when telling a story, as in *Isabella and the Pot of Basil* and now in *Pandora* (unlocated, possibly destroyed), one of the pictures modeled by Very for the 1898 Salon. The painting portrays the ancient Greek myth of the irresistible Pandora as she is about to open a container and unleash evil spirits upon the earth. As she extends her arm, the container, like the black cat, becomes the determinant for the manipulation of the figure. She is wearing a white flowing gown in tints of yellow, slipping off the shoulders to expose the breasts. Strong contrast of light and shade capture the mood of what is about to happen. Such a dark theme and a semi-nude was a departure for Alexander. The painting was never exhibited again, which gives credence to his wife's notion that he did not like it and had it destroyed.[79] The multiple sepia drawings that reveal his persistence in seeking the desired position and movement may also imply a sense of dissatisfaction.

Child with Doll (Figure 52) was a charming curiosity, differing as it did from his extravagantly twisted female figures. Eleanor Alexander, daughter of Henry Addison Alexander and a playmate of the artist's son, is placed in a domestic interior with a credenza, candelabra and chandelier.[80] The ten-year-old is dressed à *la mode* for a child of the 1890s wearing stylish clothing at least one size too large as she mothers her doll. For the culturally enlightened, the bouffant white dress is a tribute to Velázquez's Infanta. At the time Velázquez was all the vogue and ever more so with the 1891 publication of Oscar Wilde's collection of fairy tales, of which "The Birthday of the Infanta" was one. Eleanor crouches facing her doll, a miniature version of herself, in a white dress with a

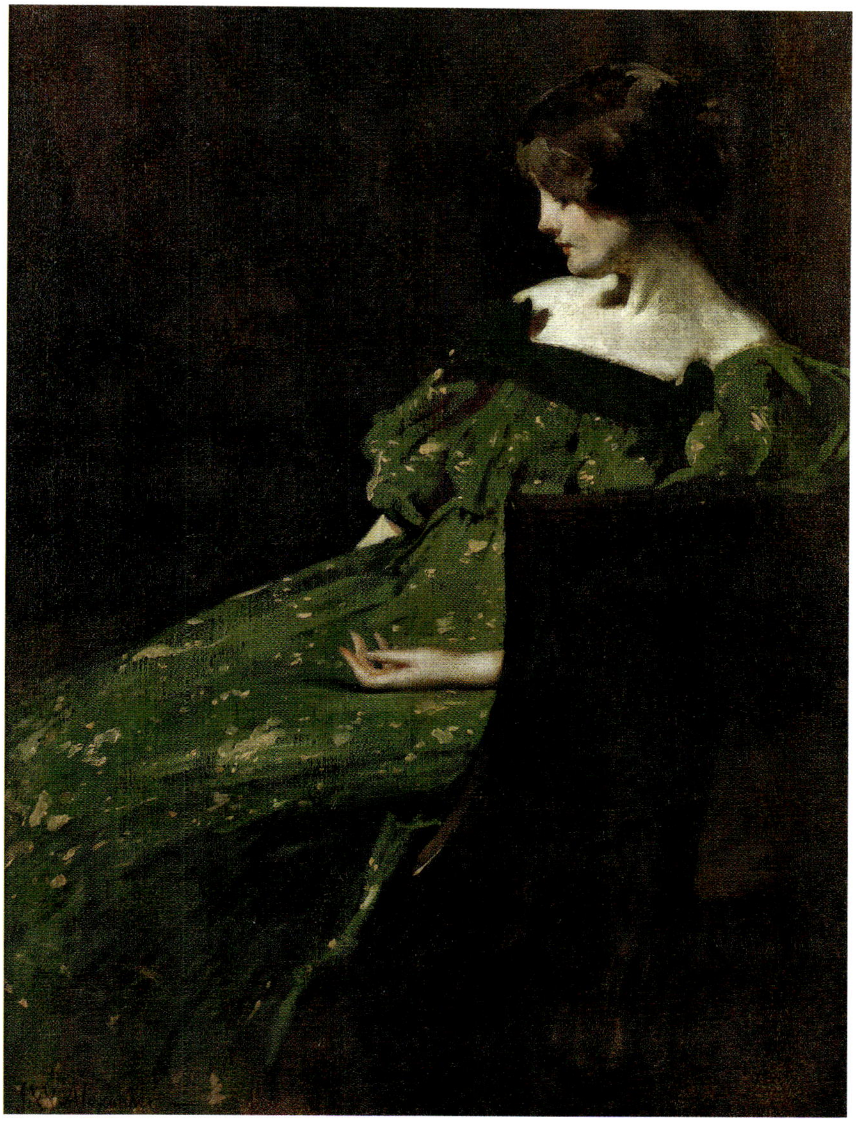

51
Green Girl, 1897,
oil on canvas, 47¼ × 35 in.
(120 × 88.9 cm.),
unknown private collection

bow in her long blonde hair. More than a decade earlier, Alexander had painted portraits of the Gilder and Clarke girls acting appropriately like children. Now he was posing young girls as little adults in over-size clothing, as in a portrait of Eleanora Sears (1895, unknown private collection) and Louise White (1896, collection of John Mann). *Child with Doll* was well received by the public at home and abroad and mentioned frequently by the critics in Paris, and later, when exhibited in Pittsburgh and Philadelphia.

Retreating to Seabright for the summer of 1898 may no longer have been an option for Alexander. His father-in-law had sold, or was about to sell, the

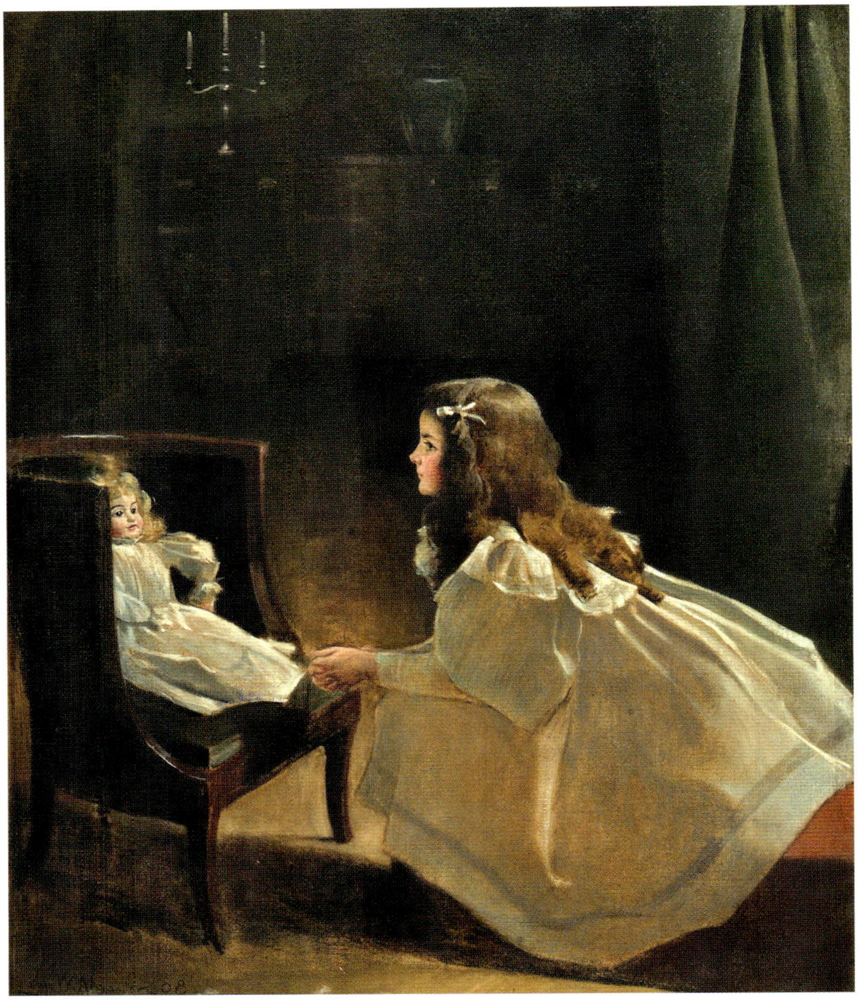

52
Child with Doll, 1898,
oil on canvas, 64⅜ × 53¼ in.
(163.5 × 135.3 cm.),
private collection, Maryland

property; in August he purchased a new property in Onteora, Tannersville, in upstate New York. So instead, Alexander remained in Europe and rented a house from a French friend in Val-de-la-Haye, a few miles from Rouen on the Seine; and he brought his Paris model with him.[81] Juliette Very appears in four new paintings, *A Ray of Sunlight* (Figure 53), *The Toiler* (Smithsonian American Museum of American Art), *L'Attente* (The Ann and Tom Barwick Family Collection), and *The Rose* (unlocated). The latter three were reserved for the exhibit of the Société Internationale de Peinture et Sculpture at Galerie Georges Petit in late 1898 and *A Ray of Sunlight* was the sole entry for the 1899 Salon. This group of pictures shows no uniformity of tone or costume, such as had come to be expected. *The Toiler* is a brown-toned painting of a milliner finishing off the trim for the hat resting in her lap. In *L'Attente* (also known as *The Café*), the

53
A Ray of Sunlight, 1898,
oil on canvas, 48 × 34¾ in.
(122 × 88.4 cm.), Ann and
Gordon Getty, San Francisco

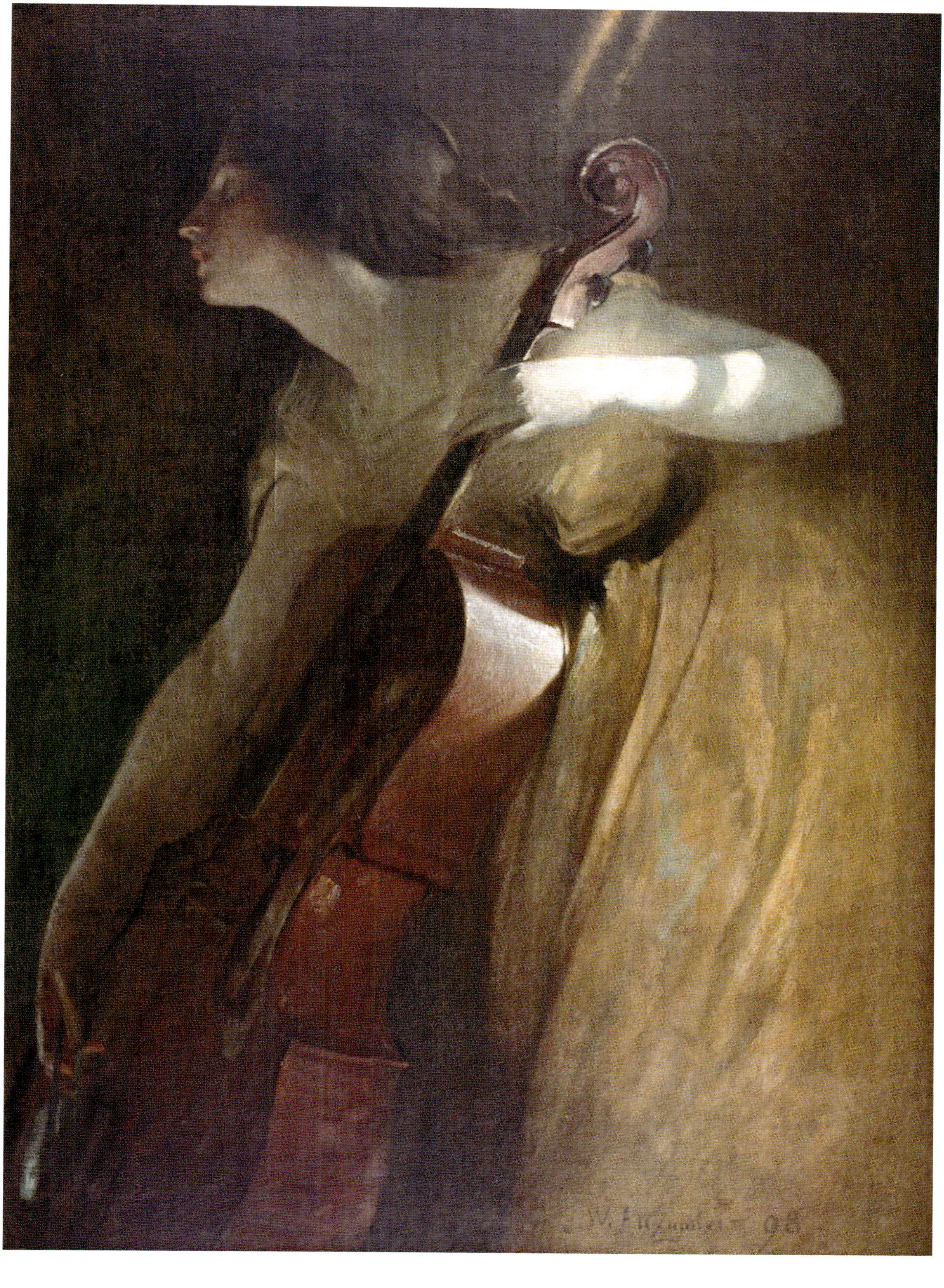

woman occupies a rational space composed on the diagonal, seated behind a white linen-covered table, in front of a mirror in which her profile is reflected. The feel of linen is tactile and the glass carafe and drinking glass on the table sparkle.

The one new painting that pushes spatial conventions is *The Rose*. The seated figure twists her head toward the viewer; the body is pushed into the chair; she is locked in a tight space. As for *A Ray of Sunlight*, it was first exhibited at the Pennsylvania Academy in January 1899 and awarded the Walter Lippincott prize. A critic for the *Philadelphia Enquirer* admired the "streak of mellow sunlight" streaming into the room. "It is no mean workman who can set himself a task like that and accomplish it without faltering."[82] The public's reception of the mannered affectation of the pose in tandem with the cello, the graceful line and the lighting would be repeated in France the following spring.

Before the third Carnegie International – the second with a peer review committee – a significant effort was made in early February to resolve lingering issues of contention. A survey was sent to advisory committee members seeking consensus over the eligibility of pictures already sold and the three-year rule for awarding prizes and medals. On the London committee, Edwin A. Abbey asked what was the point of prizes and awards if so many pictures were ineligible.[83] George Boughton complimented Beatty on a "carefully considered plan" for his management of the International.[84] From the Paris committee, Walter Gay urged that all committee members be American and spoke in favour of lifting the three-year rule, and also to cash awards.[85] J. J. Benjamin-Constant had decided never to exhibit again, yet he continued to serve as a Paris advisor through 1902.[86] The thorn in Alexander's side for 1898 was John Humphreys Johnston. There was a difference of opinion about inviting him to submit. Beatty thought his pictures were too dark and he lacked skill in drawing. Meanwhile Johnston was discussing with Alexander an installation plan that required far more space than would normally be allocated to a single artist. Nevertheless, Beatty took Alexander's advice and invited Johnston, because in the end the pictures would be "a feature of your exhibition."[87]

Having delayed his return from Val-de-la-Haye until late September, Alexander quickly had to organize the Paris committee for the upcoming Carnegie International. Paintings had to be collected, a date had to be set for the committee to judge the submissions and approved paintings had to be shipped to Pittsburgh. With the November 3 opening looming, the imminent problem was Frits Thaulow. He needed to get to Pittsburgh to perform his duties as a member of the Jury of Award but was "scared to death to cross the ocean."[88]

Alexander had to go to Thaulow, who was in Dieppe, and literally see him to the boat. Alexander did not follow until mid November because he had to meet his obligation as a member of the Société Nationale des Beaux-Arts to walk in the funeral cortège of Puvis de Chavannes.[89]

Once back in New York, Alexander was ill, for how long is unknown, but it was to Harrison Morris that he confided in December that he was again laid up with the gripe.[90] It was serious enough that Bess took the initiative to write Morris the next day explaining that her husband's condition was affecting his work and that her father's house, where they were staying, was like a hospital.[91] About three weeks later there was correspondence about an entirely different matter. Morris was writing about Alexander for *Scribner's* and was worried that his friend might be displeased. Alexander promised "that no matter what you have said in it my friendship for you is the same."[92] This warmth and depth of character moved Morris to posthumously ascribe to Alexander a "manly sweetness," accepting of whatever criticism Morris would present, yet willing to still remain friends.

Morris's article was the first professional feature article about Alexander.[93] He began by identifying three defining characteristics, "quality of line, candor of impression, and novelty of tone." Morris explained what he meant by quality of line: it "is the grace which lies hidden from the unobserving in the sweep of contour. The artist feels it when he looks at a beautiful object, he can express it only when his hand has found unswerving skill." On the one hand Morris was complimenting Alexander for "defining beauty by line;" on the other, now going to Alexander's weakness, he cautioned, "It is only when line in a portrait detracts from the prerogative of color or usurps the place of character" that line must be sacrificed. Morris continued that this rarely happened in the "well-balanced conceptions" of Alexander, "a penetrating student of human nature."[94] Morris couldn't resist adding a warning in the article against lost opportunities when great American pictures end up in foreign collections, a point for which Alexander was in total agreement.

Alexander continued to benefit from his wife's family's connections when it came to the future and plans for a permanent return to the United States. Arrangements were being made for a new studio in New York, with the help of Clinton Ledyard Blair. James Waddell Alexander, Sr. was a Princeton trustee along with Ledyard's father, DeWitt Clinton Blair, and DeWitt's father before that. The Blair family wealth came from railroad development in the western United States by Ledyard's grandfather John Insley Blair, who had been president of sixteen railroads concurrently, and the largest private owner in the world of rail miles.[95] Ledyard was friends with Elizabeth's cousin Maitland and brother Henry M. Alexander, and was in the same graduating class at Princeton as the latter. With this kind of wealth and the friendship with James Waddell Alexander, Sr., it seemed only natural to offer to add a studio over the carriage house Blair was having built at 123 East 63rd Street for his friend's son-in-law. Elizabeth Alexander, in her matter-of-fact way, recorded this largesse as mere happenstance: "John happened to say to Ledyard one day that he could not find a studio and Ledyard said, 'why I will build you one over our stables.'"[96] This benevolent project did not escape the attention of the press, with the *New York Mail & Express* (May 6, 1899) covering the story.[97]

Before returning to Paris just in time for the 1899 salon, Alexander finished two portraits. One was of David Haight (University Club, New York), yet another associate of his father-in-law. Instead of the bravura brush and dark palette of the Munich style that Alexander usually reserved for male portraits, this time the execution is seemingly thinly brushed (the pigment having been absorbed by the coarse canvas). In Whistlerian spirit, the background is lighter and tonally varied. Haight is at ease, artfully dressed in a boxy smoking jacket, holding a cigarette in his left hand. Once again, the jacket's elegant line lends itself to great artistic effect, as it did in the portrait of Thaulow, and would again in that of Rodin. The other commission that kept him in New York longer than he had wished was a portrait of Levi Morton (Albany Institute of History & Art). Morton was former Vice President of the United States and ex-Governor of New York, and the portrait had been commissioned for the state's Governors' portrait collection. Preparing to return to Paris on the first of February, Alexander gave in to Morton's wishes, finishing the portrait and even traveling to Albany to supervise the installation. Departing for France on SS *La Touraine* on April 22, he arrived back in Paris within days of the opening of the Salon.[98]

The favorable, even laudatory opinions about Alexander's sole entry for the Salon, *A Ray of Sunlight*, only added to his stature. It was considered fresh, charming, mysterious, an effective play of light, a fine tonal study, and more. A revealing, raking gleam of light streams across the left side of the figure, grazing the left top of the cello while leaving the right side in dim light. The strongest light falls on the bent left forearm, in an otherwise warm and low-key goldish-brown palette. It was especially refreshing to see the reintroduction of the dramatic affects of streaming sunlight, something Alexander had painted most effectively in the large body of work produced in the summer of 1894 at Étretat. The pose is one that only Juliette Very could carry off as she leans into the instrument, her right arm attenuated, her body an analogue to the shape of the cello. Her head is thrown back exposing the flesh of the throat with sensual abandon reminiscent of *Alethea*. What is new and fresh about this picture is the slightly "mannered", distended body.

The art world soon turned its attention to one of the defining events of the century's end, the Exposition Universelle in Paris that would replace the annual Salon on the Champ-de-Mars for the year 1900. It was to be a showcase for the achievements of participating nations in all disciplines, industrial, scientific and cultural. The presentation of American art was organized by multiple committees, and not without controversy by artists jostling in their self-importance. The prefatory statement in the official American catalogue announced that before a "conclave of nations a truly representative American exhibition" would be offered.[99] To that end, the unanimously elected Director of Fine Arts, John B. Cauldwell, strove "to assure that discernibly American people and sites would predominate." It was stipulated that entries had to date from 1889 and that 70 per cent of the paintings had to be based on realist precepts and to have been created in America.[100] This did not sit well with some Americans based in Paris. Cauldwell was rightfully concerned about the Paris Society of American Painters led by William Dannat, himself appointed a Paris juror, who were lobbying for their own pavilion.[101]

Whether as administrators or exhibitors, all the familiar American faces were involved in some way with the Exposition Universelle. Coincidentally or not, Cauldwell had just finished serving on the Jury of Award for the 1899 Carnegie International, as he had done the previous two years. John Wesley Beatty and Harrison S. Morris were named to the National Advisory Board. Twelve days after the close of the 1899 Carnegie International, Cauldwell appointed selection juries based in Chicago, New York and Paris. Several of the Chicago jurors appointed to assure representation from the western states had lesser international profiles, John George Brown, the ultimate realist, being one. The foreign selection jury was predictable, with Alexander, Dannat, Harrison, Melchers, and Julius Stewart in Paris, and Abbey, Francis Millet and Sargent in London. The other great expatriate, Whistler, had no official position, but wisely – at the request of Cauldwell, and to the dismay of the British – exhibited three paintings as an American: *Brown and Gold*, a self-portrait based on Velázquez's *Pablo de Valladolid*, *The Andalusian* and *Symphony in White, No. 2 (The Little White Girl)*.

Cauldwell made sure that control of the juries was in the hands of those based in America, though many in fact had European sympathies. The Paris

Society of American Painters felt betrayed by their diminished influence.[102] The bad feelings were exacerbated by the allocation of space, even though it was not an American decision to make but that of the host country. Alexander was accused of being complicit with Cauldwell for controlling representation and for not giving into demands from the Paris-based artists for prime hanging locations.[103] Uncharacteristically entering into the public fray, Alexander held to his convictions in a story for the *New York Herald*, in which he was quoted as saying that Cauldwell should be allowed his so-called favoritism, to "even up" the fight for those American-based artists discriminated against in the Exposition of 1889.[104] Because of his support for Cauldwell, Alexander received a presumptuous letter on July 3 from Walter MacEwen, secretary of the Paris Society of American Painters, "inviting" his resignation.

The extent of Alexander's political savvy and covert intervention on behalf of the American delegation will never be known, but it was effective. It could only help that his cousin-in-law Henry Addison Alexander was counsel to the U.S. Embassy when government representatives were negotiating for additional space. Also, Alexander had been cultivating a friendship with André Saglio, a professor at the École des Beaux-Arts, who would be appointed to the French decennial committee for contemporary art for the Exposition. Alexander had known Saglio since at least November 1897 when he hosted him at a tea in honor of William Dean Howells who was passing through Paris.[105] Again, in the summer of 1898 at Val-de-la-Haye, Alexander was strategizing with "a french man who is in the Beaux-Arts and a government official" (probably Saglio) about the 1900 exposition.[106] When the time came to negotiate officially for additional space, the results were mediocre until Saglio intervened.[107]

Writing for the official publication, *Fine Arts Exhibit, United States of America*, H. Hobart Nichols stated that "Since the Exposition of 1889 American art has to a great degree emancipated itself from foreign trammels, and entered upon a career of its own – expressing American thought and reflecting American nature."[108] Nichols was not alone in his opinion. The French also recognized a new confidence. For the *Gazette des Beaux-Arts* Léonce Bénédite wrote that "the most interesting phenomenon to note is the beginning of their tentative but decisive emancipation."[109] While praising a growing independence from foreign influences, Fourcaud went further, predicting the ascendency of American Art. And again, Georges Lafenestre spoke of liberation from European training.[110] Conversely, however, the American Ellis T. Clarke, called the supposedly truly representative American exhibit "un-national" and "un-American," pointing to expatriation as the cause of an "alien element" devoid of discernibly American people and sites.[111]

Sincere, wholesome, earnest, and fresh was how the French summed up the inherently American traits. Georges Lafenestre observed, "the common character … is energy, sanity and intensity of impression, by very simple and clean expression … the dilettantism of the old world myth, religion and fantasy, do not have a large place in the new world."[112] Given the emphasis on American precepts, Alexander's three submissions for the American section were a calculated strategy, going contrary to expectations. They were all painted in France, the sole portrait being of a French sculptor wearing his red rosette of the French Légion d'honneur, while the other two paintings are more French than American.

54
Portrait of Rodin
(*Portrait de Rodin*), 1899,
oil on canvas, 66 × 48 in.
(167.6 × 121.9 cm.),
JP Morgan Chase
Art Collection

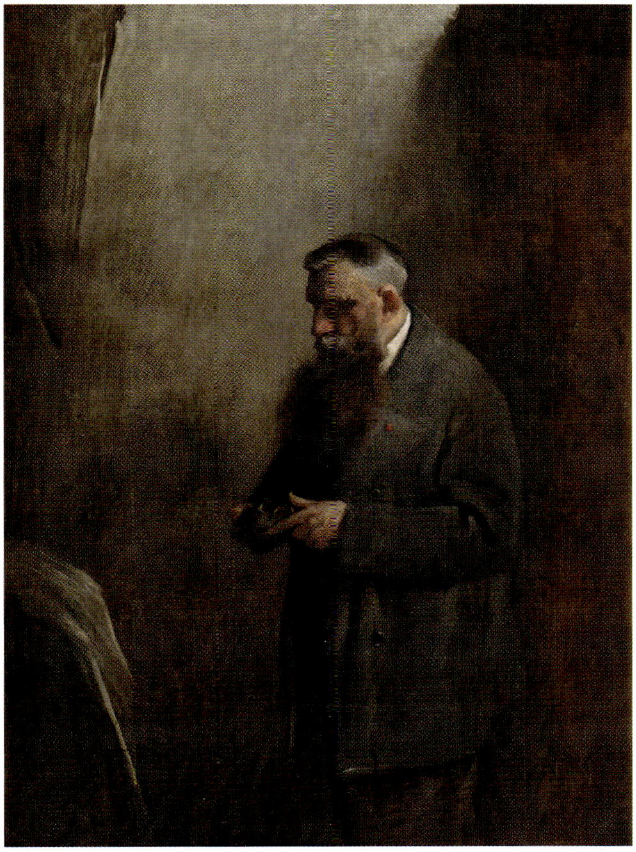

Given that Auguste Rodin's studio was teeming with activity in preparation for his most ambitious project to date, it is a mark of his friendship that he acceded to Alexander's request to pose for a portrait for the Exposition. For on July 12, 1898 Rodin had received approval for his own exhibition – in his own pavilion of his own making on the Place de l'Alma – so close to the entrance to the Exposition Universelle that the public mistook it for an official pavilion. Alexander's hulking image of the sculptor reveals the essence of a man carrying the burden of a lifetime's struggle for recognition (Figure 54). It is an introspective characterization of the artist as one would come upon him in his studio, dressed in his boxy jacket, ceaselessly working a piece of clay as he was wont to do. The incarnation of Rodin as Prédolé in Guy de Maupassant's short story *Notre Coeur* (1890) was just as in Alexander's likeness: "a large man of indeterminate age, with the shoulders of the son of the soil. His big head … and his features were heavy and coarse. His enormous hands … were broad and thick with hairy, muscular fingers; they were the hands of a Hercules."[113]

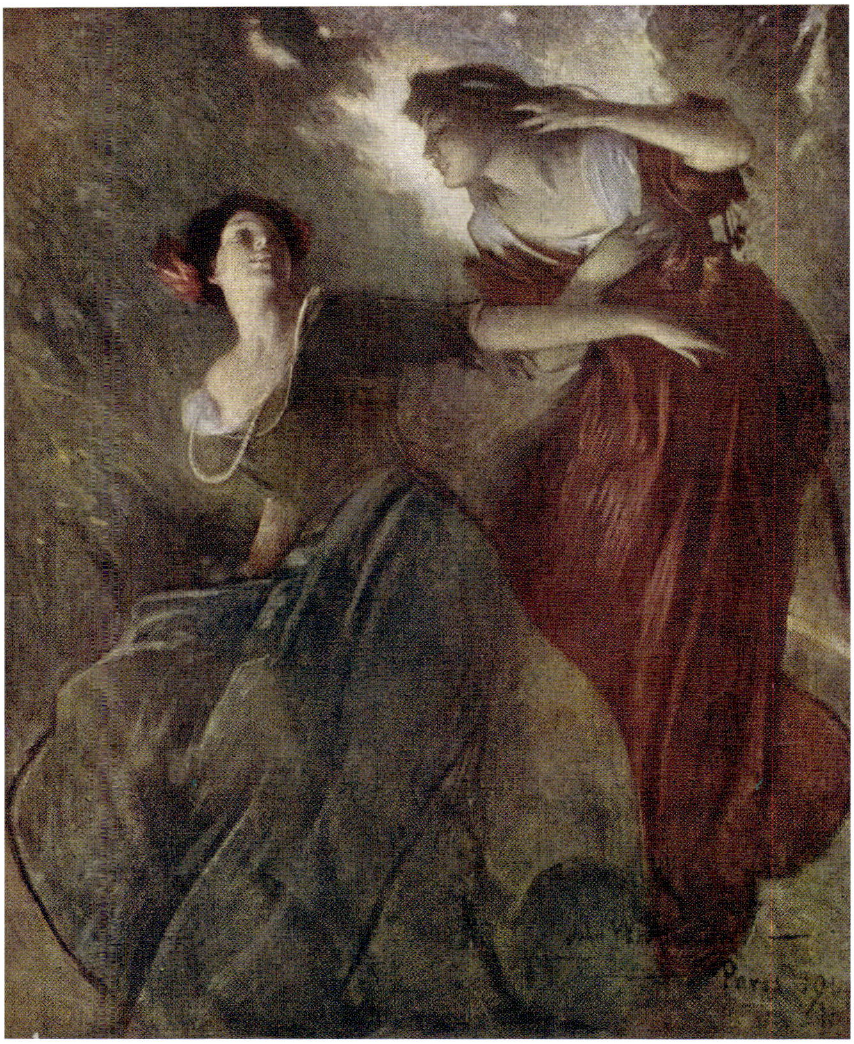

55
Automne (Autumn), 1900, oil on canvas, 64 × 54 in. (162. 6 × 137.2 cm.), unlocated. Color reproduction courtesy of the author

Perhaps a glass was raised to the portrait's success when Rodin and Octave Mirbeau visited Alexander's new studio on the Boulevard Malesherbes. Alexander introduced them to the American highball, for which they showed their distaste by "making faces."[114] As a token of friendship, Rodin was more than generous, presenting black-and-white photographs of his sculpture inscribed to both Alexander and his wife, some of which can be identified as *Balzac*, *Fugit Amor*, *Jeune Fille Confiant son Secret*, *La Vague*, *Les Sirenes*, and *Thought*. And there was more. Rodin gave them a three-foot-high terracotta version of *Jean d'Aire* and additionally offered an unidentified large-scale torso that they declined because of its size.[115]

The representation of a leading French sculptor by an American expatriate hanging in the American section was complemented by two other works submitted by Alexander that were anything but inherently American. One was the masterful *Automne* (formerly C. Ledyard Blair collection, Figure 55) and the third, *La Mère* (John White Alexander great-granddaughters). For the third year in a row Alexander's principal submission, *Automne*, was a painting ripe with the sentiment of *décadisme* embodied by his model, Juliette Very. Both figures in the composition wear a dress in contrasting autumnal colors, with the billowing skirts undulating in signature Alexander fashion. The figures levitate among branches with leaves the color of fall, with their inevitable symbolism of death and dying. If the arc of the heads, the angle of the gazes and the pursing of the lips suggest an erotic sensuality, it is chastened by the cool flesh tones of the two figures. The composition is a decidedly un-American picture indebted more to French than American types. A French precedent with which a comparison is informative is Henri Martin's decoration for the Salle des Illustres in the Toulouse Capitole, featuring ascendant allegorical figures. The arrangement of figures would have been fresh in Alexander's mind, as it had been exhibited in the Salon of 1898 and, more to the point, he had mounted a reproduction of it in his picture album (Figure 72).[116] In his third submission, *La Mère*, Alexander uncharacteristically depicts a tender moment between a mother and her baby lying on a sofa. The soft brushwork in "grays and dull buff with a strong note of brown in the woodwork of the sofa" is closer to the French painter of mothers and babies, Eugène Carrière, and lacks the wholesomeness of pictures by Alexander's American contemporaries Mary Cassatt and Elizabeth Nourse.[117]

In addition to serving on the Paris selection committee for vetting American participants, Alexander was appointed an International Awards Juror for etching and engraving. This was to his advantage when it came to the eligibility of *Automne* for a prize in the painting category. The print committee of four included Linley Sambourne who earned his reputation as a cartoonist and illustrator for the satirical magazine *Punch*, along with a Belgian and a Dutchman.[118] Looking at and making judgments about prints must have conjured up memories of his days in Venice with Whistler and Duveneck. Several of the award-winners from Britain – David Young Cameron, Frank Short, and the Anglo-American Joseph Pennell – were associated with Whistler. Serving on the print committee may have been the motivation Alexander needed to try his hand at monotypes, although, if Otto Bacher is correct, it was with the medium of monotype, and not etching, that Alexander first "amused" himself in Munich and Florence when part of Duveneck's circle. While Whistler, Duveneck and Bacher were essential to the etching revival, Alexander was not.[119] But in 1900 he tried making monotypes again. Some were new compositions, and others were based on paintings such as *Landscape, Le Pouldu* (Mary Anne Goley) and *Young Woman Arranging Her Hair* (unknown collection).[120]

Alexander's actions and his stature in Paris in late 1899 and 1900 were not that of a man packing to leave and burning his bridges. After all, days after returning to Paris in mid 1899, the family changed residence, moving to 190 Boulevard Malesherbes, a short distance from where they had been living.[121] Though busy with his submissions for the Exposition Universelle, he also exhibited with a new alternative group, along with American expatriates Walter Gay and Eugene Vail. Founded by the art critic and litterateur Gabriel Mourey, the Société Nouvelle de Peintres et de Sculpteurs was deemed to be a secessionist group. Members were a mixture of high and mid-profile international artists who regularly showed at the French Salon. There was no lack of superlatives by the critics to describe the inaugural exhibit. Of merit was the strong execution by Henri Le Sidaner, the varied light effects in Aman-Jean's pastels, the "très jolies" heads of infants by Henri Martin and the interesting studies of Breton subjects by Lucien Simon. One critic used the overused word "remarkable" to describe the work of Alexander, Charles Cottet and Gaston Latouche.[122]

The seven paintings Alexander exhibited were a mélange of types – a portrait of Richard W. Gilder, a still life, a marine picture and four figure paintings – some of which were more "remarkable" than others.[123] The 1889 portrait of Gilder was an odd choice. But none was more remarkable than *A Flower* (Figure 56), modeled by Very, that was the most talked about of the seven. Parisianized and modern, it has the mannered effect of *A Ray of Sunlight*, with the fleshy neck and the ever so slightly attenuated arms of the figure, and legs of the table. It is a masterful composition of parallels, between the sweep of the figure and the legs of the table and between the nearly horizontal upper torso and the tabletop. Tension is created by the sharp gesture of the index finger of the right hand as she balances herself on the table.[124] The sum of the parts has a contorted effect as if seen through a looking glass.

Alexander's modern leanings had become apparent from one salon to another and they were recognized by Armand Dayot (still the Inspector General of the Ministry of Fine Arts). In an article for English readers about his recent visit to the Royal Academy in London, Dayot framed his argument in terms of his disappointment in what he saw.[125] He sadly concluded that the "painter of

56
A Flower, 1899, oil on canvas, 47½ × 35 in. (120 × 88.9 cm.), private collection, California

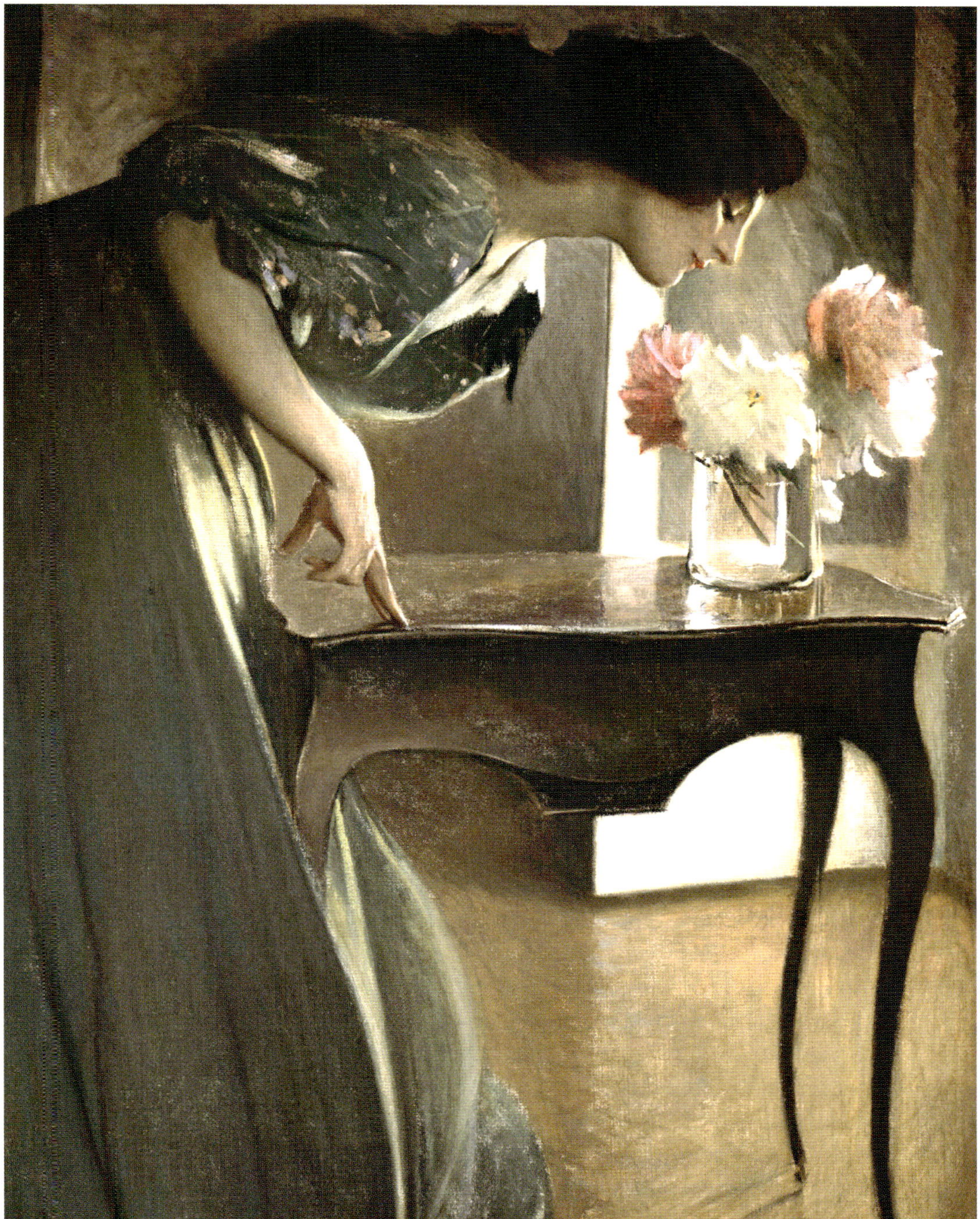

the modern woman has very nearly disappeared in England," but not so in America: he cited four Americans – Whistler, Sargent, Alexander, and Dannat – whose women, unlike those of Rossetti and Burne-Jones, were essentially modern, but who at the same time showed the proper respect for "the old masters, Velazquez, Van Dyck and Gainsborough." Referring to Alexander's debut paintings as well as *Isabella* and *Pandora*, Dayot attributed the artist's success to "the study of line and a skillful juxtaposition of harmonious colors." By being modern, with a deft hand at the flowing line, Alexander need not worry about alienating either American or French tastes. If a writer for *Current Literature* can be believed, "Mr. J. W. Alexander, too, has been Parisianized, but not too much."[126]

Alexander's decision to send new work to the Société Nouvelle and the Exposition was at the expense of other venues. He sent nothing to the Carnegie International and sent only previously exhibited works to St. Louis and to the Exposition Quadriennale in Ghent. Yet, somehow he was able to find time to complete portraits of the children of several Frenchmen with whom he had developed close relationships. He painted the daughters of Frantz Jourdain (Memphis Brooks Museum of Art), an official for the French delegation to the Exposition, a progressive with regard to the fine arts who was outspoken about the Dreyfus Affair, and of Lucien Simon and Fernand Révil. Simon, in particular, was enchanted by Alexander's depiction of his young daughter, *Lollotte* (unlocated), a child seen in profile from her right, a bow securing her short hair and wearing a dress with a balloon-shaped skirt.[127]

A year after Dayot's article came one by Gabriel Mourey for *International Studio*. Also writing in praise of Alexander, he admired "A very special sense of feminine grace, at once most decorative and intensely modern" that sprang from his "genius" for restraint, composition, use of color, and an innate simplicity in drawing, and separated him from the ordinary. Mourey credited Alexander's success to benefiting from the best of both worlds, with yearly trips to New York while thriving in the international community in Paris.[128] But without dispute the "best of both worlds" was his Parisian model who would remain behind in Paris and could never be replicated once the artist was back in New York. Alexander owed his success to Juliette Very, a quintessential artistic collaborator who infused his late Parisian compositions with a sensual *décadisme*. It was Rodin who said that the value of the right model is essential: "A model may suggest, or awaken and bring to a conclusion, by a movement or position, a composition that lies dormant in the mind of the artist."[129] Juliette Very was that essential element in the most modern of Alexander's paintings such as *Repos*, *Alethea*, *La Robe Jaune*, *A Ray of Sunlight*, *Peonies*, *Le Bol Bleu*, and *A Flower*. Very is the reason Alexander's Parisian work, beginning in 1894, put him at the threshold of innovation – modernism, even – but, without her once back in the States, it is not a position he was able to sustain.

Days after Mourey's article appeared Alexander left for Scotland, where he remained for about two months to paint at least seven portraits of members of the John James Cowan family.[130] Putting into effect plans to return to America, the family belongings had been packed and his wife and child sailed for New York on July 21. It was not until the first week of October that he himself crossed, on the SS *La Touraine* along with Alexandre Harrison and Anders Zorn who were traveling to Pittsburgh to serve as Carnegie International jurors. At a time when his art and reputation were far from that of the paragon of Americanness, and having just been named to paint the French President, he crossed over to the side of the Atlantic from whence he came, able to seamlessly resume his work in a new studio.[131] No matter what was the public explanation for his return, his decision was one that must be made by every parent. As early as 1897 in a letter to Colonel Allen, Alexander anticipated returning to the States for the sake of his boy's education.[132] This has a greater ring of truth than the posthumous recollection of his widow in 1926 that he returned "because he felt that being an American he must do what he could to advance American Art."[133] To his credit, Alexander assiduously applied the truism "leave when you are on top."

5

A MUCH ANTICIPATED RETURN

ALEXANDER'S DECISION TO RETURN TO AMERICA, already planned before the Exposition, came at a time when all the world was talking of "la formidable république americaine ... cet état des états."[1] Whether in the field of commerce, industry, science, philosophy, literature, or the fine arts, the Exposition bore witness to the global economic and cultural might and expanding influence of things American. It was the "Americanization of the world," noted the English writer, W. T. Stead;[2] the awakening of a sleeping giant. It was a time of political and cultural alignment in articulating the American experience, both nationally and internationally. The President himself, Theodore Roosevelt, well understood the value of cultural diplomacy as America sought its rightful place among the great and enlightened civilizations of the world. American innovation was heralded as an example of progress and modernity.

Alexander's so-called return was neither clear-cut nor absolute. In particular his work for the Carnegie International would take him back to Paris in the summer of 1901. Riding the crest of his 1900 success in Paris, he assumed a more public role at home, something that he had not sought as an American in Paris. In a few short months he laid the groundwork for issues on which he would campaign for the remainder of his life, such as art education in public schools and a repeal of the tariff on import of art by American artists. Of utmost concern was the need for more opportunities for artists to exhibit, be it an American Salon, a national museum or a dedicated building for the National Academy, inclusive of all artists regardless of nationality or subject matter. To this end, he, along with Whistler, Sargent, Melchers, Beckwith, and Blashfield lent their names to an effort to establish a National Museum of Art in America, a concept born of a new national pride. Francis Howard, an American-born Victorian genre and portrait painter, who at the time was Honorary Secretary of the International Society of Sculptors, Painters and Gravers when he came to America from London where he was living, agitated for the plan in November 1900. Their shared opinion was that if America was to join the ranks of civilized nations, government support mattered. President McKinley and Secretary Hay were sympathetic but the project was never realized.[3]

A few weeks later Alexander made news again with his call, using the most inclusive of terms, for an American Salon. From his citing the Paris Salon as an example, a press report inferred that since it was not exclusive to French artists, all who participated made up the French experience no matter the country of their birth. Likewise, an American Salon should be open to all. It should not favor "home scenes," nor discriminate against artists "going to foreign fields, and, like Washington Irving, getting inspiration from abroad."[4] Taking a public stance in favor of inclusiveness, Alexander disavowed notions of nationalism and isolationism; America already had a venue in the National Academy for exhibiting solely American artists. Six weeks later, after the opening of the Carnegie International for which Alexander served as a Paris advisor, he was headlined in the *Philadelphia Press*, claiming "We are attaining an enviable position."[5] The Carnegie International was the American version of the Société Nationale des Beaux-Arts in that foreign artists were among the jurors, exhibitors and those eligible for awards. Its enviable position, however, did not include being based in New York City.

Soon after his return, Alexander had an assignment from R. H. Russell, an art publisher. Russell produced high-quality art books and posters admired for their sense of restrained design that respectfully balanced text and white space – as for example the book *Eden Versus Whistler: The Baronet & the Butterfly; A Valentine with a Verdict* (1899). It is unclear if Russell commissioned Alexander to paint Maude Adams as Napoleon II in Rostand's *L'Aiglon* (Utah Museum of Fine Arts, Salt Lake City) and E. H. Sothern as Hamlet, but he did publish posters of the paintings. They were finished during or just after each performance. *L'Aiglon* opened in the Knickerbocker Theatre on October 22, 1900 for a ten-week run. The Charles Frohman production was so successful that it went on a national tour; Russell advertised a reproduction of the portrait in the spring of 1901.[6] Likewise Russell reproduced Alexander's painting of Sothern as Hamlet (possibly destroyed by the artist), a performance that opened and closed in the first week of its debut on September 17, 1900 due to a freak accident that incapacitated Sothern. The reproduction was ready by June 1901, if not earlier.[7] In both compositions, the full-length figure is set in an austere space articulated by subtleties of tone so that the atmosphere envelopes the figure, just as Whistler would have done – and, of course, Velázquez. With these theatrical projects a collaboration began between Alexander, Adams and Frohman that would be renewed in 1904.[8]

With friends like Harrison Morris, transitioning back to America was made easier. Once again, Morris showed his unyielding favoritism by singling out eleven canvases by Alexander for a special room at the Pennsylvania Academy of the Fine Arts 70th Annual Exhibition. (Was Morris feeling guilty about his article in *Scribner's* two years earlier?) With his recent relocation from Europe, Alexander relied heavily upon previously exhibited decorative pictures to represent him in exhibitions. He sent his three greatest hits from the Exposition Universelle to Philadelphia: *Autumn*, *Portrait of Rodin* and *The Mother (La Mère)*. They were featured along with others that can only be tentatively identified, such as "an exceedingly clever and simple little still life, a misty little marine, and a simply treated impressionistic landscape," and three portraits of children, a girl in gray, a boy and a third child.[9] As for new work, it was heavily weighted toward portrait commissions to the disadvantage of decorative pictures, in part explained by the absence of a muse to replace Juliette Very. There was no one to take her place for the near term except his wife.

Two days after the close of the Academy Annual, the American press broke the story of a simmering row from the previous July between Alexander and the Paris Society of American Painters, about who asked whom to resign. The society felt they had no choice but to "invite" Alexander to resign in light of his complicity with Cauldwell over control of jurors for the 1900 Exposition. Alexander kept his counsel and took no action at the time except to frame the "invitation" from Walter MacEwen, the Society's secretary. An ocean was not wide enough to separate the two factions, only delay the public acrimony. The invitation to resign was dated July 3, 1900. Possibly the October announcement that he would paint a portrait of the French President followed by being named a Chevalier of the Légion d'honneur in the new year stoked the embers of jealousy. It was compounded by a statement by John Cauldwell at a dinner in his honor on January 7, 1901, at the Salmagundi Club. Cauldwell explained how the Paris Society of American Painters tried to usurp his management of the American section of the Exposition Universelle, and acknowledged Alexander's support.[10]

Now more than six months later and several weeks after Cauldwell's comments, the American press began to pay attention. The New York *Mail & Express* broke the story on February 25, followed the next day with upwards of eight articles in major newspapers. This must have compelled the society to decide to release the letter, but without the postscript written by MacEwen: "Our conversation at the Palais des Beaux arts a few weeks ago. I told the society about." Upon learning this, Alexander immediately published the entire letter including the postscript, as he felt that to exclude the postscript mischaracterized the resignation.[11] The postscript made clear that "the society sent its demand in order to forestall him" from acting on his private conversation with MacEwen in which he had been "considering a resignation."[12] Press coverage continued daily until March 4 and thereafter slackened, though there was still another article on April 24.[13] The artist Ralph Curtis wrote a satirical letter to the editor of the *Paris Herald* ridiculing the "annual epidemic of virulent 'potintina'" and with the prediction that Alexander would be vindicated from "this stuffy situation, hermetically closed since last July."[14] Meanwhile in Buffalo those organizing the Pan-American Exposition were fearful that the situation would affect the number of "contributions from the Paris men."[15]

A sure way to redirect headlines to a less frivolous subject, but perhaps even more provocative, was Alexander's public comment about New York falling behind in art matters. Other cities like Pittsburgh, Philadelphia and St. Louis did more, he said. They actively kept abreast of what was being produced in Paris by the younger artists, and arranged for pictures to be secured for their annual exhibitions. Alexander went further, bemoaning the fact that schoolchildren did not avail themselves of the collection at the Metropolitan Museum. He accused New Yorkers of indifference and, in fact, of being behind the times. Because of, or in spite of, the debate over his differences with the Paris Society of American Painters, the timing of a debate over New York's place in the art world may have been a deliberate distraction. If Alexander intended to supplant one set of headlines by the other, he succeeded. It also marks his first efforts to advocate for art education in public schools and the start of what would be an unsuccessful attempt to promote a new building for the National Academy of Design.[16]

Gradually other news helped to ameliorate the battery of sensational articles. Alexander and Edwin A. Abbey were elected associate members of the National Academy in mid March. The Carnegie prize ($500 cash) from the Society of American Artists was the second award for *Autumn*; John Wesley Beatty announced the purchase of a painting for the Carnegie collection,[17] and Princeton requested Alexander's presence at the June 1902 commencement to receive an honorary master of arts degree.[18] What a welcome home!

Just in time for all this press attention, Alexander had a new set of publicity photographs made by portrait photographer Zaida Ben-Yusuf. Back in America and wanting to make his presence known, he chose to patronize a young photographer, whose career had been given its first boost by Alfred Stieglitz only four years earlier. Her ability to capture her subject in a natural pose was just the sort of thing that would appeal to Alexander. As noted by art historian Frank H. Goodyear III, "His wool suit and tweed overcoat peg him as practical and down-to-earth while his sweeping mustache and trim Van Dyck beard give a hint of European flair. The overcoat and wrinkled pants suggest a traveler just recently arrived" (Figure 57).[19]

Busy with private commissions in 1901 and 1902, Alexander rode the wave of his Parisian success by rotating previously exhibited work among American venues; but he never again sent new work to the Paris Salon. Three pictures for the Pan-American Exposition in Buffalo (1901) earned him a gold medal: *Autumn, A Ray of Sunlight* and *Child with Doll.* For a fair designed to celebrate progress in the Western Hemisphere, inclusive of Canada and Central and South America, it nevertheless was more favorable towards the United States. Like so many others, Alexander was represented by works not made in America, but in France. Critic S. Swift reinforced that point when he wrote that the Vedders, Harrisons and Alexanders were well known and decidedly "more French than American."[20] To the Sixth Annual Carnegie International he sent the by now much exposed Rodin portrait and the less familiar *The Rose* showing Juliette Very seated and seen from her left sniffing a rose (1898, unlocated).[21] The latter found a buyer in Mrs. William Thaw Sr., a Pittsburgher and great-aunt of Alexander's old friend Thomas Shields Clarke. To the National Academy of Design 77th Annual Alexander sent *The Piano.* Representation at the Pennsylvania Academy 71st Annual was limited to an 1899 portrait of A. Newbold Morris (unlocated) and two canvases, *The Mother* and *The Black Cat* were sent to the Society of American Artists.

In the fall Alexander tried teaching, an entirely unexpected departure at this stage of his career and something he seldom talked about. At the Art Students League he joined a roster of instructors in "illustration, composition and the sketch" that included Kenyon Cox, Irving Wiles, George Grey Barnard, Frederick Dielman, and Arthur W. Dow. For the school year 1902–3, Alexander conducted evening classes where he offered critiques of students' compositions and studies.[22] And then for

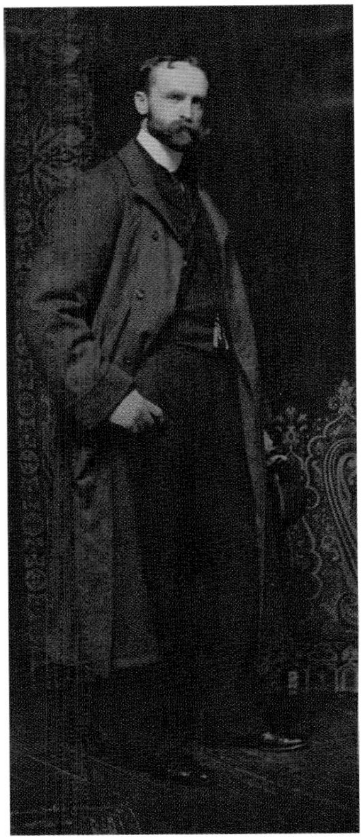

57
Zaida Ben-Yusuf,
John White Alexander, 1901,
platinum print, 9 3/8 × 4 in.
(23.8 × 10.2 cm.), John White
Alexander papers, Archives
of American Art,
Smithsonian Institution

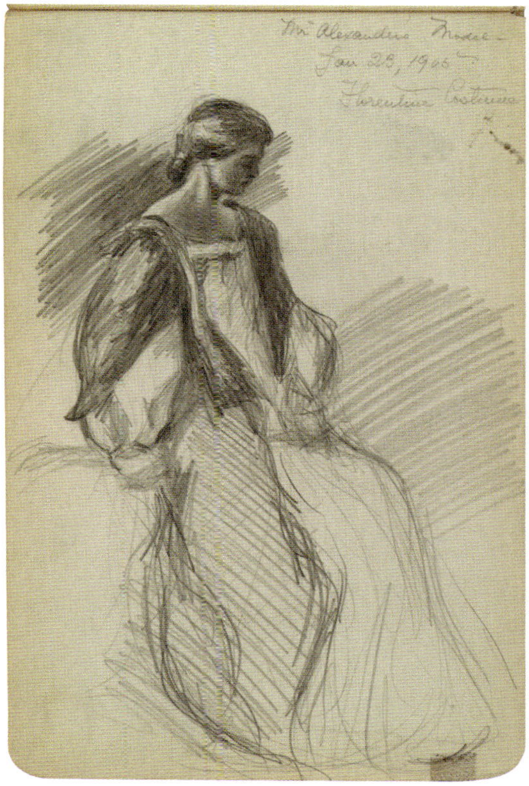

58
Malvina Hoffman (1885–1966), *Mr. Alexander's Model/Jan 23, 1905/Florentine Costume*, 1905, sketchbook page, pencil, Malvina Hoffman papers Series VIII.A. Sketchbooks, 1901–1964, box 174, container 1, Getty Research Institute, Los Angeles (850042)

the school year 1904–5, he joined the faculty at the Veltin Studio for Girls, an exclusive finishing school where he conducted life classes.[23]

Of his pupils, there is one standout, Malvina Hoffman. She studied with him at the League and then at Veltin; she may even have studied with Alexander as early as 1901.[24] Her sketchbooks, bearing annotations "Alexander Class" or "Alexander model," provide evidence of his teaching practices and preferences.[25] Pencil sketches show attention to shading of dark and light. Models are seated or standing. Men are dressed in a classical garment or a contemporary suit and tie and females are in "Florentine" costume (Figure 58). In sketches Hoffman annotated as Florentine, the flowing gowns were gathered below a square or a sweetheart neckline with full sleeves gathered at the shoulder.[26] This Florentine type can be found in two of Alexander's paintings, *Memories* (1904) and *Aurora Leigh* (1904).

The year ended on a high note, a solo two-week exhibit at the New York branch of the commercial gallery Durand-Ruel and a flattering, but unsigned article in *Harper's Weekly*.[27] The exhibition at Durand-Ruel, with both paintings and photographs of paintings, amounted to a mini-retrospective. Five were mainstays from the Paris salons. Four were new decorative pieces, *A Quiet Hour* (Figure 59), *Study in Tone* (unlocated), *The Rose* (unlocated, and not the 1898 painting with the same title), and the portrait of his wife. *Study in Tone* seemed to have been mostly ignored by the New York press; subsequently exhibited at the Boston Art Club, it was left to the Boston critics to call out its weaknesses, that being the "ghastly sort of moonlight tint" falling on the bare shoulders of the model.[28] A new costume was introduced in *The Rose*, a green and black striped skirt and a decorated bodice, that would become infamous in 1907 when the model wearing the same dress in *Study in Green and Black* (Metropolitan Museum of Art) was mistakenly taken for Evelyn Nesbit, the wife of Henry K. Thaw (the son of Alexander's patron Mrs. William Thaw, who in the "scandal of the century" had murdered the architect Stanford White the previous year in a *crime passionnel* over White's earlier relationship with Nesbit).

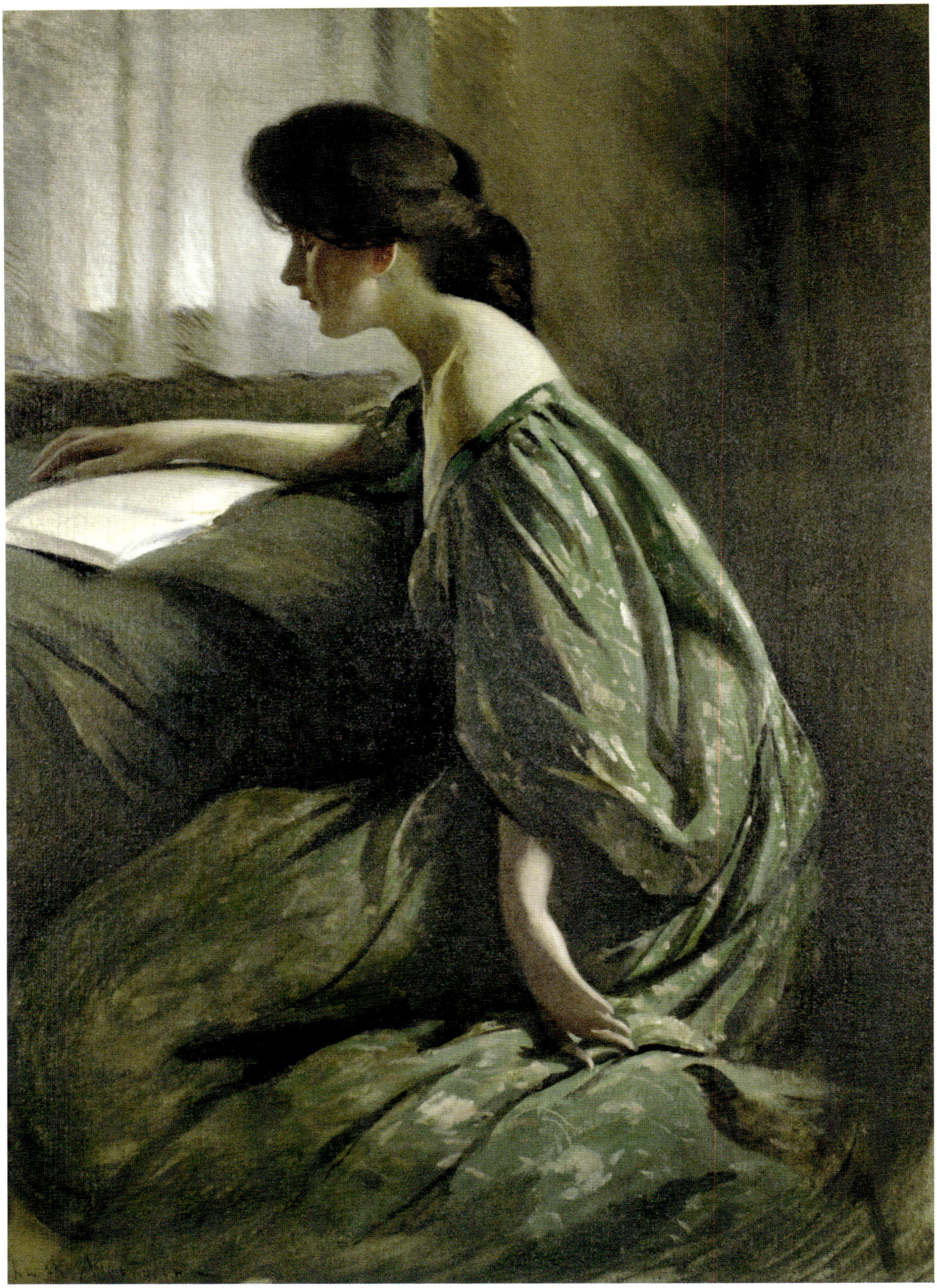

59 *A Quiet Hour*, 1902, oil on canvas, 48 3/8 × 35 5/8 in. (122.9 × 90.5 cm.), Pennsylvania Academy of the Fine Arts, Joseph E. Temple Fund, 1904.6

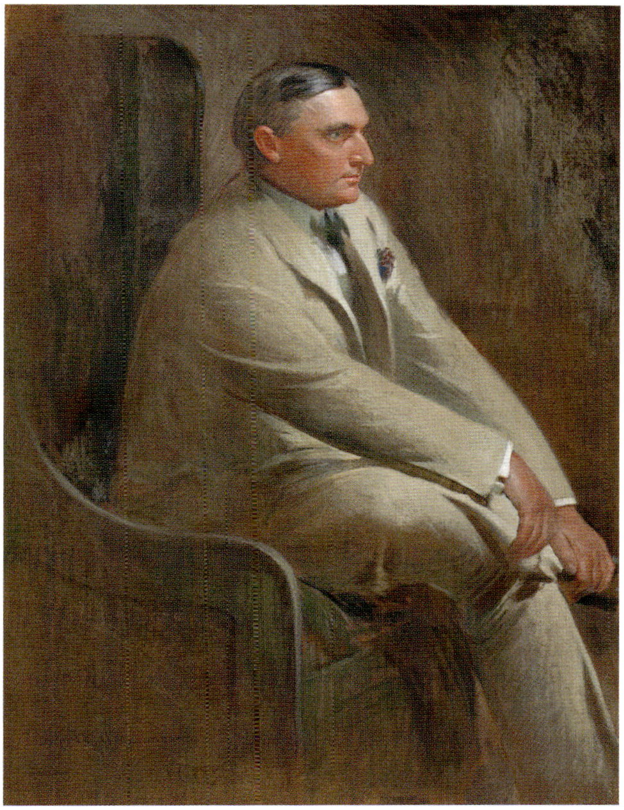

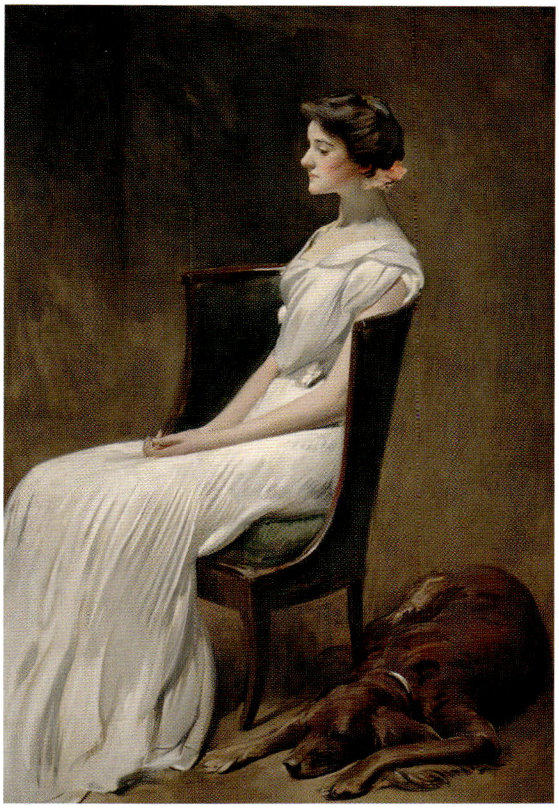

61
William Croghan Denny,
1902, oil on canvas,
48 × 36 in. (121. 9 × 91.4 cm.),
John and Lorraine Anderson,
New Jersey

60
Miss Dorothy Quincy Roosevelt, 1902, oil on canvas,
60 × 40 in. (152.4 cm. × 101.6 cm.), Dallas Museum of Art,
gift of the Pauline Allen Gill Foundation in memory of
Pauline Gill Sullivan, 2007.36,
image courtesy Dallas
Museum of Art

Other than the four new decorative works, it was new portraits of the powerful and influential in society that made up the majority of the exhibit. It probably cannot be overlooked that the stature of his father-in-law, President of the Equitable Life Assurance Society since the death of Henry Baldwin Hyde in May 1899, was a factor. An increase in high-society commissions included a portrait of Mrs. C. Ledyard Blair (Russell B. Pyne, California), whose husband had financed Alexander's new studio, and who would later own *Autumn*. The decorative effect of this portrait is unsatisfactory, with the lines of her skirt failing to achieve the sensuousness of the flowing line that distinguished the artist's Parisian figure paintings. The ravishing redhead Mrs. Herman B. Duryea, whose husband became one of the leading thoroughbred racing owners in the country, had been a neighbor in Monmouth County, New Jersey, adjacent to Seabright (The Philbrook Museum of Art). The positioning of Mrs. Duryea seated in an empire chair, and the sweep of the skirt with its appliqué hem across the floor, has a bold and decorative effect. The Roosevelts would become extended family once Eleanor Butler Alexander, daughter of Henry Addison Alexander, married Theodore Roosevelt, Jr. in 1910, but the ties with them may have formed as early as the portrait of a subdued Dorothy Quincy Roosevelt seated in the now familiar empire chair (Figure 60). The lovely Mrs. Hastings was the wife of the renowned architect Thomas Hastings of the firm of McKim, Mead & White, and later Carrère & Hastings (National Academy Museum and School). She was the daughter of Elias Cornelius Benedict, a prominent New York banker and close friend to U.S. President Grover Cleveland. And a portrait that was barely dry when it was sent to Durand-Ruel was that of ex-President Patton of Princeton dressed in his professorial robes.[29]

Two portraits, that of William Denny (Figure 61) and Geraldine Russell (Metropolitan Museum of Art), reflect ties to Onteora, a gated community in the Catskills founded by Frank Thurber and his sister Candace Wheeler. In need of a summer place away from the pressure of city life, Alexander followed his in-laws who had originally acquired property in Onteora in August 1898.[30] Onteora would become Alexander's retreat, possibly for part of the summer of 1902 when the Denny and Russell portraits were painted there, followed by the summers of 1903 and 1904, and again in 1910, when the Alexanders either leased a cottage or were houseguests, and from 1911 in their own cottage after Bess acquired The Bushes.[31] Little is known about William Denny who sat for his portrait in a summer suit, appropriate attire for a stay in Onteora. As for Charles H. Russell, he was a lawyer from New York City who built a cottage in Onteora in 1894–5.[32] His daughter's portrait, and subsequently his own, were painted there.[33] High-society portraits such as these would become – not exclusively, but often enough – the cynosure of the last fifteen years of Alexander's life; less so, the artful, decorative study of the anonymous female as she twists and turns in a shallow space.

The consensus regarding the Durand-Ruel exhibit was laudatory despite the familiarity of *Autumn, Child with Doll, Portrait of Rodin, The Mother*, and *A Ray of Sunlight*. The portraits of Mrs. Hastings and Elizabeth Alexander were the standouts. The vivacious Mrs. Hastings is poised on the edge of her chair in a painting that was described as "brilliant in execution" with a "color scheme of subdued greens and grays and such cleverly managed light as to make it almost a tour de force."[34]

Without a steady studio model, Alexander turned to his wife to pose for one of his finest decorative pictures since Paris (Figure 62). The affinities to the grand manner of portraiture exemplified by Thomas Gainsborough are obvious, specifically Gainsborough's *Portrait of Mrs. Thomas Hibbert* (1786). In both pictures the women are seated amidst a canopy of leafy tree limbs under a moody sky that is – in Alexander's case – a reprise of the light effects from

62
Portrait of Mrs. John White Alexander, 1902,
oil on canvas, 62¼ × 52⅛ in.
(158.2 × 132.4 cm.),
Los Angeles County Museum of Art, gift of Dr. and Mrs. Matthew S. Mickiewicz, M.81.182

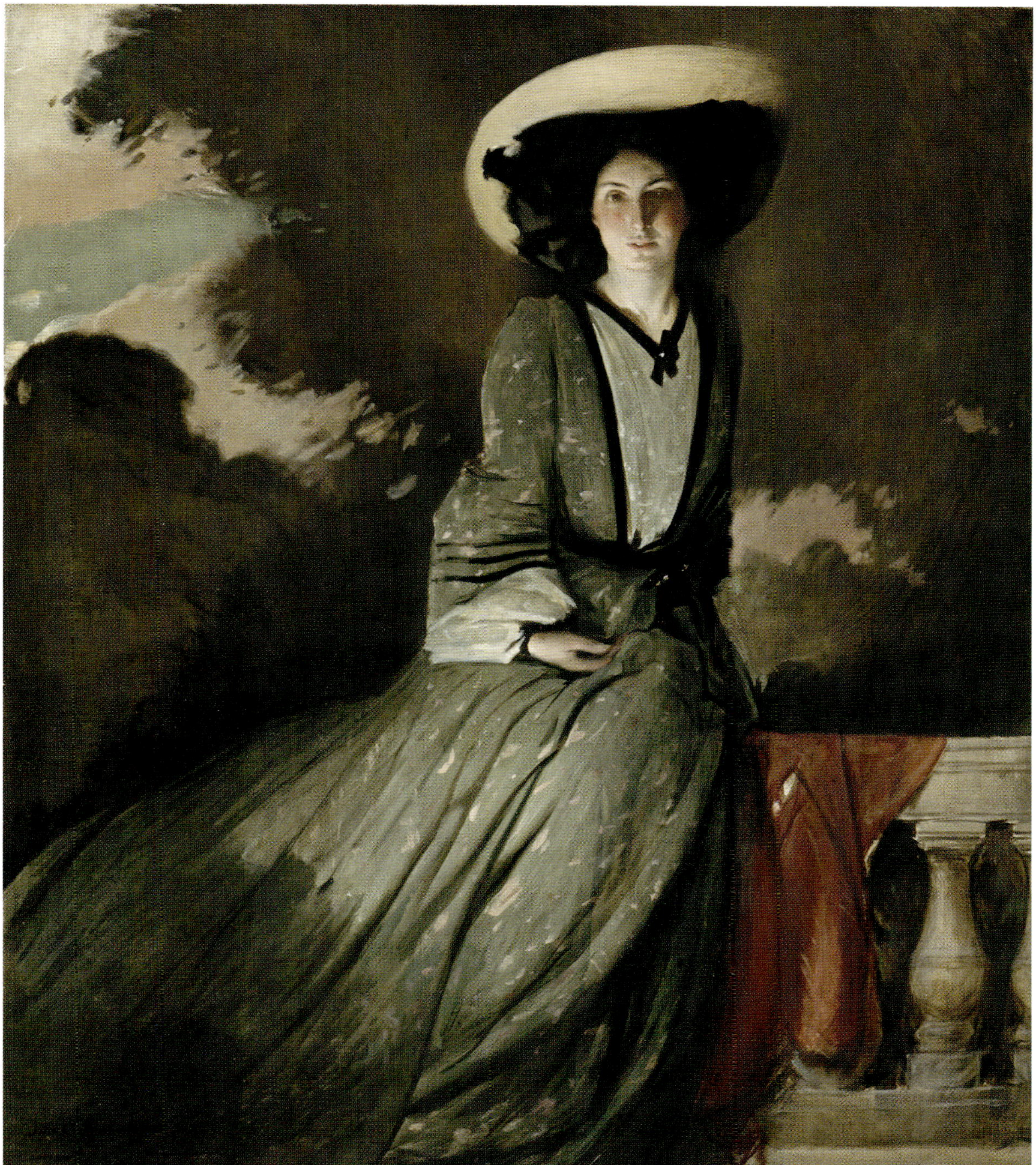

Autumn, Alexander's Salon success of 1900. Gainsborough was recently on Alexander's mind having been the feature of a tableau vivant to benefit charity held at a private residence in February of 1901. Together with his fellow artists J. Carroll Beckwith and William M. Chase, they arranged a series of tableaux on subjects including, but not limited to, colonial pictures, Gainsborough's portraits of the Duchess of Devonshire and Lady Sheffield, reproductions of Old Masters, and Japanese scenes.[35] In her portrait Elizabeth Alexander models a Gainsboroughesque broad-brim hat and is dressed in the all too familiar floral-pattern dress. This iconic patterned dress had not in fact been used since *Peonies*; its last appearance would be in *A Quiet Hour* (Figure 59), another painting the press found "delicious in tone and silvery light effect."[36]

A project in 1902 that allowed for almost complete freedom of imagination was a mural decoration for the Pennsylvania State Capitol building. Under a new governor a new commission was formed and a competition announced for a new building. With the specific stipulation that only a Pennsylvania architect could qualify, the project was awarded to Philadelphian Joseph Miller Huston in December 1901. His design drew on his admiration for the Italian Renaissance, in this case, St. Peter's Basilica in Rome. It couldn't be a better symbol of America's coming of age with artists expressing the national mood by taking inspiration from the classical past. The building embodied the essence of the "formidable république americaine." In mid 1902 Huston announced his selection of painters and sculptors to decorate the building. Again, the selection had to be limited to Pennsylvanians. The bulk of the project, the rotunda, the house and senate chambers, and two court chambers, was awarded to Edwin Austin Abbey. Though Abbey's overriding style was that of historical narrative, he did not completely disregard allegorical conventions, at times intermingling both in the same decoration, as in the *Apotheosis of Pennsylvania* in the house chamber. Inexplicably, while contracts for other locations throughout the complex were signed by Violet Oakley, William B. Van Ingen, and the sculptor George Grey Barnard, there is no record of a contract signed by Alexander, though he had been named to decorate the lower level of the North corridor.

Harrisburg was only Alexander's second attempt at designing murals; and circumstances beyond the artist's control were such that in the end he never got beyond preparatory work in the form of a few pencil sketches and five watercolors.[37] His charge was to illustrate the physical change in the state in the course of its industrial and mechanical development. The theme was *The Evolution of the State: The Industrial Development of Pennsylvania*. Alexander titled the fourteen lunettes, *Landscape*, *Smoke*, *Clearing*, *Logging*, *Rafting*, *Farming-Plowing*,

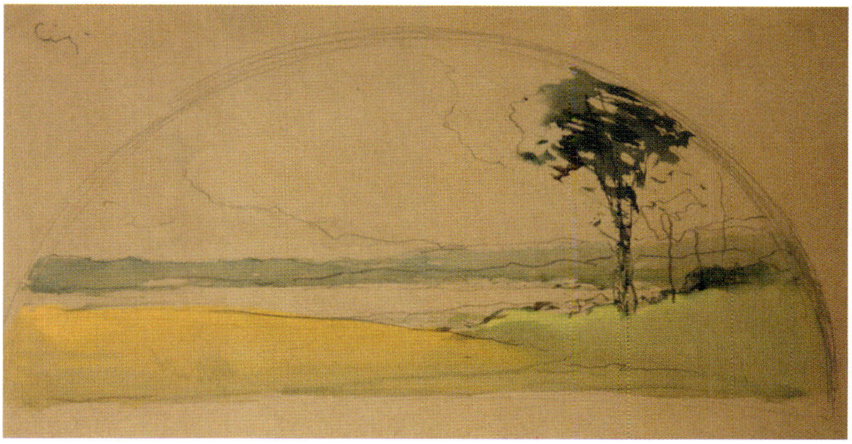

63
City (sketch for *Evolution of the State: The Industrial Development of Pennsylvania*), *c.*1902–5, pencil and watercolor, 9 7/8 × 13 7/8 in. (25.1 × 35 cm.) (sheet), John White Alexander great-granddaughters

Farming-Grain, *Oil*, *Boats-River*, *Coal*, *Building*, *City* (Figure 63), *Steam*, ending with *Capitol*. As was his custom, he no doubt began thinking about the project the moment he was named. Unlike his colleagues who used the historical narrative, Alexander tells the story of Pennsylvania through the landscape genre alone, devoid of figures. While landscape was an unconventional choice, even more so given his reputation as a figure painter, he responded to his assigned subject with an inspired decorative scheme. Judging by the watercolors, his intent was a Whistlerian approach, applying color in harmonious variations of tone to landscape forms. To appreciate this decorative scheme, at once pastoral, arcadian, and romantic, is to imagine how different it would have been from other decorations in the same building as well as in the Boston Public Library, the Library of Congress and ultimately his own "Apotheosis" cycle for the Carnegie Institute in 1905. No one would have been prepared for the originality and poetic beauty of the design. If it had been executed, there would have been no parallel in the history of American mural decoration.

Alexander's recent decorative pictures, *A Quiet Hour* and *Portrait of Mrs. John White Alexander*, helped sustain his place in the public arena in 1903 while he suffered from yet another debilitating setback in his health. For all of 1903 he relied upon previously exhibited work to represent him at the annuals at the Pennsylvania Academy, Society of American Artists, Art Institute of Chicago, Carnegie International, and a one-man show at the St. Botolph Club in Boston. The exceptions for the year were a few recent portrait commissions and three decorative pictures. Introduced at the St. Botolph Club in early spring, they were *A Rainy Day* (private collection, Virginia) and two that are only known by descriptive titles, "sketch of girl with hair down" and "sketch of a seated figure with spots of sunlight".

The one bright spot in his artistic production for 1903 came from spending the summer in Onteora. He either leased from, or was a guest of, Colonel James Kimball at Buford Lodge, that Kimball had built the previous year.[38] The lodge was named after Fort Buford in the Dakota Territory where Kimball served as an army surgeon and wrote an autobiography of Sitting Bull. One can only imagine the conversations he and the widow of George A. Custer, who also was in Onteora that summer, must have shared. Onteora was a special place, perhaps over-romanticized by founding member Candace Wheeler who opined: "Dear Onteora! whose primitive garb has changed at the touch of the many-braided wand of the world, as Cinderella's rusticity fell from her when she felt the touch of the fairy's wand. And yet it was the rustic simplicity, the attempt to materialize a dream of natural life, which brought together the dear souls who first peopled it."[39] Among the dear souls who continued to populate Onteora in the summer of 1903 were literary figures such as Laurence Hutton, an essayist, critic and former literary editor of *Harper's Magazine* and a close friend of the artist's father-in-law, also in residence. There were a number of female authors including Ruth McEnery Stuart and two writers of children's books, Mary Mapes Dodge and Susan Coolidge. The society matron, Mrs. J. N. A. Griswold (née Emmet), who spent her time both in Onteora and Newport, was there. William Denny, who had sat for Alexander the previous year, was there as was Charles Howland Russell, current President of the Onteora Club, and Maude Adams. It is possible that John Burroughs, the eminent American naturalist and nature essayist was also in Onteora that summer.[40]

Generations of New York power brokers, lawyers, publishers, writers, musicians, and actors "peopled" this rustic corner of the Catskills in the summers. Cottages without amenities had picturesque names like Lotus Land, Pennyroyal, Skylark, Harebell, Chipmunk, and The Birches. Guests and renters were welcomed throughout the season by cottage owners; otherwise, the Bear and Fox Inn took in guests. Marking the entrance to the inn was a sign designed by Dora Wheeler that captured the essence of the place. A bear and fox walked hand in hand in the moonlight silhouetted against the nearby mountain peaks. Community activities abounded with theater, concerts, the garden club, and programs at the library. If anyone dared to be distracted by the need to make a telephone call they had to go to nearby Tannersville.

Each summer at the end of the season Onteora hosted a county fair that was an exercise in creativity far above your garden-variety county fair. Take for example the fair of 1903. It opened with a parade of over 250 persons with many of the residents and guests unrecognizable in their artistically designed costumes. Participants donned "queer costumes" such as a mummy (Alexander), Minnehaha, an "Occidental," a jester, a six-foot Pierrot, and Nero (William Denny). Alexander's ghostly mummy costume required a good deal of preparation. Starting with white muslin, it was soaked in coffee and while drying on the grass sprinkled with ashes to achieve the "unholy mixture of tints." Instead of a mask Alexander painted his face with watercolors and then sprinkled it with ashes.[41]

The fair was laid out in an oval bordered by booths selling various sundries announced by a poster and decorated with flags and pendants. Everything was for sale from baked goods, handmade quilts, and Turkish cigarettes to old straw hats. Posters were painted for the various attractions by Alexander, Clara McChesney, and Elsie Roberts.[42] Of the so-called "posters" by Alexander, two were over-life-size canvases for the Fancy Work booth (Figure 64). One was of a stick-thin woman wearing an apron standing and knitting, and another, a man with a "five o'clock shadow" in a jaunty pose smoking and leaning on a walking stick. Additionally there was a pirate (Onteora Field House) and a gypsy, and possibly one of a corncob man.[43] Finally, there was a poster of Cupid carrying a bow and arrow, suggesting there was a booth to beget love and friendship (Lansing and Iliana Moore, Onteora). In each of these posters Alexander renders his subject with a sure and quick hand in the manner of a caricaturist. None of the posters were intended for exhibition nor destined for a patron, which may explain why they were painted with such fluidity and freedom of execution. Completed just for the county fair in 1903, this volume of work for a summer respite was unparalleled.

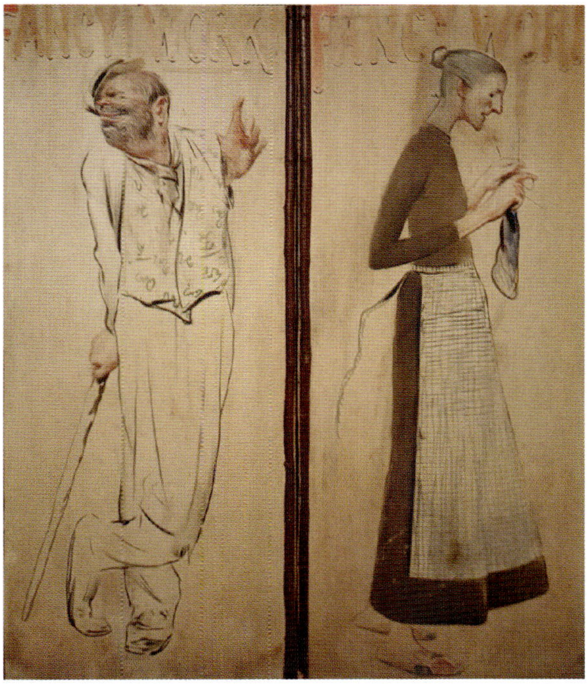

64
Poster, Fancy Work Booth, Onteora Fair, 1903, oil on canvas, 72¼ × 30 in. (183.5 × 76.2 cm.), Michal Hendrych, Onteora, New York

A signature feature of Alexander's decorative figurative paintings during his Parisian years had been costumes employed to mask movement. They were not couturier gowns but rather of his own design, in a style suited for at-home wear, loosely fitted, secured at the waist and uncorseted. For example, the two dresses in *Panel for Music Room* begot the costumes in the Étretat pictures and *Repos*. The floral pattern in the Parisian pictures, *Peonies* and *Green Girl*, were used again back in New York in the *Portrait of Mrs. John White Alexander* and *A Quiet Hour*, with the difference being in the color of the background. These costumes served as a leitmotif for his body of work at a given moment in his development.

In 1903 a new type of green dress made its appearance in *A Study* (Figure 65). It had a fitted bodice and was worn seductively off the shoulders with heavy trim at the neckline and richly embroidered sleeves with white ruffles. Seated in profile, bare shoulders in light and shadow, the figure leans forward with apprehension, hands clasped in her lap. The painting earned praise for its "certain delicate appeal in the lightly drooping figure" and its "peculiar indefinable charm."[44] The source of its so-called charm was the suffusive warmth of the light filtering through a curtained window. The costume, with its emblematic decoration of the sleeves and the bodice, appears again in another painting also of 1903, *The Green Gown* (unlocated).

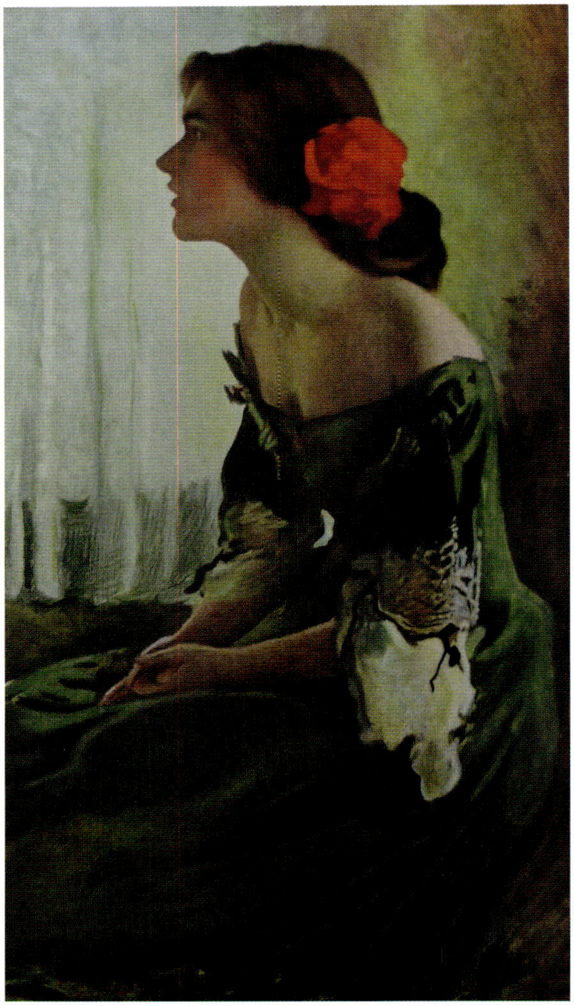

65
A Study (*The Girl in the Green Gown*), *c.*1903, unlocated. Photograph courtesy of the author

Alexander was prescient in devising this charming visual construct – a figure in soft light with a curtained window – that was subsequently explored by his contemporaries. The Ten and the American Impressionists devised their own iterations, as for example in *The New York Window* (1912) by Childe Hassam. *A Study* debuted at the Sixteenth Annual Exhibition in October at the Art Institute of Chicago. It is one of Alexander's best examples since resettling in New York – and nearly his last – of the emotive power of sentiment, in which the figure is constrained by its space and limited in its movement. The painting met with such favor that it was made into a calendar and offered for sale by the Osborne Company as "The Girl in the Green Gown."[45] In addition to a new idea for posing a figure and introducing a new costume, Alexander also found a new muse in Anne Raynor

Ward, a family friend, who would model for some of the artist's most important paintings again in the 1910s. A similarity of hairstyle and profile in *A Study* and *A Quiet Hour* leads to the likelihood that the same model posed for both.[46]

Alexander scored a Gold Medal at the 73rd Annual exhibition at the Pennsylvania Academy of the Fine Arts in late January 1904 with *Memories* (Figure 66). The discretionary award was the Academy's most prestigious honor in recognition of the highest professional achievement. Of a total of five submissions by Alexander, four had been previously exhibited. He was still working on the new picture, *Memories*, five weeks before the opening.[47] While to some critics *Memories* was "haunting and stimulating", to others it was "namby-pamby."[48] Neither interpretation did it justice. In *Memories*, as well as in *A Quiet Hour* and the painting of his wife seated on a balustrade, Alexander reimagines the decorative. He has abandoned contorting the figure in a shallow space in favor of a more three-dimensional space. Rather than the figure being imprisoned by her dress, she has more control of her body, with the skirt draping it more naturally and gracefully. In *Memories*, the plain dress of the figure on the left, is contrasted with a new floral-pattern dress worn by the figure on the right. The bodice and sleeves are fitted, tied below the bustline and around the upper arm. With the introduction of depth of field in the picture with its background landscape, it becomes difficult to refute Charles Caffin's characterization of *Memories*: sentiment is no longer expressed by an isolated figure trapped within its space.[49] In this two-figure composition sentiment becomes interactive, expressed by the unspoken word between the two.

References to Onteora permeate *Memories*. The silhouetted mountain range echoes the sign for the Bear and Fox Inn. The right figure is seated on a rocky outcrop of the landscape with a view across the Hudson River to the Berkshires. One can imagine the left figure in a state of reverie listening to the words of Dora Wheeler's ode to Onteora being read from the book in the hand of her companion, or remembering music performed by some of Alexander's fellow residents in the summer of 1903, including Mary Knight Wood, Heinrich Meyn or Greta Torpadie.[50]

Within weeks of the close of the 73rd Annual, the Academy decided to purchase one of Alexander's pictures. The Gold Medal picture, *Memories*, was not their choice, rather it was the more graceful *A Quiet Hour*. In doing so they declined – given the originality of *Memories* – one of Alexander's last great decorative pictures, one "with a mood of eroticism and languor and a quasi-symbolist overtone," in favor of a less esoteric and less "Parisianized" work.[51] In making their decision the Academy actually arranged an exchange, returning *The Café* (*L'Attente*), an earlier purchase made in 1900 for the Temple collection, for *A Quiet Hour*.[52]

Meanwhile, Alexander was one of six speakers scheduled for the presentation of his portrait of Pittsburgh Central High School Principal Benjamin Cutler Jillson to the school on January 29, 1904. In addition to the unveiling of the portrait, there were five speakers on the program representing the class of 1875 (including Alexander, though he was not a graduate) to give testimonials.[53] The alumni never forgot that it was Jillson's heavy-hearted task to preside over the dedication of the new Fulton Street school building on October 13, 1871, when he stood in place of the man he succeeded, Philotus Dean, who died in his arms that summer, a victim of exhaustion and typhoid fever. Dean oversaw the design and construction of a new building with state-of-the-art features like an air circulation system, light-filled classrooms, and newly furnished classrooms, laboratories and library. Jillson, his successor, resigned in 1880 though later returned as professor of Chemistry and Geology. It was the last class of his principalship, the class of 1880, that presented Alexander's three-quarter length portrait (unlocated) standing beside a desk with a document in his hand.

Beginning in 1904 through May, Alexander's physical state was such that he was still unable to work steadily, making it likely that he cancelled his trip to Pittsburgh for the presentation of the Jillson portrait. Having missed the opening of the 73rd Annual of the Pennsylvania Academy on January 25, he and Bess wanted to visit even for a few hours but were overly optimistic about his ability to withstand the rigors of a trip.[54] There was a strong incentive for going because of the award for *Memories*. In a letter written by Bess to her husband's trusted confidant Harrison S. Morris, she disclosed the severity of Alexander's condition and the impact on his work: "Mr. Alexander is still far from well & has not gone back to work. He has arranged with his sitters here to postpone their sittings but has one coming on from Grand Rapids this week which he cannot postpone." The sitter coming from Grand Rapids was probably Mrs. Dudley Waters. Two portraits of her children had been completed by the close of 1904 but hers was still to be done.[55] Bess held out hope that her husband could work a short time each day, yet she doubted that he could even accomplish that much. Their objective was to do everything for him to improve in advance of a planned trip to Boston in March 1904 to take on an important commission with the promise of others.

Not fully recovered until May, he finally undertook the journey to Boston, a ten-day working trip during which time it appears he completed two portraits.[56] The day after his arrival, he was introduced to his first sitter, Mrs. Sarah

66
Memories, 1904, oil on canvas, $62^{1}/_{16} \times 52^{1}/_{16}$ in. (157.7 × 132.3 cm.), Brooklyn Museum of Art, Museum Collection Fund, 22.75. Photograph: Brooklyn Museums

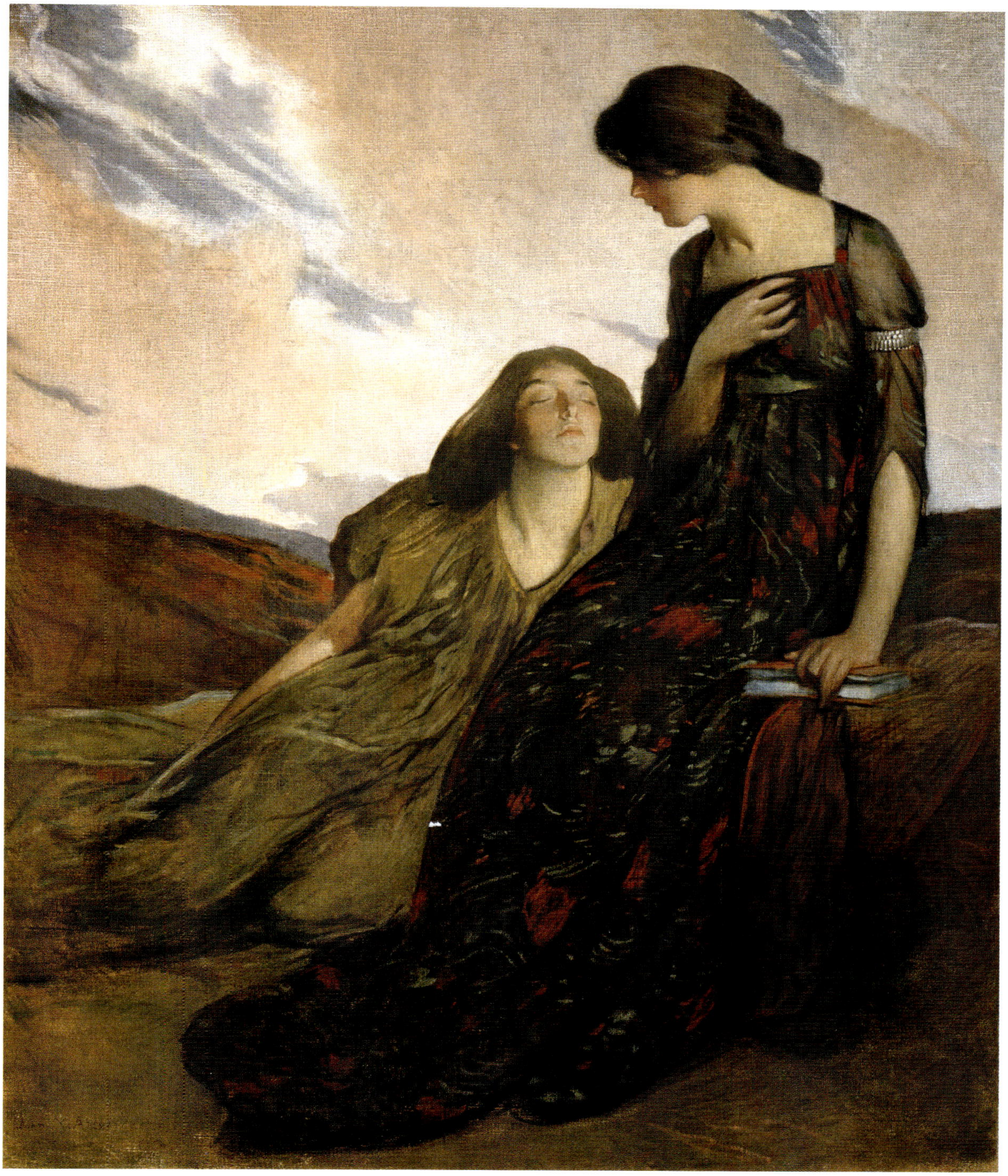

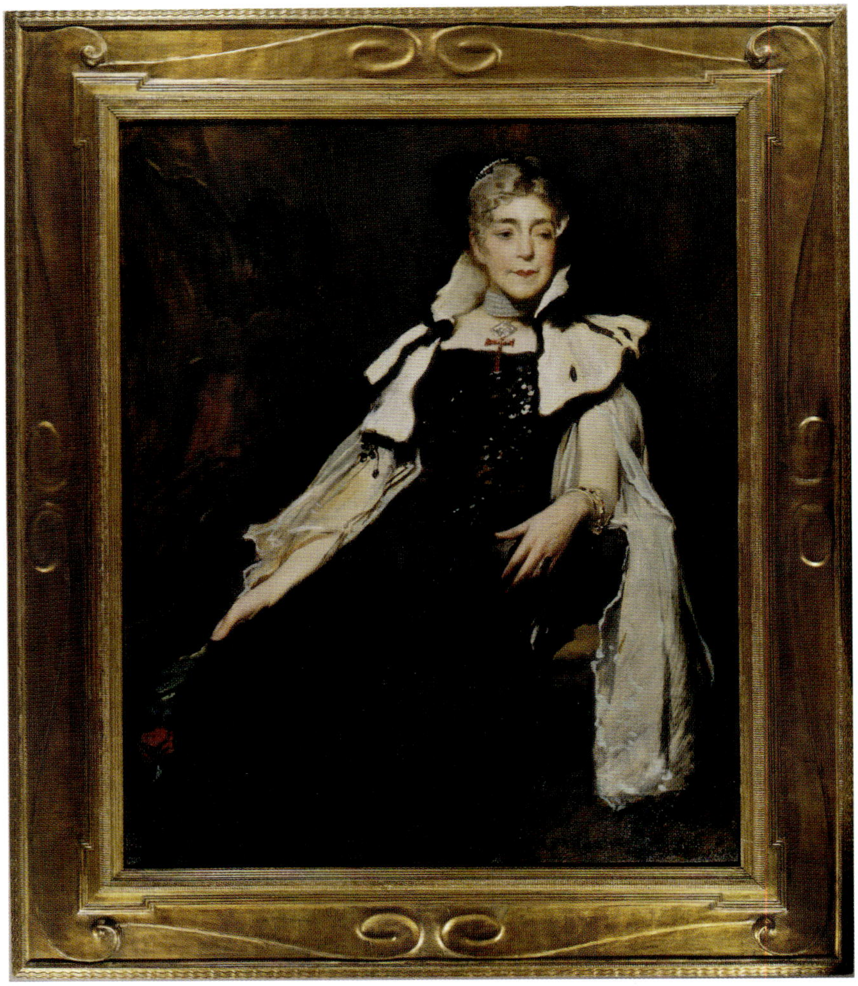

67
Mrs. Sarah de St. Prix Wyman Whitman, June 1904,
oil on canvas, 50 × 40 in.
(127 × 101.6 cm.),
unknown private collection,
New England

de St. Prix Wyman Whitman (Figure 67).[57] The choice of Alexander to paint her portrait, destined for Radcliffe College, was decided by the sitter herself as a result of his successful exhibition at Durand-Ruel.[58] It may also have had something to do with his month-long stay in Boston the previous year during a one-man exhibition of his work at the St. Botolph Club.[59] Upon first meeting Mrs. Whitman, he described her just as she was, literally in the throes of dying: "cheeks and lips purple, a semi-demi-blond grey wig and no shape at all," sitting in a room heated to a temperature of 83 degrees.[60] Her deathly pallor illuminated by "a cold, hard North light" was "about as severe a thing as I know."

Alexander "was shocked by what he was up against." He was afraid that "if he looked away he might look back to find that she had died." Mrs. Jack Gardner or a Mrs. Parkman alternately chaperoned the sittings. They were so exhausting, both for the artist and the sitter, that on one occasion Alexander had to be taken to the country to recuperate. None too soon, for Mrs. Whitman did indeed die within weeks of the completion of the picture. A second portrait, that of Israel Munson Spelman, may have been the "less important work" inferred in Bess's letter to Morris.[61] A civil engineer by training and a railroad man, Spelman was a long-serving trustee of Mount Auburn Cemetery. The commission was arranged by a two-man committee of the cemetery corporation, J. Montgomery Sears and Charles Francis Choate.[62] The Spelman portrait made such a good impression that a discussion ensued about painting Choate. Alexander demurred, explaining that he had two portraits to close out in New York before he could take on another.[63] A portrait of Choate was never realized.

Alexander was accorded all the hospitality expected for one of his stature and he relived every moment of it in his daily letters home to Bess. He described his stay at the private Somerset, St. Botolph and Union Clubs and dining in the homes of Boston's first families – Gardner, Putnam, Codman, Endicott, Forbes, Parkman, Sears, and Sprague. He was a victim of rivalry between Mrs. Jack Gardner and Mrs. Sprague who, he wrote, "are fighting for a bone of a painter."[64] He also mentioned seeing "a lot of the fellows," among them the brother of Francis Davis Millet, Charles M. Loeffler and Wilfred von Glehn who was in Boston to marry Jane Emmet. Wilton Lockwood he would see again in November as an award juror for the Carnegie International.[65] He stopped by the museum to see *Isabella*, which he thought "looked quite well." A visit to the Boston Public Library to see the Puvis, Sargent and Abbey murals made sense in view of his imminent Harrisburg project. He "confessed to finding the Abbeys better than expected" and the Sargents not so good. He shared the opinions of others about the color of Puvis's mural that clashed with the yellow marble and could have been ameliorated if only Puvis had visited the library. Notwithstanding, when it came to Puvis, "'toute' was very fine."[66] As remained to be seen, Puvis's decorations would have some bearing on the scheme for the Carnegie commission awarded to Alexander the following year.

Given the state of his health in the first half of 1904, Alexander must have made a great effort to present fresh works for the Ninth Annual Carnegie International in November. Previously in 1901 he had shown French-made pictures. With the exception of a specially prepared portrait of Andrew Carnegie (unlocated), there was no need to present new decorative pictures in 1902 because

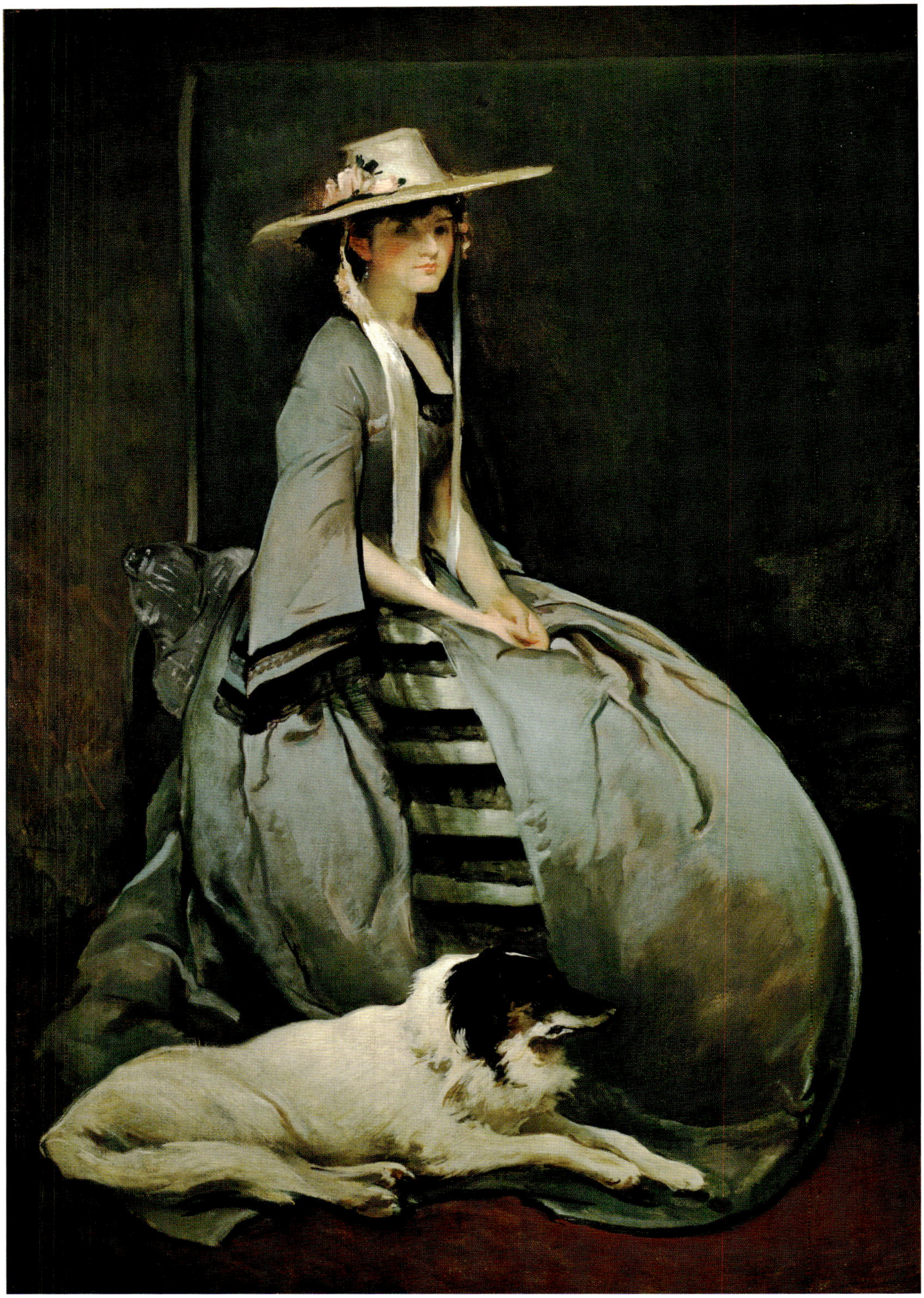

68 *Aurora Leigh*, 1904, oil on canvas, 76 ⅜ × 52 ⅜in. (194 × 133 cm.), Carnegie Museum of Art, Pittsburgh, gift of C. Bernard Shea in memory of Joseph B. Shea, 1940.4

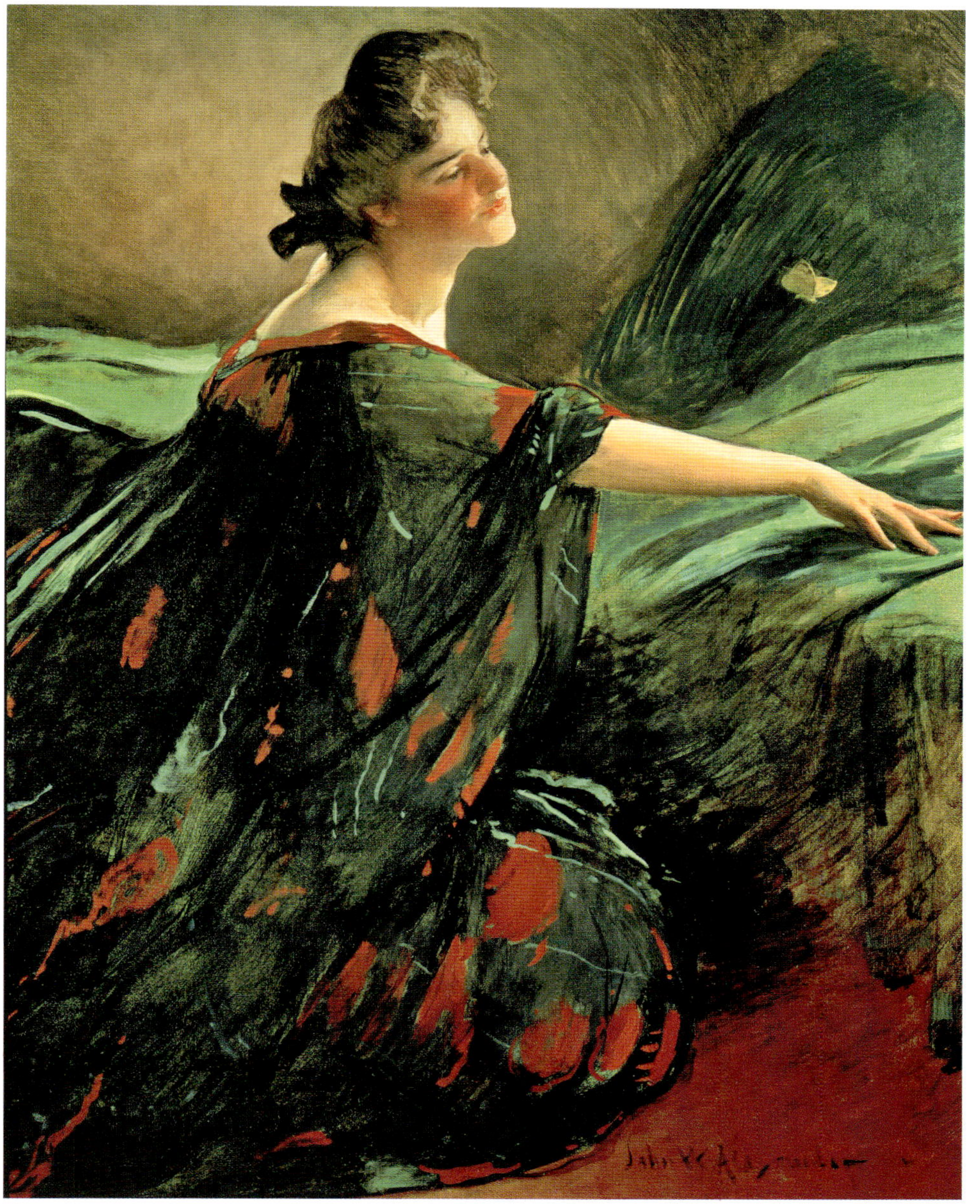

69 *A Butterfly*, 1904, oil on canvas, 50 × 40 in. (127 × 101.6 cm.), unknown private collection, Pittsburgh

John W. Beatty curated a loan exhibition in lieu of hosting an International. In the 1903 International, Alexander showed *Autumn*, which was being exhibited for the sixth time to an American audience since his return from France. Perhaps because of self-imposed pressure to exhibit something new in 1904, he presented three new paintings, none of which were portraits.

Neither strictly a portrait nor a figure painting, *The Family* (American Academy of Arts and Letters) was a sentimental recreation of his own nuclear family – father, mother and infant. In a pyramidal composition, the artist places himself at the peak with his family nestled beneath him. The other two pictures, *Aurora Leigh* (Figure 68) and *A Butterfly* (Figure 69), had been started in the summer in Onteora. Once again Alexander looked to literature for his subject, in this case Elizabeth Barrett Browning's poetic romance *Aurora Leigh* (1856/7). He depicted a passage in which the twenty-year-old Florentine dresses the part of a (somewhat genteel) shepherdess, in an iridescent gown of shades of green, blue, gray and peach, wearing a broad-brim hat with her shepherd dog at her feet. The dress worn by the model was borrowed from Mrs. J.N.A. Griswold of Newport and Onteora and was from her trousseau dating from around the same time as Browning's poem.[67] As for the third picture, *A Butterfly*, it is a reprise of the purely decorative picture, a type seen less frequently since 1900. In the same patterned dress as *Memories*, the graceful figure is placed on her knees next to a divan with her right arm extended, gazing at a butterfly. It is a dynamic composition with a masterful convergence of diagonals: the angle of her back, the crush of the divan pillows and the extended right arm together forming an X in the center. The model for these purely decorative pictures was Anne Bradley, a small-time actress, who came to spend the summer of 1904 in Onteora for that express purpose.[68] She and Alexander probably met through a common association with Charles Frohman, the American theatrical producer, and Clyde Fitch, the writer for the Broadway stage. [69]

It sometimes happens that artists find themselves party to the extreme consumption of wealthy clients. A case in point was Alexander and James Hazen Hyde. Hyde was the son of the founder of Equitable Life Assurance Society, the firm now headed by the artist's father-in-law following the death of the founder in 1899. In the midst of a simmering coup, Hyde, the major stockholder, who allegedly spent company funds as if they were his own, held a costume ball for 600 at Sherry's Hotel on January 31, 1905. The hotel was familiar to many guests as the place where their daughters debuted. A dedicated Francophile, Hyde chose as the theme Louis XV's court at Versailles, no doubt drawing upon his memory of a special tour of Versailles four and a half years earlier; on May 1,

1900 Hyde, with an entourage consisting of Ferdinand W. Peck, United States Commissioner for the Exposition Universelle, and individuals on committees or having special interests in the Exposition, among them Maurice Binder, René Nagelmackers, Horace Rogers, Charles H. Simons, M. P. Peixotto, Mr. and Mrs. Thomas Hastings, Henry A. Alexander (Elizabeth's cousin) and John and Elizabeth Alexander, was given a private tour of the palace and the Le Nôtre gardens by the Conservateur of Versailles, Pierre de Nolbac.[70]

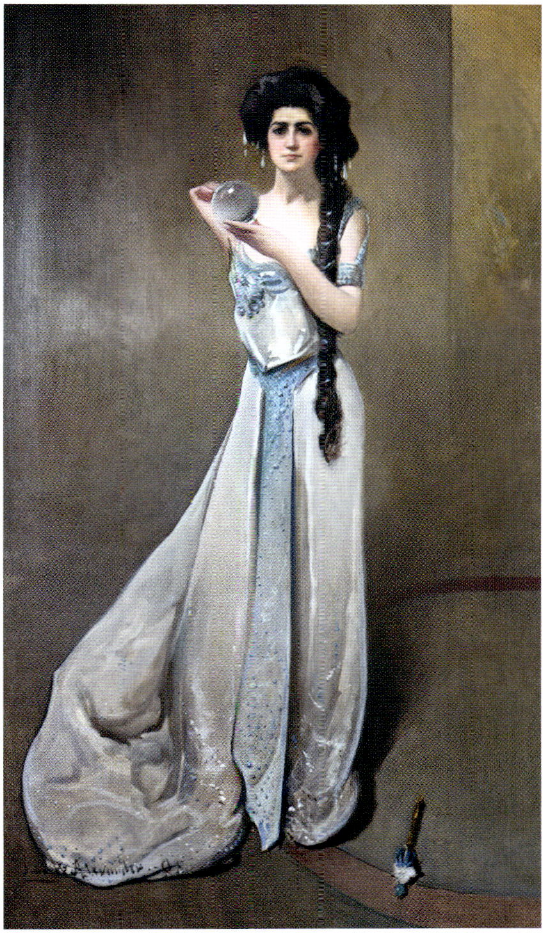

70
Mrs. Clarence Mackay, 1905, oil on canvas, approx. 90 × 53 in. (228.6 × 134.62 cm.), Mackay School of Earth Sciences and Engineering, University of Nevada, Reno

This visit spawned the idea for a costume ball the likes of which had never been seen in America. The level of excess was to the standards of the court of the *ancien régime*. Food, drink, jewels, and costumes in the spirit of the period were more than lavish. Guests were attended by liveried staff. Bugles announced dinner on the third floor under a canopy decked out with arbors of roses, fountains and turf simulating the landscaping of Versailles. Forms of entertainment included a ballet, music by the Metropolitan Opera Orchestra and a comedy performed by the legendary Madame Réjane brought from Paris for the occasion.

The showstopper, however, was not on the official program, but rather a guest, Mrs. Clarence Mackay, not just because of the flash and weight of her jewelry, for which she required the assistance of two footboys, but for the originality of her costume (Figure 70). She dressed as the eighteenth-century actress Adrienne Lecouvreur in the title role of Racine's *Phèdre*, wearing a draped gown inspired by antiquity. "She wore two large breastplates of turquoise, silver sandals, and a tiara of turquoises and pearls. A necklace of the same completed her costume."[71] Unlike other guests, her hair was not powdered, but braided, falling over her shoulders and intertwined with turquoise. In her hand she held a scepter. Pressure was applied by the client on the painter to complete the portrait so that she could announce it to the press prior to the ball.[72] It was a calculated move by a member of genteel society to capitalize on the anticipated press coverage of the Hyde ball.

The ball was the talk of the town, not just for its own sake, but for what followed. The Equitable board accused Hyde of paying for the ball from company funds, the sum involved ranging from, at the most absurd of estimates, a quarter million dollars to the more conservative calculation of $70,000. Charges and countercharges ensued in a public spectacle played out in the press and subsequently in the New York State Assembly in Albany. It was a matter of syndicates, retainers and nepotism, symptomatic of industries such as railroads and banking that "had mushroomed from small companies into an industry dominated by giants" with no federal or state government regulation.[73] After spectacular growth, Equitable was one of the three giants of the insurance industry under the absolute control of its founder. The real money was in the huge pool of capital which was invested in financial subsidiaries and syndicates of which Equitable officers were not only shareholders, but were paid to serve on their boards. They availed themselves of the pool of capital, borrowing at low rates and making loans at higher rates, even back to Equitable.

"The Equitable fight was an accident waiting to happen."[74] After the death of the founder, the presidency was assumed by James Waddell Alexander, Sr. with the understanding that it would revert to James Hazen Hyde when he turned 30 in 1906. The Hyde ball had collateral implications, causing an implosion not only at Equitable but for the insurance industry in general. Just days after the ball, President Alexander acted quickly to discredit Hyde at a board meeting on February 8. The Equitable battle was all the news for weeks as an internal committee debated, and then issued a report on May 31, that was a condemnation of both Hyde and Alexander. On June 3, the Equitable board voted against both men. Meanwhile, in mid July, New York State launched an investigation of the entire insurance industry. Subjected to extreme pressure, and having been removed as President by the board, Alexander fell ill. He first took refuge at the home of his son-in-law, then in a sanatorium in Bay Shore.[75] Under such stressful conditions, John White Alexander's ability to shelter and tolerate an imperious father-in-law reflects admirably upon his non-judgmental character. (An example of Alexander, Sr.'s imperious attitude was his stern admonishment to a new member of the Equitable fiscal committee, saying it was "not their province to go into the management of the company, or to express opinions about methods."[76]) The Equitable scandal put in motion a chain of events that led to state and national reforms of the insurance industry. As for the cost of the ball, it was subsequently revealed that Hyde financed it himself.

Alexander, the artist, benefited handsomely from the family association with Equitable, painting portraits of board members and their families. In the

1890s, he had painted the founder, Henry Baldwin Hyde (unlocated), Marcellus Hartley and family members, and Henry Marquand. General Louis Fitzgerald's portrait (unlocated) was completed by March 1901. Mrs. Samuel Untermyer, whose husband defended Hyde in the scandal, posed in 1903–4 (unlocated). Presumably there was no talk of Equitable when George Theodore Bliss (Yale University Art Gallery) posed during the time the scandal was brewing, or when Alexander was working on a portrait of Richard Aldrich McCurdy (unlocated), president of an Equitable subsidiary, Mutual Life Insurance Co., who faced conspiracy charges in April 1906. One friendship that proved to be resilient was that between Mrs. E. H. Harriman, whose husband intervened in the Equitable scandal, and Elizabeth Alexander who later engaged in a business partnership with Harriman's niece in 1915.

While the scandal was James Waddell Alexander's to rebut, his case may not have been helped when his son-in-law exhibited a reminder of the Hyde ball, the Mackay portrait, at the 27th Annual Exhibition of the Society of American Artists. The exhibit opened March 25, while news of the scandal was ongoing. Despite its being given the place of honor, the press showed no mercy toward the portrait. The painting was recognized for its strengths, but more often for its weaknesses: "It is as dry and as empty a canvas as we have seen in a long time."[77] Another called it "the most superficial piece of work."[78] The left arm holding the crystal globe "has the unfortunate effect of a deformed stump growing from the shoulder."[79] There were others who thought it a "tremendously strong bit of work."[80] Yet there was much to criticize, starting with how to pose the very tall Mrs. Mackay. It would have made a better composition if she had been seated. Her braid is far too long and interrupted by the awkward left arm, whereas the placement of the right arm is left to the imagination. With her torso pivoted slightly at the waist, the figure seems unnaturally thin. Moreover the portrait is a virtual sea of turquoise. A reviewer asked why a painting that was not worthy of the place of honor was so honored. One explanation offered was because of the "magnificent sculpturesque frame."[81] Indeed, it was not just any frame. From the studios of Stanford White, the frame was a very grand and imposing surround for a 7½ by 4½ ft. canvas.[82]

At the annual exhibition by the Art Students League Fakirs, the Mackay portrait found itself the subject of student parody by no less than six students. The headline in the New York *Sun* of April 25 proclaimed "Alexander's portrait of Mrs. Mackay the Chief Butt," continuing as follows: "a shot putter with the title 'Get back in the Ring'; as an advertisement for hair restorer with the legend 'Mackayrine grew this hair and I can prove it;' with the lady as a ball player, a real ping pong ball half protruding from the canvas; as a person about to take a huge liver pill; and as a young woman, presumably a domestic, who has dropped a lot of glassware."[83] No matter, Mrs. Mackay must have had a sense of humor, as she purchased Will Howe Foote's parody for $50.[84]

In early 1905, for a span of two and a half months, the Alexander name was everywhere – and not just about insurance, but also about painting. News of the Mackay portrait dominated from the time of the Hyde ball through the Fakirs Annual, with the latter overlapping the Society's Annual toward the end. On April 11, the Pratt Institute in Brooklyn opened a 26-piece, one-man show of the "eminent artist." Coming about two and a half years after the Durand-Ruel exhibit, it was an affirmation of Alexander's high rank among modern painters, as one who "occupies a unique place because of his distinctive style, his individual treatment of color and line, and his particularly delightful personal rendering of the human figure, whether in portraiture or pictorial composition."[85] The exhibit was larger than the one at Durand-Ruel, naturally including recent portraits, but with at least six decorative pictures, most from the Parisian years, that had already been exhibited in America at Durand-Ruel. Three recent male portraits were of William Bunker, a New York businessman (New-York Historical Society), Dr. Walter B. Gunnison, commissioned by Erasmus High School, Brooklyn (unlocated), and Colonel George Harvey, editor of *Harper's* (unlocated). Reviews were mostly positive, singling out the already familiar "grace in form and harmony in color," the "originality and daring" of the poses of women, and complimenting the "opulence of the greens."[86] On the other hand, the Bunker portrait was mocked for the rigidity of the suit, landscapes were "out of key," and the position of the figure in *A Flower*, it was said, would horrify the likes of Reynolds and Van Dyck. It was *Memories* that was praised as a "truly meritorious work."[87] Because of insufficient information, curiosity about two of the decorative pictures, *Girl with Hat* and *Study in Light Green*, that are only known by their title, must go unsated.

If work is an indication of recovery, then by any measure Alexander's commitments in the first half of 1905 were a sign of a robust return to health. He was busy with a staggering number of portrait commissions as well as the Harrisburg mural commission, all the while continuing his teaching at the Veltin Studio. Not one but two articles recounted the number of sales as well as a litany of sitters.[88] *A Quiet Hour* had been sold to the Pennsylvania Academy, *A Ray of Sunlight* to the Minneapolis Fine Arts Museum, *Portrait of Rodin* to the Cincinnati Art Museum, and *The Blue Bowl* to the Rhode Island School of Design. Paintings that were originally exhibited in Paris and not sold had been brought home and were repeatedly exhibited in American venues. For example, it took exhibits in Philadelphia, Pittsburgh, New York, and Boston before there was a buyer for the Rodin portrait, that sold to Cincinnati in July 1903. *The Blue Bowl* was exhibited in Philadelphia, Vienna, New York Boston, Chicago, Lincoln (Nebraska), and then Providence where it was acquired by the Rhode Island School of Design in October 1904.

As for portrait commissions, there were more than twenty in the studio in varying stages of completion. He must have been the envy of his colleagues when they read accounts of his being "so busy that it is necessary for him to have four sitters a day, sometimes." The list of sitters included Dr. Charles Frederick Chandler, Columbia University (April 1905, unlocated), Clarence MacKay (unlocated) and Mrs. MacKay, Dr. Clarence Webster, distinguished Chair of Obstetics and Gynecology at Rush Medical College in Chicago (1905, unlocated), Chancellor William Magie of New Jersey (Princeton University Art Museum, 1904), Cornelius N. Bliss, dry goods merchant, politician and member of the board of Equitable Life Assurance Society, for New York Hospital (1905/6, unlocated), Dr. Gunnison, Marion Haven, later Mrs. Forsyth Wickes, patron of the Boston Museum of Fine Arts (1904/5, unlocated), and Judge Van Syckel (November 1904) of the Supreme Court of New Jersey. Three versions of the Van Syckel portrait were made, one for the Trenton State House, one for the bar association of Elizabeth, New Jersey and the third for the family. Not mentioned in the press, but nevertheless part of the group of twenty, were portraits of William Bunker, D. Webster King (1905, unlocated), Miss Ryerson (unlocated), and Mrs. Clarence Webster (New Brunswick Museum, Saint John, Canada).

With the demands of his portrait obligations and concern for his father-in-law's well-being, came the added pressure of the headline news of June 10. Without competition, Alexander was awarded a $175,000 commission by the board of the Carnegie Institute to execute mural decorations for an extension, a combination library, music hall, natural history museum, and art gallery.[89] Timing of the announcement was strategic if not provocative, usurping the news the previous day that gave a detailed account of the scheme for the Harrisburg State Capitol lunettes.[90] The conflicting priorities now vying for Alexander's attention were alluded to, but it was made clear which one would take priority. One sentence in particular could have raised the ire of those in Harrisburg, stating that the artist "will devote himself exclusively" to the Carnegie commission, "as he will have no time for anything else."[91] Alexander's Pittsburgh contract was the largest contract to cover the largest amount of space ever in the short history of the American mural movement. Covering

5,100 square feet of wall, it was to be completed in eighteen months for a Founder's Day celebration in November 1906. Given the public announcement of the theme of the decoration for the Harrisburg Capitol, the challenge would be to come up with fresh ideas for Pittsburgh and avoid duplication.

Signed July 5, the Carnegie contract was generic as to subject but specific as to the space: three floors of the entrance hall of the library extension leading to the Arts and Science departments clustered around an atrium.[92] While no general theme was given, it did have to be approved by the board. William N. Frew, President of the board, and Alexander were publicly discussing the decoration in terms of the economic success of Pittsburgh, for which it was undeniably in large part indebted to Andrew Carnegie. There was talk of the "great producing and transportation powers of Pittsburg getting to coal, steel making, rivers and railroads and a further series devoted to showing the progress made in literature, music and arts as made possible by the immense production of the city."[93] To prepare, Alexander would take the advice he had suggested to John W. Beatty for Frits Thaulow's 1898 visit to Pittsburgh: go "out to the Steel works some night – I have long wanted to do that myself – there are thousands of good things to be done about every living city."[94] Paradoxically, the theme for the first floor echoed the Harrisburg project with the requisite depictions of coal processing, rivers and railroads. For the time being the concept for the second and third floors would remain unclear.

Two questions Alexander had to answer for himself were where to do his painting and how to organize the theme. He left little doubt as to the first, assuring the public that within fifteen minutes of arriving in Onteora, which was again his destination for the summer, he would begin work.[95] Once he was settled, his thoughts would turn to resolving the organizing principle. His vision of the living city that was Pittsburgh in 1906 – a civilized metropolis built on honest labor, despite an industry that was filthy dirty and belittling to the human spirit – began appearing in the press in early 1906.

> The first sketch, which is rapidly taking form, illustrates the idea of fire as applied to iron ore, its product, and the result of the industry to the city where it is carried on. From the base of one of the panels are seen the ascending flames of the furnace fires, and rising from their centre appears an allegorical figure of Pittsburgh holding in his hands the product of the furnaces. On the other panels are seen the nations of the earth coming forward with rich gifts. Above them are other figures typifying the arts and civilization that come to the city as a result of the Iron industry.[96]

This description is corroborated by a handful of undated small pencil sketches, little more than scribbles, yet not so different from the final version.[97] The one significant change from the sketches is the elimination of a shield held by the ascending figure.[98] Symbolic of Labor, he is surrounded by trumpeters to his left announcing his coronation by a figure holding a laurel wreath (Figure 71). The next three panels to the right are rich in groupings of winged figures symbolizing the "nations of the earth" bearing gifts, garlands, a figure of victory, and palms.[99] Behind, in the upper right, rears the mythical winged horse Pegasus who, as legend has it, was a source of inspiration every time his hoof struck a hard surface. And once again there is a place for a cupid like the one he painted for the Onteora fair the previous summer, this time without a bow and arrow.

At the heart of the project was Andrew Carnegie, the benefactor of the institute that bore his name and commissioned the murals. A Pittsburgher, he had used ruthless business tactics to the detriment of the weak and poor to amass uncommon wealth. After selling his business in 1901, he turned to philanthropy that theoretically benefited those who were victims of his ruthlessness. As a philanthropist he practiced what he preached, with the most important pulpit being his book, *The Gospel of Wealth*. He espoused the notion that wealth, wisely administered, should be given back for the common good. He famously wrote, "The man who dies thus rich, dies disgraced." If any one person personified the meaning of the fruits of labor it would be Carnegie. The shape of his face with its trim mustache and beard is clearly visible in the figure of Labor and recalls Alexander's portrait of the steel magnate. Yet the metaphor of Carnegie as the spirit of Pittsburgh was not mentioned by the press, or by the artist for that matter.[100]

Alexander's plan for an "Apotheosis of Pittsburgh" contextualizes Carnegie's vision of the rewards of hard labor. The premise was to depict Pittsburgh being transformed by the fruits of the efforts of its citizens. They rise up from the gritty gloom of steel mills, railroads, shipyards, coal processing plants, and construction sites, to the crowning of their labor.[101] The theme was one of man's triumph over labor rather than the other way around. This was the essence of the lower panels, which in Alexander's own words, captured "the spirit of force and the nobility of labor." Sarah J. Moore has written, "Through careful observations of men at work Alexander imbued the first floor murals with a sense of realism and topical relevance whose quasi-documentary nature was unprecedented in American mural painting."[102] From the lower floor, long horizontal panels, composed on the diagonal, sweep the viewer up in the vortex of the whirling shapes. The billowy smoke then leads the eye up to the second floor comingling allegorical symbolism with the realism of milling steel.

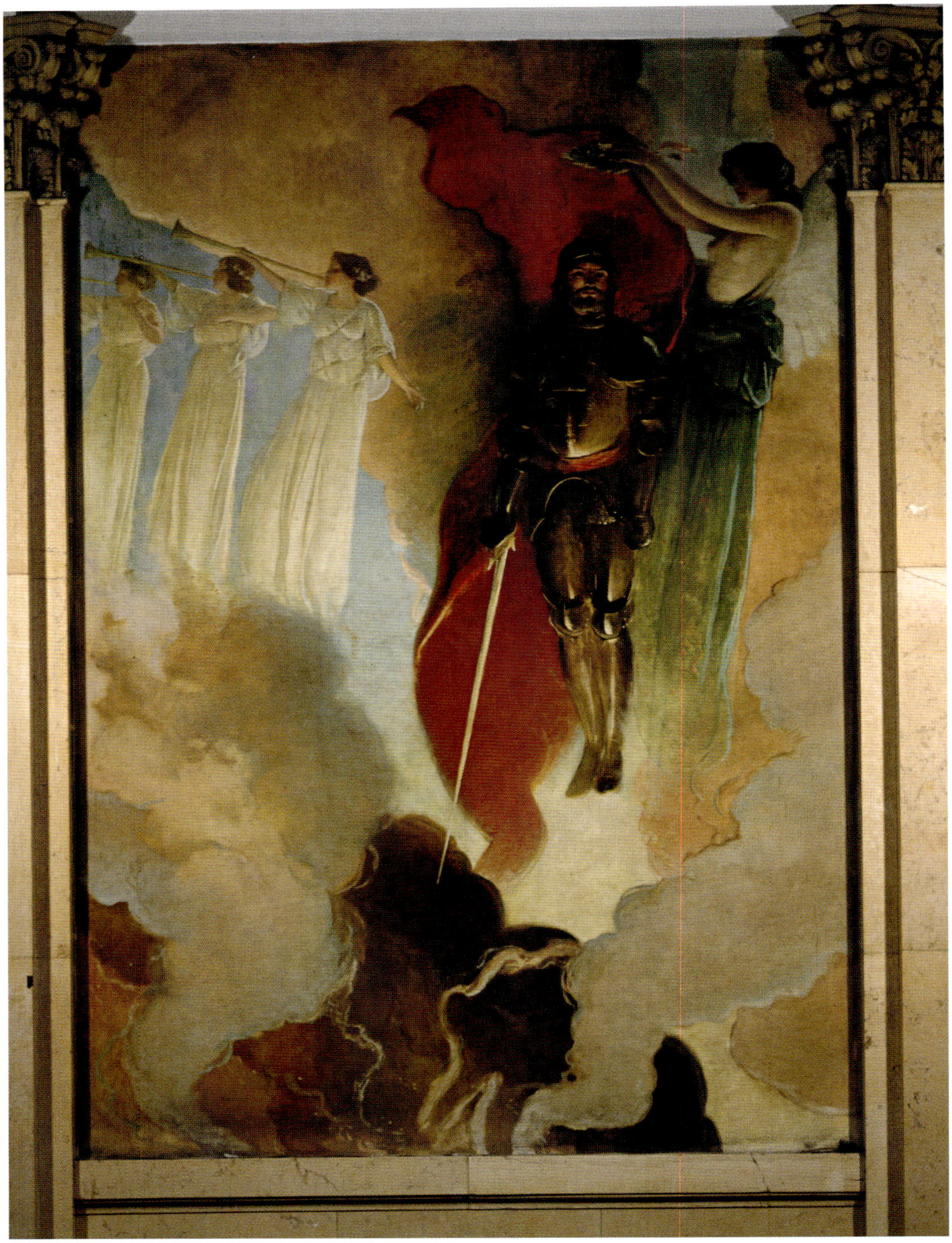

71 *The Crowning of Labor*, 1905–8, oil on canvas, wall measuring 170⅝ in. × 115⅝ in. (433.4 × 293.7 cm.), Carnegie Institute, purchase, 1907

Once Alexander settled on the concept of an apotheosis, he drew from a reservoir of experiences and images. The choice to depict an ascending figure surrounded by allegorical figures bearing gifts determined the images he would look to for inspiration. It is reasonable to expect he knew of Constantino Brumidi's *Apotheosis of Washington* (1865) in the U.S. Capitol, John La Farge's *Ascension* for the church of that name in New York (1888), and William Morris Hunt's atmospheric *The Flight of Night* in the New York State Capitol Assembly Chamber (1878). Yet, essential to his image making, not just for the allegorical decoration, but the other panels, were his years in Paris, not America, and examples by three Frenchmen: Puvis, Albert Besnard and Henri Martin.

Alexander's writings dating from the 1890s leave no doubt as to the importance of these three. He minced no words about Puvis as "undoubtedly the greatest painter of the century."[103] The value of Puvis when producing large-scale decoration, he wrote, is found in simplifying line and a lack of unnecessary detail. Alexander would have known of Puvis's work at the Panthéon and of *The Sacred Grove* for the Museum of Fine Arts, Lyon, with its airborne figures. The latter was the highlight of the 1884 Salon, and as such was so admired that Toulouse-Lautrec parodied it later that same year and hung it in his Paris studio until 1897. A reduced version of the original painting found its way to America by 1890 as part of the Potter Palmer collection in Chicago.[104] Another, *Dramatic Poetry*, with its bevy of levitating figures surrounding the chained Prometheus was featured in the 1895 Salon and destined for the Boston Public Library. Ten years later, after Alexander had had the chance to visit the murals in situ, their central section, *Muses Welcoming the Genius of Enlightenment* with levitating, long-robed attendants bearing attributes, resonates in Alexander's design for *The Crowning of Labor*.

Regarding Albert Besnard's series of decorations for the vestibule of the École de Pharmacie, Kenyon Cox, the American artist and writer, commented on the "frankly and even painfully realistic subjects."[105] This echoed Alexander's own praise of Besnard's realism and contemporaneity: He "has shown what a great decorator can do with the most commonplace subjects, scenes from an almost squalid phase of modern life."[106] In his decoration intended for the building for the faculty of medicine, Besnard had rejected the idea of allegory.[107] Instead, the storyline tells of the humanity of daily life and compassion for the sick, using science to find cures: a doctor tends to a patient, the patient convalescences, the botanists search for plants, and the scientist conducts laboratory tests. This idea of "la vie quotidienne" helps explain the "painfully realistic" figures in Alexander's decorations for the first floor, where bare-chested laborers toil with dignity while engulfed by smutty fumes. It was Besnard's example that freed Alexander to see the value of modern life as a decorative subject. To that end he actually visited a steel plant in Trenton, New Jersey to find the quintessential steelworker to model for him.[108] Alexander and Besnard were products of their time, expressing in their art Darwinian notions of the survival of the fittest. Labor is the foundation of Pittsburgh's material wealth and that is what is being celebrated in the murals. In an article for the May issue of *Harper's*, Charles Caffin did not miss the distinction between the allegorical and the reality of "la vie quotidienne." "It is not only that the male types represent a conception of their rights and possibilities of labor that is a part of our present-day understanding of democracy ... the girl types are drawn from such as we can see around us."[109] Caffin concludes that Alexander is "unequivocally modern."

A third French muralist, Henri Martin's symbolist pictures, exhibited at the first Salon de la Rose Croix and at the new Salon, also left a lasting impression. Of those continuing Puvis' tradition of mural decoration, Alexander thought Martin "one of the first painters living."[110] *L'Inspiration*, featured at the 1895 Salon, with three figures bearing symbols hovering above a cloaked troubadour, was relevant to the design for the Pittsburgh decoration, as was Martin's entry for the 1898 Salon. The latter panel tells the legend of Clémence Isaure, a figure from medieval times in Toulouse, flanked by heavenly attendants in an apparition before cloaked and hooded troubadours (Figure 72). Part of a series, it was destined for the Salle des Illustres in the City Hall of Toulouse. Alexander kept a reproduction of it mounted in a photo album.

Having to fit his designs within an architectural setting for the Carnegie project, Alexander was bold in the orientation of the panels and wise in avoiding Puvis's pitfall. The extension, like the Boston Public Library, had a grand staircase leading to a column-lined second floor at the top of which he placed the central decoration. However, the placement of the key panel does not conform to classical convention like the Boston Public Library, but rather is placed off axis to the left of center. Yet balance and unity of the overall decoration are maintained in a rich layering of forms and movement based on the diagonal that visually connects one panel to another. As for color, having seen for himself the discordance between the color of the marble in the Boston Public Library and the color of Puvis's decoration, Alexander shrewdly decided upon a tone that would harmonize with the yellowish-gray marble.

From the summer of 1905 until the installation in February 1907, Alexander's primary focus was the Pittsburgh commission. Yet during this time he did not completely abandon portrait commissions or figure painting. He

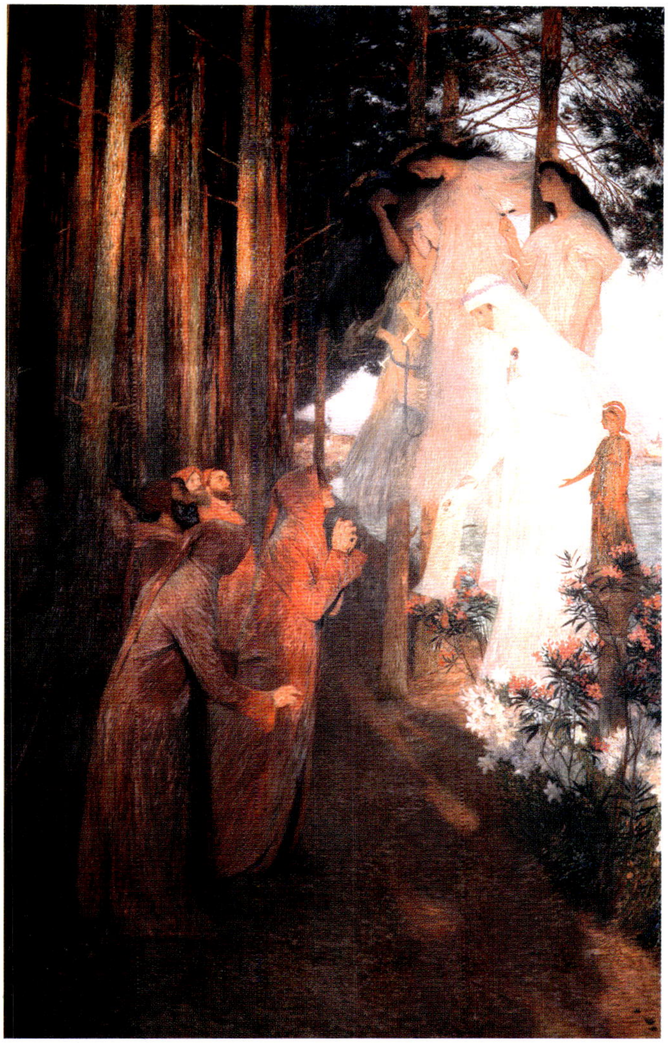

72
Henri Martin (1860–1943), *L'Apparition de Clémence Isaure aux Troubadours*, 1898, Salle des Illustres, Capitole, Toulouse, France. © Ville de Toulouse

completed two pictures of note, one being *Maude Adams as Peter Pan* (Utah Division of Arts & Museums Fine Art Collection). During the summer of 1905 while he was in Onteora working on the *Apotheosis of Pittsburgh*, Alexander's neighbor, the actress Maude Adams, discussed the need for a costume for her role as Peter Pan in the first American production of J. M. Barrie's play. She wanted "a look as if Peter Pan had flown in and out of the woods."[111] Alexander made a sketch and then volunteered his wife to make the costume. To get the effect Adams wanted, maple leaves were stenciled, embroidered and appliquéd onto a textured green fabric. Bess designed the little green cap with a red feather and the flat "Peter Pan" collar that became thereafter associated with all things Peter Pan. Alexander depicts her elfin figure in costume ascending above the earth holding the pipes of Pan. Adams's Broadway performance was already a success by the time the picture was displayed in the lobby of the Empire Theater during the 1905–6 season.[112]

In a second picture, Alexander returned to decorative figure painting. The model in *Study in Green and Black* (Figure 73) is wearing a striped dress that was introduced in 1902 in *A Rose* (unlocated) and reappeared in *The Green Gown* in 1903.[113] Whistlerian in manner, the title establishes the decorative intent, with the dress as the instrument of the narrative. After describing it as a "stunning" work, the writer for the *Buffalo News* then proceeded to discuss the dress as if a specialist in the study of marine life.[114] The embroidered or appliquéd fitted bodice transitions to the skirt with the effect of a "santanic [sic] like dress of brilliant lizard green, striped with black." There is an elegance and tenderness to the arc of the bent head that obscures the face, unlike in *The*

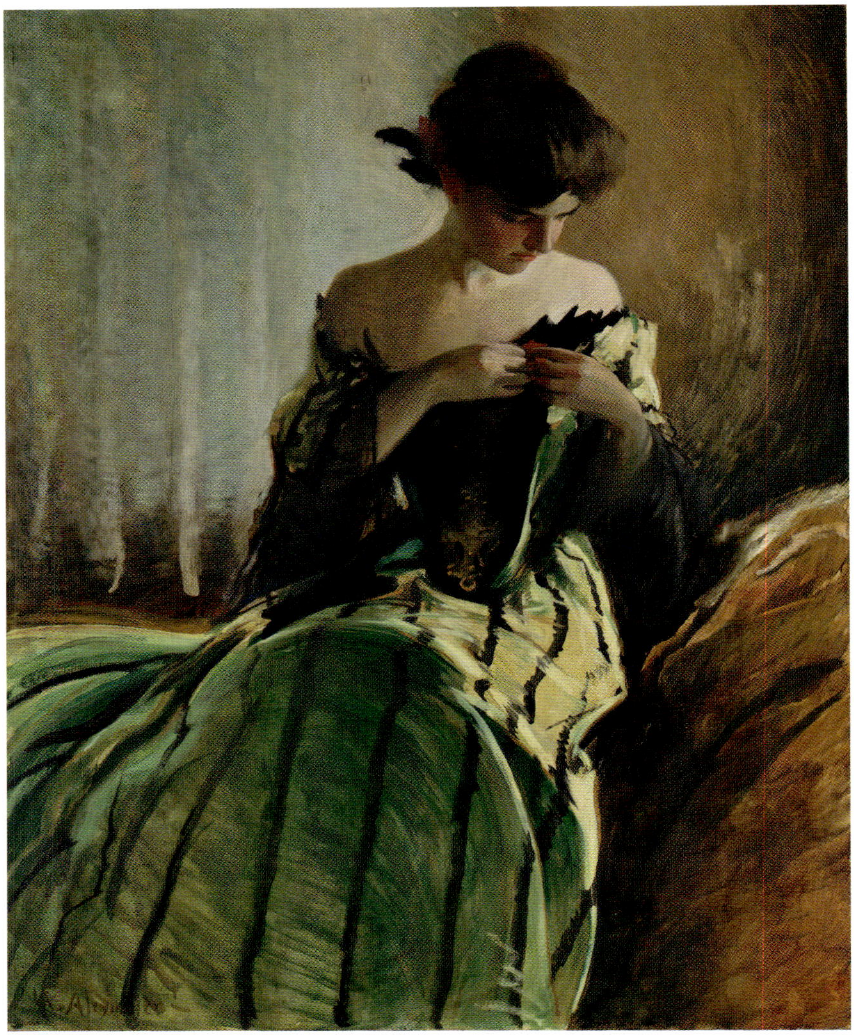

73
Study in Green and Black, 1906, oil on canvas, 50 × 40⅛ in. (127 × 101.9 cm.) The Metropolitan Museum of Art, George A. Hearn Fund, 08.139.1 (as *Study in Black and Green*)

Green Gown. Movement had always been the key to Alexander's originality, but now it is natural, not mannered, no longer a matter of constraining or contorting the figure within a tight space. There is a natural ease to the bowing of the head and positioning of the arms to pin a flower on the dress. As for the costume, while the model is wearing a striped skirt, she is no longer engulfed by the volume or decorative sway of the skirt. Though one of Alexander's important decorative works from 1906, it nonetheless does not rise to the level of inventiveness of his Parisian pictures. Scandal would later attach to this painting over the presumed identity of the model (see p.150).

Alexander required three studios for the Carnegie project. For the winter of 1905–6, he arranged with his friend Charles Dana Gibson, with whom he had shared good times in Paris in 1894–5, to lease Gibson's unoccupied studio in Carnegie Hall.[115] Alexander would also lease another studio, the large Vanderbilt Gallery in the Fine Arts Building, where sometime in June he planned to transfer work from the smaller Carnegie studio and make the finishing touches.[116] The third was a new studio in Seabright.[117] By summer 1906 the customary reason to summer in Onteora was no longer relevant. Once his mother-in-law sold the cottage, and his father-in-law removed himself from the public eye by embarking on a two-and-a-half-year world tour without his wife, Alexander substituted Seabright for Onteora where he stayed in Ward Cottage.[118] The Wards, a founding family of Seabright, were friends of long standing of Alexander, Sr. The Ward generation of 1906 included Edward Overton Ward and his daughter Anne Raynor Ward, who had already modeled for some of Alexander's paintings.

In late June 1906 Alexander traveled to Pittsburgh to meet with the president of the Carnegie Institute board, William Nimick Frew. If any decision was made at that time to delay the date of the dedication which had originally been planned for Founder's Day in November 1906, it was not newsworthy until late in November at which time it was reported, almost parenthetically, that the dedication would be the following March.[119] With the dedication now set for April 11, 12, and 13, Alexander traveled to Pittsburgh several times in the first four months of 1907. The first was in late February to install the murals.[120] The second was to fulfill his obligation as Chairman of the jury of award for the Eleventh Carnegie International. The committee of William M. Chase, Cecilia Beaux, Ben Foster, Gari Melchers, Irving Wiles, Henry Oliver Walker, George Hopkinson, and two foreign jurors, René Billotte, and Emile Claus, awarded three medals. The recipients were the Frenchman Gaston La Touche for *The Bath* (formerly University Club, Pittsburgh), the American Thomas Eakins for *Portrait of Professor Leslie Miller* (1901, Philadelphia Museum of Art) and the Polish Olga de Boznanska for *Portrait of a Woman* (unlocated).[121] During the week of the dedication Alexander arrived early to participate in ancillary events. He, Andrew Carnegie and Henry O. Tanner were three of 28 "distinguished sons of Greater Pittsburgh" to be honored at a banquet hosted by the Chamber of Commerce.[122] Alexander also lectured on mural painting before the Art Students League of Pittsburgh.[123]

The main event, celebrating the gift of a building dedicated to Literature, Science and Arts from Andrew Carnegie to the people of Pittsburgh, took the form of a three-day convocation. Invitees included many foreign dignitaries. Special trains brought visitors from New York and Chicago. The printed program was eighteen pages in length listing speakers, speeches and dedications, but there was no mention of the mural decoration, *The Apotheosis of Pittsburgh*, or its creator.[124]

The honoree, Andrew Carnegie delivered his address on the first day, preceded by an organ chorale, an invocation and the reading of a letter from President Theodore Roosevelt. Following Carnegie's talk there was an address by the German Minister of State, with a somewhat self-serving title, "The Popular Significance of the Carnegie Institute," and the presentation of prizes for the three best paintings in the International. On the second day, there was the pomp and circumstance of addresses from international representatives of universities, colleges, museums, and learned societies on applied science, natural science, electrical engineering, natural history, philosophy, geology, agriculture, and more. For example, in the lecture hall could be heard talks on "French Sculpture of the Middle Ages" by the director of the Trocadéro Museum, Paris, and "Dunfermline's Son" by the Provost of the Town of Dunfermline, Scotland, Carnegie's birthplace. In the afternoon of the second day the varied programming included "German Military Constitutions" by His Excellency Lieutenant General Alfred von Loewenfeld, Adjutant General of His Majesty the Emperor, followed by "The Mission of an Art Museum" by Léonce Bénédite, Director of the Luxembourg Museum, Paris. On the third day, honorary degrees were conferred by the Western University of Pennsylvania. The absence of representation from the Philadelphia Museum of Art and the Pennsylvania Academy of the Fine Arts may be explained by the competitiveness between the Eastern and Western parts of the state. Chase and Bénédite both considered it one of the best Internationals they had ever seen, and one marking "the real awakening of the artistic sense of the community;"[125] Pittsburgh was now positioned to host the most notable exhibitions in America. What Carnegie had done for Pittsburgh was unmatched in America.[126]

There was a plethora of coverage about the murals by the local press, some in New York and Boston, but not so much in Europe. On the Sunday before the dedication, both *The Pittsburgh Dispatch* and the *Pittsburgh Gazette Times* featured reproductions of the first and second-floor panels with headlines like "notable" and "splendid." There was also an immense sense of pride in a hometown boy who was so honored. Alexander met the highest expectations of the citizens of Pittsburgh who were ecstatic over his ability to embody in his decorations that which made Pittsburgh distinctly Pittsburgh, "strong, pulsating with life and vigor, and bright prospect."[127] On the day before the dedication Alexander was quoted in *The Pittsburgh Dispatch*, "I have attempted to represent no special industry but rather the spirit of force and the nobility of labor. An attempt to give this a literal interpretation would interfere with the artistic possibilities."[128] Thus, by his own account, intentionally or not, the issue of a specific identity for the male figure of *Labor* was nullified. In the May issue of *Harper's Monthly*, the earliest feature article for a national magazine, Charles Caffin admired Alexander for keeping "clear of heroics," "sentiment," "pomp," and "affectation," and he thought Alexander courageous in avoiding the cliché of "embodying the city as a woman."

As for the iconography of the decoration, an effective way to consider *The Apotheosis of Pittsburgh* is autobiographical. Alexander surely took into account the common circumstances of his upbringing and good fortune with that of Carnegie. Both were of Scottish descent, both grew up in Allegheny City, the wrong side of the tracks on the outskirts of Pittsburgh, and both found jobs as messenger boys for a telegraph company. In the decorations for the first and second floors, and continuing up the stairs to the third, Alexander reimagined his youth, connoting labor's social and economic promise in the image of the hardworking men and women of Pittsburgh. As a native, Alexander personally witnessed the transformation of Pittsburgh. In school he benefited from the visionary Principal Philotus Dean and his building design for a state-of-the-art high school. He walked the city as a messenger boy for Pacific & Atlantic Telegraph. As an illustrator for *Harper's*, he was their man when it came to stories about Pittsburgh. He covered the great strike of 1877, witnessing the mobs and their burning of the Pennsylvania Railroad depot and surrounding area. He was sent again to Pittsburgh in late 1880 to document a union dispute that never materialized. The trip with C. Fred Muller to illustrate "King Coal's Highway" for *Harper's* began in sight of Pittsburgh's perpetual cloud of smoke. His success in life was shaped by his boyhood in Pittsburgh just as he hoped for and imagined it could be for the people of Pittsburgh in 1907.

It was as if Alexander's allegory was the antidote to the collective distrust of Pittsburghers toward their government and business leaders. Lincoln Steffens's survey of political corruption, "Pittsburg: A City Ashamed" (1903), chronicled Pittsburghers' muted exasperation at the state of their government. In 1905, *The Bulletin*, a magazine of Pittsburgh arts and society, propagandized the value of hard work – lots of it.[129] Under the cloud of the Thaw murder trial in New York, the *Newark Monitor*, in the harshest of rebukes, reminded the public of what they despised about Pittsburgh plutocrats, especially Harry Thaw and William Corey. The *Apotheosis*, it said sarcastically, "should have another series of mural decorations representing Harry Thaw, Corey, and the rest of the greedy leeches and gilded parasites who have escaped from the smoke of Pittsburg to the scented atmosphere of the actress' dressing room."[130] Thaw and William Corey were two of a kind. When Corey became President of U.S. Steel he moved to New York City while his wife remained in Pittsburgh, and he proceeded to party on a scale equal to that of Thaw. He made headline news not as a murderer, but by divorcing his wife and remarrying at a cost of half a million dollars in 1908.

The Bulletin – the same magazine that praised the value of hard work – also broke the scandal of the alleged identity of Evelyn Nesbit Thaw as the model for *Study in Green and Black*.[131] The painting had been exhibited twice before becoming the artist's bête noir of 1907. The model's identity was never an issue in Buffalo or Philadelphia. It became one on April 11 when it was exhibited in Pittsburgh at the Eleventh Annual Carnegie International and *The Bulletin* made its allegations. Coincidentally, jury deliberation over the guilt of her husband Harry Thaw in the murder of Stanford White, Nesbit's former lover, occurred on the same day. After forty-seven hours the jury in the "trial of the century" emerged deadlocked, resulting in a second trial nine months later. The alleged identity of the model became public only in the days after the close of the International by which time all the visiting dignitaries had since departed. Pittsburgh society balked and the conservators of morality had their say. There would be no room in the museum collection for the portrait of the "shameless little strumpet."[132] Wisely, there was no public comment from the gallery or from Alexander who smiled and said nothing when asked.[133] The issue of the model did not deter Chicago from showing the picture in October. With high praise, one critic said that the "distinguished Pittsburgher has never done a better piece of work than this. The charm of its refined color, of its harmonious arrangement, of its subtle interpretation of the sitter's character, stamp it as a distinct contribution to American art."[134]

As for the allegation that Nesbit modeled for the painting, it cannot be substantiated. Multiple and contradictory claims, beginning with the mothers of those vilified, only served to inflame the debate. Nesbit's mother claimed that her daughter had modeled for the painting and cited a letter from the artist to that affect.[135] Thaw's mother denied that Alexander had ever met Nesbit.[136] Then and now, opinions that favor Nesbit as the model are based solely on comparing the painting to photographs. While archival records make it clear Nesbit is not the model, they add to the confusion by proposing, not one, but two other possibilities. In the Alexander papers there is a reproduction of *Study in Green and Black* annotated "Miss Bradley" who also modeled for *Aurora Leigh* and

A Butterfly.[137] Anne Bradley could have been in Onteora in the summer of 1905 when Alexander could have begun painting *Study in Green and Black*.[138]

Equally credible are two letters from Overton Ward, the half-sister of Anne Raynor Ward, naming Anne as the model.[139] Ward listed several paintings by Alexander, whom she described as a family friend, for which Anne posed. They were *A Quiet Hour* (*c*.1902), *The Favorite Corner* (*c*.1903), *The Green Gown* (1903), *Study in Green and Black* (1906), *The Ring* (1911), and an unknown *Portrait*.[140] Comparison of the paintings is fruitless given the artist's predilection for types rather than likenesses. There is nothing in the decorative figure paintings to definitely distinguish Anne Bradley from Anne Raynor Ward or to account for aging between 1902 and 1911. It is a reasonable assumption that Anne Raynor Ward is of the Ward family of Seabright. In the summer of 1906 Alexander was working in Seabright and staying at Ward Cottage. But if Ward modeled for *Study in Green and Black*, it would have to have been before the summer, as the painting was first exhibited May 31 in Buffalo. There is the possibility that in planning for the summer he reconnected with the Ward family earlier in the year when Anne may have made herself available to model. Nevertheless, the secret of the identity of this American muse is now narrowed down to two possibilities; but neither of them is Nesbit.

The sensationalism of the socially vindictive claims of 1907 seemed to matter most in Pittsburgh. By the time the painting was exhibited at the National Academy in the spring of 1908, past allegations did not prevent the Metropolitan Museum of Art from acquiring it.[141] It was also the object of burlesque by more than one student fakir in their 1908 exhibition. If Nesbit was the subject, it was of no importance to the students at the League. First prize went to G. Robbins Brandlen's parody *Study in (Green – indicated by a stroke of color) and (Black – indicated by stroke of color)*. Possibly motivated by class distinctions, if not racial divides, the subject is a black woman with a halo above her head, administering castor oil to her sick infant, while another figure is sleeping behind her; a bottle of gin is at the foot of the bed.[142]

After the Carnegie dedication in April, Alexander focused on the next phase scheduled for installation in October 1908. He continued his work on the murals in Seabright – that is, when he was not suffering from back pain.[143] The debilitating pain in the lower torso was probably induced by work on the murals over the previous eighteen months. Considering the size of the task, it was even more physically onerous for the artist because Alexander did not employ assistants. He had to do it all himself because he was a "lefty," and no assistant could imitate his stroke.[144]

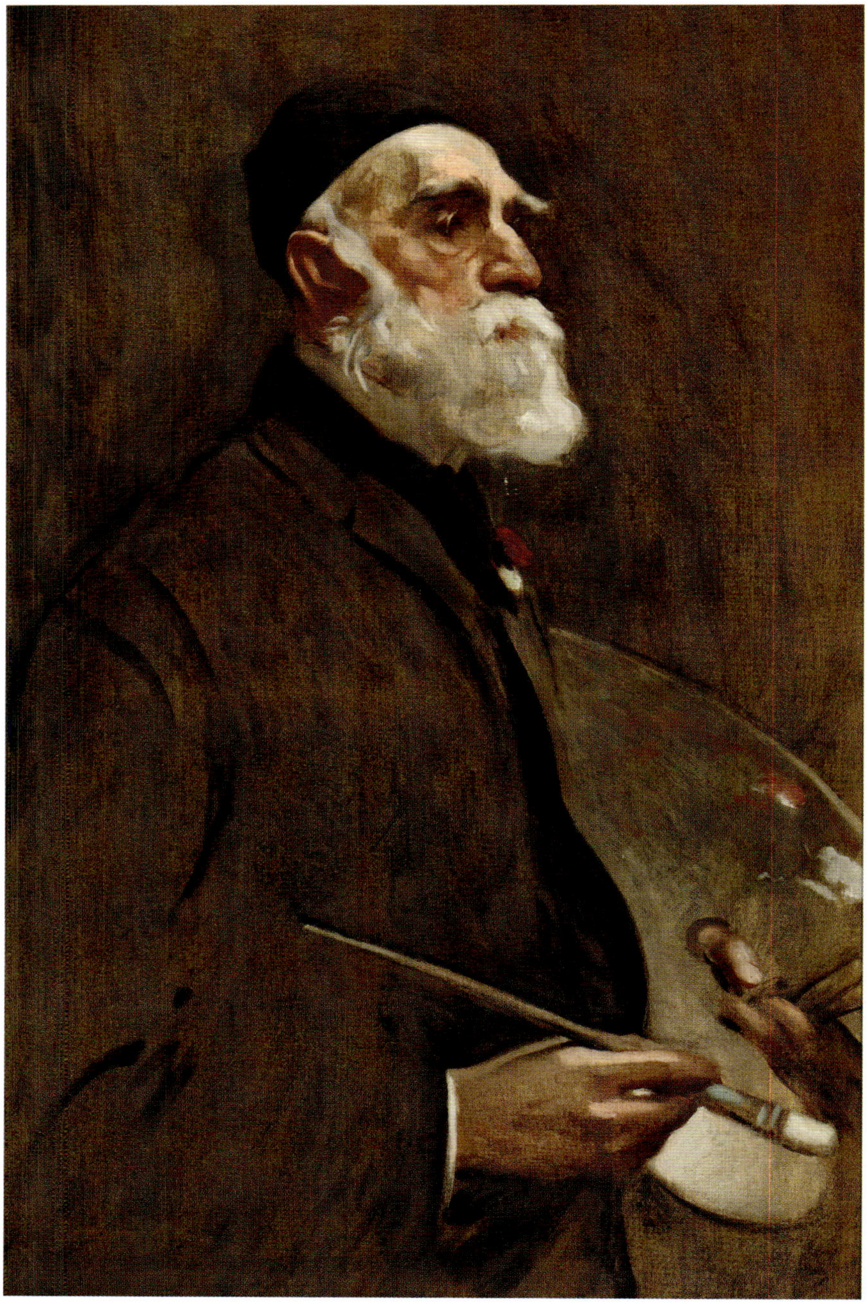

74 *Worthington Whittredge*, 1907, oil on canvas, 39½ × 25⅝ in. (100.3 × 65.1 cm.), courtesy of the Century Association, New York, John Bigelow Taylor, photographer

Progress slowed on the murals as well as easel painting for several months. When Alexander resumed easel painting, the first to be completed was a portrait of Worthington Whittredge (Figure 74). It was the new picture for the season shown briefly in November at the Century Club before being sent to the Winter Exhibition at the National Academy and then to the Pennsylvania Academy of the Fine Arts in early 1908.[145] It was universally praised for its "economy of strokes," showing all the "brio" and "swiftness" of a sketch infused with a "primal freshness."[146] As would be expected, in contrast to his ongoing work on the murals or his decorative painting, Alexander reverted to his Munich style for the likeness of the living *eminence grise* of the Hudson River School, dressed the part of an artist with palette and brush in hand. In a magnanimous gesture Alexander offered to undertake the portrait and make a gift of it to the Century Club. The club acted on Alexander's offer in early March just weeks before Whittredge's 88th birthday.[147] On April 25, Alexander was on the program for a birthday celebration hosted by the members of the Highland Club, a gentlemen's club in Summit, New Jersey where Whittredge was living.[148] Birthday toasts were delivered by John Burroughs and current and future presidents of the National Academy of Design.

Other easel pictures were mostly of friends. He could hardly say no to Maude Adams who posed in costume for her role in *The Jesters*, a Charles Frohman production that opened in New York on January 15, 1908. A portrait of Helen Beatty, daughter of John W. Beatty, Director of the Carnegie International, was probably started and completed in Pittsburgh. Alexander's fealty to Princeton no doubt swayed him to offer to paint the portrait of Isabella Guthrie McCosh, widow of Princeton's eleventh president.[149] It was started at the end of the year and may have been in anticipation of, or was the reason why Alexander was awarded a second honorary degree at commencement in 1909. Two portraits, that of Professor John Howard Van Amringe (unlocated) for the Columbia University Club and *The Skinner Sisters* (Yale University, Musical Instruments Collection), daughters of William Skinner, a wealthy textile manufacturer in Holyoke, may have been the only commissions.

During this time Alexander undertook several figure paintings on a variety of themes. *Marjorie*, known only through press accounts, was a "full length of a young girl in white." It was sent to the "Exhibition of Fair Women" sponsored by the International Society of Sculptors, Painters and Gravers in London in February 1908.[150] And for perhaps the only time, he experimented with a colonial revival picture, *At the Window* (Figure 75), in which the dress and tall case clock evoke the colonial era. The soul of the picture is in the decoding of the

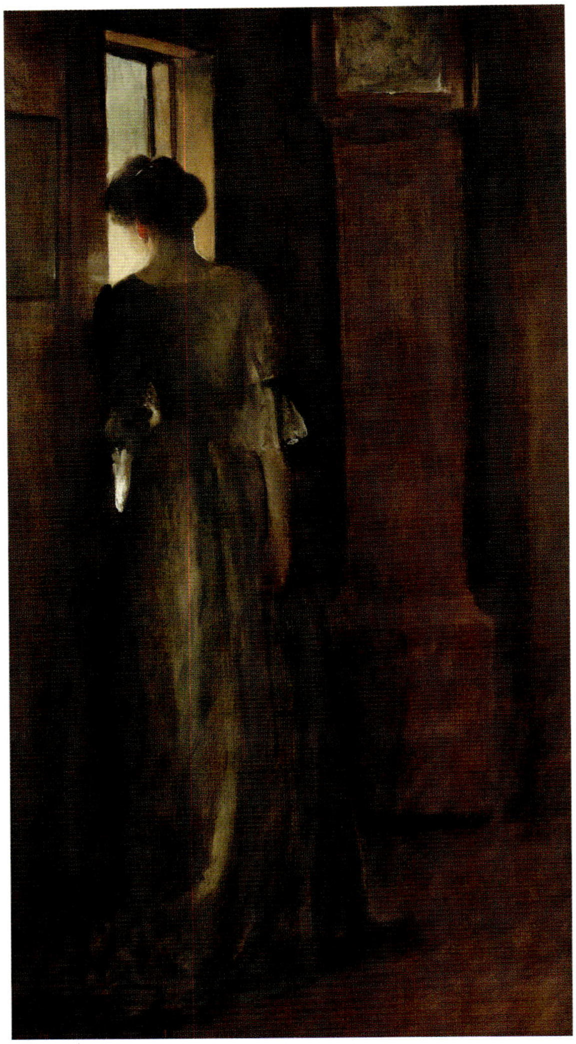

75
At the Window, 1908/9,
oil on canvas, 40 × 22 in.
(101.6 × 55.9 cm.),
Tina and Joe Pyne, Houston

sentiment of reverie. Seen from the back, the figure, slackening, head tilted, staring out the window with her full weight leaning into the window frame, stands in contrast to a ramrod-straight clock.[151] Adding to the variety of themes, Alexander looked to antiquity for *Aurelia* (John White Alexander great-granddaughters). In a pose reminiscent of *Pandora* (1898), the seated figure is seen in profile turned to her left. Her dress, with a décolleté neckline, is roughly sketched in. Aurelia was the name of Julius Caesar's mother, a well-regarded, intelligent, and independent beauty. The canvas is in a largely unfinished state, and there is no record of it being exhibited in Alexander's lifetime.

On several occasions in 1908 Alexander was in demand as a master of a different art form, the tableau vivant. The first, "Arrangement from Old Masters," was scheduled to benefit the MacDowell Club of New York. It was cancelled due to the death on January 23 of the composer Edward MacDowell in whose honor the club was founded. Five weeks later Alexander staged another for the private social club for women, the Colony Club, to benefit the St. Catherine's Home for Girls. The hostesses were pillars of high society, Mrs. Thomas Hastings, Mrs. J. Borden Harriman and Mrs. John Jacob Astor.[152] Finally, at the end of the year he was called upon to stage a second tableau vivant for the benefit of the MacDowell Club, once again on the theme of "Arrangements from Old Masters."[153] Performing in a tableaux after Veronese were both Mr. and Mrs. Langdon Geer (she, née Roosevelt, had been painted by Alexander in 1901) along with Katherine Rhoades, an artist of the Stieglitz circle, and others. The Misses Eleanor Butler Alexander (future Mrs. Theodore Roosevelt, Jr. and daughter of Bess's cousin, Henry A. Alexander) and Helen Morgan appeared in "Lady Washing her Hands" after Gerard ter Borch. Marian Beckett, also of the Stieglitz circle of artists, appeared in "Lady with Fan" after Lorenzo Lotto. Presenting tableaux vivants during the Christmas season to benefit the MacDowell club would become a tradition for Alexander continuing through 1913, during which time he also served as club president. For a club whose membership was made up of talented musicians, artists and writers, tableaux vivants were a fitting genre.

Tableaux vivants had grown in popularity since the 1890s. They could be staged on an intimate scale in a home or artist's studio, or on a larger scale in the home of a socially prominent family, or even grander, in places such as Sherry's ballroom. As an historian of the form describes it, they were "Also referred to as living pictures, [in which] live actors posed for a period of thirty seconds to ten minutes in imitation of scenes from history, mythology, literature, and the fine arts."[154] Manuals were published providing tips ranging from lighting and color of costumes, even giving "painterly" advice, for example "downstage figures wear darker colors" to achieve depth of field. While they were ostensibly for an altruistic purpose, supporting a charitable cause such as education, homes for the elderly or orphans, the opportunity to be seen by one's peers was not a negligible incentive. When a Mrs. Astor, a Mrs. Hastings or a Mrs. Harriman was a hostess, the press took notice. Being mentioned in print as being associated with a charitable cause, in addition to the fine arts, only added to one's prestige. This temporary diversion "into the titillating world of Bohemia" was an occasion to dress in one's finest and to be seen as a professional beauty, and an advertisement for the unmarried.

While the Carnegie mural project was well advanced at the end of 1908, the same could not be said of the Harrisburg project. It was deadlocked in a quagmire of Pennsylvania politics and budget appropriations, the victim of an ugly contracting scandal that enveloped the project since the October 1906 dedication of the Capitol building. Charges of defrauding the Commonwealth, filed against the architect and subcontractors, were not settled until April 1910.[155] Though fully conceptualized by Alexander prior to the announcement of the Pittsburgh commission, the Harrisburg decorations were still merely an idea sketched on several pieces of paper.

Alexander was free to devote his energies to completing phase two of the Carnegie murals. For the remaining decorations on the second floor, he abandoned allegory for the realism of an industrial landscape that was Pittsburgh in 1906. The panorama of this smoky city on the banks of the Monongahela that he knew intimately is dotted with factory buildings and trains at the river's edge, waiting for coal barges and riverboats to pull into port to offload or to take on cargo. In the far distance rise the hills of South Pittsburgh. On the opposite wall a shed occupies the foreground, behind which is a blast furnace, hot-air boilers and towering stoves. In the tall vertical panels in the alcoves, laborers are hard at work among steel beams, iron girders, scaffolding, and cranes. For authenticity, Alexander took the unusual step of constructing a wooden structure resembling a girder and convincing workers from a construction site behind his New York studio to come to the studio and model for him.[156] In a stroke of genius, Alexander brings unity to the panels that ring the second floor, combining the allegorical with the realism of everyday life. Exquisite color effects of hot air and soot-filled, billowing clouds assume a pure art nouveau shape (not unlike images of Loie Fuller in motion), serving as visual attendants to the apotheosis. The murkiness of the smoky city is visually transformed into beautiful artistic effects. The scheme for the second floor combines allegory with a modern American industrial landscape, contrasting an old industry with the new. The composition recalls Besnard's elevated vista of an urban port in the horizontal panel *L'Homme Moderne* for the École de Pharmacie.[157]

The industrial theme concludes with the changing skyline of Pittsburgh. In words sounding more like Carnegie's than his own, Alexander described a march of "humanity, unrestrained, sweeping along to a far off goal, never tired, never resting, never forgetful of its aim."[158] Filling twelve panels situated about the third floor stairway are ordinary men, women and children, no longer tired and dirty, but with clean faces and ruddy complexions. No one is old. A multitude of over 400 in a ceaseless forward surge conveys a collective sense of optimism. In an article for the popular *Scribner's Magazine*, William Walton reminds us that Alexander "always had something of an instinct that the ugly is not meant for his art."[159] In Walton's arresting description of the creative process, "the working man" could sympathize with how seriously Alexander took his work. He "sits down empty handed before his great panel of white canvas and looks at it, for hours if necessary; finally, with a piece of charcoal tied to the end of a long rod, he suddenly draws a line." Walton had high praise for what he called "great decorative painting that is as logical as it is beautiful." Referring to the third and final phase designated for the third floor, but not yet completed, the artist would have been Walton's source for the description of a "frieze of panels … representing in many and ingenious forms of allegory personifications of the arts, the sciences, the letters."

The logic of the third floor allegory completes a narrative that began with the realism of an industry founded upon the sweat of the laboring man and culminates with the dream of prosperity for all. Reverting to the classical canon for the third floor decorations, Alexander sketched robed figures signifying

Painting, Sculpture, Literature, Music, Science, Justice, Law, Truth, Manufacture, Agriculture, Mining, Coal, Oil, Navigation, Labor, Capital, Telegraph, Traffic, Chemistry, Electricity, Poetry, Drama, and Architecture, with their corresponding attributes.[160] Enclosed in a rectangle, a single figure is depicted seated or standing. There is little or no information in these quickly rendered sketches as to context, no bellowing furnaces or billowing clouds. Despite the third level not being completed, this unconventional combination of allegory and realism prompted Birge Harrison to say of the grand scheme, "There is certainly a strange picturesqueness in some of our modern steel-mills, with their cyclopean forces at work against backgrounds of whirling steam and flowing furnace."[161]

Presumably Alexander was working diligently on the final phase of the Carnegie project following the installation of phase two in October 1908. Expectations were that the decorations would be completed by Founder's Day in April 1909, however, it was not to be.[162] The question then becomes: with little evidence of actual work, what was he doing? The answer was a myriad of distractions, including two operations that can account for the lack of progress.

The greatest of the distractions was his acting as a public voice for a cause of significance to the New York art community. Alexander was a strong advocate of the need for more exhibition space in the city. As a member of the city improvement commission and party to its report of March 1907 to Mayor McClellan, he was in a position to know the status of the city's buildings and grounds.[163] He acted upon this information in early 1909 when he saw an opportunity for the future growth of the Academy on the site of the arsenal in Central Park that no longer served its original purpose. As a council member of the National Academy and with the sanction of its President Frederick Dielman, he floated a proposal: using Academy funds, raze the old arsenal and construct a two-story building in its place. In exchange, the city would maintain the new building that would house the police and Parks Department on the first floor. The Academy would administer the second floor and from time to time make the space available to sister institutions. The council technically had the authority to make the decision, but nevertheless, it was put to a vote and was approved by the membership. One of the more colorful objections by the opposition was the proximity "with the police and monkeys" in the nearby zoological gardens.[164] Because the plan required approval from Albany, in consultation with city government, two bills were sent, one to the state Senate on February 16 and the other to the Assembly on February 17. Though the bill did not pass, Alexander was already being talked about as the next President of the National

Academy because of his obvious leadership in championing the Academy's most pressing need.[165]

Efforts to secure the arsenal site were just one of many milestones in 1909 that distracted Alexander from finishing the Carnegie murals. Another was a major retrospective at the National Arts Club opening on February 23, days after the bill for the arsenal site was introduced in Albany. Curated by the president of the club, J. Nilsen Laurvik, it consisted of 63 works, supplemented by 30 photographs. The earliest work was a sketch of J. Frank Currier (1870s, unlocated); the most recent, *At the Window* and the portrait of Helen Beatty (unlocated), were from the second half of 1908. The majority dated from the 1890s and after, but given titles such as "portrait," "sketch," and "landscape" it is difficult to accurately characterize the nature of the exhibition. Watercolors of flowers would have dated from the mid 1880s and 1890s. There were the occasional marines and landscapes, also unidentifiable. Two pictures represented Brittany. Mrs. William Thaw lent two paintings, *The Red Box* (unlocated) and probably *The Rose*. Several news articles mentioned the theatrical portrait of Joe Jefferson despite the fact that it was not mentioned in the checklist.[166] The absence of his breakthrough picture, *Azalea* (1885), is puzzling given that Robert Abbe, brother of the sitter, attended the opening. This, and the lack of major loans from Boston, Paris, Providence, St. Petersburg, and New York, limited the breadth of the retrospective. There was both adulation and honest criticism from the press. Herman Bloch faulted Alexander for resisting the innovations of modern movements, but on the other hand, "his sense of the decorative movements is so fine that it evokes … the sense of the beautiful." *Memories* was an example of the latter. One picture Bloch particularly did not like was no. 42, *A Study*, the identity of which is unknown, but to him the portrait of Rodin was a masterpiece.[167] Later that year, Laurvik, in an analysis shared by most, wrote that regrettably "In the whole history of art one looks in vain for anything approaching his inimitable skill in the arrangement and play of his figures."[168]

The opening of the retrospective was the social event of the season, attended by friends, patrons and people who had sat for a portrait. The many distinguished guests comprised a litany of names on the social register and from public life: President Woodrow Wilson of Princeton, Senator Chauncey Depew, Mayor McClellan, Archbishop Farley, E. H. Harriman, William Dean Howells, Clyde Fitch, Charles Scribner, Joseph Choate, J. Henry Harper, John Cadwalader, Mr. and Mrs. Clarence Mackay, and artists George G. Barnard, Cecilia Beaux, J. Carroll Beckwith, Gutzon Borglum, William M. Chase, Kenyon Cox, Albert

Herter, and Walter Shirlaw.[169] If anything, this event substantially elevated the perception of power and influence wielded by Alexander, coming at a time when the National Academy would be looking for its next leader.

In the few weeks after the opening of the retrospective at the National Arts Club, the milestones came thick and fast, continuing through June 20. The Thirteenth Annual Carnegie International opened on April 29, but this time there were no additional murals to celebrate. Rather he submitted a portrait of Helen Beatty and once again served on the jury of awards with foreign jurors Alfred East (British) and George Breitner (Dutch). When asked about the murals, he stated that his intent was not to go abroad for the summer, but, instead, to focus on completing them.[170] There were however major distractions despite his good intentions. Immediately after the International, he began rehearsals with Maude Adams on the design for the stage set for her upcoming re-enactment of Joan of Arc. The very next day, May 13, he was elected President of the National Academy.

Alexander did not presume a right to the presidency, yet Frederick Dielman may have felt the pendulum swinging away from him and toward Alexander. At a closed council meeting on April 5 Alexander did everything to persuade Dielman to remain.[171] Dielman was renominated on the first ballot by the ten council members. Several made speeches to convince Dielman to reconsider, but he remained resolute. When the slate was presented to the membership, once again, members including Alexander spoke in favor of Dielman. In the most understandable of explanations Dielman said the work "had grown more exacting and arduous." He felt he could not give it the attention it deserved.[172] Between the election and assuming the Presidency on June 7, Alexander discreetly slipped away from the public eye to have not one, but two operations on his throat.[173]

While in recovery Alexander's proposed design for a mural competition for the Federal District Court in Cleveland was approved by the Supervising Architect, James Knox Taylor, on May 28, 1909. Since the Tarsney Act of 1893, the Supervising Architect of the Department of Treasury had administered competitions for design and construction of new federal buildings, instead of their being designed by staff. The courthouse was the first public building erected as part of Cleveland's City Beautiful movement. The team of experts was Daniel Burnham of Chicago and Arnold Brunner and John Carrère, both of New York. The architectural team's recommendation for a classical style carried considerable weight in the choice of muralists.[174] Obvious candidates practicing a classical style were Edwin Blashfield, Kenyon Cox and Will Low. Alexander was the outlier. Nevertheless, his approved design, *Justice*, was both a model of classicism, taking into consideration the building's purpose and function, and a feat of originality – just as much as his decorations for the Library of Congress, Harrisburg and Pittsburgh. The central figure, Justice, is in a forward motion tending to the right with the right arm raised, probably to hold scales. Slightly lower on the same raised platform are two figures flanking her. On the right, the helmeted figure, probably Law, holds a sword. It is unclear what the sketchy figure on the left signifies. Also consistent with a classical program is the use of primary colors instead of a soft palette, such as he planned for the Harrisburg project, or dark colors, as he chose for the Library of Congress.

Even within an hieratical arrangement, Alexander is capable of the unexpected. The scheme is all about movement. Countering the forward motion of Justice to the right is the frieze at the bottom extending the full width of the composition with figures surging to the left. The concept of multiple figures moving in unison that appeared in this presentation piece is a distinct change from a pencil study that shows all of the figures lined up, rigidly in place.[175] Other differences from the pencil sketch are the clouds fanning out from behind Justice like a Rorschach test and open colonnades framing the edges on the left and right. The generalization of the figures in the frieze is such that it is unclear whether they are meant to be real or idealized people. In the presentation piece Alexander's originality breathes life into what could have been adherence to a stereotypical classical canon, and it is the sense of movement, instead of the central figure being static, that distinguishes his *Justice* from that of another courthouse commission in the same year, Kenyon Cox's *The Judicial Virtues* for the Luzerne County Courthouse, Wilkes-Barre, Pennsylvania. In fact, in criticizing the "academic and conservative" murals for Wilkes-Barre, a sharp-eyed critic noted that they "lacked the sweep of imagination and emotional suggestion" that could be found in Alexander's design for Pittsburgh and Harrisburg.[176]

With Alexander's election as Academy President came a flood of congratulatory letters. Members and non-members had great expectations for the new appointee. "You're the man for the job," wrote Charles Dana Gibson, from whom Alexander was currently leasing a studio.[177] Robert Reid noted, "Many of us long ago decided you were just the man."[178] Adele Herter wrote on behalf of her husband and herself, calling him "gifted and so modern."[179] The likes of Samuel Swift, William L. Harris and Harrison S. Morris couldn't help but note the luck of the Academy in convincing Alexander to serve. Even Charles Frohman, the eminent theater producer, sent congratulations.[180] The most poignant letter was sent by Leon Dabo who perhaps best summarized the collective sentiment: "most important of all you, your personality – your great talent, should impress the art world of our country that there is no need for a 'Secession' for a rival institution in our midst – but that the academy will admit that there are many expressions of beauty – that 'art' is not in the keeping of a few gentlemen, no matter how refined their taste, nor how profound their learning."[181] Alexander had long been convinced that the risk of a so-called "secession" could be much reduced by having a larger and better exhibition space, and this is where he put his energy. If he had succeeded, there very well may never have been an Armory Show. As for his winning personality, it is the key to whatever success he achieved in life. He was non-judgmental as well as a keen and sympathetic observer of human behavior. To be able to mix comfortably with the effete of Paris, to call Oscar Wilde, Henry James and Whistler friends, to gain the admiration of the fishermen of Seabright and the construction workers of New York, to befriend Ole Hanover, on the one hand, and Richard Watson Gilder on the other, is the mark of an equalitarian.

Alexander's star had been on the ascent after the installation of the Carnegie murals and Charles Caffin's favorable article for *Harper's Monthly Magazine* in May 1907. This was followed with some frequency by feature articles full of praise by the most venerable of critics. In May 1908, Arthur Hoeber wrote a flattering review of an artist who "has forged his way to the front rank of his profession through hard work."[182] In September 1908 Christian Brinton characterized as modern his "esthetic expression of contemporary femininity."[183] In January 1909 William Walton recounted the circumstances of the Carnegie decoration and Alexander's qualifications that produced "an inspiring" result.[184] In March 1909 Charles de Kay rehabilitated the concept of "beauty of line."[185] And in December 1909 J. Nilsen Laurvik ranked him as "pre-eminent as a delineator of feminine beauty and charm" and as such "Mr. Alexander has done more than any other modern painter to demonstrate that modern dress is not wholly devoid of pictorial possibilities."[186]

Alexander spent a few days in Princeton in June 1909. He was made an honorary member of the American Whig Society of Princeton and attended the Annual Banquet of the Quadrangle Club. At the 162nd commencement on June 15, he was awarded an honorary Doctor of Letters for his "vivid, impressive, and finished excellence" as an artist.[187] As in 1902, the 1909 procession ended at Alexander Hall, a reminder of the Alexander family legacy, honoring his wife's great-grandfather, Reverend Archibald Alexander, first professor of the Princeton Theological Seminary, and financed by his grandson Charles B.

Alexander. The difference between the commencements in 1902 and 1909 was that as President of the National Academy, Alexander was on equal footing with the Presidents of Princeton and Harvard. He had been invited by Princeton President Woodrow Wilson to speak at the Alumni luncheon, the chief event of the day that followed the conferring of degrees.[188] At the lunch the theme of the remarks by President Abbott L. Lowell of Harvard and President Wilson was "that American universities should take a greater interest in the intellectual side of college life" instead of concentrating on the scientific.[189] Being a representative of the non-scientific community, Alexander was asked to say "a few words" on a topic of his choice.[190]

Alexander may have gone directly from Princeton to Cambridge to meet up with Maude Adams and Charles Frohman and where he would again be in the company of Harvard President Lowell.[191] Ever since *L'Aiglon* in late 1900, Alexander was a constant in Frohman's productions of Adams's performances. Now he was part of the team for Frohman's one-night, open-air pageant on June 22 in Harvard University Stadium. Adams performed as Joan of Arc based on the play *The Maid of Orleans* by Friedrich Schiller. Under the auspices of Harvard's German Department, and at Adam's insistence, the Germanic Museum would benefit from the proceeds. Heralded as the "Biggest Cast in World's History" numbering 1,300 with 60 principals, it required orchestration "like an army."[192] Since the announcement in March 1908, Alexander assumed responsibility for costume design, selection of color, groupings of tableaux, and lighting while his wife supervised the making of the costumes.[193] At Elizabeth Alexander's disposal was Charles Frohman's vast inventory of costumes.[194] Getting the costumes historically correct was paramount, none more so than Joan's battle armor which was modeled after a sculpture, *Joan on Horseback* (1889), by the Frenchman Paul Dubois.

Sets were designed by Ernest Gros with the two major sets being the battle scene between the French and English and the coronation of King Charles VII at Rheims Cathedral.[195] The battle scene consisted of 100 men on horseback and took almost 30 minutes. It was inspired by Ernest Meissonier's painting *1807, Friedland* in which Napoleon views a battle from the crest of a hill. The scene was a great worry to Frohman as Adams had to gallop down a 30-foot-high hill directly into man-to-man battle. Adams was a stickler for detail, and in this case, her personal safety. She practiced on her horse, devising distractions such as noise-making metal objects tied to the saddle, shots fired and banners waving in order to condition the horse not to spook. The coronation scene was inspired by Boutet de Monvel's recently completed *The Crowning at Rheims of the Dauphin*. In the closing act the mortally wounded Joan was carried off the battlefield to the sounds of Beethoven's "Eroica" Symphony to which an audience of approximately 15,000 in Harvard stadium cheered.

Besides the skill it took to direct such a formidable cast, the performance stood out for two technical innovations that would have a lasting effect on stagecraft, lighting and stage sets. The decision to use a single set on which props would be rotated was an innovative departure for Adams and Alexander in 1909 when realistic sets for each scene were the norm.[196] Lighting consisted of an arc of lights of 2,000 candle power placed at intervals in the top of the stadium. Additionally, there were two gigantic searchlights with thirty-inch openings with lenses six inches wider across than those found on any battleship. Color painted on the lamps not only served as a source of colored lighting but became a code for alerting performers to make their stage entrance. Alexander was in his element, experimenting with and refining the use of color and the effect of lighting in a dramatic performance.

It so happened that interest in Joan of Arc was heightened by the international movement for her sainthood, and the fascination she correspondingly exerted on a number of American literary figures and dramatists, some of whom were personal friends of Alexander. One of Mark Twain's least successful novels was *Personal Recollections of Joan of Arc by Sieur Louis de Conte (Her Page and Secretary)* (1896). Twain was obsessed with Joan's story, leaving no doubt as to his admiration in a December 1904 article in *Harper's Magazine*: "We know what she was like, without asking – merely by what she did. She is easily and by far the most extraordinary person the human race has ever produced."[197] Then in 1906 there was a Broadway production of *Jeanne D'Arc* by Percy MacKaye with Julia Marlowe as Joan. Having studied Joan's life, Adams admired her essential traits of goodness, "mysticism," "frailty," and "spiritual heroism."[198] Joan was beatified by the Catholic Church in 1909 in the first step toward canonization. For Americans, however, the story was a secular one, important for her patriotism and idealization of womanhood.

There was good reason for Alexander to describe the past few weeks to Harrison Morris, his ally as chairman of the Ways and Means Committee at the Academy, as a "confused jumble."[199] One after the other, he moved from Princeton to Cambridge, and then Seabright where he relocated his family for the summer. He was always of a fragile constitution and even more so now, given which his accomplishments had been nothing short of formidable, and they continued with new work once he was back in Seabright. Several new decorative paintings were started in the summer for show at the end of the year.

It is likely that Alexander's participation in the Fourth Annual Exhibition of Selected Paintings by American Artists in Buffalo in May led to a retrospective exhibit later that year, with ten of the 43 pictures shown dating from his time in Paris. Additionally, several new decorative paintings were started in the summer for the Buffalo venue at the end of the year.

Of the three new pictures, *Phyllis*, *The Tenth Muse* and *Summer's Day*, two manifested Alexander's love of Velázquez's somber tones, empty spaces and light reflecting off surfaces.[200] The alluring *Phyllis* (Figure 76) looks the part, in a fantasy of a well-to-do country maiden wearing an off-white dress trimmed in black with ruffles at the neckline and sleeves, a black ribbon at the throat, and a yellow straw hat framing her head like a halo.[201] The artist reverts to a familiar technique, the flowing black line, to articulate the folds of the skirt. As a study of tone and mood, it is in the best Whistlerian tradition, yet also cognizant of Velázquez's lessons with the figure emerging from the shadows.

Even more reminiscent of Velázquez is *The Tenth Muse* (Figure 77). The picture is a tribute to the noble profession of being an artist in the guise of a tribute to the Spanish master. As in *Las Meninas*, the artist, in this case Alexander, inserts himself in the composition, staring out from behind a stretched canvas, and invites the viewer into a mysterious space under half-light and half shadow. In a rare public display, Alexander presents himself with authority, at the top of his game, dressed in a suit while surrounded by the tools of his profession: a brush and palette, a studio manikin and a stretched canvas, the edge of which catches the light.

A third new painting was *Summer's Day* (Figure 78), a large and complex composition of two figures, a still-life and a cat. (This should not be confused with *A Summer Day* dated *c.*1912.)[202] In the manner of *Study in Green and Black*, figures are enveloped by sunlight filtered through a curtained window. While it was on exhibit at the Albright Art Gallery, one reviewer described *Summer's Day* perfectly: "The sun streams through the long low window in the background and touches the edge of the drapery on each girl. It also casts a glow over a bowl of nasturtiums that is placed on the window wall. The composition is superb and the tone of the picture is most harmonious."[203] Once again, the success of the picture is based on the soft, suffused light enveloping the space. The context for the painting is the Seabright studio, not the one from the 1890s, but the one Alexander occupied in the new century, furnished with a long low window and a bench built into the wall.[204]

There is yet another picture that pays tribute to Velázquez, which may have been painted in 1909, a "sketch" of Mark Twain (Figure 79). The bonds

76
Phyllis, 1909, oil on canvas,
84 × 46 in. (213.4 × 116.8 cm.),
Swope Art Museum,
museum purchase

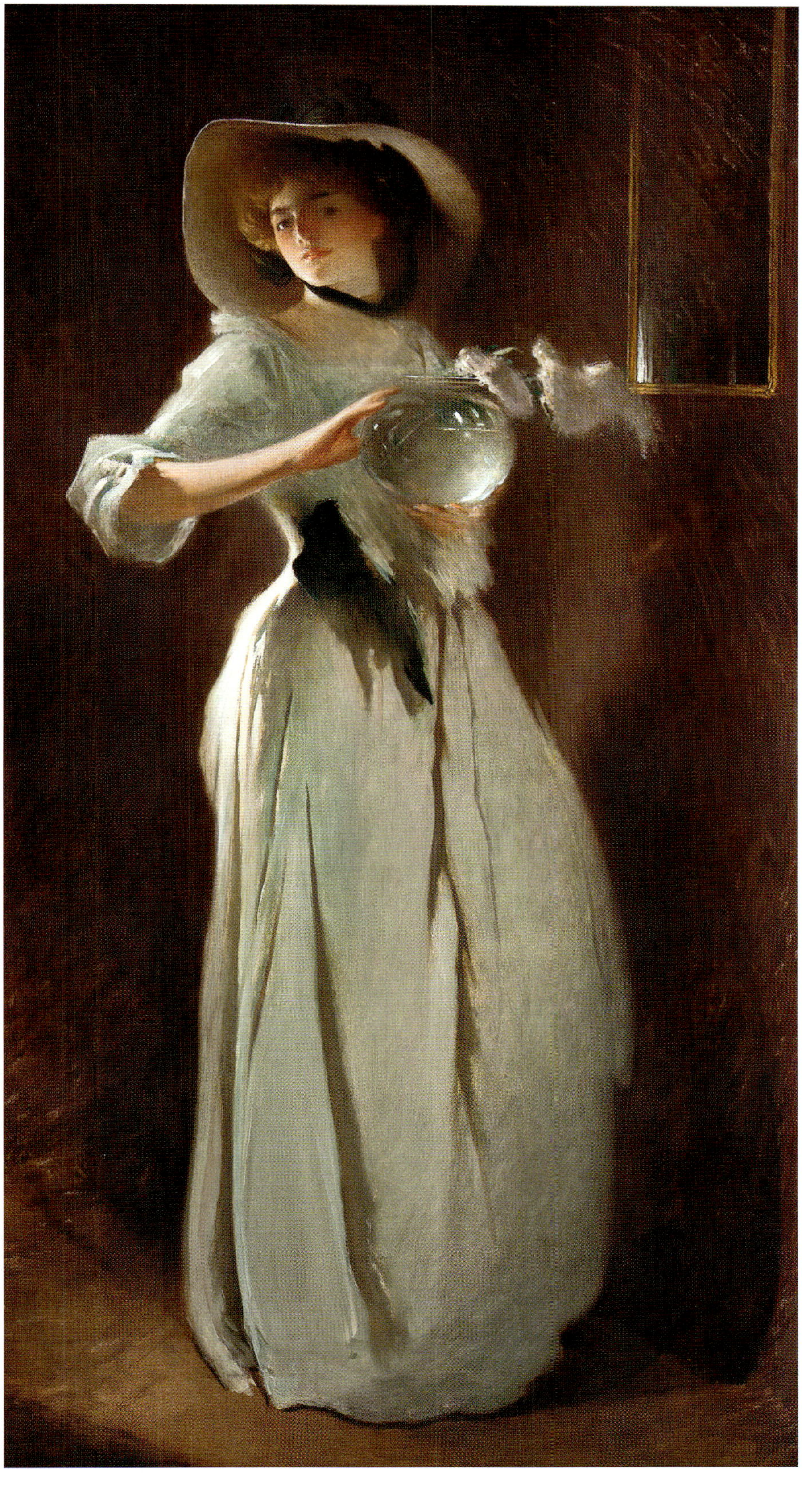

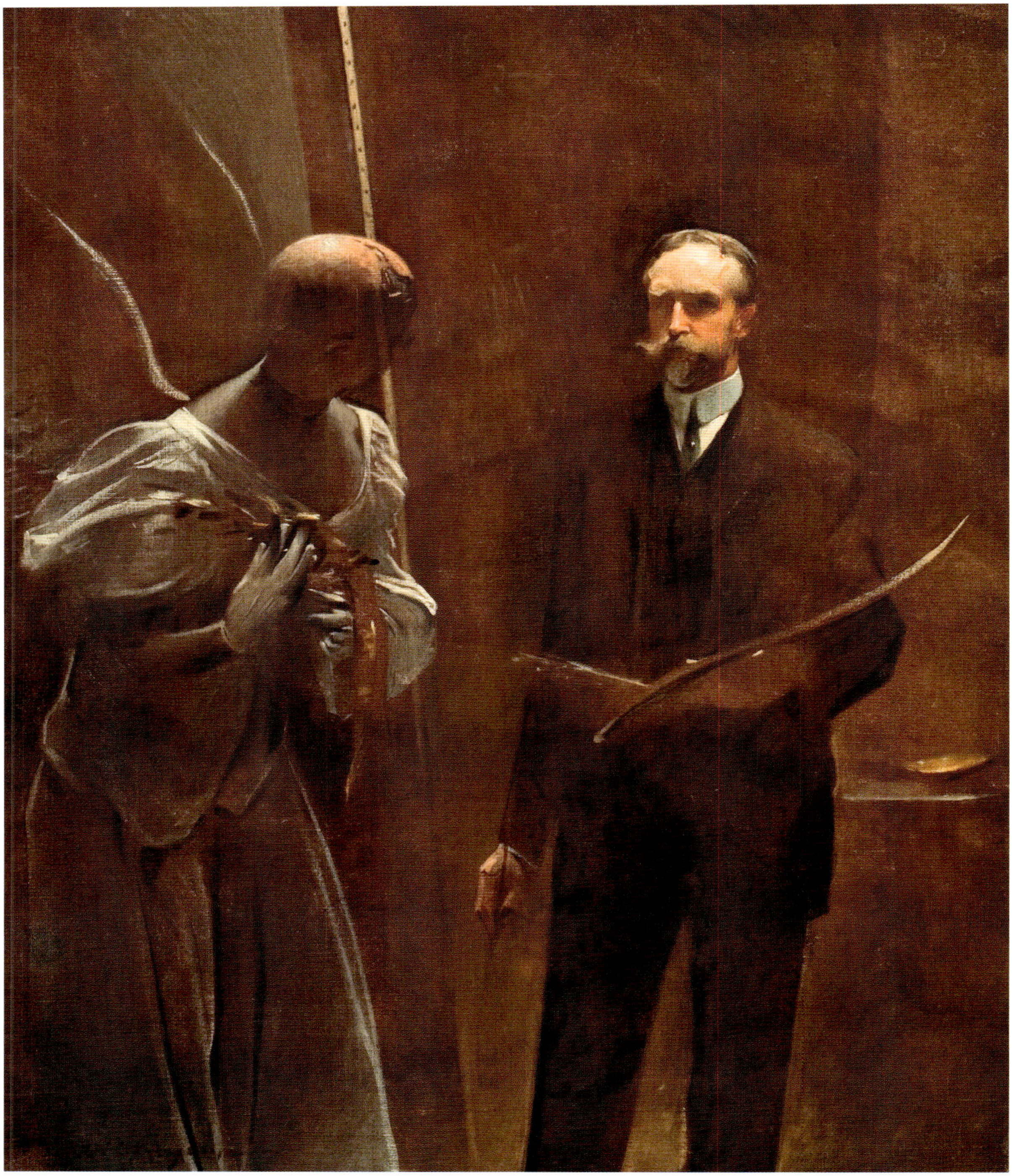

77 *The Tenth Muse*, 1909, oil on canvas, 62½ × 52½ in. (158.8 × 133.4 cm.), The Hevrdejs Collection, Houston

between the Alexander family and Twain ran deep. The artist and the writer shared ties to *Harper's*, beginning in the 1870s. On Bess's side of the family, as early as 1886, if not earlier, Henry Martyn Alexander of Alexander & Green advised Twain in negotiations with his nephew and partner, Charles Webster.[205] The painter attended Twain's 67th birthday party and the grand 70th birthday party at Delmonicos in December 1905.

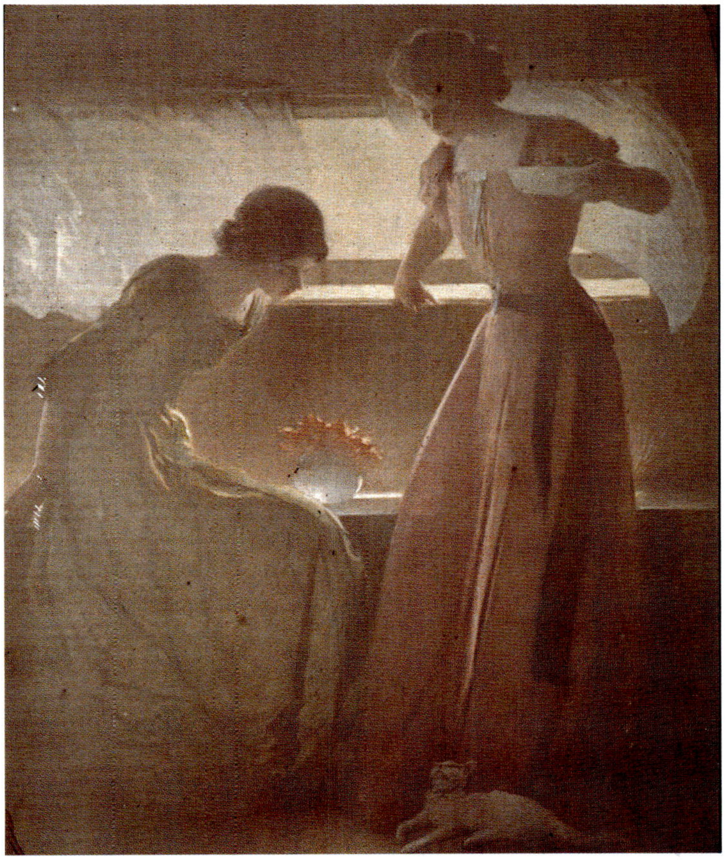

78
Summer's Day, 1909, oil on canvas, unlocated. Photograph courtesy of the author

The earliest talk of Twain sitting for Alexander was in Paris in 1894, but it appears to have been premature.[206] A pencil sketch that first appeared in *International Studio* in May 1908 could have been a preliminary attempt at a portrait and an indication that the artist and the author were weighing the idea. In greetings for the 1909 new year, Twain invites Alexander to come and paint him.[207] This raises the likelihood that the portrait may have been the result of a visit to Redfield, Connecticut, sometime in early 1909. In the portrait the aged but intellectually alert and energetic author stands wearing a dark suit and holding what looks like a pen in his right hand. Twain is depicted as he would want to be remembered, not in the saddened state he was reduced to by the death of his wife in mid 1904 and the prolonged epileptic suffering of his daughter Jean who died on Christmas Eve 1909.[208] Posing the subject in a dark suit is curious as Twain started appearing in public in a white suit in late 1906. Nevertheless, a 1909 date for the portrait fits stylistically with Alexander's other paintings. Invoking the Spanish master once again, Alexander anchors the figure of Twain firmly to the floor by means of the black shadow of the right foot. In subtle tones of color the floor recedes into undefined space with no clear delineation of floor or wall.

The Velázquezness of it all, the sparse interior and close tonal range, is as stylistically different as can be from Twain's portrait in Gari Melchers' mural for the Missouri State Capitol (1922). Decorations for the Governor's Reception Room called for figures of significance to the history of Missouri to be featured, one in each of the four panels. The author is posed, standing erect in the pilothouse of a riverboat wearing his iconic white suit. A late work by Melchers, it is painted in high-key colors rather than the soft tones of his earlier murals for the Library of Congress (1896). What does not escape either artist's attention is the indefatigable nature of their subject, energetic and robust.

Another exhibition Alexander had to prepare for was the Academy's winter show. As President, he must have felt the pressure to exhibit his best new work knowing that he would be subject to additional scrutiny seeing as almost every review reminded readers of his position. Another study of light and (mostly) shadow was *Sunlight* (Figure 80), completed during the previous six months. The figure is seen from the back looking down at the streaks of sunlight coming from an unseen source. The dress has been variously described as white and green. Alexander once again places a red flower against the dark hair to provide a color accent, as he had done years before in *Portrait Gris* and again in *A Study* (1903).

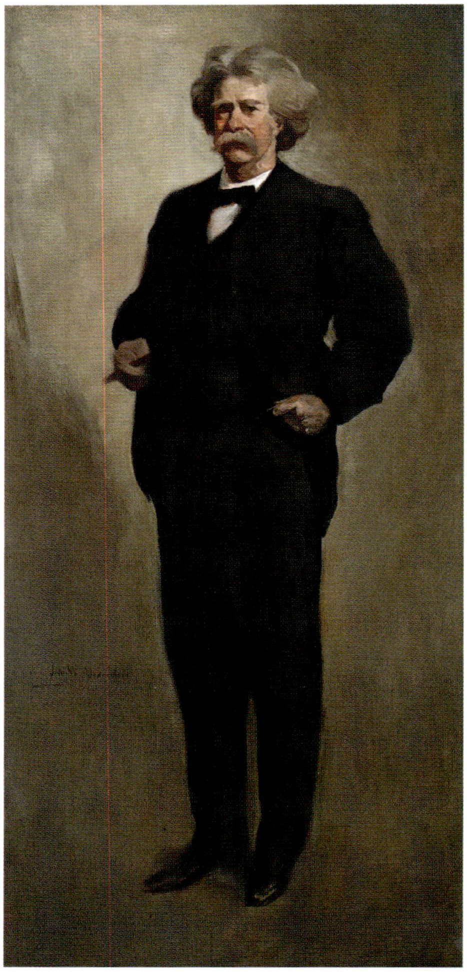

79
Sketch of Mark Twain, *c.*1909, oil on canvas, 72½ × 36 in. (191.7 × 91.4 cm.), National Portrait Gallery, Smithsonian Institution, 81.116

This new work prepared for exhibitions at the end of 1909 anticipates the future. Alexander turned once again to the convention of manipulating light for effect, be it raking light, natural or artificial, a device that began with the portrait of Joe Jefferson in 1881. It became a theme of the body of work from the summer in Étretat in 1894 and reappeared in *A Ray of Sunlight* in 1898, *A Study* in 1903, *Study in Green and Black* in 1906, *Summer's Day* and *Sunlight* in 1909, and then in a series beginning in 1911 in Onteora.

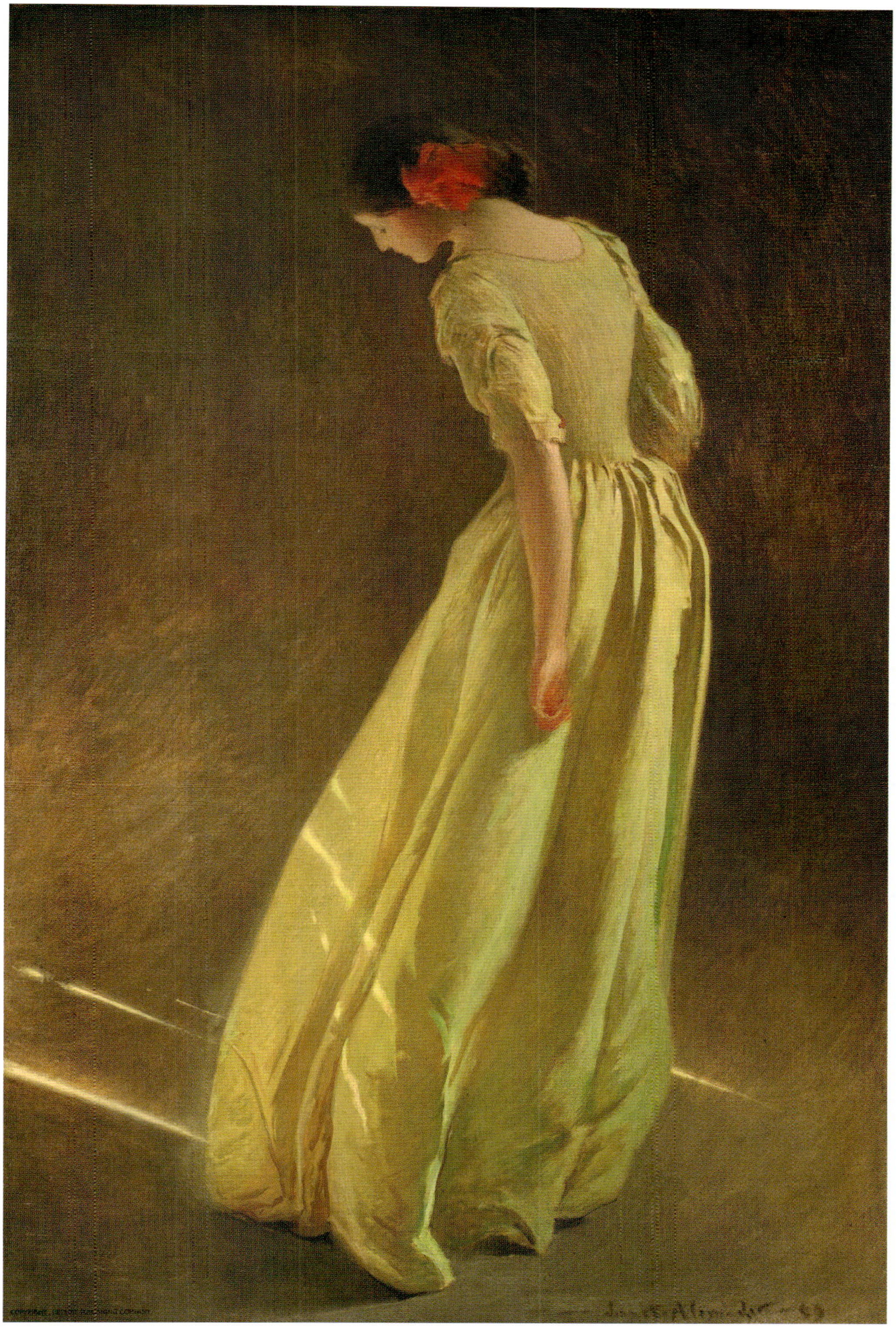

80 *Sunlight*, 1909, oil on canvas, 83½ × 55½ in. (212 × 141 cm.), unknown private collection

6

PRESIDENT OF THE NATIONAL ACADEMY OF DESIGN AND CAMPAIGNER FOR GOOD CAUSES

WITH THE PRESIDENCY OF THE ACADEMY came new obligations as a public figure and a spokesman that Alexander enthusiastically embraced. Yet privately, because of his health, he must have had to be selective about all that he did in 1910 and the early months of 1911. In late January he was absent from the National Arts Club dinner on January 12 honoring William M. Chase. His prepared remarks were read by another. Out of necessity, priorities were shifted from portrait commissions to public appearances. For the remainder of the year the severity of his ongoing undiagnosed condition was mitigated by skillfully interspersing public statements with absences. He finished no new decorative work in 1910, sending work from the second half of 1909 to the various annual exhibitions. For example, between February 2 and 17, he maintained a very public stance about the need of the Academy for additional exhibition space. "New York should be the salon of the whole country," was his topic when he addressed graduates and former students of the School of Science and Architecture of Columbia University at their annual dinner. The speech could well have been the basis for an article for the March 1910 issue of *The Craftsman*, the contents of which became his clarion call during his presidency.[1] He then traveled to Pittsburgh to make a presentation before the Historic Society of Western Pennsylvania together with Percy MacKaye about a Fourth of July pageant that they would both organize for the summer of 1911. After this he absented himself from further public appearances.

On doctor's orders Bess sent him off without her to rest with friends in New Smyrna, Florida. Rest was imposed for a month by withholding news and correspondence. Bess confided to Morris that her husband had lost twelve pounds and that after two consultations total rest was the prescription, but she wished he was not so far away.[2] The alleged success of the respite was lampooned in a photograph obviously intended for family and close friends, of Alexander nattily dressed seated at a table laden with an oversize soup bowl and a compote.[3] Next to him are two women offering him even more nourishment, perhaps with the hope that he would gain back the twelve pounds.

Upon his return on or about March 26, he was in the news again for a collaboration with Charles Frohman and Maude Adams on the costumes and scenery for her performance in *Chantecler*. After his re-election to the presidency of the Academy in May he underwent repeated surgeries. In a succession of letters to Harrison Morris, Bess went into detail, bemoaning how "just as he feels better, a little stronger, they operate and knock him out again." It had been an "anxious Spring," and he still was "not out of the woods."[4] The next week he had a fever and had been "knocked out by a surgery he had the previous Sunday."[5] And finally a week later, having not worked for the past four months and having been in severe pain but now with his temperature gone, he got out of bed for the first time in ten days.[6] Even when a dear friend like John Beatty inquired about portraits for friends, Bess wrote that her husband was to rest for the summer and could not consider new commissions until October.[7] Plans for the summer would take the Alexanders to Paris and Munich and probably other cities on the Continent with the expectation of returning in September.[8]

Before going off to Europe for a rest, Alexander must have taken satisfaction in his contract with the Detroit Publishing Company for which he would earn royalties. They were the purveyors of high-quality art reproductions for schools and libraries. At their W. 38th Street galleries they mounted an exhibit of paintings, studies and facsimiles of Alexander's work.[9] A two-week solo exhibition at this venue that was neither art gallery nor museum served a second purpose other than an exhibition of his work. The majority of the exhibit was made up of reproductions, and the show was a marketing tool to sell the products. Available for purchase were reproductions of fifteen paintings, plus six details of the Carnegie mural. The highest level of full-color reproduction was known as a "Thistle Facsimile". *Isabella and the Pot of Basil* was offered in eight variations according to size, quality and price including as a Thistle Facsimile.[10]

Crossing over to Europe with the Alexanders were Mr. and Mrs. Thomas Hastings, Maude Adams and Alf Hayman, business partner to Charles Frohman. Ostensibly the reason for going abroad was to study costumes, scenery and lighting in preparation for Adams's upcoming performance in Edmond Rostand's *Chantecler* in New York.[11] Stage lighting had been of interest to Alexander for a long time. "I have built models of stage settings and experimented with the lighting. The many tableaux which I have directed I have worked on merely to lead up to the kind of work which I now am doing for the professional stage." His aim was for simplicity of scenery, costume and light so that the actor became the dominant note on the stage, and not subsumed by the scenery. Lighting was applied like a painting by Whistler with an eye toward composition and color. It was all about tone with no one strong color standing out to distract from the dramatic performance.[12]

A second reason for the trip was to study "exhibition buildings in Europe" in his capacity as President of the Academy.[13] Though efforts to secure the Central Park site had been abandoned, the fundamental need for an appropriately sized exhibition building had not. Alexander toured European cities and admired many examples of civic museums, particularly those in Munich.[14] He had returned from Europe by early September seemingly even more resolute to solve the problem, knowing strategically that if it were solved, the threat of secession would be defused. The message for the American public was that New York lagged behind Europe in large exhibition spaces and that even a Midwestern town such as Richmond, Indiana, could better accommodate large exhibitions. He voiced his opinion whenever he could; the salient points in his article for *The Craftsman* titled "The Need of a National Academy, and its Value to Growth of Art in America," formed the basis of his public statements. In the article he posited that institutions are formed out of revolution, which he described as a "nursery of ideas," but cautioned that over time they could become resistant to change. The progress of the arts in America had advanced in the last twenty years to the point that artists did not need to be driven abroad to seek a European education. "We have become genuinely convinced of the great educational value of the fine arts in their relation to our people." In turn, what artists needed was an "ever-widening opportunity" to exhibit, not just at the Academy.[15] He gave as an example the frustrating circumstances of the recent winter exhibit at the Academy where 1,600 pictures were submitted, many of high quality, but because of limited space even some approved pictures could not be exhibited.

Only after his return did the press seem to make much of what was perhaps the real reason for the trip, for consultations about his health. While he repeatedly referred to the multitude of art galleries that he saw in Munich, the mystery remains as to how much time he spent consulting with doctors while there and what treatments he underwent. One clue is his wife's recollection of consulting with a Dr. von Muhler.[16] He is also reported to have been taking the baths in an unnamed German city.[17] Upon his return, the personal reason for his trip was revealed. Prior to his trip the press had not known that he needed to recuperate, but now they were making the point that he was "improved" after having gone abroad primarily to recover from a serious unidentified illness.[18]

Spending a month in Florida and the summer in Europe took its toll on picture making. Commissions progressed in fits and starts or not at all. Probably all the portraits from that year were worked on in the last quarter of 1910. The portrait of William De Witt Hyde, President of Bowdoin College, which had been agreed to in 1909, had to wait for over a year, with Hyde finally sitting in November 1910.[19] Grover Cleveland's posthumous portrait (Grover Cleveland Birthplace Memorial Association, Caldwell, N.J.) was announced in January 1910 for completion the following spring.[20] Also announced in 1909, but not finished until 1911, was the portrait of the wife of Mr. Ambrose Monell, the man in whose honor monel nickel alloy was named.[21] Portraits of A. Barton Hepburn, a banker and politician, and Mrs. F. W. Hallowell were probably begun in late 1910. While no decorative figure painting can be firmly attributed to the year 1910, there is one anomaly, the so-called "posters" for the end-of-season fête in Onteora. Within days of returning from Europe Alexander was in Onteora, as whose guest it is not known. For the Shakespeare-themed fête, Alexander completed what he called posters, but were actually paintings, one of a knight on horseback and another of a bearded man drinking from a mug (Onteora Club collection). As if to announce himself, both are boldly dated "Sept. 10, 1910" on the face of the painting.

The "Secession" Dabo had referred to in his flattering and encouraging letter of congratulation was ongoing, with the community of New York artists roiled by struggles to find a larger place to exhibit. The privilege of exhibiting at the Academy meant being approved by one's peers, a membership of 125 painters, 25 sculptors and 25 architects. Each academician and the unlimited number of associates were entitled to exhibit one picture exempt from the jury. Solicited works were guaranteed acceptance. Unsolicited works were subject to review by a jury.[22] When Alexander assumed the presidency, he was well aware of the festering dissatisfaction among the new men at the vetting process. As an alternative, artists felt compelled to act independent of the Academy. A breakaway group, The Eight, led by Robert Henri, organized and had already staged an exhibit at the Macbeth Gallery in 1908. This was followed by the Exhibition of Independent Artists in 1910. Both were staged in borrowed spaces and not in a permanent facility of their own. The Eight became a symbol of revolt and this is most likely what Dabo was referring to.

With a fear of secession and the campaign for a larger exhibition hall, it was the role of the President of the Academy to lead, and Alexander did so fearlessly. For example, he took advantage of the platform given him as the honoree at the December 19 Salmagundi Club dinner to make a provocative prediction that would frame the ensuing public debate. He pronounced, on what basis is not known, that the city would give the Academy a site within the next three months.[23] The *Evening World* reported on the dinner with a head-scratching statement: "A lay member, Dr. Coffin showed an x-ray picture of the interior of Mr. Alexander's skull. What we would like to know is did he find there a single valid reason for the eminent artist's confident presumption … that New York City is going to give the academy a choice site for a new building, preferably the little that is left of Bryant Park."[24] Having lost the battle for a site in Central Park, Alexander had shifted his attention to a site on the west side of Bryant Park between 40th and 42nd Streets.[25]

Always on point, Alexander had another opportunity to press the need for a building large enough to accommodate multiple interests. He was quoted in an article with the headline, "French Art Not Coming."[26] This was a reference to an exhibition of the Société des Peintres et des Sculpteurs (formerly the Société Nouvelle) organized by Cornelia Sage, Director of the Buffalo Fine Arts Academy. With bronzes by Rodin and paintings by Aman-Jean, Besnard, Jacques-Émile Blanche, Eugène Carrière, de La Gándara, Martin, Simon, and other foreign artists on show, Alexander was truly among friends when he exhibited *At the Window*. The American Walter Gay was a member and Sargent was mentioned as a member but did not exhibit. The point Alexander was making was to ask why "one of the most important displays of contemporary foreign art" was not traveling to New York. It was about to open in Chicago and then travel to St. Louis, with Boston a late addition. The quick-witted Alexander was quoted as saying, "The exhibition will undoubtedly come here, but with a difference. It comes as it first arrived, boxed up and crated."

The plan then shifted strategically to one that would accommodate all artistic organizations in the city in one building. This was the purpose of a meeting called by the Academy in mid February. Attending were representatives from all the art societies of New York City: the Society of American Artists, Society of Mural Painters, National Sculpture Society, American Watercolor Society, New York Watercolor Club, Society of Pastelists, Architectural League, Institute of American Architects (New York City and Brooklyn chapters), Society of Beaux-Arts Architects, and the Municipal Art Society. All were invited to join forces to persuade the city to donate a site. At this meeting yet another site on the east side of Fifth Avenue facing the New York Public Library was added as a possibility.

Alexander spoke of the proposal repeatedly, first at the late February meeting of the Republican Club of the City of New York, at the late March meeting of the Artists' Suffrage League and at the League of Political Education in early April. In a description worthy of a Nast cartoon, it was reported, "The most persistent exhibition booster for a new exhibition building in which all artists of New York may show their pictures at proper times and seasons, is John W. Alexander ... so bent on his project that the park commissioner Stover is almost afraid to leave the city parks out over night for fear that Mr. Alexander may seize a site in one before dawn."[27] The commissioner may have had enough; just a month before the public opening of the New York Public Library, it was reported that while discussing landscaping with Thomas Hastings, the architect of the library, Stover happened to pronounce that there would be no building in Bryant Park.[28] This was classic political theater, with the park commissioner trumping Alexander's publicly stated presumption. Meantime Alexander was being the exemplary citizen, personally hanging the art collection of the New York Public Library prior its public opening on May 23 and then lending his name to a joint effort for an open-air theater for the citizens of New York City led by none other than Maude Adams and Charles Frohman.

In another capacity, Alexander used his position as President of the MacDowell Club to further the needs of artists. That the President of the self-perpetuating Academy also presided over the progressive MacDowell Club, whose exhibition policies were sympathetic to the young struggling artists snubbed by the Academy, was a tribute to the character of the man who held the positions simultaneously. In 1911 when the Club relocated to a new location at 108 West 55th Street, one of the first initiatives was to inaugurate a democratic system of exhibitions: "Groups of not less than eight nor more than twelve artists shall pass judgment on all pictures submitted for exhibition. If one artist desires to hang a picture, he can invite seven other artists to form a group, and his right as a member of the group, to contribute his picture to any one of the exhibitions will be recognized by the Club." A trial series of fifteen exhibitions for which artists could form their own groups was scheduled from October 19, 1911 to June 1, 1912. Alexander explained, "We are trying to form a plan that will work all around for the benefit of painters."[29] To do so, he adopted the Robert Henri template: no jury, no prize. Whatever the terms of a revolt against the Academy, it was (in the words of historian Milton Brown) "as yet directed against the organizational restrictions and not against the artistic principles of academic art."[30] The principle of organizing art exhibits introduced at the MacDowell Club was one example of ever-widening opportunities for artists that was at the core of Alexander's article for *The Craftsman*. The article was less about nationalism and more about shaming New York into resolving the insatiable demand for a facility large enough to accommodate all who wished to exhibit. Meanwhile, in spite of the differing positions, D. Putnam Brinley, George Bellows, Randall Davey, Robert Henri, and John Sloan all volunteered to pitch in to prepare for the upcoming Christmas Festival at the MacDowell Club.[31]

Though the worrying state of Alexander's health was not cause for public alarm, it was not a secret. In a letter to Alexander, Birge Harrison expressed his concern. It was more a case of Alexander overdoing it, he said, but nevertheless it foreshadowed the end of a life cut short too soon.[32] Harrison both praised Alexander and counseled him

> How on earth do you manage it – in the morning & afternoon the big painter turning out big canvas work all the time, in the evening the brilliant society man seen everywhere, and heading all sorts of "movements," and all the time the only real president the Academy has ever had.

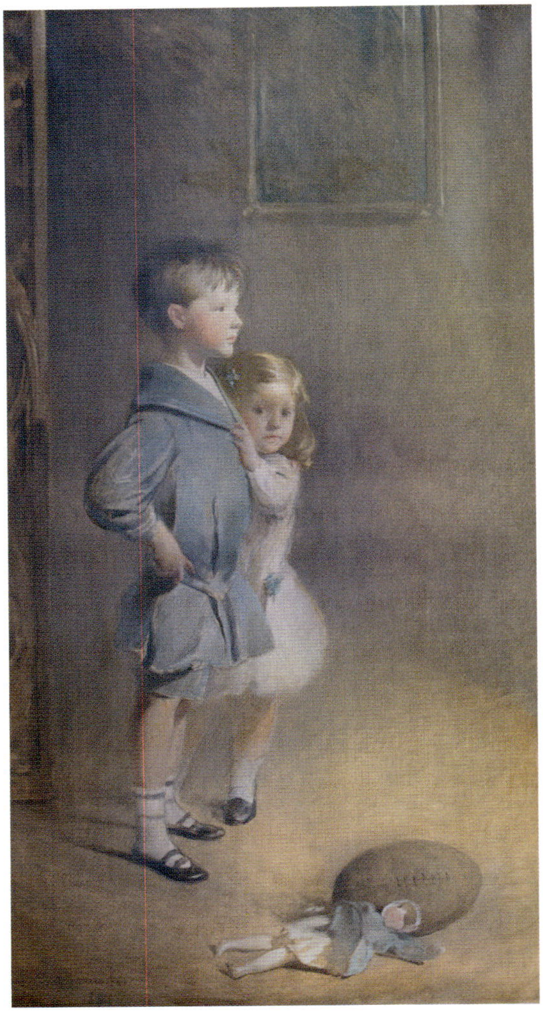

81
Robert Stewart and Elizabeth Kilborne, 1911, oil on canvas, approx. 74¾ × 41½ in. (188 × 104.1 cm.), descendant of the subjects, California

Harrison contrasted him with their mutual friend, Robert Louis Stevenson, saying that the writer "did not fight the stand-up battle that you are fighting. Let all this extraordinary production and vitality of life in spite of a constitution that has never apparently been rugged, and health that has never been perfect."

Further, Harrison urged him to "husband his strength" and slacken "his prodigal outlay of vitality in all things & all people." Yet, as the leader of the Academy, official duties necessitated his presence at various public and private functions. He was named to memorial committees for Mark Twain, Francis D. Millet and Winslow Homer. He was an honorary pallbearer for John Carrère's memorial that took place at the New York Public Library (a Carrère building) before it was opened to the public. At times, he was an honoree, as in the case of the Salmagundi Club.[33] Though he cancelled his $10,000 contract for the mural for the Cleveland Court House days after Harrison's letter, he nonetheless succumbed to the lure of other mural commissions in 1911. When Harrisburg finally approved a $22,000 expenditure Alexander was ready to sign a contract.[34] In August his friend, architect George B. Post prevailed upon him to agree to three murals for the Senate Chamber of the Wisconsin State Capitol.[35] Nonetheless, neither project was realized. Like Harrisburg, the Wisconsin contract got mired in politics, but the difference is that Alexander withdrew from the project.

This so-called perception of a "prodigal outlay" did not however extend to an excess of painting in 1910, though appearances may have suggested otherwise. Alexander relied on two decorative pictures to represent him in the cyclical exhibitions at the National Academy, the Pennsylvania Academy and the Carnegie International. *Sunlight* debuted at the National Academy in December 1909 and toured through April 1911, including exhibits in Berlin and Munich before being purchased by the Friends of American Art of the Art Institute of Chicago in October 1910.[36] *Summer's Day* toured to four venues from December 1909 through December 1910. In the meantime, he sent previously exhibited pictures to Buenos Aires, Rome and even Terre Haute, Indiana.

The pace of portrait commissions picked up in the last quarter of 1910 and through the following year. Most likely these commissions were generated by patrons seeking a portrait by a distinguished painter. Patrons included Mrs. Hunt Henderson (unknown), Mr. Houston Lowe, a Dayton manufacturer of paint and varnishes, and his wife (collection of Dayton History), President William De Witt Hyde of Bowdoin College (Bowdoin College Museum of Art), Jefferson Davis McLean (Modern Art Museum of Fort Worth) of Texas, a full length of a Mrs. Mitchell (unknown), Judge Frederick A. Ward (unlocated) of the Second District Court in Brooklyn, and President Mary Emma Woolley of Mount Holyoke College (Mount Holyoke College). Woolley's portrait was completed in time for the 1911 commencement.[37] A repeat client, the Skinners of Wisteriahurst, Holyoke, Massachusetts, commissioned a double portrait of the children of Mrs. Robert Stewart (née Skinner) (Figure 81). There was a copy of a portrait of Henry H. Porter, a Chicago railroad man and industrialist (unlocated), made from another painted two years earlier.[38] McLean's portrait occupied Alexander for the entirety of 1911. The subject was a Fort Worth County Attorney, who was tragically killed at age 36 during a raid on an alleged gambling house. Because it was a posthumous portrait based on photographs, family and friends were so relentless in their insistence as to how the likeness should look that the portrait was returned for alterations.[39] A portrait of

Charles Edward Garman, Professor of Moral and Mental Philosophy at Amherst (Mead Art Museum) was begun in 1911 but completed in 1912. Lastly, there were at least three portraits generated by friendship or family: a portrait of Helen Gertrude, daughter of Henry M. Alexander (collection of Mr. and Mrs. Joel Leitner), a portrait of Bess and a full-length portrait of Maude Adams (unlocated) in character as Maggie in *What Every Woman Knows*.

Little did Birge Harrison realize how prescient he was in his admonition to Alexander to "husband his strength." The circumstances in which Alexander carried on with his work while fulfilling his public engagements were Herculean by any measure given the increasing fragility of his health. Several weeks before his talk at the Republican Club, Alexander was ordered to rest by his doctor having been ill for most of February.[40] In late May, having hung the paintings at the New York Public Library, having spoken on "The Art Outlook" for the annual meeting of the American Federation of Arts in Washington, and having attended the opening of the New York Public Library, he was home recovering from a serious operation.[41] On June 1 he lectured on "Individuality in Art" at the invitation of the School of Fine Arts at Yale University. By July he and Bess were in Onteora where he was seriously ill, suffering from an ear infection and not working.[42] He began the summer residing at Treetops and then by August moved to The Bushes. This became their first permanent residence in Onteora, where he began a new body of work that investigated the dramatic effects of sunlight filtering through a curtained window onto a figure seated on a banquette. In November Bess was the purchaser of record for The Bushes; it was not an uncommon practice for a woman to be a property owner in Onteora.

The restorative powers of a summer in Onteora cannot be overestimated, allowing time for both rest and for experimentation. In the summer of 1911 techniques of stagecraft inspired Alexander's new work, techniques perfected while in Paris the previous summer and executed on stage for the Frohman production of *Chantecler* early in 1911. As has been seen, stage lighting had been an interest of Alexander's for a long time, honed by building models for stage sets and experimenting with lighting while directing and producing tableaux vivants (see p.154).

Alexander applied the same ideas that he had developed for lighting to designing stage sets. He devised a new method of stage scenery for *Chantecler* that would revolutionize the industry.[43] This latest achievement by a "man of wonderful energy and an ardent worker in the cause of America's artistic achievement along many different lines," came as a surprise, wrote the *Pittsburgh Independent*.[44] His innovation was simple, practical and cost-efficient:

> scenery is made of filmy gauze-like hangings against a background of black velvet … The hangings which are transparent and thinner even than tissue paper, are toned and tinted with colors sprayed on to represent the scene to be pictured. Most of the light is thrown forward from the rear instead of back from the footlights … The result is that the light filtering through the tinted hangings against the black background causes everything … to stand out. Thus we gain that illusion of atmosphere and perspective …[45]

Alexander's approach is an adaptation of a technique he observed in the performances of Loie Fuller in Paris in the 1890s. While her system involved the projection of rotating disks of varying color, his variant projected light onto thin hangings sprayed with color. Like in Fuller's sets, the colored hangings were in front of black velvet.

The figure paintings begun in the summer of 1911 and continuing until the summer of 1914 show an adaptation of his stagecraft to picture-making and represents a new and final serialization of a favorite theme – dreamy, atmospheric sunlight. The theme of sunlight, be it soft or raking, was hardly new to Alexander. It was an intermittent one ever since the 1880s beginning with *Girl with Teacup* and reappearing in *Brittany Sketch, In the Orchard*, and others from the summer of 1894 in Étretat, and continuing with *Sketch of Sunlight* (lost at sea in 1997) and *A Ray of Sunlight*, both from 1898, *A Study* (1903), *Study in Green and Black* (1906), and *Sunlight* (1909). The latter is the last example of a major work showing a harsh raking light. Now, taking a new direction, Alexander creates an evenly toned and tinted surface suffused with light. Light is the continuum and the curtained window that walls off the figure becomes the instrument of his narrative. Alexander adopts a secular, indoor version of the hortus conclusus within which the quiet figure "expresses no particular activity beyond that of appearing most comfortably 'at home.'"[46] An important example known only through written accounts, *Primrose* (1911), shows a woman standing in front of a window holding primroses. At the Pennsylvania Academy annual, the painting was described as a "suffusion of greenness."[47] The same critic elevated *Primrose* to the rank of a "masterpiece."

"Suffusion" best describes this new body of work in which a soft natural light acts as a cocoon inhabited by the figure. The overall tone of *The Ring* is a suffusion of yellow with the model subjected to the warmth of the yellowish summer sun (Figure 82). Light finds points of contact, with the strongest being the luminous curtain, the pillow and the dappled effect as it traverses from the right edge of the skirt to the banquette seat. The costume no longer alludes to

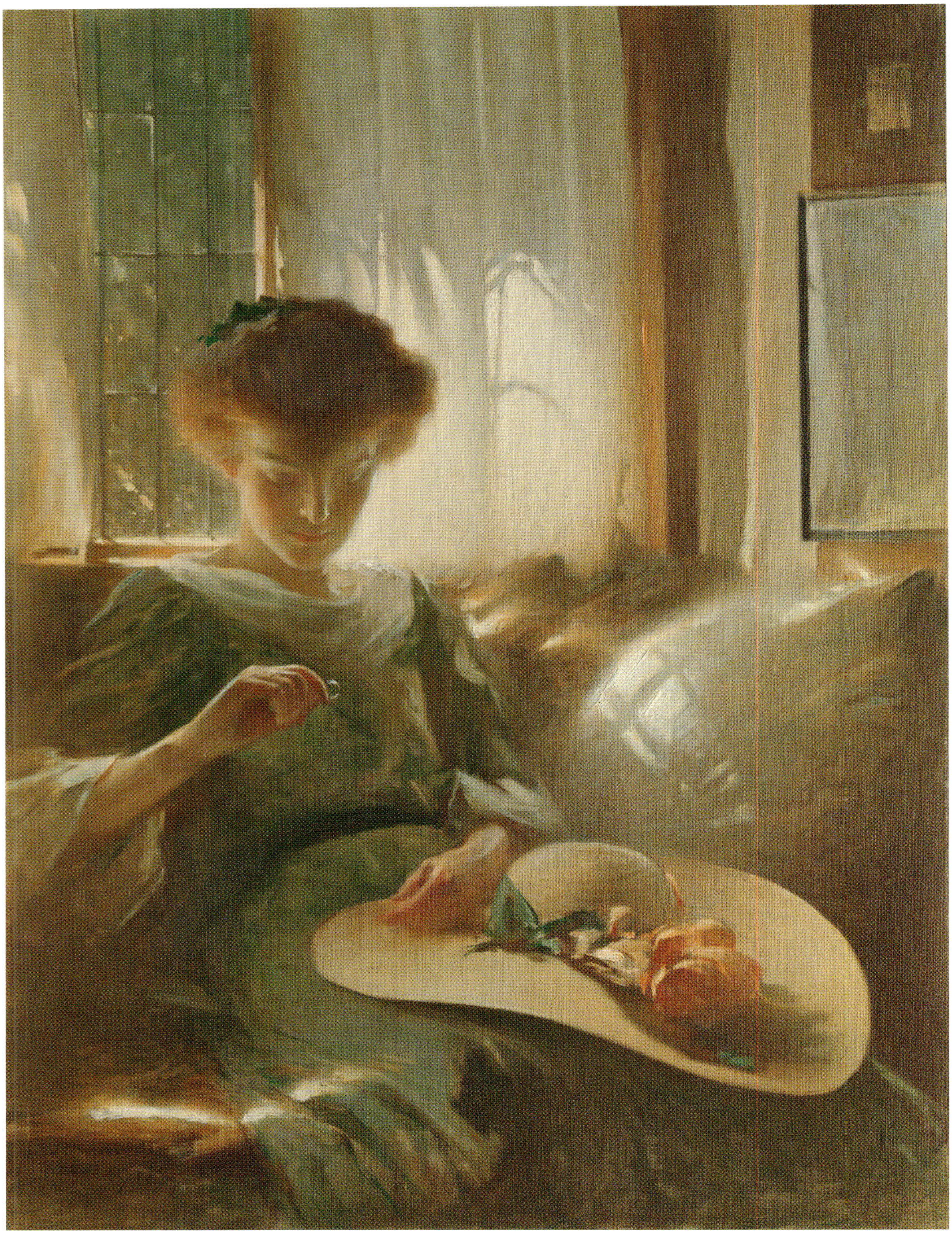

82 *The Ring*, 1911, oil on canvas, 48¾ × 36 ⅜ in. (123.8 × 92.4 cm.), The Metropolitan Museum of Art, gift of Mary Hearn Greims in memory of Arthur Hoppock Hearn, 1912.12.

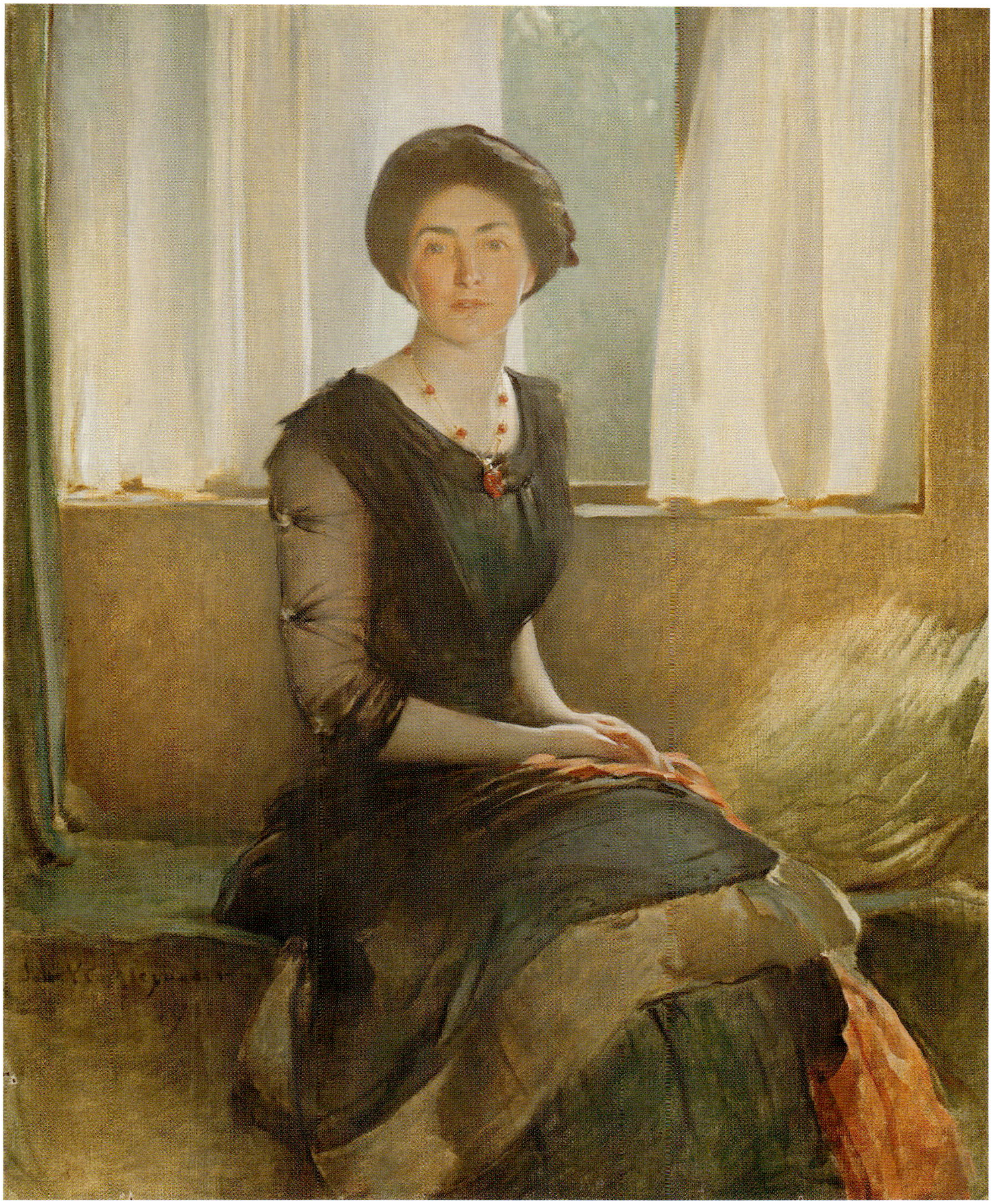

83 *Portrait of a Lady* (Elizabeth A. Alexander), 1911, oil on canvas, 50 × 40⅛ in. (127 × 101.9 cm.), John White Alexander great-granddaughters

antiquity. Seemingly more contemporary, it is of the country not the city. Composed on a grid, this painting rises to a new level of complexity. The curtained mullioned window dominates the top half while the head of the girl links the two halves. In the lower half, the rounded form of the straw hat is complemented by that of the pillow. Adding to the complexity is the vertical shape of a frame to the far right that interjects another dimension into a picture that is overtly sentimental. The soft enveloping illumination enhances the symbolism of the woman reflecting upon the meaning of the ring in her hand.

As for the other picture from this summer, a likeness of Bess (Figure 83), it was clearly meant as a portrait though it is also decorative. Alexander almost always depicts his wife from the front with an intellectually alert expression. This time her face is fuller and more matronly. Her hair is shorter and rolled back off the face. Her costume suggests that she is dressed for a special occasion or to receive guests. The dress design was not *à la mode* but more of an aesthetic style with its multilayered skirt, black chiffon outer layer and chiffon sleeves (she is holding a red shawl).[48] The quality of the light coming from the window behind does not suffuse as evenly as in *The Ring* and there are contrasting colors in a higher key. In an otherwise finished canvas the pillow to the right is deliberately left unfinished, perhaps a nod to modernity.

This is the portrait that Alexander sent to the inaugural exhibit of the newly formed National Association of Portrait Painters. This disparate group of 27 artists banded together, in Sarah J. Moore's words, "to present cohesive, well installed displays of the various trends in contemporary portraiture from the aesthetic and decorative to the realistic, and included internationally known and acclaimed artists."[49] Most importantly, it offered yet another among the ever-widening opportunities for artists of differing ideologies to exhibit together and to dissuade the public away from the "tiresomely conventional and perfunctory portrait."[50] The critics had admiring words for Alexander's portrait, "in his best vein – reserved, dignified and like all of Alexander's work, ineffably gracious."[51] They may as well be speaking of the model herself, the artist's wife. This venue, that could contain two portraits as different as Alexander's of Bess and George Luks's painting of two young brothers in clown costumes with a jack-o'-lantern, was representative of a more inclusive and less hierarchical process to qualifying, one which Alexander advocated.

The crusade leading up to the International Exhibition of Modern Art (the Armory Show) was marked by the polarity between the progressives and the traditionalists, or "truth versus beauty". Alexander fell into the latter camp, though he did everything he could as a leader to avoid revolt by the former.

Representations of both types hung side by side at the annuals in Pittsburgh, Philadelphia and New York. During this transitional time, from "art for art's sake" to modernism, even a year could make a difference.

For the generation in pursuit of beauty – the American Impressionists (Dewing, Frieseke, Hassam, or Richard Miller) and the Boston group The Ten (Benson, DeCamp or Tarbell), the artistic status quo involved a more genteel characterization of women as subject. At the most viable and vital American venue, the Carnegie International of 1909, a time when Alexander's murals in both symbolist and realist styles was attracting all the attention, he exhibited a more conventional portrait of Helen Beatty, while Childe Hassam exhibited *Spring Morning*, a decorative figure painting of a woman of a genteel character in a refined interior illuminated by light from a curtained window. By contrast, in 1910 Robert Henri showed *The Equestrian*, a ribald record of modern life executed in a slapdash stroke, of an Asian model from a lower social class wearing an elegant riding outfit. Aesthetically, it was as far removed from Hassam's *Spring Morning* as two pictures can be. By the time of Hassam's *Spring Morning* of 1909 or Alexander's *The Ring* of 1911, the curtained window formula was overworked. The redeeming value of *The Ring* is the suffusive light, an effect that Alexander explored over the next three years. For Hassam, *Spring Morning* evolved into the popular "New York Window Series." Stylistically, Hassam represented the past and Henri the near future, while abstraction pointed to the unknown future. Both the Hassam and Henri pictures were acquired for the Carnegie collection.

Since Alexander's invitation to lecture on June 1, something had been afoot on the part of Yale University School of Fine Arts. Either because of a brilliant speech, "Individuality in Art," by "one of the greatest painters of the twentieth century" or because of his inherent leadership skills, Yale identified him as a talent whom they would like to see reshape the School of Fine Arts.[52] Yale began a recruiting campaign to woo Alexander to succeed J. Ferguson Weir whose retirement was pending. Weir visited Alexander three times, twice accompanied by Yale President Arthur T. Hadley.[53] Concessions were tendered including a salary higher then Weir's. Alexander would report directly to the President and have the freedom to continue his own work. The courting of Alexander most likely took place after his return from Onteora. Alexander wisely, perhaps even unselfishly, declined, knowing the truth about his health, and Weir reluctantly accepted his decision in a letter of November 28.[54] Had he accepted one can only imagine the future for Alexander, Yale and the New York art world.

Yale's loss meant that Alexander was still a force to reckon with in New York City when it came to efforts to rectify the lack of exhibition space. Since a single organization, the National Academy, had been rebuffed by the city over two sites, the arsenal in Central Park and the Fifth Avenue site opposite the Library, all of the city's art societies now joined forces to form a federation called the National Academy Association. With plans for incorporation, Alexander was named the temporary President and Henry Watrous, Secretary. An executive committee comprising of William A. Boring, Cass Gilbert, Herbert Adams, and Bert Hanson, a lawyer for the Municipal Art Society, was appointed. The committee was charged with devising a plan of action and writing a charter. Always the optimist, Alexander was convinced that the National Academy of Design had made headway in its jury procedure, even at times excluding submissions by jurors and including outsiders. However, as he saw it, the future lay in a federation with a new building and a promise of frequent – even daily! – exhibits.[55] The stakes were raised by going to the state assembly to seek incorporation of the new federation.

Though Alexander was doing everything to stave off the insurgency, he did not succeed. He and the sculptor, Gutzon Borglum, vice-president of the Association of American Painters and Sculptors, were "the chief fighting men" of their respective camps. Speaking for the record, Borglum accused the Academy of trying to maintain control. Alexander assured the opposition that they could have all the gallery space in the new building that they required.[56] Despite Alexander's assurance, the insurgents continued to organize. Their purpose, as drawn up by Henry Fitch Taylor, Jerome Myers, Elmer MacRae, and Walt Kuhn, was to form a society that exhibited "works of progressive and live painters, both American and foreign, favoring such work usually neglected by current shows and especially interesting and instructive to the public."[57] At the first meeting of the newly formed Association of American Painters and Sculptors (AAPS) on December 19, 1911, there was at least one admitted admirer of Alexander in attendance, Leon Dabo. Another, J. Alden Weir, was elected President *in absentia*. Not exactly an obvious choice, Weir was taken by surprise and quickly announced his resignation.[58] Arthur B. Davies replaced him. Coincidentally, on the same evening as the first organizational meeting of the AAPS, the MacDowell Club was celebrating their Christmas festival. Of the rival group, Bellows, Davey, Henri, and Sloan were not on the AAPS register of attendees, meaning they would have met their commitment to assist in the *Midsummer Night's Dream* at the MacDowell Club. Brinley opted out to attend the meeting of the rebellious group though he still contributed to the Christmas festival.[59]

The opposition group would go on to organize only one exhibit, but it was one that would cause seismic change not only in accepted norms of style and exhibiting practices, but also the art market and collecting.

Walter Pach, who was not present at the initial meeting of the AAPS, but nevertheless fulfilled an essential role in organizing the Armory show, had a multifaceted career. One was as a writer on art. In the January, 1912 issue of *The Outlook* he wrote an evenhanded, if not a mostly non-acrimonious, assessment of Alexander in the form of an interview titled "Art and the Average Man."[60] A proponent of modern art, Pach did not show his secessionist hand. He did not attack Alexander or the Academy, though he did not shy away from the problem. In the give-and-take of the interview, Pach elicited a response from Alexander about the issue that divided the two sides. To Pach's statement, "there was a definite attitude among the members, especially the older ones, that the Academy was their private club, and non-members (the new men) were to show their work there only on sufferance," Alexander simply replied, "We must give the young men their chance." Addressing the current factionalism Pach wrote, "It has been a particular mission of John W. Alexander's to make the heterogeneous group of men who are producing our art act in unison," despite having been trained differently and representing different traditions. In the spirit of educating the public as to what artists are doing and simultaneously teaching the value of art as an enhancement to life, Alexander envisioned exhibitions touring the country. In turn, this would give artists what they needed, an ever-widening opportunity to exhibit. Pach closed with a positive summation of Alexander as a man who touched the lives of the American public in a variety of ways: as a mural painter, advising on plays, speaking out publicly, and as an advocate for art in schools. Pach's profile of Alexander, the President of the conservative National Academy of Design, was as a "man for all seasons," a man of conviction.

A key step for the traditionalist camp was the introduction of a bill for the incorporation of the National Academy Association on February 13 by state Senator Wainwright. While the legislative process was making its way through committee in Albany, and while proponents of the American Association of Painters and Sculptors were strategizing, it seems that some rivals were able to set aside differences in the name of collegiality and amusement. The occasion was the Fifth Annual MacDowell Club dinner. Thirteen artists of varying styles, working mostly in charcoal, labored for twenty minutes at a "speed of 60 miles per hour" to create a 70-foot-long mural.[61] The thirteen artists – George Bellows, Nell Brinkley, H. B. Eddy, James Montgomery Flagg, Henry "Hy" Mayer,

F. Luis Mora, Wallace Morgan, Boardman Robinson, John Sloan, Dan Smith, Irving Wiles, Art Young, and Alexander – were all skilled illustrators.[62] The result was a procession of themes in a profusion of styles. Because they were still "favorably known to each other," the progressives put aside their differences for the holiday season.[63] The secession could wait another day.

Within a week of the state Assembly forwarding the act for incorporation to the Governor on March 29, James Huneker's article, "What is the matter with our National Academy?" appeared in *Harper's Weekly*.[64] It was a thoughtful piece and less incendiary than it could have been. He granted there had been changes for the better in the past five or six years, but nevertheless, the spring Annual was particularly "spiritless" and even harsher, of "dispiriting mediocrity." There was always 291, Alfred Stieglitz's gallery, "to slake your thirst for eccentricity." He did not see increasing the size of the exhibitions or the space as the solution. The core of the problem was "narrow and antiquated policies … that bar the young talent." The prime artistic curse was "academic privilege which transcends the will of the jury of selection." Huneker echoed the Pach interview: the problem was the older members who treated it like a private club. The solution, he advised, was to "weed out the superannuated men" and "inject fresh blood." While he found Alexander standing for progress, he still asked the question: what can be done? Huneker cleverly posits his argument in rhetorical fashion thus mitigating the accusatory tone. For example, he states that if the academy was "run by a clique of painter politicians," – a charge he was not prepared to make – he is certain Alexander would resign "if he thought there was the suspicion of truth in such a charge." Meanwhile the road to the future had reached a fork, with the incorporation of the National Academy Association on April 13 and Walt Kuhn's negotiations on April 19 for a

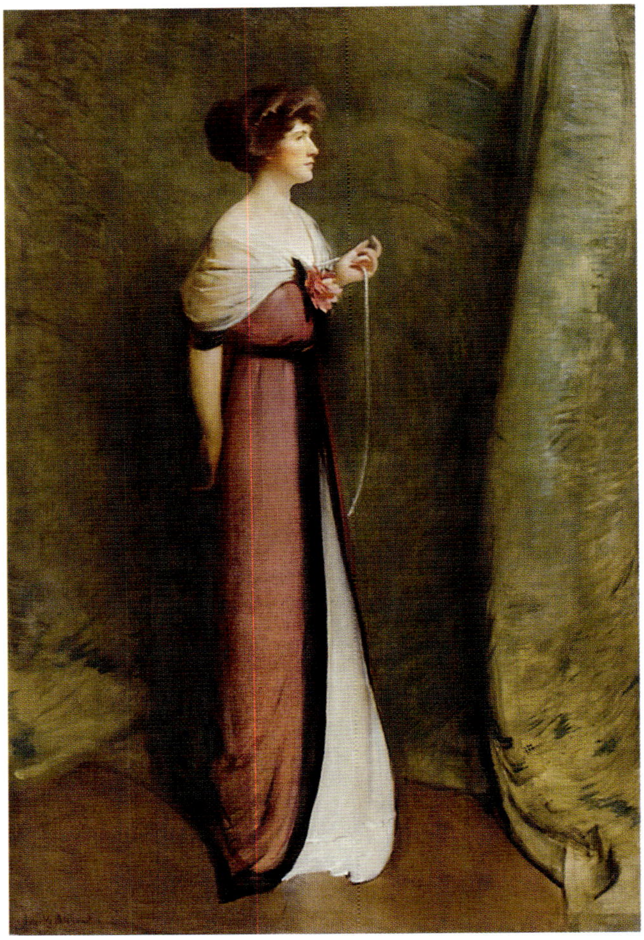

84
Portrait of Mrs. Ashton Potter, 1912, oil on canvas, 95 × 55 in. (241.3 × 139.7 cm.), Honorable Marilyn Logsdon Mennello and Michael Mennello collection, founders of the Mennello Museum of American Art, Orlando

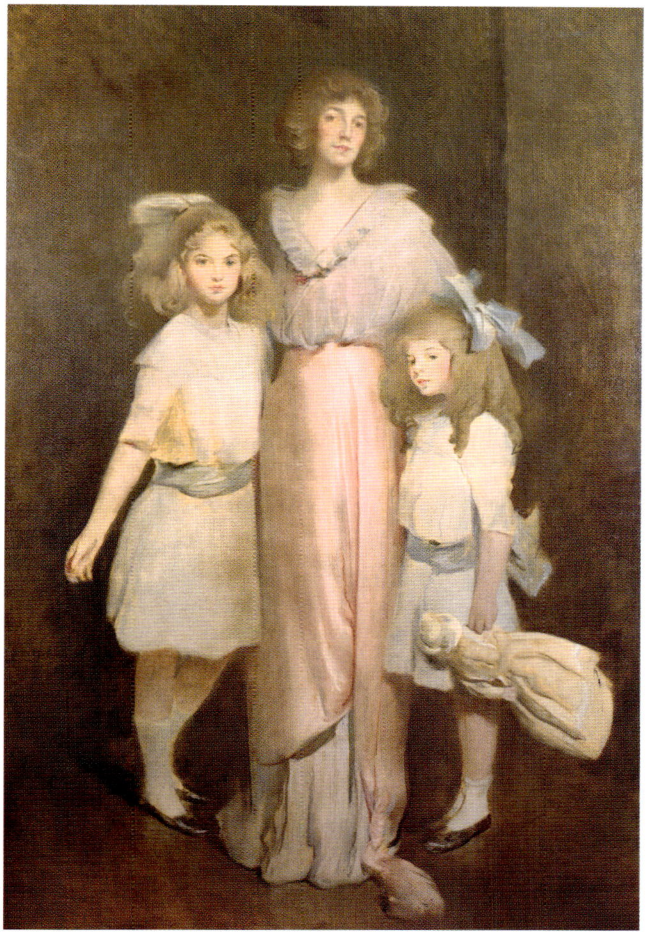

85
Portrait of Mrs. Florence Goodyear Wagner Daniels and Children, 1913, oil on canvas, 95 × 55 in. (241.3 × 139.7 cm.), Board of Governors of the Federal Reserve System, Washington, DC, gift of Ira Spanierman

lease for the 69th Street Armory that would be the site of the Armory Show.[65]

The campaign for a new and large fine arts building consumed most of Alexander's energy and was a frequent topic of his public statements. That and the state of his health both contributed to the slackening of his own work. Only one new picture, a portrait of Maude Adams, was shown before the summer of 1912. He had been working on it over the past twelve months or so and still did not consider it finished. Nevertheless he relented when Beatty pleaded with him to send it to the Carnegie International, which he did along with *Phyllis*.[66] Alexander was right. Bearing the brunt of much criticism, the Adams portrait was called "anemic and insipid."[67]

In late spring Alexander accepted a sizable and important portrait commission from the Frank H. Goodyear family of Buffalo.[68] At the time of Goodyear's death in 1907, his estate was valued at $18 million. He had been president of the Buffalo and Susquehanna Railroad, the Buffalo and Susquehanna Iron Co., and the New Orleans Great Northern Railroad as well as having extensive holdings in steamship, leather and banking industries. Mrs. Goodyear engaged the artist to paint her two surviving married daughters and a posthumous portrait of her husband (the whereabouts and details of the portrait of Mr. Goodyear are unknown). The portraits of the daughters are masterly, both as likenesses of women of substance as well as decorative figure paintings. Alexander gave much thought to the positioning of the figures and the attributes, in these, his two largest commissions ever completed.

In the portrait of Grace Goodyear Depew Potter (Figure 84), there is something familiar in the undulating line that invites comparison to *Isabella and the Pot of Basil*, the sensation of the 1897 Paris Salon. Both figures are arranged in profile facing right. Mrs. Potter's white dress with a rose-colored over-garment

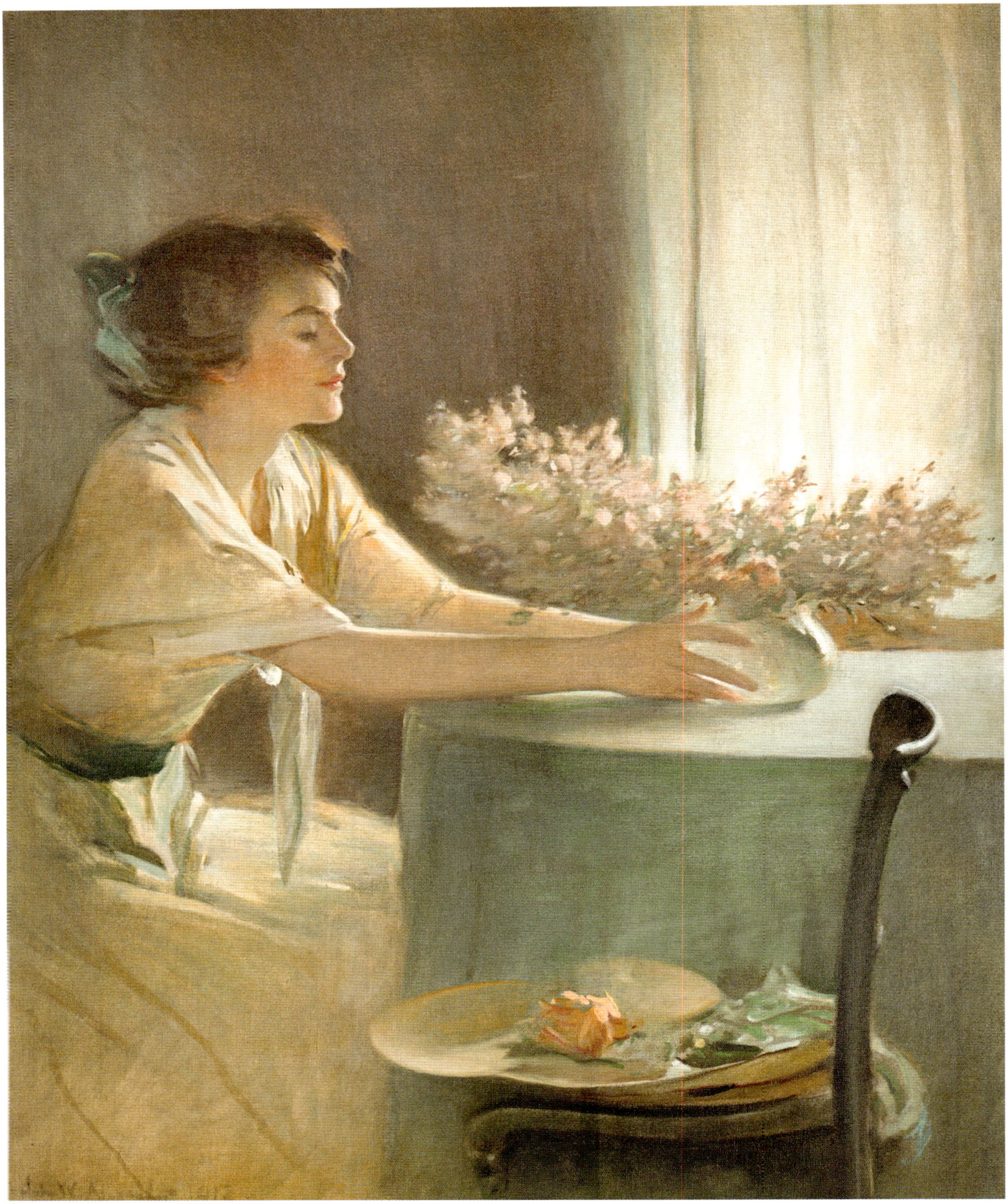

with black trim around the waist and falling to the hem echoes Isabella's costume. The two, however, could not be more different in sentiment. The Parisian picture, executed at the height of Alexander's avant-garde powers, was born of the secessionist and art nouveau milieu, while the later picture was a product of turn-of-the-century America with all the trappings of a modern American woman who happened to be extremely wealthy. Is there any doubt that the long undulating string of pearls around the neck, a token of her wealth, are genuine? Admirers called the painting "a simple and rhythmic work with a distinctive decorative note."[69] Naysayers called it "empty of human interest."[70]

The portrayal of Grace's sister, Florence Goodyear Wagner Daniels and her two daughters (Figure 85), is not just that of any mother. Three statuesque figures in white and off-white dresses accented by pastel colors are carefully arranged in a triangular, hieratic configuration. The two daughters are positioned as attendants to their mother, the central figure. The composition and the choice of colors exude a sense of innocence, worldliness, confidence, and forthrightness. Mrs. Daniels is a secular madonna presented as a signifier of the modern woman and the new American aristocracy. The portrait took some doing, as her mother expressed displeasure that "it is not at all like them," but she did like Grace's portrait.[71] She asked Alexander to make Florence's portrait "right," which he must have done, as it was subsequently exhibited. Having been reproduced in the *Evening Sun* with the headline, "Have You a Mind? Then Cultivate It if You Wish to Be Beautiful," it was taken for a symbol of the modern woman.[72]

Once again Onteora offered Alexander a summer respite, which he surely deserved. As the new owner of The Bushes, he added on a studio, one specifically designed to accommodate varying light effects.[73] Measuring 55 by 40 by 23 feet, "it had every kind of lighting that was ever known, so you could paint and shade things and get different effects." The summer of 1912 would be productive, with at least five new decorative pictures and a portrait of Dean John Ferguson Weir. With enhanced lighting capability he set about testing different effects. For example, the intensity of light was cooled in *A Meadow Flower* (Figure 86), warmed in *The Gossip* (Figure 87), and turned up in two paintings simply entitled *Full Length Study*. All in all, the lighting effects appear more natural than in *The Ring*, and light does not diffuse form to the same degree.

The subtlety of composition, using geometric shapes, that distinguished *The Ring* is manifest again in *A Meadow Flower* and *The Gossip*. In the former a stack of circular shapes – the hat, the circular tabletop and the flower arrangement – offset the verticals of the curtains, tablecloth, the chair back and a dangling end of the girl's shawl. Seated at a table with a curtained window behind,

86
A Meadow Flower, 1912,
oil on canvas, 50½ × 40½ in.
(128.3 × 102.9 cm.),
Joan and Bernard Carl,
Washington, DC

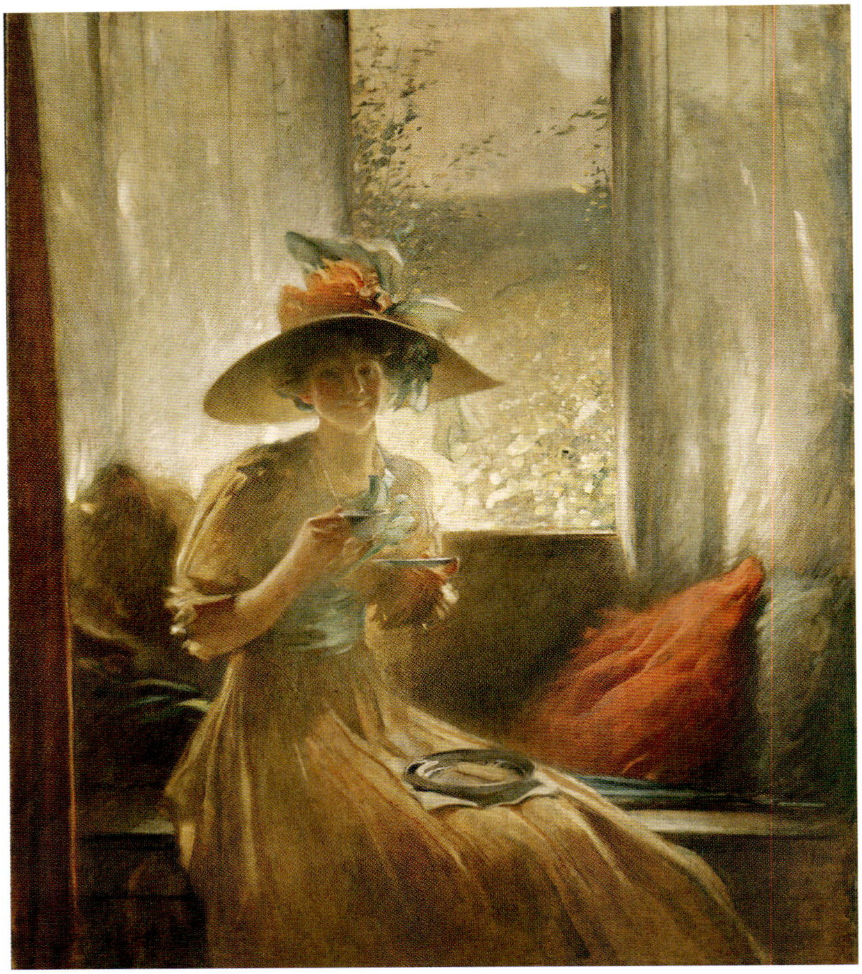

87
The Gossip, 1912, oil on canvas, 63 5/16 × 54 in. (160.8 × 137.2 cm.) Philadelphia Museum of Art, The Alex Simpson, Jr. Collection, 1928

the figure leans forward with outstretched arms similar to *Azalea* and *An Idle Moment*. Spatial depth is blocked by the juxtaposition of the darkened interior wall and the curtained window. In *The Gossip* a figure dressed for teatime, wearing a hat top-heavy with flowers and ribbons, is seated on a banquette before a window. The composition is a study in verticals (curtain and window frame) and horizontals (the edge of the seat, the back of the banquette and the horizon), again offset by the round shapes of the brim of the hat, the saucer and the plate. Unlike *A Meadow Flower*, where the curtain closes off the view, the narrative in *The Gossip* is extended through an open window on the right looking out onto a landscape.

A third painting known only through a black-and-white photograph shows a seated female seen from the back, hair piled up on her head.[74] The arrangement is an inspired orientation of point and counterpoint. The head is listing slightly to the left while the lower torso moves to the right. Tucks at the waist form folds in the skirt that undulate over the lap. While no observations can be made about color, there is a graceful rhythmic flow to the composition, worthy of a painting by Artemisia Gentileschi.

Two very large pictures are also thought to be products of this summer. Other than size, what they have in common, and what distinguishes them, is their adherence to the rules of perspective in the planning of an interior space occupied by a single figure. In *Full Length Study, Onteora* (unlocated), the size of the room runs deep, unlike the other *Full Length Study* (Joan and Bernard Carl, Washington, DC).[75] In the former, the interior space with a figure holding a vase of flowers is articulated vertically and horizontally with furniture and furnishings. *Full Length Study* differs in that it is organized according to one-point perspective, articulated by a sequence of vertical signposts: a standing figure in a long flowing skirt, the edge of the wall, floor-to-ceiling drapes, and the curtained window. In the former there are touches of color in the flowers. In the latter the palette is limited to shades of brown, red-brown and white. Following upon Alexander's mastery of large canvases in the Goodyear commissions, these two decorative pictures were even larger.

New to this body of work was the model, Belle Edson, the daughter of a local farmer from the neighboring valley. This was her second summer modeling for Alexander and she would continue to be his muse for two more.[76] She would be the last of his models and also the most conventional; adopting ordinary poses, sitting or standing, she lacked Juliette Very's originality, her ability to strike a pose and get into character, whether directed by the painter or of her own doing. Once Alexander returned to America, it took some time to find a model to replace Very – but "replace" is not the right word. One of Very's successors was Anne Raynor Ward who modeled for paintings that did invoke a certain edginess, such as *Study in Green and Black* and *The Green Gown*. But none of the American models had that certain *je ne sais quoi* between them and the artist, like his French model, Juliette Very.

In just over six weeks, from first discussion to sitting, Alexander took on a portrait commission for Yale University of John Ferguson Weir (the man who had hoped Alexander would succeed him) (Figure 88).[77] Weir and his wife traveled to Onteora for the sitting, registering as guests at the Bear and Fox Inn on July 25, 1912.[78] Those raising the funds for Alexander's $2,500 honorarium requested a large canvas with Weir posed in cap and gown in honor of his status as Founder and Director of the Art School.[79] Still adhering to the Munich style for his male portraits, the artist placed his subject in a dark interior. In this case the artist was circumscribed by the color requirements of academic dress, thus the choice of a brown gown which adds to the overall dark palette that is relieved by the white hood.[80] Again, following the precepts of the Munich canon, the strong and revealing light falls on the very fine face. The framed print in the upper right is not an arbitrary choice but an insightful one. As the founding Dean of Yale's School of Fine Arts, Weir earned a reputation as an art educator with an emphasis on the importance of the old masters. No doubt out of respect, Alexander chose to add Goya's print after Velázquez's portrait of Philip IV of Spain as a signifier for all that Weir stood for as a teacher. Compositionally, the framed print was the perfect foil to open up the otherwise shallow space. Alexander had done it before, for example, in *Azalea* and in the portrait of Henry G. Marquand.

Towards the end of 1912, Alexander was highly active, lecturing, exhibiting, making public statements, and presiding over three organizations as president. The new work for the season was all from the summer. *The Gossip* was his submission for the Corcoran Fourth Annual and *A Meadow Flower* for the Winter Annual of the National Academy of Design, both in December. The portrait of Mrs. Potter was featured at the National Association of Portrait Painters exhibit at Knoedler & Co. in February 1913. As President, he presided over the 1912 annual Christmas pageant sponsored by the MacDowell Club, which, it was said, "far exceeded in beauty and details and gorgeousness of decorative effects any that had been presented before."[81] At the gala, the conventionally dressed mixed with poseurs costumed as gigantic beefeaters, Celtic barbarians, Canterbury pilgrims, Druid priestesses, Don Quixote, King Arthur, Cleopatra, and figures from paintings by Veronese, Watteau, and Gainsborough. "The real artistic thrill" was Alexander's "living picture tableau, 'The Star of Bethlehem' … posed and draped with masterly skill, the rich deep colors brilliantly lighted."[82]

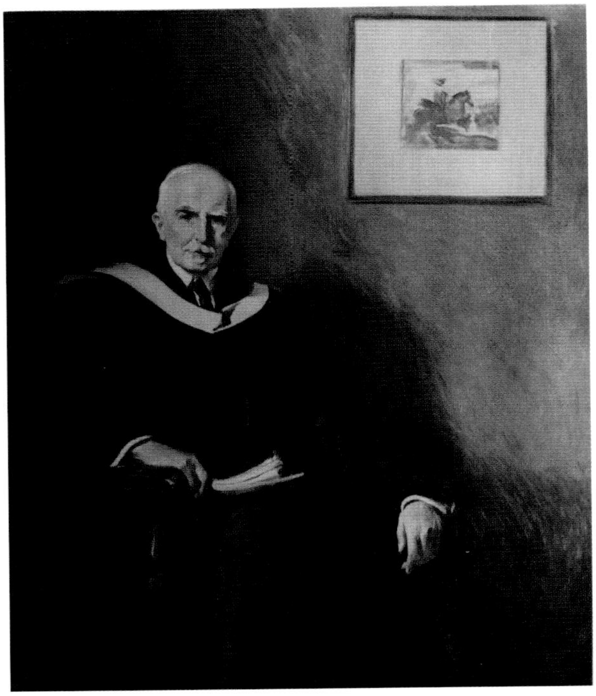

88
Portrait of John Ferguson Weir, 1913, oil on canvas, 64½ × 54 in. (163.8 × 137.2 cm.) Yale University Art Gallery, 1913.681

Looming over everything else in the last few months of the year was news of the Armory Show. During the MacDowell holiday festivities, how could the conversation among artists not have veered to speculation about the invitations from the AAPS to exhibit at the International Exhibition of Modern Art? Invitations were issued around the first of December and loans began to be negotiated about the twelfth, at which time a publicity campaign was launched.[83] While the press was "crazy for stuff" to print, other newsworthy events included the MacDowell Club gala. The conciliatory Alexander used the occasion of the gala to publicly frame the debate and attempt to ease friction between the academicians and the revolutionaries by invoking Edward MacDowell's dream:

> that somewhere in this big city a number of people could be brought together, all having the true artistic spirit but who might have sought different methods of expression, and that these people should lose, by this companionship, the narrowness that comes from too close an adherence to a single line of thought.[84]

Alexander was not speaking in a vacuum when he invoked MacDowell. Rather, he was acting as a strategic and magnanimous leader. On the other hand, however, Alfred Stieglitz was both firing a salvo and encouraging the public not to miss the Armory Show: "The dry bones of a dead art are rattling as they 'never rattled before.' Yet the Chase School and Henri Academy and the Alexander Manufactory will go on doing business at the old stands. Sometimes the dead don't know they're dead."[85]

Once the Armory Show opened, just about everyone formed an opinion about modern art, egged on by the press. Art societies took sides but the President of the National Academy was a model of discretion. It remains to be confirmed whether Alexander visited the show, but if he did, he would have been reintroduced to his past. He would have faced reminders of the origins of his coarse-weave canvas adopted after meeting the Nabis in Le Pouldu, reminded of Juliette Very (who could very well have been the model for the seven drawings exhibited by Rodin) and seeing for the first time the Cézanne landscape he would approve for purchase in his capacity as a trustee for the Metropolitan Museum. Because of his position, but just as likely because of his character, he refrained from incendiary or accusatory statements. Conveniently or not, he was scheduled to be in Chicago during most of the Armory Show to deliver the annual Scammon Lecture series. Discussions had been ongoing with William M. R. French, Director of the Art Institute of Chicago, since the previous October.[86] Simultaneously, the Art Institute mounted an exhibition of twenty-eight of his pictures. Alexander was in Chicago from at least February 20 through March 9, and possibly longer.[87]

The Scammon Lectures were intended for the students of the School of the Art Institute of Chicago though museum members were also welcomed. Thus, the themes of the lectures were appropriately designed for art students. Alexander followed Edwin Howland Blashfield, who the previous year spoke on "The Classic Point of View." Alexander's theme was "Painting as a Profession," with four lectures addressed "To the Student," "To the Artist," "To the Critic," and "To the Public."[88] In his remarks he counseled students to take their profession seriously, learn technique and learn from the old masters. With the modern exhibit in New York perhaps in mind, he advised, "the artist must know the rules before he can break them."[89]

Alexander's one-man exhibition at the Art Institute was interesting for both what was included and what was not. It was his first one-man show since the Albright Gallery in December 1909. Nine of the 28 pictures were the same as in the 1909 exhibit; there were no portraits of men. Based on the list of identifiable pictures, the most current was *A Meadow Flower* and the oldest, *Brittany Study*. With just a handful of pictures from the 1890s, the selection was dominated by pictures made since his permanent return to America. One picture titled "Unfinished" teases the question, why show it? There was one portrait of a lady who was not identified by title but all Chicagoans knew her to be Mrs. Clarence Webster. She is leaning forward in a chair with an abundance of personality, beauty, youthfulness, and brains, the same attributes that characterized Alexander's depiction of his own wife. Webster's husband was a distinguished citizen of Chicago, a gynecologist at Rush Medical College (affiliated with the University of Chicago) and with other affiliations with local hospitals. The Webster portrait (1905), and others including the *Portrait of Mrs. John White Alexander* (Los Angeles County Museum of Art), *A Meadow Flower*, *Other Days*, *The Gossip*, *Memories*, and *A Butterfly*, were among the many "transcendent beauties" extolled by the press.[90] But one observer could not avoid the fractionalization going on in New York, contrasting the "dream world" of Alexander's paintings with the "vigor of executive force which the painter exhibits in his dealings with the Academy, the Federation, the Institute of Arts and Letters and other working organizations."[91]

Alexander was a gentleman to the "finger tips: restrained, diplomatic."[92] It was not in him to make enemies. When it came to the shocking works on view on 69th Street that would upend the course of American art, he tended to express his opinion in deeds rather than in words. If Alexander was persuaded that the Armory Show would "begin a new epoch," as Walt Kuhn predicted, he rarely admitted to it at the time.[93] In his view, progress lay in a permanent facility large enough to accommodate all who wished to exhibit. The fact is that the 69th Street Armory building was a leased facility for one exhibition. The need did not go away. Two indicators of Alexander's so-called "executive force" in following through on his convictions occurred immediately upon his return from Chicago. A new plan was now advanced, that had been the result of daily negotiations since probably the MacDowell Club gala and continuing while he was in Chicago.[94] The latest plan was for the National Academy Association to purchase land adjacent to the Fine Arts Building at 215 West 57th Street.[95] In going public it was also announced that the art collector George A. Hearn had pledged his "zealous interest." The extent of Mr. Hearn's pledge in a January 28 letter to Alexander – $10,000 toward a total of $200,000 – was not part of the announcement, but an appeal to the general public was.[96]

Mockery of The Armory Show took many forms: cartoons, editorials, articles, and actual burlesques. The most hilarious of the "mock" events that clearly made the point by example was an exhibit at the so-called Academy of Misapplied Art hastily organized by the Society of American Fakirs. To add to the irony the event was hosted at the newly opened Lighthouse of the New York Association for the Blind. Opening on March 22 was an "exclusive exhibit of works of the most distinguished American artists of the cubistic, post-impressionist, futuristic, neurotic, psychopathic and paretic schools."[97] A majority of these so-called "distinguished artists" were from the establishment, who on an annual basis found themselves the subject of parody by the Fakirs, but this time they joined ranks with the students. The aim was to "outcube the cubists and put the futurists in the middle of the past tense." The display included atypical cubist-style canvases by Alexander (*Horse Drinking from a Tin Pail*), Kenyon Cox (*An Old Man with a Tooth Pick*), and Edwin Blashfield (*A Milking-Stool in the Gloaming*). Other participants included Karl Bitter, George Bellows and Cass Gilbert. A jury of award was made up of the local policeman and the janitors and blind residents of the Lighthouse![98] The serious reason for the Association's lending their facility was that it benefited from the 25 cent admission fee which would be applied to reducing its sizable debt.[99]

Alexander's obligation as a juror for the Carnegie International required him to be in Pittsburgh on April 3, thus removing him from the ongoing ruckus surrounding the Armory Show. The International had been the place to see the most current examples of European art, having earned a reputation as the premier annual venue in the country – until, that is, it outlived any sense of currency. Its situation was not dissimilar to the National Academy of Design. With Beatty still at the helm, what had been novel in 1896 was no longer so in 1913. His tastes had not changed with the times, still favoring the work of artists who "sought truth through the close observation of nature" (not in any Ruskinian way) and the avoidance of "violence or passion or even obvious unpleasantness."[100] Over the years there were exceptions, such as Winslow Homer's *The Wreck* in 1896, John Sloan's *The Coffee Line* in 1905, Stanhope A. Forbes' *The Village Industry* in 1909, and George Bellows' *The Circus* in 1913, for which he was awarded an honorable mention. When works by Matisse were shipped from abroad in 1912 they were put in storage instead of being displayed.[101] In 1913, the first, second and third medals were awarded to Glyn Philpot (British), Henri Martin (French) and Gifford Beal (American), respectively. Other than Bellows, the most avant-garde artist to receive an honorable mention was Arthur B. Davies. One reviewer, Anna Seaton-Schmidt, observed, that overall, "True, they do not possess the excitement and curious effects produced by a Nude Descending the Stairs," but they did meet the test of "solidly good workmanship which the Duchamp painting did not."[102]

As for the Carnegie International, according to Vicky A. Clark, "as concepts and styles in paintings diverged more radically … new aesthetic avenues were conspicuous by their absence."[103] Where the system failed was with the foreign advisors. After 1900 those who were advisors were the new men of the 1880s and 1890s who were no longer at the cutting edge, men such as B. J. Blommers in the Hague, John Lavery in London, Franz von Stuck in Munich, and Edmond Aman-Jean in Paris. They tended to ignore the more radical artists in the independent and secessionist exhibitions. Beatty's expectations may have had something to do with it. Critics began leveling the same criticism against the Carnegie International as they had against the National Academy. For example, in 1911 a critic complained that "nothing new is expressed save in a few canvases."[104] Christian Brinton concluded in an article in 1913, "During the seventeen years which have elapsed since the inauguration of this splendid series of exhibitions there have been no surprises, no brusque departures from precedent, and no signs of retrogression."[105] When the jurors convened on the evening of April 3, 1913 over a game of pool, the conversation turned to the Armory Show. Alexander was not yet "ready to say that cubism has come to stay or will revolutionize art."[106] On the other hand, he predicted that the exhibit would "wake people up" and that "American art will be the better for their influences if the influence is not allowed to go too deep."[107] He would not live to see how deep the influence would go.

In an attempt to avoid the impending reaction to the status quo, the National Academy Association did what the reticent National Academy of

Design could not or would not do. It took steps to refresh its leadership, mixing new blood with those who assumed a sense of entitlement. On May 6 the trustees amended their charter to enlarge their number by 17, making way for fresh blood and fresh ideas, while accepting non-artists who had an interest in the arts.[108] This strengthened the Association's position as they set about matching the pledge from Mr. Hearn. A provision of the charter that remained unchanged was for one representative each from the Metropolitan Museum, the New York Public Library and the Chamber of Commerce. As President of the National Academy of Design. Alexander's position was assured as he spearheaded the strategy by the National Academy Association to secure a new building.

In the months leading up to the summer break, Alexander had several portrait commissions to tend to, one more demanding than the other. Before leaving for Chicago he committed to doing the portrait of William T. Manning, Rector of Trinity Church, a leading ecclesiastic who would become the Episcopal bishop of New York. Progress, however, languished and at the time of the artist's death the portrait was not finished.[109] Demanding his immediate attention after returning from Chicago was a portrait of President Slocum of Colorado College.[110] The college offered to pay Alexander's expenses to travel to Colorado Springs but instead Slocum came to New York for a sitting during Easter vacation. The understanding was that the portrait be completed by the third week of May. A commission for a less demanding client – but of an equally important personage – was for the Stevens Institute of Hoboken, New Jersey, one of the first technical schools in the country. Their commissioning of the portrait of President Alexander C. Humphreys was announced in February with the work continuing until the end of the year.[111] Humphreys was renowned for his collection of American art, which was exhibited in February 1914 at the Carnegie Institute in Pittsburgh at the time his portrait was on view in New York.[112]

There were signs that Alexander was slowing down during the summer break of 1913 in Onteora, with just two new significant canvases at his easel for the upcoming exhibition season. Both *June* (Figure 89) and *Her Birthday* (Figure 90) were continuations of the "sunlight" series that featured light filtering through a thinly veiled window. Belle Edson was the model. In *June*, she stands beside a table holding a glass vase with a single peony, perhaps a seasonable flower in the northern climes of the Catskills. Another vase rests on the table with a selection of peonies and probably azaleas. In *Her Birthday*, Alexander challenges himself to master space in a canvas that was even larger, at 80 by 64 inches, than the two from the previous summer. Instead of the three figures

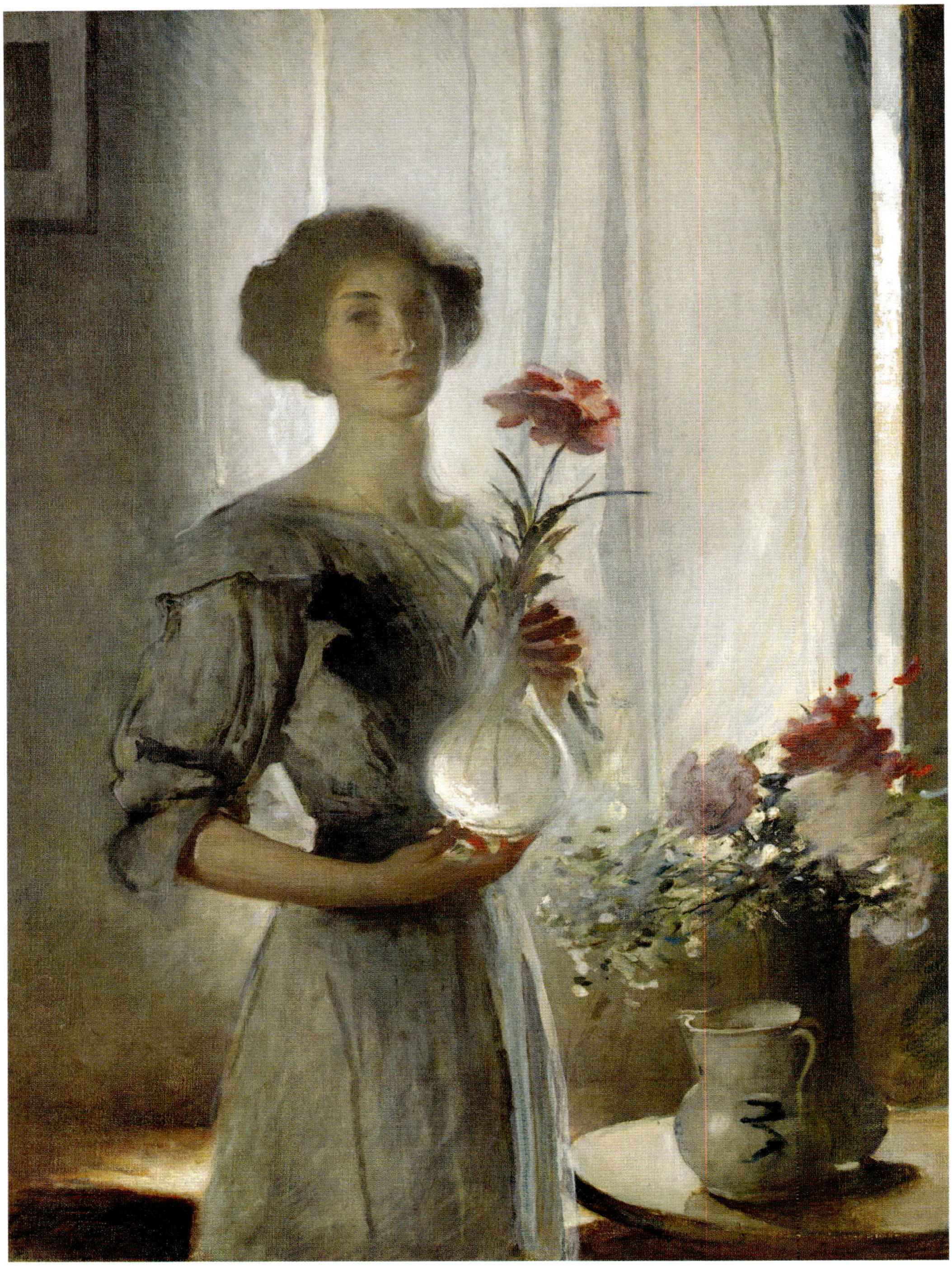

89 *June*, 1913, oil on canvas, 48¼ × 36 in. (124.3 × 91.6 cm.), Smithsonian American Art Museum, gift of William Alexander, 1916.10.1

comingling through gesture or body movement, they serve as three separate vignettes, each in their own world. What is intriguing about this canvas is that Belle Edson is the model for all three vignettes.[113] The lower right corner of the painting was unfinished despite the fact that it was signed, dated and exhibited. The picture was considered "not worthy" of the artist when it was shown in the Twenty-Sixth Annual Exhibition at the Art Institute of Chicago. One astute observer did not miss the singularity of the vignettes, noting that the upper right corner, with a woman standing behind a table laden with an assortment of vases filled with flowers, could stand alone as a complete picture.[114] The same could be said of the other two figures.

Aside from painting, the summer of 1913 was marked by two significant developments. Now at the pinnacle of his career, Alexander was invited by John Trask to organize a selection of his work for a dedicated gallery at the upcoming Panama-Pacific Exposition.[115] The exposition would be an opportunity for an international audience to see what critics Sadachichi Hartmann and Charles Caffin were writing about. Surveying Alexander's artistic achievements, Hartmann elaborated upon his distinction between portraiture and decorative painting, preferring the originality of the latter: "he uses his sitters as objective facts, he sees them as curious and unusual shapes and emphasizes every beauty of form that will help him toward some new and charming linear interpretation."[116] Less than a year later, in a second insightful article, Charles Caffin's observations were not materially different from Hartmann's: "When he can choose his model and dress and place her in accordance with the composition of line, form, and color that he has imagined, then his gift of inventiveness is displayed in all its originality and spontaneousness."[117]

A second development in the summer of 1913 was the breaking of a story that hinted at a resolution of the protracted Harrisburg commission. Every two years the question of appropriation and signing of a contract had been reconsidered. Now on September 12, 1913, it was reported that the Harrisburg Capitol Public Grounds and Buildings Commission was ready to meet with Alexander.[118] The end to this protracted stalemate would only come with the death of the artist.

Low productivity continued into the fall and early winter of 1913. In a letter to Harrison Morris of March 16, 1914, Alexander wrote, "I have been shut up practically all this winter … am beginning to feel quite like myself again."[119] By this it could be inferred that he had been shut up since his return from Onteora in early October. Collectively, official duties for the Academy, public speaking, social activities, and his own work suggests that the hardy "all's well" was an illusion, one perpetuated with finesse. He ended 1913 by posing two tableaux, one in a private home and one for the MacDowell Club, and began the new year socializing at the premiere for Maude Adams's *Leonora*, a performance for which he had assisted.[120]

In the beginning of 1914 the pacing of his activity and productivity implies that while maintaining the appearance of being fully engaged he allowed for appropriate pauses in between. He had to contend with an insurrection from academy members, in part of his own making. Some members who had been accepted for the Winter Annual did not have their work hung because of limitations of space. Alexander sympathized, labeling the situation "atrocious," though he was not one who suffered, as he had not exhibited at the Academy at all in 1913. With President Alexander's encouragement, it was announced that an alternative location would be found to mount the excluded pictures.[121] Two weeks later, in spite of his assurances to Morris that he was feeling normal, he cancelled a trip to Pittsburgh to serve on the jury of award for the Carnegie International which this year included the new men, Robert Henri and Elmer Schofield.[122] In the months that followed, Alexander found time to instruct elementary school children and had lectured five times by the end of March. He was represented in at least twelve exhibitions before the summer, although they included only three new works between them.

One year after the Armory Show, Robert Underwood Johnson, successor to Richard Watson Gilder as editor of *The Century*, decided to devote the April 1914 edition to the theme of "The Transitional Age in Art." He commissioned five essays by Alexander, Edwin Blashfield, Ernest Blumenschein, Walter Pach, and Jay and Gove Hambidge to "consider dispassionately all of these phases ... from the conservative to the radical."[123] Alexander's essay was first with "Is Our Art Distinctly American?" He took the high ground, choosing not to add to the mass of "purposeless and superfluous criticism." Instead he gave an overview of art in the United States and how it came to be distinctly American. After years of sporadic efforts in the young nation, mostly imitative of foreign influences, the National Academy of Design was founded and became the stalwart of American art. Somewhat apologetically, he put the Academy's current crisis in human terms, citing the difficulty of working by committee to reach a "consensus of opinion of a jury of thirty men of widely differing tastes and ideals."[124] Nevertheless, he emphasized that the Academy must continue to recruit so-called liberals. He compared the organizers of the Armory Show with those of the Society of American Artists. Both were trying to "find an audience for their new message." He reminded the reader that Sargent in his

90
Her Birthday, 1913,
oil on canvas, 80 × 64 in.
(203.2 × 162.6 cm.),
unknown private collection.
Photograph, J0019560,
© Peter A. Juley & Son
Collection, Smithsonian
American Art Museum

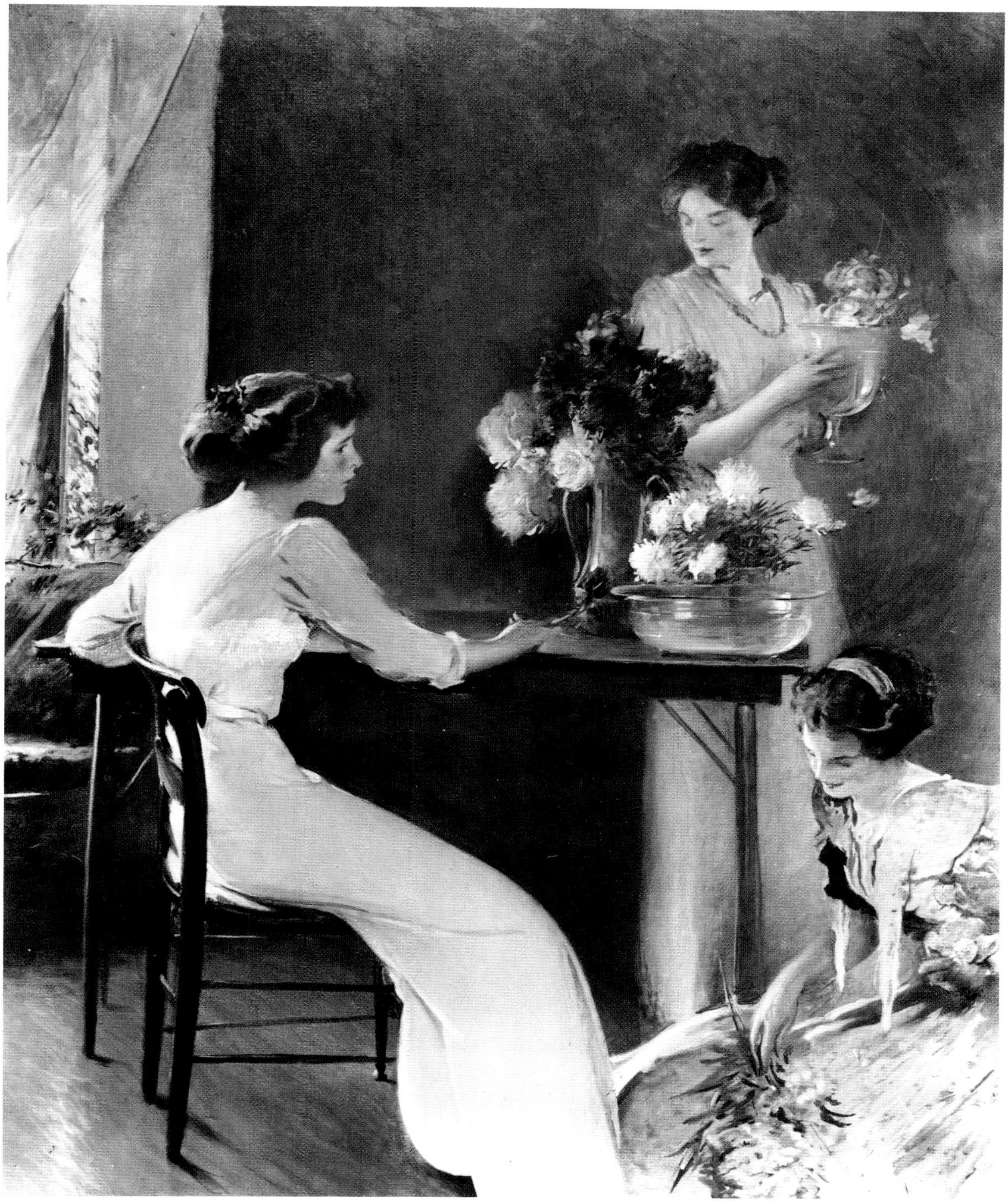

day "excited the same acrimonious discussion" as the Cubists. He predicted, "Some of us may live to see the day when the much discussed 'Nude Descending the Staircase' may come to be regarded by those who keep really up to date as too commonplace for serious artistic consideration." He closed with a paragraph on the lack of public appreciation of art made in America, citing the neglect of Whistler as an example. Times had changed since the 1880s when the portrait of his mother, a great modern work, was exhibited in New York and no buyer stepped forward to purchase it; today, he said, it could easily find a purchaser. In its way, the Armory Show went a long way toward demonstrating the "substantial beginning of art that is national." By this Alexander was making a distinction between a style that was distinctly American and an ideology that was nationalistic. Alexander was not one for ideology.

The essays followed one after the other in deliberate sequence. Writing on "The Painting of Today," Blashfield, unlike Alexander, barely contained his disdain. Although a classicist, he allowed that the new movement "has potential for good in its concentration upon color and light."[125] Eschewing intolerance of the past, he argued, there were "no reasons why 'the vigor and freshness acquired should not be applied to correct proportion, correct forms, and correct values.'" Next came an essay by Blumenschein on "The Painting of Tomorrow."[126] He advised patience for the new and considered the difference "a very healthy affair, the influence of which will work for good in the art of to-morrow." He made a distinction between the post-impressionists who painted in a "simpler" style creating "large flat masses of color," and the academic technique of "subdividing a hundred colors to produce one large tone." He declared that, "A new truth had been added to our knowledge, and *one which will be welded into all future art.*"

Then followed two essays on behalf of the modernists. Pach put forth "The Point of View of the 'Moderns,'" attributing the beginning of the present era to Cézanne, the "greatest master of modern times."[127] He used the phrase "supremacy over realism" to trace the diminution of realism. He began with the classicists versus the romantics, advanced to the realists, impressionists, and then to Cézanne. The latter was far beyond his time in the diminution of form over realism. For him a picture does not have to look like nature. The evolution of cubism was indebted to "the composition of the volumes" in the work of Cézanne. Pach made his point by illustrating Joseph Stella's *Battle of Lights, Coney Island* (Yale University Art Gallery). Painted after the Armory Show, the caption read, "Had he merely represented the physical appearance of the American fiesta, he believed he could not have given the rhythm of the scene, which transforms the chaos of the night, the lights, the strange buildings, and the surging crowd, into the order, the design, and the color of art."

The final essay, by Jay and Gove Hambidge, made a case for geometry in art.[128] According to their view, the circle and square were fundamental to art as far back as the pre-Christian era. Egyptian sculpture was given as an example, where the parts of the body are cut "in flat planes." From the late Middle Ages to the High Renaissance, during the time of Cimabue, Giotto, Raphael, and Durer, these artists blocked out their forms in geometrical shapes. The ancient Greek philosopher and mathematician Plato reduced all things ultimately to ideal geometric forms. Bringing their argument to the present, the Hambidges posited that "Plato is reborn in Picasso."

By publishing these essays in a magazine with a national circulation the debate was moved outside New York, reaching a popular audience. Articles in local newspapers such as the *Youngstown Telegram* drew attention to the special issue and encouraged the public to read it.[129] The *Cleveland Leader* was somewhat sensational with its headline, "Shock your Grandmother School of Art," noting the paradoxes and contradictions represented in the collection of essays.[130]

The summer routine in Onteora did not begin as usual. Alexander's wife, accompanied by her mother and a suffragist friend, Ruth Noyes, went up earlier than usual and registered at the inn.[131] It is not certain when Alexander joined them, nor how long Bess stayed at the inn. Perhaps he required solitary rest at The Bushes. Once in Onteora Alexander managed to complete two portraits, one being of Julia Gilbert (unlocated). As soft light falls on the upper torso, Miss Gilbert stands facing left holding up a single peony as if it is a prayer offering. In a note to the painter, the father of the sitter, the architect Cass Gilbert, praised the three-quarter-length portrait, saying, "It has all the charm of the refined and beautiful nature which you have so fully understood and so delightfully suggested … No one can do this sort of thing as well as you."[132]

This would also be the summer of what was most likely Alexander's final commission, a posthumous portrait of Lieutenant General John M. Schofield ordered by the widow.[133] Schofield was a graduate of West Point and a war veteran, having served in the Civil War and afterwards assuming commands on the frontier, and in Missouri and Ohio, and having achieved the rank of Commanding General of the United States Army by the time of his retirement. In full dress uniform, he wears four decorations: the first on the left is unidentified; the others from the left appear to be the Society of Cincinnati, the Medal of Honor, and the Loyal Legion.[134] He is silhouetted against a blue sky and pinkish clouds. The probability that the portrait was started, if not completed, in Onteora, is hinted at by the sky in the background, which is very similar to two Onteora pictures: the portrait of Geraldine Russell (Metropolitan Museum of Art) and *Memories*.

Sometime after Alexander's return to the city, there were discussions about the commissioning of two portraits of U.S. President Woodrow Wilson.[135] The fact of his illness came up in a letter arranging how and when Wilson would sit for his portrait.[136] He admitted to the President that he had been ill, but was now improved, but there is no telling how long he had been ill, nor how sustainable would be the recovery. At the end of October, in another sign of slowing down, Alexander resigned from the Pittsburgh Arts Commission.

Nevertheless, Alexander continued to be busy supporting other causes of importance to him. There was reason for renewed optimism about a building site for the National Academy with the news that the Parks Department would finally abandon Central Park.[137] Though America had not yet entered the Great War there was a war effort underway on the part of American artists for their French colleagues who were at the front. Alexander took part in sales exhibitions to raise funds for the so-called French soldier artists. For a statewide campaign in support of the suffragette movement for which Bess was chairman of the art committee, he allowed his painting *The Mother* to be used as a poster.

In all of the normal frenzy, Alexander kept himself busy with projects and issues that were less physically taxing. Using the bully pulpit of the printed word for his cause célèbre, in yet another article Alexander answers the question "What is the Matter with American Art?" Pointing his finger at the American public, he argues for the need for a building that would be the showcase of an American Salon. There is "nowhere else such a lack of real intelligent appreciation, although Americans talk a great deal about art."[138] Meanwhile, he remained a constant collaborator in the productions of Maude Adams, his vision evident through the handiwork of his wife in the costumes, and in his design for stage sets for *The Ladies' Shakespeare* that opened in Philadelphia on January 18, 1915. He continued to send works to exhibitions, but now it was exclusively previously exhibited work. The Panama-Pacific Exposition opened without a room dedicated to his work, though there had been talk of one as recently as early January. Unable to organize a group of pictures due to his illness, he was represented instead by a single picture, *Phyllis*.[139]

With Alexander's work and ability to exhibit sidelined by illness, Bess felt a curious yet prescient need to enter into a business venture. She became the proprietor of an art gallery, partnering with Elizabeth B. Averell, a niece to the wealthy widow of Edward H. Harriman who took considerable interest in her niece's gallery.[140] The gallery was named Arden, a reference to the Harriman estate near Newburgh, N.Y. Meanwhile, in an exchange of letters in mid February, Bess informed John Wesley Beatty of her husband's recovery.[141] Beatty swiftly countered with "sincere affection" and an invitation which was not accepted, for Alexander to join him for a rest in South Carolina.[142] If, in fact, he was convinced of his recovery, why on March 10, at a meeting of the board of the National Academy of Design, did he announce that he would not be a candidate for President? Having made that decision, he made it clear to the public in a lengthy article that he had not given up on the campaign for a new building and site.[143] He also confessed his desire to return to painting, which he said he had not done for about a year. Optimism for the future amidst adversity had always been the mark of this man. He was relieving himself of responsibilities to others so that he could return to painting full-time. But was he fooling himself, knowing that for the past five years any exertion prostrated him and he spent the larger part of the day on the sofa.[144]

Alexander's final days were recorded in poignant letters from Bess and John to the Allens, the Pittsburgh couple who had taken him in as a youth. On May 22 John wrote to Mrs. Allen that he and Bess had a "strenuous winter" compounded by the fact that her critically ill father had been with them for over three months and that the house was "full of nurses, and confusion and anxiety." Though he had been near death, his father-in-law recovered. As for himself, "Taking altogether I am doing well. Resigning from the presidency of the Academy was 'a very great relief.'"[145] He wrote to Mr. Allen on the same day reassuring him not to worry in the least and that he was otherwise content. The very next day Bess wrote to Mrs. Allen of symptoms remarkably similar to when Alexander took ill in the home of Robert Louis Stevenson in 1886. "An hour or two after John had written to you yesterday he was taken very ill."[146] The family was sitting together in the library when he said he felt "queer & then he fell over & was unconscious for about three quarters of an hour." It was "evidently a convulsion produced by some interference with his circulation," a condition which today would be called hardening of the arteries.

Several days later in a letter to Mrs. Allen, Bess reported that John was very weak but getting the best care.[147] "The situation with him is puzzling to the doctors who cannot account for his seizure." She commiserated with Mrs. Allen that they both were burdened with family illnesses and financial troubles, hers over the last ten years (thus the explanation for her starting a business). In her post-mortem summation, at once clearheaded and reflective, Bess wrote the Allens of how the end came.[148] After the convulsion on May 22, Dr. Pearce Bailey, a specialist in neurology, was consulted, who was inclined to treat his patient somewhat leniently because his general condition was good. He was sent home under the care of a nurse. A week later on May 30 the patient seemed much improved and James, their son, now a professor of mathematics at Princeton, left early to prepare for classes. The next day Bess was so confident that she allowed the nurse to go out for the afternoon. However after dinner Bess noticed a strange expression. Her husband could not respond to her questions. Taking her hand in his he pressed it and then lost consciousness followed by another convulsion. The doctor was called and took his pulse which was "very remarkedly good" so they thought he would revive. An attack came about 7.45 and he died at 9.20. Bess reflected, "I hope he did not suffer. He looked, where he lay on his bed, just as if he was peacefully sleeping & I cannot bring myself to feel I could call him back even if that were possible because he suffered so." For a married couple who represented a harmonious complement of two, Bess's words were heartbreaking: "He filled every interest in my life & the world is so empty without him for me that I would gladly follow him if it were not for my boy." She added in a postscript that she was thinking of the near future, writing that she would have liked to sell the house but "times are too bad."

7

FROM THOSE WHO LOVED HIM, TRIBUTES

WITH ALEXANDER'S DEATH came a flood of tributes from admirers, addressed to his widow. Remembrances, both warmly expressed and even emotional, that captured his essential character were sent from long-standing friends to the most recent of acquaintances, from artists and representatives of art organizations, and from a former employer. Collectively, they are testimonials to a "useful citizen" and his place, as Harrison S. Morris put it, in the "Valhalla of our American genius". Beginning with a verse by Alice Cary quoted by Howard Giler, a selection follows, in order of date.[1]

Whatever men say in blindness
And spite of the fancies of youth –
There's nothing so kingly as kindness
And nothing so royal as truth.
Howard Giler, undated[2]

June 1

He has left a name that will live in the history of his country's art.
Charles Dana Gibson (undated but probably June 1)

The world of art has sustained a great loss.
George Wharton Edwards, Greenwich Society of Artists

Am profoundly impressed with passing of the earliest nobliest last of my school board friend.
Edward Elisha Phelps

On earth he lived; He did not merely stay.
Harry Watrous, quoting Elihu Vedder

For he is a world possession – he was so delightful in his personality, so free from eccentricities of genius.
Edward A. Woods

June 2

He has been to everyone radiant with energy which while it consumed him – shed light and helpfulness on everyone about him.
Robert Abbe

A kind of keystone to our arch. He worked too hard almost, in helping every good cause.
Edwin Blashfield

Altruistic devotion to the cause of Art was arduous unremitting and of large result.
Robert Underwood Johnson, American Academy of Arts and Letters

He was the soul of chivalry, the essence of nobleheartedness … you will be uplifted always by the radiance of his pure fame and the place he will hold in the Valhalla of our American genius.
Harrison S. Morris

J. Alden Weir (postmarked from the Panama-Pacific Exposition, San Francisco) informed the widow that the international jury of award for painting authorized placement of a memorial wreath.

June 3

… great admiration for his achievements as an artist, and … sincere affection for him as a man.
Edwin Baldwin, for The Century Association

Art has been deprived of one of her most radiant champions and his place made vacant cannot be filled.
Earl Stetson Crawford, for the National Association of Portrait Painters

What a lovable & manly character, & influence for good, he has bequeathed to his friends & fellow artists.
J. Henry Harper

My heart is too full for words.
William Laurel Harris

Mr. Alexander was one of our great men. His life was devoted to the improvement of his fellowman particularly in the elevation of the art of paintings … Through his great talent and leadership American art has risen to a much higher level.
Mr. and Mrs. Adolph Lewisohn

His place in our country as its most distinguished painter can not be filled and the academy lost its "greatest President."
Irving Wiles

June 4

We have all followed his brilliant career with the highest admiration. There was a quality of gentleness in his nature which endeared him to all who knew him.
S. H. Church, President, Carnegie Institute

I have again and again admired his public spirit and devotion to duty, even when by reason of health conditions duty must have been difficult to perform.
Robert W. De Forest

His noble life and character … he was in <u>many</u> ways an honor to his profession and this is widely recognized in the hearts of all who knew him.
John F. Weir

June 5

Our relations were of the character to bring out the tenderness of his heart for those in distress.
William Bailey Faxon, Artists' Aid Society

June 8

… exceptional rare spirit of the man.
Ruth McEnery Stuart

June 14

I never saw the church so largely filled with men, nor with sincerer evidences of the deepest sorrow … embodiment of life and spiritual vigor.
Gerry S. Grant, The Church of the Ascension

June 26

I can scarcely believe my eyes or realize that it can be.
Charles Deering (from Sitges, Spain)

July 6

[The trustees] appreciated not only his great talent and all his efforts to increase Art in our country, the many encouragements he gave to young artists, but also his great kindness to all who came in contact with him.
McDougall Hawkes, President, Museum of French Art

July 15

We could ill spare in this world such men as your husband and mine, gentle leaders in their art and working so for the good of it.
Augusta Saint-Gaudens

November 30

He had a width of interest which gave him an unusual capacity for leadership and a sympathy with the varied purposes of art, which enabled him to help many causes at once, of Art in the galleries, in the museum, in the art schools, in the public schools and in the clubs.
Fine Arts Federation of New York, signed by Edwin Blashfield, Herbert Adams, Kenyon Cox and Joseph Howland Hunt

CHRONOLOGY

1856

October 7: born Allegheny City (today Pittsburgh)

1860s

Frances Smith Alexander and son reside with her parents; John is about five when she dies

*c.*1868

leaves school to work for Pacific & Atlantic Telegraph Co.

1870

June: household census of Colonel Edward Jay Allen, Secretary and Treasurer of the Pacific & Atlantic Telegraph Co., records his wife and four children, plus two English domestics and the mother and brother of Mrs. Allen; Colonel Allen assumes guardianship of the young Alexander sometime after the census; Grandfather Smith dies shortly thereafter

1870–1

may have attended School of Design

1871

spring: Kentucky painter Robert Burns Wilson sets up a studio in Pittsburgh with Alexander; probably at this time executes a *Wedding Album*

September: Wilson leaves Pittsburgh and Alexander enters Pittsburgh Central High School; fellow student Edward Elisha Phelps becomes a lifelong friend

October 13: Pittsburgh; dedication of new high school building on Fulton Street

1873

April: leaves high school without finishing

1874

December: travels with Robert Burns Wilson down the Ohio River in an "open boat"

1875

February 2: Alexander to leave for New York City "next week"

February 26: initially resides at Lafayette Hotel; looks for work and attempts to enroll in classes either at the National Academy or Cooper Institute

April 28: moves to a boarding house

May 3: shows his work at *Frank Leslie's*, *The Graphic* and *Harper's*

May 19: hired as an office boy by Charles Parsons of *Harper's*

June 14: Parsons retains him as an illustrator

December 14–January 2, 1876: in Pittsburgh for Christmas; consults with Colonel Allen about going to Europe

1876

January 31: resides at 137 MacDougal Street; John Wesley Beatty, stops in NYC on way to Munich

June 11: *Harper's* sends him to the Centennial Exposition

October: meets Allen family in Philadelphia at Centennial Exposition

1877

August 11: illustrations for "The Great Strike" in Pittsburgh appear in *Harper's*; Charles Reinhart introduces Alexander to his brother Ab; they plan to travel to Europe together

August 16: Ab Reinhart issued passport

August 18: sails on the SS *Indiana* from Philadelphia; eight-day crossing; docks in Liverpool then train to London; visits National Gallery and Doré Gallery; a few days later crosses the Channel to Dieppe and then to Paris; stays with Charles Reinhart family for a few days; dissatisfied with the École; he and Ab depart for Munich

September 8: Munich; Alexander and Ab share a room for 10 marks ($2.50); monthly expenses below $20

October 10: qualifies for drawing class in the Munich Royal Academy; enrolls in class of Gyula Benczúr; a Mr. Crawford from Pittsburgh commissions portraits. Reading George Eliot, Longfellow, Schiller and Goethe

1878

February 17: seeks permission from Allen who is paying the bills to enroll for the next term; John Hammer, a friend of Charles Reinhart, mentors the boys taking them to opera, concerts and the beer garden

April 14: first in drawing but also for conduct and attendance

April 28: begins Life Class under Professor Ludwig von Löfftz

by mid June: moves to Polling before school term ends in late July; cost of living about 50 cents per day; boards at home of Herr and Frau Josef Seitz; studios were in the old cloister

midsummer: Frank Duveneck, William M. Chase and John Twachtman return to Munich from Venice

July 6: Chase stops in Polling en route to US to teach at the Arts Students League

July 27: awarded bronze medal by Munich Royal Academy for drawing

August 3–September 8: Duveneck in Polling

August 17: Chase's Abschied starts at train station in Weilheim and continues into Polling

end of December: A Centenarian (unlocated) exhibited at W. W. Barker, Pittsburgh

1879

February: Mark Twain hosted at the Rathskeller, Munich

March 16: from Polling to Munich to view Old Masters at Alte Pinakothek

June 1: sketching trip to Murnau with Ab Reinhart and probably Louis Moeller

September 1: leaves Polling and returns to Munich

October 1 (on or about): accompanies Duveneck to Florence along with Louis Ritter and possibly two others

December 24: Christmas Eve spent at the home of Mr. Boott and Christmas at the home of Elizabeth Blood

1880

March 4: portrait of Larkin Mead exhibited in Duveneck's studio

May 1: accompanies Duveneck to Venice; during summer Duveneck paints portrait of Alexander in top hat with a red beard (Cincinnati Art Museum)

July 19: Whistler begs money from the "boys"

August: The "boys" give a sendoff for Alexander along the canals of Venice

October: arrives in Pittsburgh on assignment for *Harper's* probably to cover the dispute between Waverly Coal & Coke Co. and the miners union; stays with Colonel Allen; executes family portraits

1881

March 21: travels with G. Fred Muller by boat from Pittsburgh down the Ohio and Mississippi to New Orleans and back on *Harper's* assignment

in New York; rents Saint-Gaudens' former studio in the German Bank Building

July 2 and August 11: illustrations of the Pittsburgh Flood published in *Harper's Weekly*

sometime in the summer: in Newport to paint the portrait of Mrs. Samuel Tilton

fall 1881 or January 1882: Princeton School of Science, drawing instructor (probably September–December (first term), January–mid April (second term) and late April–June (third term)

1882

January: Harper's New Monthly Magazine publishes G. Fred Muller's "King Coal's Highway" with illustrations by Alexander

January 2: Oscar Wilde's first trip to US; Alexander first meets him in New York City

March 7: Alexander illustrates the cover of the inaugural issue of *The Princeton Tiger*

March–April: exhibits at 57th Annual Exhibition, National Academy of Design

May 1–20: Society of American Artists, Fifth Annual Exhibition, exhibits *32 Pounds Massa*

July 31–August 5: in Port Jefferson, Long Island sketching with John and Edward Moran and Thomas S. Clarke

1882–83 school year: drawing instructor for a student Sketching Club at Princeton

October 24–December 9: exhibits at 53rd Annual Exhibition, Pennsylvania Academy of the Fine Arts

1883

January 25–February 17: exhibits at Boston Art Club

March 5: planning a trip to Pittsburgh in a few weeks; stays at the home of Charles Clarke, father to Thomas Shields and Mabel; preparing to paint Mabel's portrait; sketches "blast furnaces in operation at night"

March 26–April 28: Society of American Artists, Sixth Annual Exhibition, exhibits *Portrait*; tours to Boston from May 7 to June 4
April 2–May 12: exhibits at 58th Annual Exhibition, National Academy of Design
August: to Yellowstone National Park on assignment for *Harper's*
October: Mabel Clarke portrait exhibited at the National Academy according to the press but not listed in NAD exhibition records
November 10: Yellowstone illustrations appear in *Harper's Weekly*

1884

April 7–May 17: exhibits at 59th Annual Exhibition, National Academy of Design
May 2–June 21: Society of American Artists, Seventh Annual Exhibition, exhibits *Portrait* (Mrs. Tilton), tours to Inter-State Industrial Exposition of Chicago, September 3–October 16, but with a different portrait
May 9 or 10: sails with Tom Clarke and Louis (?); destination Gibraltar; visits Prado in Madrid
May 23: Tangiers
June 18: aims to be in Paris by this date to see Salon that closes on June 20; expects to go with Stanley Reinhart to nearby artists' colony (possibly Grez-sur-Loing)
July 16: Dordrecht
August 16 (on or about): leaves from Liverpool for New York; sometime this year travels with William Alexander (Elizabeth Alexander's uncle) to Millboro, Virginia, to visit William's mother of the Cabell family and to meet Dr. James Lawrence Cabell
December 29: writes Edward Phelps (now of the Office of City Controller, Pittsburgh) that he is engaged

1885

September 29: in East Gloucester, Mass. with Ross Turner, John Leslie Breck and Frances C. Lyons Houston
November: exhibits at American Art Galleries

1886

January 9 and 15: Henry Martyn Alexander of Alexander & Green (great-uncle to Elizabeth) advises Mark Twain on business matters
February–March: series of drawings of distinguished authors commissioned by *The Century* magazine; February 13: John Burroughs; February 22–4, Camden: begins portrait of Walt Whitman; February 25: Frank Stockton; March: John Milton Hay
April 5–May 15: 61st Annual exhibition, National Academy of Design; exhibits *Flowers* and *Portrait of Dr. James McCosh*
May 3: Society of American Artists, exhibits landscape
June (probably)–before November 12: The Century magazine assignment to illustrate prominent literary figures takes him to London, Paris and Ireland; July 4, Bournemouth to sketch Robert Louis Stevenson; accompanied by Charles de Kay travels to the West, North and South of Ireland including County Cork primarily to illustrate an article by de Kay; London: dinner party at Mrs. Gordon's (mother of Alexander's student in Florence in 1879) with guests Lady Colin Campbell (former student Gertrude Elizabeth Blood), Albert Ludovici and John O'Connor
November: meets James Gordon Bennett, President of New York Herald Co. on return trip; illustration for the New York *Evening Telegram* appears in November and again in January 1887

1887

early in the year: takes a studio in The Chelsea Building, 222 West 23rd Street
May 19: Elizabeth's father, James W. Alexander of Equitable, approves engagement
May 21: Seabright: Louis C. Tiffany also in Seabright
May 26: Seabright: expects to close with the builder this afternoon on a large summer studio
September 24: addresses 4,000 wedding invitations; after this date can be reached at The Chelsea Building
November 2: married by Rev. C. C. Tiffany, rector of Zion Church, Madison Avenue and 38th Street, New York; Dr. Robert Abbe best man; bridesmaids Carrie Hoe and May Palmer; ushers were the bride's brother, Henry M. Alexander, Jr., uncle, William Alexander, and cousins, Samuel and Maitland Alexander; invitees were Mrs. Henry Draper; Mr. and Mrs. Courtlandt Palmer, Mr. and Mrs. Henry B. Hyde, Henry B. Hyde, Jr. , Mrs. Jeremiah Milbank, Mr. and Mrs. Parke Godwin, Mayor and Mrs. Abram S. Hewitt; reception at the home of the bride's parents, 50 West 54th Street; housesitting for in-laws
December 5: Society of American Wood Engravers folio illustrates *Portrait of a Child (Mabel Clarke)*

1888

after February 9: resided in the old Wyoming Building, 55th and 7th Avenue
May 3: attends First Annual Dinner of the American Watercolor Society along with Samuel L. Clemens, A. A. Anderson, Edwin

Blashfield, J. Henry Harper, Louis C. Tiffany, C. Y. Turner, J. Alden Weir, Irving R. Wiles, and others
by May 5–October 25: Seabright
July 23: Courtlandt Palmer dies of peritonitis; Alexander's portrait featured at the memorial
September 19: Seabright: birth of son, James Waddell Alexander, Jr.
October 25: returns to New York City from Seabright

1889

March 29: *Old Cole* exhibited at the Fellowcraft Club
May 31: Camden; attended 70th birthday celebration for Walt Whitman
by July 6: Seabright for most of the summer; portrait of Mrs. Stewart née Williamson, rejected by the family
August: greater part of month on St. Lawrence River at Alexandria Bay in the Thousand Island region of the Adirondacks painting Van Wagenen portrait
November 16: New York; Fellowcraft Club for journalists, artists and illustrators; annual Dinner; Richard Watson Gilder, founding President; Alexander and Mark Twain spoke; Henry Harper attended

1890

January 30–March 6: exhibits at 60th Annual Exhibition, Pennsylvania Academy of the Fine Arts
February: inaugural exhibit at Aldine Club includes Alexander's portrait of *William D. Howells*
February 20: Fellowcraft Club; Richard Watson Gilder reelected President and Alexander elected Vice President; Alexander's portrait of Gilder presented to the club
by May 30: Cornish, N.H.; boards for the summer at Stephen Alden Tracy farmhouse; Saint-Gaudens, Thomas Dewing, Charles Platt, Henry Walker, Henry and Edith Prellwitz in residence; Dennis M. Bunker leaves after 3 weeks; August 9: attends Charles Beaman picnic; September 11: attends house warming party for High Court

1891

elected member Society of American Artists
February 18 or 23: New York, succeeds Richard Watson Gilder as President of the Fellowcraft Club
April 25: Ernest Longfellow sublets Alexander's studio in The Chelsea
April 28: Walt Whitman portrait given to the Metropolitan Museum of Art by Mrs. Jeremiah Milbank
April 29: last dinner of the season for Fellowcraft Club and farewell by President Alexander; presented to the club was his portrait by Benoni Irwin and his own portrait of George Washington Childs; Chauncey Depew, Richard Watson Gilder, Charles de Kay, and Julian Ralph among attendees
May 2: sails for Europe on *Old Burgoyne*; met by Elizabeth's mother and younger brother in Paris
May 21: Paris; Whitelaw Reid, Envoy Extraordinary and Minister Plenipotentiary issues Seal of Legation of the United States
May 23: Seal of Legation stamped for entry into Germany
June 18–20: Polling; registered guest at Streicher Inn; thereafter in Polling until mid July; spends time with Max Bohm, an American in Polling and his aunt Anna Stuhr; plans trip to Ettal and Oberammergau
Paris: Ivan Pranishnikoff helps find living and studio accommodations for the Alexanders at 31 Boulevard Berthier; Alfred Roll, Alfred Stevens, Walter Gay, Albert Besnard, and Puvis de Chavannes are neighbors
November 13: Paris; following months of recuperation begins hosting open house on Saturdays

1892

sometime in 1892: Paris; to Théâtre Français to see Jean Mounet-Sully perform in *Oedipus* as guest of Henrietta Reubell along with Alexander Harrison, Oscar Wilde and John Boit (brother to Edward)
March 10–April 10: First exhibition of the Salon de la Rose Croix at Galerie Durand-Ruel; attends March 10 opening
end of May–October: Le Pouldu, Brittany; resides in Goulven Inn

1893

March 25: Anders Zorn arrives in New York on his way to Chicago; James Waddell Alexander, Sr. looks after Zorn and his wife who are quarantined
May 10–c.July 10: Paris; exhibits at Société Nationale des Beaux-Arts
June 2: elected associate member of the Société Nationale des Beaux-Arts
by July 12–September: New York and Seabright; portrait commissions for Marcellus Hartley, Joseph Mosenthal, James Waddell Alexander and Chief Justice Mercer Beasley of New Jersey
July 16: Munich Secession; exhibits *Portrait Jaune* and *Portrait Noir*
August 18: Seabright; writes to Phelps of his intent to settle in Paris and remain for several years
September 30: sails for Paris

1894

January 3–March 3: Century Club, monthly exhibitions: exhibits portraits of James Waddell Alexander, Sr., Chief Justice Beasley and Joseph Mosenthal c.*January 13:* Grafton Gallery, London: exhibits *Portrait Gris* and *Portrait of Mrs. Paul W. Bartlett*

April 25: Paris: exhibits at Société Nationale des Beaux-Arts

June 16: elected *Sociétaire* of the Société National des Beaux-Arts, with "hors concours" privileges

summer: Étretat; also in Étretat were Eugène Boudin, Mark Twain and Henry Bacon

October 29–December 17: Seventh Annual Exhibition of Oil Paintings and Sculpture by American Artists, Art Institute of Chicago, curated by Sarah Hallowell; exhibits *Portrait–pink* (*Portrait of Mrs. John W. Alexander in changeable silk dress*), *Portrait–gray* (*Portrait Gris*), *Portrait–black* (*Portrait of Mrs. Paul W. Bartlett*), *Portrait–yellow* (*Portrait Jaune*), *Portrait–man in profile* (*Portrait of Frits Thaulow*), *Portrait–painter* (*Portrait of Ivan Pranishnikoff*), *Portrait–lady in profile*, *The Mirror*, and *The Piano*

December 31: Paris; Elizabeth Alexander to Edna Allen: John "has found an almost perfect model," Juliette Very

1895

sometime in 1895 exhibits in Dusseldorf (cannot confirm Elizabeth Alexander's notes): exhibits *Portrait Jaune*, Mrs. John White Alexander in changeable taffeta dress and portrait of the painter Pranishnikoff

February 1: Paris; invitation to paint murals for the Library of Congress

March 7–April 5: Paris, Exposition Internationale de Peintres et Sculpteurs, Galerie Georges Petit; exhibits *Etude* (*Sunlight in Mirror*), *Girl in Black with Red Bows*, *Green Girl*, and a landscape

April 22–October 22: the first Venice Biennale; exhibits *The Piano* and *Repos*

April 25: Paris, Société Nationale des Beaux-Arts; exhibits *Repos*, *Alethea*, *Panneaux* (*In the Orchard*), *Etude* (*Sunlight in Mirror*), *Red Girl on Divan*, *Devant la Glace*, *Green Girl*, *Justine* (semi-nude), *Woman in Black*, and *Woman in Figured Dress on Divan*

May 1–September 29: Grosse Berliner Kunstausstellung, Berlin, exhibits *Portrait of Mrs. John W. Alexander* (with columns), *Portrait of the painter Ivan Pranishnikoff* and *Portrait Jaune*

by June 9: New York, arrives on *La Gascogne*; summers in Seabright; works on Library of Congress murals; goes back and forth to New York City frequently; many communications with John W. Beatty regarding the 1895 Loan Exhibition to Carnegie Art Gallery

October 2: New York; takes receipt of foreign shipment of paintings for the Carnegie 1895 Loan Exhibition

October 7: Seabright; John working on illustrations for Elizabeth's stories for *Harper's*; traveling to Washington frequently regarding the Library of Congress murals

October 11: Pittsburgh

October 30–December 7: Loan Exhibition of Portraits for the Benefit of St. John's Guild and the Orthopaedic Hospital at the National Academy of Design; exhibits *Portrait of James Waddell Alexander, Sr.* and a portrait of the artist's son in a sailor suit

November 5: Pittsburgh; dedication of Carnegie Library with speech by Andrew Carnegie; program includes loan exhibition of works by Rembrandt, Gainsborough, Tadema, Constable, Inness, Millet, Munkácsy, Whistler, Abbey, and *Harmony* and a portrait by Alexander

November 15: New York; resides at 4 East 64th Street (residence of father-in-law); writes Beatty that Harrison S. Morris, managing director of the Pennsylvania Academy, will take all his Carnegie pictures

weeks before December 7: visits Thomas Eakins in Philadelphia who is working on a portrait of Frank Hamilton Cushing

December 7: Pittsburgh; Mrs. Allen hosts reception at Edgehill for John and Elizabeth Alexander

December 9: Pittsburgh, Two Hundred and Fourteenth Reception of the Art Society, the first in the new Carnegie Music Hall and Art Galleries; special exhibit of 22 paintings by Alexander

December 23–February 22, 1896: 65th Annual Exhibition, Pennsylvania Academy of the Fine Arts

December 28: Alexander's 22 canvases from Pittsburgh arrive in Philadelphia to be hung in the annual, among them *Repose*, *Alethea*, *At the Piano*, *In the Orchard*, plus *Red Bow* and an additional painting

1896

sometime in 1896 exhibits in Cologne (cannot confirm Elizabeth Alexander's notes): *Portrait Jaune*, Mrs. John White Alexander in changeable taffeta dress and Portrait of Pranishnikoff

March 2–23: Boston, Loan Collection of Portraits for the Benefit of the Associated Charities and the North End Union; exhibits *Portrait of James Waddell Alexander* and portraits of Helen Manice and James

c.*March 21:* New York, sails for Paris

April 25: Paris, Société Nationale des Beaux-Arts, exhibits *Etude* (portrait of his wife in pink gown with black trimmings)

April issue of *Harpers New Monthly Magazine* publishes first of seven short stories written by Elizabeth Alexander and illustrated by John

Mid April and throughout the year: Paris agent for interests of the Carnegie International
May 3–September 30: Berlin, Internationale Kunstausstellung, in celebration of the 200th anniversary of the Royal Academy of Arts, exhibits *Le Piano*, *Repos* and *Girl in the Orchard*
July 25: arrives New York City on way to Washington
August 1: Munich, Verein bildender Künstler Münchens, Secession, exhibits *Portrait of Mrs. John White Alexander* (with column); *Portrait of the painter Pranishnikoff* and *Alethea*
by August 9: New York, sails for Paris
early September–mid October: St. Louis Exposition; exhibits *Woman in Gray*, *The Black Dress*, *The Black Cat* (*Le Chat Noir*), *A Portrait (Profile of James)*, *The Divan*, *A Study in Red*, *The Guitar*, and *The Bronze Bowl*
October 5–9: Czar Nicholas II and Czarina visit Paris seeking to negotiate a loan from France; Elizabeth Alexander serves as hostess at the American embassy for Ambassador James Biddle Eustis; Henry Addison Alexander, cousin to Elizabeth, is counsel to the U.S. embassy (1892–9)
November 5–January 1, 1897: exhibits at Pittsburgh, First Annual Carnegie International
November 7: sails from Paris accompanying shipment of Library of Congress murals
November 14: arrives New York on SS *La Touraine*
November 16: Washington; installs *Evolution of the Book*, six lunette shaped murals at Library of Congress
November 17: Pittsburgh for single day, leaves immediately for New York to dine with his father-in-law on the 20th; travels again to Washington
November 24: New York; sails for Paris
December 6: Paris, Fourteenth Exposition, Internationale de Peintres et Sculpteurs, Galerie Georges Peitit; exhibits *A Study in Pink*, woman reading on a couch and a third canvas
December 12: Carnegie forwards paintings to Philadelphia before close of International
December 21–February 22, 1897: 66th Annual Exhibition, Pennsylvania Academy of the Fine Arts; exhibits *The Mirror* (awarded Temple Gold Medal); *Red and Black*, *The Yellow Girl* (Woman in Yellow with Black Cat), *Peonies*, *Portrait* (Head of James), *The Black Dress* (Charles and Emma Frye Art Museum, Seattle), *The Black Cat*, *The Divan*, *The Guitar*, *The Bronze Bowl*, and *Woman in Gray*

1897

January 27: Paris; besieged by angry artists over lack of sales at the Carnegie International
April 24: Paris, exhibits at Société Nationale des Beaux-Arts
spring: New York; 19th Annual Exhibition, Society of American Artists, exhibits *Portrait Gris*
April–October: Venice, Second International Exposition; exhibits *Portrait* and *The Mirror*
May 1–October 31: Nashville, Tennessee Centennial and International Exposition; exhibits *Portrait of Mrs. John W. Alexander in Changeable Silk Dress*
May 1–October 31: International Exposition, Copenhagen (entries cannot be verified)
May 15–October 1: Stockholm, Allmänna konst-och industriutställningen (Exhibition of Arts and Industries), exhibits *Le Repos*, *Sunlight in Mirror* and *Girl in Green (Sketch)*
c.June 1: south to Saas-Fee, Canton Valais, Switzerland
July 22: Paris; William Turner Dannat, President of Paris Society of American Painters, writes regarding problems with Alexander's membership
by September 1: Paris; returns from Saas-Fee
September 8–October 27: 14th Annual St. Louis Exposition, exhibits *Peonies* and *The Yellow Girl* (*Woman in Yellow with Black Cat)*
September 16: Paris; Carnegie jury Benjamin Constant, Charles Sprague Pearce, Walter Gay and Alexander meet; Léon Lhermitte, Émile-René Ménard, Henri Martin, Jacques-Émile Blanche, Gari Melchers are no-shows; Puvis de Chavannes could not attend, Dagnan Bouveret never responds to invitation
November 2–December 12: Chicago, Art Institute of Chicago, Tenth Annual Exhibition of Painting and Sculpture by American Artists, curated by Sarah Hallowell, exhibits *Peonies*, and *Woman in Yellow with Black Cat*
November 4–January 1, 1898: exhibits at Second Annual Carnegie International and acts as Paris advisor
November 6: Krefeld, Kunstaustellung 1897, inauguration of Kaiser Wilhelm Museum, exhibits *Portrait Gris* and *Dame Rouge*
November 21: Paris; Elizabeth Alexander hosts Mr., Mrs. and Miss Howells, Mr. and Mrs. Robert Underwood Johnson of *The Century* magazine, Harriet Monroe of Chicago and her sister Mrs. Root; Mr. and Mrs. Albert Herter, Mr. Saglio (André?), attaché of the Beaux-Arts, Dr. Shepheard, Mr. George Howland, and Mr. and Mrs. Pomeroy
December 2: Paris; French court awards Whistler the portrait of Lady Eden; Mr. and Mrs. Alexander attend trial
December 4: Paris, Exposition Internationale de Peintures et de Sculpture, Galerie Georges Petit; exhibits *Rouge et Noir* and *Green Girl*
December 15: Ludwig Dill and Arthur Langhammer apologize for not yet listing Alexander as a corresponding member of the Munich Secession

1898

January 10–February 22: exhibits at 67th Annual Exhibition, Pennsylvania Academy of the Fine Arts

February: Lille Exposition (de la Rue Negrier), exhibits *Rouge et Noir, Le Piano* and probably *Femme Jaune* (this information cannot be independently verified)

February 24: Brussels, exhibits at La Libre Esthétique

March 19–April 23: 20th Annual Exhibition, Society of American Artists, New York; exhibits *Peonies (Pivoines), Woman in Yellow with Black Cat* and *Isabella and the Pot of Basil*

March 25–June 15: exhibits at First Vienna Secession (Kunst-Ausstellung der Vereinigung bildender Künstler Österreichs)

April 5: Austrian Emperor tours the Secession with Gustav Klimt and Carl Moll

c.*April 19:* Society of American Fakirs annual exhibition parodies *Isabella and the Pot of Basil*

May: London, first exhibition of International Society of Sculptors, Painters and Gravers; Whistler, James Guthrie, John Lavery, and Albert Ludovici, executive committee; Alexander an honorary member; exhibits *Green Girl*

May 1: Paris, Société Nationale des Beaux-Arts, exhibits *Child with Doll, Femme au Noeud Vert (The Green Bow), Femme Jaune (Juliette with Flowers), Sketch of Old Ladd, Juliette in Pink, Pandora, Still Life* (bowl and glass on panel), *The Blue Bowl*

May 5: Paris, *Femme au Noeud Vert* acquired by the French Government

June 1–November 1: Omaha, Trans-Mississippi and International Exposition; exhibits *The Yellow Girl* (*Woman in Yellow with Black Cat*)

c.*June 6:* summer at Val-de-la-Haye, a few miles from Rouen on the Seine, rents house from a French friend

July 28: Munich, Internationalen Kunst-Ausstellung des Vereins bildender Künstler, Secession no. III; exhibits *The Mirror*

August 23: Val-de-la-Haye; a French government official (probably André Saglio) is a house guest; they discuss strategy for 1900 Exposition Universelle

October 27: walks in the funeral cortege for Puvis de Chavannes

November 3–January 1, 1899: Paris advisor to the Third Annual Carnegie International, exhibits *Child with Doll*

November 12: New York, arrives from Paris on the St. Louis; he and Elizabeth stay with father-in-law at 4 East 64th Street

November 12–December 28: Second Vienna Secession (Kunst-Ausstellung der Vereinigung bildender Künstler Österreichs), exhibits *The Mirror*

November 20: Barnard College commissions ceiling decoration

November 23: New York, preparing to leave for Pittsburgh

November 29: Pittsburgh, dinner with Henry K. Porter; stays at the Schenley Hotel

December: Musée du Luxembourg completes exchange of *Le Noeud Vert* for *Portrait Gris*

December 5–31: Paris, exhibits at Société Internationale de Peinture et Sculpture, Galerie Georges Petit

December 14–January 14, 1899: Loan Exhibition of Portraits for the Benefit of the Orthopaedic Hospital, National Academy of Design; exhibits *James Waddell Alexander, Sr., A Child, Mrs. B* (Mrs. Paul W. Bartlett), *Miss V*, and *Joe Jefferson*

December 21: bedridden with the gripe

1899

January 16–February 25: 68th Annual Exhibition, Pennsylvania Academy of the Fine Arts; exhibits *A Ray of Sunlight* (Lippincott Prize), *Child with Doll, The Blue Bowl, Still life,* and *Musings*

February 11: New York, first annual meeting of the National Institute of Art, Science and Letters; Alexander a charter member

April 22: New York, sails for Paris stopping in London to sketch John Morley for *The Century* with possible stop in Glasgow

May 1: Paris, exhibits at Société Nationale des Beaux-Arts

May 2: Henry Baldwin Hyde dies James Waddell Alexander, Sr. becomes interim President of Equitable

June 28: Paris; Whistler invites Alexander to his studio on Thursday

August–mid September: summers in Murnau with family (first visited June 1879)

August 13–October 8: Ghent, Exposition Quadrennial de Gand, exhibits *In the Orchard* and *Repos*

September 11–October 14: 16th Annual St. Louis Exposition; exhibits *Portrait of a Child* and *Portrait of Joe Jefferson as Bob Acres*

November 2–January 1, 1900: Fourth Annual Carnegie International; Paris advisor

November 6–December 17: Twelfth Annual Exhibition of Oil Paintings and Sculpture by American Artists, The Art Institute of Chicago; exhibits *Portrait of a Child* (Eleanor) and *Joe Jefferson as Bob Acres*

December 5: Paris; Whistler at the Hotel Chatham, invites Alexander to visit

1900

January 13: New York Times: Director John Cauldwell has appointed jury for the American Section of the Paris Exposition Universelle: Edwin A. Abbey, Alexander, William T. Dannat, Alexander Harrison, Gari Melchers, Francis D. Millet, John S. Sargent, and Julius Stewart

January 15–February 24: 69th Annual Exhibition, Pennsylvania Academy of the Fine Arts; exhibits *The Café, The Toiler,* and *The Rose* (yellow)

March 8–June 6: Seventh Vienna Secession (VII Kunst-Ausstellung der Vereinigung Bildender Künstler Österreichs Secession), exhibits *The Blue Bowl*

March 10–31: Paris, Société Nouvelle de Peintres et de Sculpteurs; exhibits *A Flower; Richard Watson Gilder;* Alice sitting profile, pink; Still Life – three bowls white, green, yellow; Black study kneeling peonies, Bess; Marine; and *Femme aux Fleurs*

April 14: Paris; French President Émile Loubet opens Exposition Universelle

May 1–November 15: Paris; exhibits three paintings at Exposition Universelle

May 1: accompanies James Hazen Hyde on tour of Versailles

June 4: Paris; serves as juror for print section, Exposition Universelle; fellow juror Linley Sambourne gives Alexander an introduction to Sir George Reid, President of the Royal Scottish Academy, for his forthcoming trip to Edinburgh; *c.*June 8, Elizabeth Alexander invites the Sambournes to a reception she is hosting

June 12: Paris; French President Loubet hosts a dinner at the Elysée Palace for all the jurors including Abbey, Millet and Sargent

June 22: member of the international jury for the French entries at the Exposition Universelle

July 3: Paris; Alexander informed by Walter MacEwen, Secretary, Paris Society of American Painters, that a majority vote called for his resignation

July 21: Elizabeth and son sail for New York without John

July 24: Paris; attends dinner hosted by John Cauldwell, Director of the American section of the Exposition Universelle

c.*July 26–August 29:* Edinburgh; guest of John James Cowan at New Hall near Carlops, for several weeks to fill commission for seven family portraits

October 7: New York Journal: Alexander will paint portrait of French President Loubet

October 8: New York, arrives on SS *La Touraine*

November 1–January 1, 1901: Fifth Annual Carnegie International; Paris advisor

1901

January 4: Candace Wheeler sells Outlook cabin in Onteora to Elizabeth Beasley Alexander (Mrs. James Waddell Alexander, Sr.)

January 14–February 23: 70th Annual Exhibition, Pennsylvania Academy of the Fine Arts; exhibits *A Flower, Autumn; Portrait of Miss V* (probably *Green Girl*); *Rodin; A Mother; Portrait of Young Girl* (in grey, probably Louise White); *Portrait of a Boy*; portrait of a third child; clever & simple little still-life, a misty little marine, and a simply treated impressionistic landscape

January 26: France names Alexander Chevalier of the Légion d'honneur

February 24: New York; participates in a tableau vivant at the home of Mr. and Mrs. Joseph Stickley with J. C. Beckwith and William M. Chase

February 26: New York Herald, Paris edition, headline: "Paris Artists in trouble, Mr. John W. Alexander Requested to Leave the Society of American Painters"

March 3: has been sick for several days

March 13–May 4: 23rd Annual Exhibition, Society of American Artists, *Autumn* (awarded Carnegie Prize), *A Ray of Sunlight* and *A Flower*

March 15: elected Associate member of National Academy of Design

March 16: New York; hosts a series of informal tableaux vivants in his studio

April 3: New York; lectures at the Art Students League

c.*April 12*, but by May 1: Paris; John W. Beatty also in Paris; paints French President Loubet

c.*April 30:* New York, Society of American Fakirs, Annual Exhibition, *A Ray of Sunlight* parodied by two students: *An X Ray of Sunlight* and *Bring Your Feet to the Dance*

May 1–November 2: Buffalo, exhibits at Pan-American Exposition

c.*August–September:* Paris; juror duties for Carnegie International

September 28–October 5: sails from Paris to New York, aboard *La Savoie* along with Gari Melchers; intends to make New York City his home; resides at 116 East 65th Street

Saturday before October 16: New York; Edward Aman-Jean and Robert W. Allan arrive from Paris and London respectively; met by Alexander before taking night train to Pittsburgh to serve with Frank Benson, Thomas Eakins, Frederick W. Freer, Winslow Homer, Clarence Marshall Johns, John La Farge, and Robert Vonnoh on the Carnegie International jury

October 16–20: Pittsburgh, Carnegie International juror; lecture to Art Students' League of Pittsburgh deplores the tariff on incoming shipments of art; banquet at Hotel Schenley to honor jurors

October 31: Boston and Worcester, Mass.; visits Boston to discuss a portrait commission before going to Worcester to arrange for portrait of Mrs. Homer Gage and son; dines at Worcester Bohemian Club on October 31

November 7–January 1, 1902: Pittsburgh; exhibits at Sixth Annual Carnegie International; Paris advisor; ex-U.S.

President Cleveland speaks on "The Obligations of National Co-Partnership," and Alexander on "Our Tariff Against Art"

Chauncey Depew was a speaker, among guests were Alexander, Richard W. Gilder, Booth Tarkington, Henry Harper, F. Hopkinson Smith, Dr. Henry Van Dyke, and Hamilton Mabie

1902

January 3–February 1: exhibits at 77th Annual Exhibition, National Academy of Design

January 20–March 1: exhibits at 71st Annual Exhibition, Pennsylvania Academy of the Fine Arts; juror for painting

March 24–April 1: Paris; opening celebrations for the Musée du Luxembourg; gallery dedicated to foreign painters included Whistler's *Arrangement in Grey and Black, No. 1, Portrait of the Painter's Mother* and Alexander's *Portrait Gris*

March 28–May 4: exhibits at Twenty-fourth Annual, Society of American Artists, served on the advisory board and selection committee

March 31–April 19, Pennsylvania Academy Fellowships Exhibition: exhibits *A Breton Girl* and two extensive canvases of "arrangements of color and drapery"

April 11: elected Academician of the National Academy of Design

April 29: Society of American Fakirs Annual Exhibition, parody of *The Yellow Girl* (alias *The Black Cat*)

May 6: Worcester; Alexander juries with John Lambert, Jr. and Charles Woodbury for the June 1 Summer Exhibition; exhibits *A Mother, The Yellow Girl* (cited as the *The Black Cat*), *Mrs. Homer Gage and Son*

June 11: Princeton; Master of Arts conferred upon Alexander at the 155th annual commencement

July: one of several artists named to decorate the Pennsylvania State Capitol building

September: New York, 1902–3 school term as instructor at Art Students League; gives informal talks on composition twice a month

November 6–January 1, 1903: Loan Exhibition of Paintings over 300 years, Carnegie Institute, exhibits *Portrait of Andrew Carnegie*

November 24–December 6: Exhibition of Paintings by John W Alexander, Durand-Ruel Galleries, New York: exhibition of 18 paintings including *Still Life* (green, red and grey), *A Portrait of Mrs. V, Study in Green, A Mother, A Quiet Hour, Autumn, William Croghan Denny, Dorothy Roosevelt, Portrait of Mrs. John W. Alexander, Dr. Francis Landey Patton, Mrs. Thomas Hastings, Mrs. Clinton Ledyard Blair, The Rose, Portrait of Rodin, Study in Tone. Child and Doll, Geraldine Russell* (most likely), *A Ray of Sunlight* plus photographs of paintings

November 29: New York; dinner honoring Mark Twain's 67th birthday at the Metropolitan Club hosted by Colonel Harvey (editor of *Harper's*); William Dean Howells reads a sonnet and

1903

January 3–31: Boston Art Club, Sixty-Seventh Exhibition, exhibits *Portrait of Rodin*

January 17: Philadelphia, private reception for the 72nd Annual Exhibition, Pennsylvania Academy of the Fine Arts; January 19–February 28, exhibits *Portrait of Mrs. John W. Alexander, A Quiet Hour, Study in Green, The Rose, Portrait of Mrs. Thomas Hastings, Portrait of William C. Denny*, and *Study in Tone*; Mrs. Alexander acts an official hostess with Mrs. John Cadwalader, Mrs. Arthur Biddle and others; house guests of Mr. Edward H. Coates, President of the Academy

February 10–26: Thirteenth Annual Exhibition of The Society of Washington Artists; (at the Corcoran Gallery of Art); exhibits *Ray of Sunlight*, awarded Corcoran Prize

March 22–c.April 21: Boston; resides at the St. Botolph Club

March 28–May 3: 25th Annual Exhibition, Society of American Artists; exhibits *Portrait of Mrs. Thomas Hastings* and *A Flower* (*Femmes aux Fleurs*); serves on jury of admission

March 30–April 18: St. Botolph Club, Boston; exhibits 17 paintings: *An Idle Moment, Autumn, A Quiet Hour, A Mother, A Flower, Reverend Henry Van Dyck, The Blue Bowl, Portrait of Mrs. John W. Alexander* (as *Portrait with Hat*), *A Ray of Sunlight, A Rainy Day* (*A Quiet Corner*), *The Rose, Study in Tone*, "an old woman hurrying along the beach, her honest face screwed up by the potent sunshine," *Still-life, Still-Life with Bowl*, sketch of a girl with her hair down, and a sketch of a seated figure with spots of sunlight

May 11: Bach Festival, Bethlehem, Pa.: exhibits a portrait; William M. Chase is also an exhibiter

May: New York; completes term as instructor at the Art Students League

June 26: Onteora; guest at or rents Buford Lodge

July 8: Insurance Press (New York): *Portrait of Rodin* purchased by the Cincinnati Art Museum

September 5: Onteora; parades in mummy costume for county fair; paints at least six "posters"

October 1: returns to New York City from Onteora

October 20–November 25: Sixteenth Annual Exhibition of Oil Paintings and Sculpture by American Artists, Art Institute of Chicago, juror of selection along with Ben Foster, Jules Guerin and F. Edwin Elwell for New York; exhibits *A Quiet Hour, A Mother, A Flower, Study in Tone, A Rose, Flowers, Still Life,*

A Rainy Day, Landscape, A Study (*Idle Moment*), *Marine, Portrait of Boy* (James), *A Study, Portrait* (William C. Denny), *Portrait of A Woman* (Mrs. Alexander), *The Blue Bowl* and *A Ray of Sunlight*

November 5–January 1, 1904: Eighth Annual Carnegie International; exhibits *Autumn*; Paris advisor

November 7: Blairsden, N.J.; weekend guests of C. Ledyard Blair along with Mr. and Mrs. Thomas Hastings

November 18: American Art Galleries, Loan Portrait Exhibition; exhibits portraits of *Dorothy Roosevelt* and *Mrs. Thomas Hastings*

November 30: New York; lectures on "Art and the People" at League for Political Education

1904

January 1–30: Boston Art Club, exhibits *Portrait Study*

January 3–30; 79th Annual Exhibition, National Academy of Design; exhibits *A Rose* and *A Quiet Hour*

January 25–March 5; 73rd Annual Exhibition, Pennsylvania Academy of the Fine Arts; exhibits *Memories, The Glass Bowl, A Rainy Day, A Study*, and *Portrait of Miss Dorothy Roosevelt*; Converse gold medal

January 29: presentation of portrait of Professor B. C. Jillson at meeting of Alumni Association of Pittsburgh Central High School

February 7: Tilden-Thurber Co. art galleries, Providence, Fourth Annual Exhibition of oil paintings by New York artists, exhibits *A Rose*

February 9: writes Harrison Morris that he is unable to work

March 2–15: Loan Exhibition, Pictures by American Figure Painters, National Arts Club, one of eight artists including Tanner, Vonnoh, H. M. Walcott, Hawthorne, F. D. Marsh, Moschowitz and Potthast, exhibits *The Blue Bowl*, a landscape, a marine and three others

March 12: Mayor McClellan appoints a committee to prepare a comprehensive plan for the beautification and development of New York City including Alexander, George A. Hearn, Harry Payne Whitney, Daniel C. French, and others

March 21–April 13: Fourteenth Annual Exhibition of The Society of Washington Artists (at the Corcoran Gallery of Art); exhibits *The Glass Bowl* and *A Quiet Hour*

March 26–May 1: New York; Twenty-Sixth Annual, Society of American Artists, juror of selection

Mid April: Democratic Club of New York, exhibits *Portrait of Mrs. Eliza B. Wheaton*

April 18–May 7, 1904: New Haven Paint & Clay Club, exhibits *The Green Gown* and *A Rainy Day*

April 26: to Ed Phelps: "am fully recovered in health and harder at work then ever"

April 30–December 1: St. Louis, Universal Exposition, exhibits *Portrait of Rodin* (lent by Cincinnati Art Museum), *Autumn, A Rose, Study in Tone, Mother and Child, The Glass Bowl, Flowers*, and *Portrait of Mrs. John White Alexander*

May 15–25: Boston; commission to paint portrait of Sarah Whitman for Radcliffe; by May 16 viewed Puvis murals at the Boston Public Library

Summer: Onteora, rents Runkle Cottage; Anne Bradley models for him

September 29: returns to New York City from Onteora; shortly thereafter joined the faculty of the Veltin School for Girls

October: Fourth Annual Autumn Exhibition, Rhode Island School of Design, exhibits *The Blue Bowl*

October 22: St. Louis, Universal Exposition, *Portrait of Mrs. John White Alexander* awarded Gold Medal

November 3–January 1. 1905: exhibits at Ninth Annual Carnegie International

November 29,: Alexander absent from presentation of his portrait of Judge Bennet W. Van Syckel at the Trenton State House

December 23–January 10, 1905: Exhibition of Paintings by Ten American Artists, Detroit Museum of Art; exhibits seven works, including *Memories* and *A Ray of Sunlight*; during last days of the exhibit the Minneapolis Society of Fine Arts purchases *A Ray of Sunlight*

December 31–January 28, 1905: 80th Annual Exhibition, National Academy of Design; exhibits *A Study, An Interesting Book, A Favorite Corner*

1905

January 23–March 4: 100th Annual Exhibition, Pennsylvania Academy of the Fine Arts; exhibits *Portrait of Sarah Wyman Whitman, Aurora Leigh, Mrs. E. B. Wheaton, A Mother, A Butterfly*; juror for painting and for hanging

January 31: New York; James Hazen Hyde hosts ball; Charles B. Alexander, an Equitable Director and son of Elizabeth's grandfather's brother, attends; Mrs. Clarence Mackay creates a sensation at the ball

February 8: James Waddell Alexander Sr. acts to remove Hyde from Board of the Equitable Life Assurance Society

February 23: Philadelphia; celebration of the 100th anniversary of the Pennsylvania Academy of the Fine Arts; a special train transports guests from New York City among them Alexander, Chase, Adams, Butler, Thomas S. Clarke, and Cox

March 22–April 13: Fifteenth Annual Exhibition of the Society of Washington Artists (at the Corcoran Gallery of Art); exhibits *A Study*

March 25–April 30: New York; 27th Annual Exhibition, Society of American Artists; one of many jurors (Blashfield, Chase, Cox, Low, Wiles etc.); exhibits *A Mother, The Butterfly, Portrait of Mrs. Clarence Mackay*

April 11–May 6: Twenty-Six Oil Paintings by John W. Alexander exhibited at Pratt Institute, Brooklyn

April 19: Anne Bradley writes Mrs. Alexander of her availability to model during the coming summer in Onteora

April 19: James Hazen Hyde press release implicates James Waddell Alexander Sr. in investment syndicate scandal

April 24: Society of American Fakirs Annual Exhibition; *Portrait of Mrs. Clarence MacKay* parodied

c.*May 11:* anticipated date to leave for California for commissions; return stops planned for Grand Rapids and Chicago to varnish Mrs. Clarence Webster's portrait; no evidence of making the trip

May 24: William N. Frew, President, Board of Trustees, Carnegie Institute, requests to see Alexander in Pittsburgh in the next few weeks to discuss murals for the Carnegie

June 3: Equitable Board votes against Hyde and James Waddell Alexander

June 7: Pittsburgh Post publishes a full description of Alexander's Harrisburg mural decoration

June 8: Pittsburgh; arrives to confer on the Carnegie mural project

June 10: Pittsburgh Press announces Alexander's mural commission for the Carnegie Institute at a cost of $175,000

June 25: New York Times: James Waddell Alexander, Sr. has taken refuge at the home of his son-in-law

July 5: contract formally signed with Carnegie Institute to execute mural decorations

summer through c.Oct 3: Onteora; resides in Runkle Cottage; works on Carnegie murals

July 21: New York Times: James Waddell Alexander, Sr. recuperating at a sanatorium in Bay Shore

October 12: Pittsburgh; serves on Jury of Award for the Tenth Annual Carnegie International

October 19–November 26: Eighteenth Annual Exhibition of Oil Paintings and Sculpture by American Artists, Art Institute of Chicago; exhibits *Portrait of Mrs. W.* (e.g. Mrs. Clarence Webster)

November 2–January 1, 1906: Tenth Annual Carnegie International; exhibits *Portrait of Mrs. John W. Alexander*

November 6: New York; Maude Adams as Peter Pan opens at the Empire Theatre

November 25: New York Mail article on formation of the MacDowell Club named after Edward MacDowell; Alexander an advisor

December 23: New York; attends 70th birthday party for Mark Twain at Delmonico's; 170 guests including A. Carnegie, William Dean Howells, John Burroughs, Dr. Henry Van Dyke

December 31–January 28, 1906: 80th Annual Exhibition, National Academy of Design; exhibits *A Favorite Corner (A Rainy Day), An Interesting Book* and *A Study*

1906

January 6–February 3: Boston Art Club, exhibits *Portrait of D. Webster King*

January 21: Society of American Artists announces jury for 28th Annual Exhibition; Alexander one of 25 including Chase, Cox, Daniel C. French, Robert Henri, William Kendall, Francis D. Millet, Walter Nettleton, Henry Prellwitz

January 24: Elizabeth Beasley Alexander sells Porcupine Cottage, Onteora

March 19–April 17: Sixteenth Annual Exhibition of the Society of Washington Artists (at the Corcoran Gallery of Art); exhibits *A Mother* and *A Portrait* ("a prosperous middle-aged man clad in a gray suit and seated in a none too graceful position")

April: James Waddell Alexander, Sr. leaves on a two-and-a-half-year world tour

May 16: New York; chairs committee for the Fine Arts Federation concerning a building plan

May 31–September 2: First Annual Exhibition of Selected Paintings by American Artists, Buffalo Fine Arts Academy; exhibits *A Quiet Hour, A Mother, The Butterfly,* and *Study in Green and Black*

c.*June 23,* Pittsburgh: meets with President Frew of the Carnegie Institute Board of Trustees regarding Carnegie murals

July 14: Charles Dana Gibson offers Alexander another year leasing his studio in the Carnegie building on 57th Street

Summer and winter: Seabright; working on Carnegie murals in probably a studio he had built for the purpose

September 17: Joseph Pennell appeals to Alexander to share reminiscences about Whistler for his pending book

October 16–November 29: juror for New York representation for Nineteenth Annual Exhibition of Oil Paintings and Sculpture by American Artists, Art Institute of Chicago along with Irving R. Wiles, Kenyon Cox and Evelyn B. Longman

November 11: New York; 70th birthday celebration for Henry M. Alden, editor of *Harper's*

1907

January 21–February 24: 102nd Annual Exhibition, Pennsylvania Academy of the Fine Arts; exhibits *Portrait of Mrs. William T. Carter* and *Study in Green and Black*

January 23–April 11: trial of Harry K. Thaw for murder of Stanford White

February 7–March 9: Corcoran Gallery of Art, First Annual Exhibition, Oil Paintings by Contemporary American Artists; exhibits *The Butterfly*

c.*February 16:* Mrs. Samuel Untermyer writes Rodin about commissioning a Whistler monument for New York City and closes by saying that Mr. Alexander hopes to receive him in Pittsburgh in six weeks

February 19–23: Pittsburgh; oversees installation of murals

February 19: Rodin writes Alexander that a trip to Pittsburgh is too tiring and asks details of the Whistler monument proposal

March 4: named Chairman, Jury of Award, Carnegie Institute f or the April 11 dedication and exhibition; jury includes Chase, Wiles, Beaux, foreigners Emile Claus and René Billotte, and others

March 7–10: Pittsburgh; serves as a juror for Carnegie International

April 3: Pittsburgh; arrives in advance of the dedication; one of 28 "distinguished sons of Pittsburgh" honored at dinner on April 4 by the Chamber of Commerce

April 11–13; Pittsburgh; Carnegie Institute, Eleventh Celebration of Founder's Day, and Dedication of the New Building; five central panels entitled "The Apotheosis of Pittsburgh" installed

April 11–June 13: Eleventh Annual Exhibition, Carnegie International; exhibits *Study in Green and Black* and *Portrait of Mrs. Eliza B. Wheaton*

by May 31: Seabright: Ward's Cottage, works on Carnegie murals in studio used the previous summer; work suspended for a time due to a severe attack of lumbago

October 22–December 1: Twentieth Annual Exhibition of Oil Paintings and Sculpture by Contemporary American Artists, Art Institute of Chicago; exhibits *Study in Green and Black*

December 14–January 11, 1908: exhibits at Winter Exhibition, National Academy of Design

1908

January 15: New York, Empire Theater, Maude Adams opens in *The Jesters*

January 28: New York: a series of tableaux vivants directed by Alexander to benefit MacDowell Fund cancelled due to death of MacDowell on the 23rd

February 4–March 24: 103rd Annual Exhibition, Pennsylvania Academy of the Fine Arts; exhibits *Portrait of Worthington Whittredge* and *A Favorite Corner*; Chairman, Painting and Hanging Committees

February–March: London; exhibits at *Exhibition of Fair Women*

March 2: New York; Colony Club Benefit for St. Catherine's Home for Girls with tableaux by Alexander

March 14–April 18: National Academy, 83rd Annual Exhibition; exhibits *Study in Green and Black*

March 28: New York; President Alexander presides over annual MacDowell Club dinner

March 28: Brooklyn Times: Alexander will design costumes and scenery for Maude Adams next season

April 9: Pittsburgh; Carnegie International, Jury of Award; Albert Neuhuys and Henri Le Sidaner are foreign jurors

April 9–24: Exhibition of Paintings, Public Library, Meadville, Pa.; exhibits *A Mother* and *A Butterfly*

April 25: Summit, N.J.; The Highland Club annual dinner, celebrates 88th birthday of Worthington Whittredge

April 30–June 30: Twelfth Annual Carnegie International; Jury of Award

June 3: Boston Transcript: Alexander exhibits *A Butterfly* in Eleventh Annual Exhibition, Worcester Art Museum

Summer: Seabright, Ward's Cottage and partially in Pittsburgh regarding the murals

September 28: ships three cases of the murals from Seabright to Pittsburgh

c.*October 9–14:* Pittsburgh; installs second floor panels at the Carnegie Institute

November 10: New York; MacDowell Club Benefit; tableaux vivants directed by Alexander

December 8–January 7, 1909: Corcoran Gallery of Art, Second Annual Exhibition, Oil Paintings of Contemporary American Artists; exhibits *The Mother* (possibly same as *A Mother*)

December 21: New York; Maude Adams opens in *What Every Woman Knows*

1909

January 13: elected a trustee of the New York Public Library

February 8: Pittsburgh Press: Alexander ready to go ahead on the Harrisburg commission should appropriation be approved

February–March: multiple articles about Alexander's plan for the National Academy on the site of the old arsenal in Central Park

February 23–March 17: John W. Alexander Retrospective Exhibition, National Arts Club, includes 65 paintings and 10 photographs of paintings

March 14: President Alexander presides over MacDowell Club Annual Dinner

April 8–9: Pittsburgh; Carnegie International, Jury of Award, foreign jurors are Alfred East (British) and George Breitner (The Netherlands); Alexander named to Pittsburgh Civic Commission; may have stayed in Pittsburgh until after Founder's Day

April 29–June 30: Pittsburgh; Founder's Day, Carnegie Institute and exhibits at Thirteenth Annual Carnegie International

May 10–August 30: Buffalo; Fourth Annual Exhibition of Selected Paintings by American Artists, Buffalo Fine Arts Academy, Albright Art Gallery, exhibits *Other Days,* and *Portrait of Rodin*

May 12: New York; first rehearsal at the Empire Theatre for *Joan of Arc* featuring Maude Adams

May 13: elected President of the National Academy of Design

May 16: Alexander and Adams travel to Harvard in preparation for her performance of *Joan of Arc*

mid May: father-in-law returns from world tour; resides with his son Henry

May 28: design approved for *Justice*, a mural for Federal District Court, Cleveland

May 30: Alexander thanks Harrison S. Morris for intervening with Senator Boies Penrose on the Harrisburg project; he is better after two throat operations

June 7: assumes Presidency of the National Academy and ex-officio member of the Board of the Metropolitan Museum of Art as Chairman of Committee on Paintings

June 8: Princeton; honorary member, The American Whig Society of Princeton; June 11, The Quadrangle Club Annual Banquet; June 15 awarded Honorary Doctor of Letters; speaker at Alumni luncheon

June 20–23(?): Cambridge, Mass.; with Maude Adams at a reception on June 20 prior to staging of *Joan of Arc* directed by Charles Frohman on June 22

Summer: Seabright; Ward's Cottage at least through the end of August working on Carnegie murals

July 6: Alexander thanks Morris for interceding with the Pennsylvania Governor about the Harrisburg commission

August 29: New York for the day from Seabright

December 10–January 10, 1910: A Retrospective Exhibition of Paintings by John White Alexander, Buffalo Academy of Fine Arts, exhibits 42 paintings including *The Tenth Muse, Phyllis, Memories, Other Days, Summer's Day, Portrait of Mrs. John White Alexander*

December 11–January 9, 1910: Winter Exhibition, National Academy of Design; exhibits *Portrait of Richard Watson Gilder* and *Sunlight*

December 14: elected Corresponding Member, American Institute of Architects

December 25: James Waddell Alexander, Sr. sends letter of condolence to Mark Twain upon the death of daughter Jean on Christmas Eve

December 26: New York American: the Annual Christmas frolic of the MacDowell Club was held last Tuesday; artists caricatured old masters with Alexander as Giotto

December 31: New York; twenty-fifth anniversary of American Economic Association and American Historical Association was celebrated in tableaux on the theme of "An Historical Evening" directed by Alexander

1910

January 7: Alexander named to the Royal Society of British Artists

January 12: National Arts Club honors William M. Chase; Alexander sends remarks *in absentia*

January 23–March 20: 105th Annual Exhibition, Pennsylvania Academy of the Fine Arts; exhibits *Summer's Day* and *Portrait of Richard Watson Gilder*

February 2: New York; speaker at Annual Dinner, Schools of Science and of Architecture, Columbia University

February 17: Pittsburgh; banquet of the Historical Society of Western Pennsylvania; Alexander and Percy MacKaye speak about a Fourth of July pageant for 1911

February 22–March 26: New Smyrna, Florida for doctor-ordered rest

March 3: Jersey City Journal: Alexander among those invited to submit a mural design for the Hudson County Court House

March 10: The Craftsman publishes "The Need of a National Academy" by Alexander

March 12–April 17: 85th Annual Exhibition, National Academy; exhibits *The Tenth Muse*

March 17–April 17: Berlin; Königliche Akademie der Künste, Ausstellung Amerikanischer Kunst: toured to Kunstverein, Munich, April 30–May 19; exhibits *Sunlight* and *Portrait of Mrs. Alexander*

April 1: New York American: Charles Frohman's winter production will be Maude Adams in *Chantecler* with costumes by Alexander

May 1: Brussels, International Fine Arts Exposition; exhibits "figure with luminous light"

May 2–June 30: Fourteenth Annual Carnegie International, exhibits *The Tenth Muse* and *Summer's Day;* Duveneck exhibits *Portrait of John W. Alexander*

May 9: Elizabeth Alexander to Harrison Morris, "decision today about additional surgery"

May 11: re-elected President of the National Academy of Design

May 13–July 15: Paris, National Society of Fine Art; lends to its exhibit of paintings on the theme of children

May 17: Elizabeth Alexander to Morris: fourth and "last surgery took place on Sunday;" "feverish"
May 24: Elizabeth Alexander to Morris: Alexander got up for first time in ten days; four months since he worked; severe pain; Seabright on Sunday if strong enough
May 28: Gothamite: the previous week Mrs. Harry Payne Whitney hosted an exhibit of young artists; Alexander a juror
May 30: *Daily Citizen*: Alexander went to San Francisco to supervise the tableaux and color schemes for Maude Adams; to be accompanied by William Furst; in the end he does not go (June 6: Maude Adams as Rosalind in *As You Like It* at University of California, San Francisco)
June 1: elected member, American Academy of Arts and Letters
June 6: Elizabeth Alexander to Beatty: after his fourth and last operation Alexander was bedridden with a high temperature for 10 days
July 13: sails on *Mauretania* to Paris for the summer; went abroad for his health and to work on costume and stage designs for *Chantecler*
by September 10: having returned from Europe, Alexander is in Onteora where he painted "posters" for the Shakespeare Fête
October 18–November 27: Twenty Third Annual Exhibition of Oil Paintings and Sculpture by American Artists, Art Institute of Chicago; exhibits *Sunlight*
November 30: New York, Carnegie Hall; Tribute to Mark Twain, William Dean Howells presides, Alexander on memorial committee
November 30: Exposición Internacional de Arte del Centenario, Buenos Aires, concours award for *A Quiet Hour*
December 10–January 8, 1911: Winter Exhibition, National Academy of Design, exhibits *Summer's Day*
December 13–January 22, 1911: Corcoran Gallery of Art, Third Annual Exhibition of Oil Paintings by Contemporary American Artists; exhibits *Sunlight*
December 19: New York; Salmagundi Club dinner honors Alexander
December 20: New York; MacDowell Club, Masque Ball, costumes under direction of Mr. and Mrs. Alexander
December 30: New York Sun: Alexander will chair memorial exhibition for Winslow Homer scheduled for February

1911

January–December: President, National Institute of Arts and Letters
January 23: New York; Maude Adams in *Chantecler* opens at the Knickerbocker Theater; costumes by Alexander
February 5–March 26: 106th Annual Exhibition, Pennsylvania Academy of the Fine Arts; *Sunlight* lent by Art Institute of Chicago
February 15: New York; Alexander chairs meeting of New York art societies regarding a new site for the National Academy of Design building
February 24: elected President of the School Art League; promotes industrial design in city schools
February 25: Republican Club of the City of New York; speaks on "Can New York be Made the Art Center of the World?"
March 2: New York; The Digressionists, Fifth Exhibition & Dinner at the Century Club; jurors: Alexander, F. M. L. Tonetti, Wilson Eyre and Rockwell Kent
March 4: New York; Tribute to John M. Carrère, architect of the New York Public Library; Alexander honorary pallbearer
March 7: New York Times: Alexander taken ill and cancels $10,000 Cleveland court house mural contract
March 28: New York Times: Artists' Suffrage League meeting; Alexander speaks on individuality in art and need for an art building
March 30: one-week exhibit at Lotus Club (New York); exhibits *Phyllis*
early April through summer: Esposizione Internazionale d'Arte, Rome, exhibits *Memories* and *The Tenth Muse*
April: Art Club of Philadelphia, Second Special Exhibition of Eminent Living American Painters; exhibits *Study in Tone*
April 4: New York; Third Annual Luncheon, League of Political Education; Count Leo Tolstoy and Alexander guests of honor; Alexander speaks on the need for an art building
April 24–May 6: Detroit Publishing Co., New York, exhibits paintings, studies, color facsimiles, and carbon photographs
April 27–June 30: Fifteenth Annual Carnegie International; exhibits *Sunlight* (first class medal)
May 1: Annual Meeting, National Society of Mural Painters; delivers tribute to Francis D. Millet
May 10: Board of Trustees, New York Public Library issues resolution of appreciation to Alexander for the hanging of the paintings in the Lenox and Stuart Galleries of the library; Annual Meeting, National Academy of Design, Alexander re-elected President
May 12: Buffalo; Sixth Annual Exhibition of Selected Paintings by American Artists at the Albright Art Gallery; exhibits *Phyllis*
May 16–18: Washington, DC; Second Annual Convention of American Federation of Arts; Alexander speaks on "The Art Outlook"
May 23: opening of the New York Public Library
May 25: recovering from a serious operation
June 1: New Haven, Conn.; lectures on "Individuality in Art," Yale University, School of Fine Arts

June 23: Pittsburgh Press: $22,000 approved for Harrisburg State Capital murals; Alexander agrees to a contract

summer: Onteora; resides at Treetops; sometime in August moves to The Bushes; very ill; ear infection; not working

August 23–November 3: George B. Post, architect for the Wisconsin State Capitol, negotiates with Alexander to paint three murals for the Senate Chamber

fall: Yale University President and John Ferguson Weir, Dean of School of Fine Arts, aggressively court Alexander to succeed Weir

early October: returns to the city from Onteora

October 25: New York; Alexander named head of National Academy Association

November 1: Elizabeth A. Alexander purchases The Bushes, Onteora

November 1: Pittsburgh Dispatch: Alexander named to City Art Commission for the beautification of Pittsburgh

November 6: New York; Metropolitan Museum reception for a new Egyptian wing hosted by J. P. Morgan, Edward Robinson, Alexander, and Wilhelm von Bode from Berlin

November 14–December 27: Twenty-Fourth Annual Exhibition of American Oil Paintings and Sculpture, Art Institute of Chicago; exhibits *Primrose*

November 16–December 26: Exhibition of Works by Members of the Société des Peintres et des Sculpteurs, Albright Art Gallery, exhibits *At the Window*

November 28: Weir to Alexander, accepts his refusal of Yale deanship

December 9–January 7, 1912: Winter Exhibition, National Academy of Design; exhibits *The Ring*

December 19: New York; Christmas Festival, MacDowell Club, President Alexander contributes to costume design for Shakespearian pageant

December 19: first meeting of the Association of American Painters and Sculptors

December 23: Percy MacKaye's *The Scarecrow* about to open on Broadway with Alexander's portrait of the lead male character as a stage prop

1912

January 4–28: exhibits *At the Window* at Exhibition of Works by Members of the Société des Peintres et des Sculpteurs, Art Institute of Chicago; February 4 at The City Art Museum, St. Louis; March 8–31, Museum of Fine Arts, Boston with the addition of *Isabella and the Pot of Basil*

January 17: Washington, DC; Seventh Annual meeting of Washington Society of Fine Arts; Alexander lectures on American Illustrators

February 1: Albany; on the previous Tuesday a bill was introduced in the state legislature incorporating the National Academy Association

February 4–March 24: 107th Annual Exhibition, Pennsylvania Academy of the Fine Arts; exhibits *Primrose* and *The Ring*

March 13: New York; MacDowell Club Fifth Annual Dinner; 70 ft.-long mural created by 13 artist members including Alexander

March 18: New York Evening World "Is the Modern Woman Beautifully Dressed?" Alexander is quoted

March 18–April 6: New York; exhibits at First Annual Exhibition, National Association of Portrait Painters

March 29: Albany; legislation to incorporate the National Academy Association sent to the Governor for approval

April 2: Pittsburgh; Carnegie International Jury of Award meet: Alexander, Chase, Davis, Foster, Lathrop, Schofield, Symons, Tarbell, Sir Alfred East (Great Britain) and Henri le Sidaner (France)

April 6: attends Art Commission of Pittsburgh business meeting

April 12: Albany; incorporation of the National Academy Association approved

April 25–June 30: exhibits at Sixteenth Annual Exhibition Carnegie International

May 1: New York; Annual Meeting, National Society of Mural Painters; as First Vice President pays tribute to Francis D. Millet who died on the Titanic

May 8: New York; National Academy of Design re-elected President

May 9: Washington, DC; speaks at third annual meeting, American Federation of Arts

summer: Onteora, The Bushes

July 25: Dean Weir comes to Onteora to sit for his portrait

July 31: New York; first meeting of the directors of the Association of American Painters and Sculptors (AAPS)

October 4: returns to New York City from Onteora

December 4: New York Times: Woman's Titanic Memorial Benefit will have the "coloring" of a performance by Mr. and Mrs. Alexander and costumes by Mrs. Alexander

December 14–January 12, 1913: exhibits at Winter Annual, National Academy of Design

December 17–January 26, 1913: exhibits at Corcoran Gallery of Art, Fourth Annual Exhibition of Oil Paintings by Contemporary American Artists

December 18: New York; Annual Christmas Festival, MacDowell Club, Alexander directs costumes made by Mrs. Alexander

1913

January 20: Annual Dinner The Berkeley Institute, Brooklyn; guest of honor

February 1–14: exhibits at Second Annual Exhibition, National Association of Portrait Painters
February 4: New York; attends Louis C. Tiffany's Egyptian Fête; poses several "living pictures;" dresses as a mummy
February 11: elected to one-year term as trustee of American Academy in Rome
February 17–March 15: New York; The International Exhibition of Modern Art at the Armory
February 20–March 10: Chicago; Scammon Lecture Series on Feb 24 and 27, March 3 and 6; Alexander speaks on "Painting as a Profession"
February 24: Chicago; honoree at dinner by Chicago Literary Club
February 27: Art Institute of Chicago, reception for Exhibition of Paintings by John W. Alexander; exhibits 28 pictures
March 11: *New York Tribune*: National Academy Association has adopted a new plan for an enlarged facility by adding on to the Fine Arts Building at 215 West 57th Street
March 22–April 12: New York; Academy of Misapplied Art exhibition; exhibits "cubistic" work
April 3: Pittsburgh, Carnegie International Jury of Award meets: Alexander, Chase, Davis, Hawthorne, Henri, Schofield, Symons, Wiles, Rene Xavier Prinet (France), and Henry Caro-Delvaille (France)
April 24–June 30: Pittsburgh; Seventeenth Annual Carnegie International, exhibits *Portrait of Mrs. Thruston Wright*
May 10–August 31: Rochester; Albright Art Gallery, Eighth Annual Exhibition of Selected Paintings by American Artists; exhibits *Sunlight* and *The Gossip*
May: MacDowell Club exhibition of works on paper; Alexander exhibits two burlesques of male figures
May 8: New York; Alexander re-elected President of the National Academy of Design
summer: Onteora, The Bushes
August 23: invited to organize a group of his pictures for a dedicated gallery at the 1915 Panama–Pacific International Exposition
September 12: *Pittsburgh Sun*: Harrisburg Capitol Public and Grounds and Building Commission will meet with Alexander about the North Corridor decoration
October 4: *New York Evening Post*: free Saturday art courses for school children offered by the School Art League; Alexander instructs elementary school children
October 18: *Christian Science Monitor*: Alexander will paint U.S. President Wilson
November–December: Mr. and Mrs. Alexander assist Maude Adams in three productions including costumes for *The Legend of Leonora*
November 23: *New York Press*: Alexander poses tableaux at home of Mrs. Marshall Orme Wilson (née Astor)
mid December: Chicago, Fine Arts Building; exhibits *Her Birthday*
December 7: *New York Times*: MacDowell Club Festival will include tableaux vivants by Alexander after Hals and Watteau

1914

January 5: New York; attends premiere of Maude Adams's *Legend of Leonora*
January 9: Chicago; The Friends of American Art Loan Exhibition of American Paintings; Edward Ryerson lends two Alexander portraits
January 10: New York; speaks at presentation of portrait of Dr. Alexander C. Humphreys to Stevens Institute of Technology
January 22: Alexander re-elected President of the National Academy Association
January 22: National Arts Club sponsors an exhibit of American Art sent to Montgomery County Arts Association, Dayton, Ohio; exhibits *The Gossip*
January 24: Newport, R.I.: lectures under auspices of the Art Association of Newport
February 4: Third Annual Exhibition, National Association of Portrait Painters; exhibits *Portrait of President Humphreys;* travels to Pittsburgh
February 21: New York; American Pageant Association; Alexander a speaker
March 13: *New York Sun*: National Academy announcement that jury of awards reduced from 30 to 7 members
March 14: *Evening Post*: Parks Department vacating the Arsenal; Alexander renews effort to secure site for National Academy
March 15: *Providence Journal*: exhibition, *American Mural Painters*, at the Rhode Island School of Design toured by the American Federation of Arts; Alexander represented by sketch of *Apotheosis of Pittsburgh*
March 16: to Harrison Morris: "have been shut up practically all this winter"
March 18: *New York Evening Globe*: appointment to Carnegie International jury; foreign jurors Henry Caro-Delvaille (France) and Julius Olsson (Great Britain)
March 21–April 26: National Academy of Design, 89th Annual Exhibition, exhibits *June*
March 23: *New York Sun*: Museum of French Art exhibit of members; exhibits *The Green Gown* and *The Green Bow*
March 28: New York; Woman's Suffrage Party hosts meeting on "The Relation between the Fine Arts and Woman's Suffrage;" Alexander a speaker

April: *The Century* magazine publishes "The Transitional Age in Art"

April 3: New York; School Art League benefit under auspices of the National Academy

April 9: illness prevents Alexander from travelling to Pittsburgh for Carnegie International jury duty

April 18: *American Art News*: 23rd Annual Exhibition of Fakirs, Art Students League; *June* parodied

April 21: New York; re-elected President, National Academy

April 30–June 30: Eighteenth Annual Carnegie International; exhibits *Her Birthday*; Jury of Award; smaller version toured to Chicago in August, Detroit in October, and Indianapolis in January 1915

May 2: *Evening Star*: Alexander to paint portrait of U.S. President Woodrow Wilson for Princeton

May 2: elected President, National Society of Mural Painters

May 10: *New York Press*: *The Mother* to be used in Empire State Suffrage Campaign

May 14–October: London; Anglo-American Exhibition; serves on U.S. committee with Hugo Reisinger (Chairman); exhibits *Thurlow Weed* and *Portrait of a Lady*

May 16–August 31: Ninth Annual Exhibition, Albright Art Gallery, Buffalo; exhibits *Memories*, *June*, *A Flower*, and *Other Days*

May 18: Onteora, Elizabeth Alexander, Ruth Noyes and Mrs. James W. Alexander registered at Bear & Fox; Alexander may have gone alone to The Bushes

July 4: Nashville paper reports on summer Loan Exhibition under auspices of Nashville Art Association at the Parthenon toured by the American Federation of Arts; Alexander represented

October 14: letter from U.S. President Wilson, acknowledges Alexander's illness and sets condition for sitting for portrait

October 16: attends dinner by Society of Illustrators to honor Arthur B. Frost

October 17: member, American Artists' Committee for the Relief of the Families of French Soldier-Artists

October 26: *Pittsburgh Chronicle*: resigns from Pittsburgh Art Commission

November 3–December 4: Twenty-Seventh Annual Exhibition of American Oil Paintings and Sculpture, Art Institute of Chicago; exhibits *June*

November 8: *The World*: *Breton Peasant* and another exhibited at MacDowell Club

November 22: *The World*: "What is the Matter with American Art? The American Public Says John W. Alexander"

November 24 & 25: New York; Alexander and other jurors meet for Panama–Pacific Exposition

December 5: New York; presides over Third Annual Luncheon, School Art League

December 16–January 24, 1915: Corcoran Gallery of Art, Fifth Annual Exhibition, Oil Paintings by Contemporary American Artists; exhibits *June*

December 19: member, jury of selection for National Academy Winter exhibition

December 29: attends Christmas party, Architectural League of New York

1915

January 7–31: New York; National Arts Club members exhibit; juror

January 7–February 7: Minneapolis Institute of Arts, inaugural exhibition; exhibits *A Ray of Sunlight*

January 18: Maude Adams in *The Ladies' Shakespeare*, Broad St. Theater, Philadelphia; costumes and set by Alexander

January 21: New York; hosts reception to increase membership in School Art League

January 24: *The World*: Half Moon Club annual dinner at the University Club; Alexander attended

January 26: *Morning Telegraph*: A. E. Gallatin collection exhibited at studio of Mrs. . H. P. Whitney under auspices of the Museum of French Art to benefit French soldier-artists; includes Alexander's *Whistler in London*

February 1: Knoedler's opens sales exhibit for the Relief Fund of Families of French Soldier-Artists; Alexander represented

February 6: New York; Thirteenth Annual Exhibition, Architectural League of New York dinner; Alexander a speaker

February 9: *New York Tribune*: Fourth Annual Exhibition, National Association of Portrait Painters will benefit families of French artists; Alexander represented

by February 11: Arden Studios opens under the direction of Mrs. John W. Alexander and Elizabeth B. Averell

February 15: *New York Herald*: officers of Metropolitan Museum re-elected; Alexander on executive committee

February 20–December 4: Panama–Pacific International Exposition; exhibits *Phyllis*

March 5: *Star Independent* (Harrisburg): contract not signed for the North Corridor State Capital Building; Alexander says bond given to original contractor, John Sanderson, still valid; Harrisburg considering replacing Alexander

February 24: New York; *Sanctuary: A Bird Masque* by Percy MacKaye performed at the Hotel Astor; Alexander served on Committee of Arrangements.

March 10: New York; announces at officers' meeting of National Academy of Design his intent not to be a candidate for President

March 20–April 25: National Academy, 90th Annual; on jury of awards

March 27: New York Evening Post supplement: an interview with Alexander, "The Fight for Art in New York City"

April 14: annual meeting of Municipal Arts Society; Alexander elected a member

April 26: annual meeting of the Board of Managers, School Art League, President Alexander presides

April 27: Boston Evening Transcript reports on exhibition at Reinhardt Gallery of sculptors on the theme "What is War?"; Alexander on jury

April 28: New York; J. Alden Weir elected to succeed Alexander as President of National Academy

May 31: New York; Alexander dies at home after an operation and illness of two weeks

June 3: New York; funeral at Church of the Ascension; burial in Princeton; pallbearers Harry Watrous for J. Alden Weir, Edwin Blashfield, Edward Robinson, Herbert Adams, Cass Gilbert, Frederick Stokes, Charles D. Gibson, Charles H. Russell, Robert Abbe, and Thomas Hastings.

November 17–December 15, 1915: New York; Exhibition of Selected Works by the Late John W. Alexander, Arden Gallery

1916–17

March 1916–1917 John White Alexander Memorial Exhibition, Carnegie Institute, Pittsburgh March 1916; reduced version tours eleven museums: Corcoran Gallery of Art, May 6–21,1916, Detroit Institute of Arts, November 1916; diverted to *Special Exhibitions, The Art Institute of Chicago*, Dec. 12, 1916–Jan. 2, 1917; Cincinnati Art Museum, January 6–29, 1917; Milwaukee Art Institute, February 1917; Minneapolis Institute of Arts, March 3–28, 1917; City Art Museum, St. Louis, opens April 8, 1917; Colorado Springs Art Society, opens May 6; Cleveland Museum of Art, June 29–August 26, 1917; Toledo Museum of Art, September 1917; Memorial Art Gallery, Rochester, October 1917; Rhode Island School of Design, November 8–29, 1917

1917–18

December 29, 1917–January 10, 1918: The Century Association, Memorial Exhibition of the Works by the Late John W. Alexander, N. A.

NOTES

Preface

1 Harrison S. Morris to Elizabeth A. Alexander, June 2, 1915, Harrison S. Morris papers, Princeton University, Rare Books and Special Collections.
2 William W. Andrew, *Otto H. Bacher* (Madison, Wis., Education Industries, 1981), 262.
3 Leon Dabo to Alexander, May 15, 1908, JWA papers.
4 "J.W. Alexander, Noted Artist, Passes Away," *Pittsburgh Dispatch*, June 2, 1915, John White Alexander papers, Archives of American Art, Smithsonian Institution.
5 See *Apollo*, January 2012, 58, Fig. 1.

Chapter 1

1 "J.W. Alexander, Noted Artist Passes Away," *Pittsburg Dispatch*, June 2, 1915, Scrapbook: 1914–1915, John White Alexander papers, Archives of American Art, Smithsonian Institution (hereafter JWA papers).
2 Harrison S. Morris papers (C0003), Princeton University Library, Department of Rare Books and Special Collections.
3 "Letters – and – Art," *The Literary Digest*, June 19, 1915, 1466-8.
4 Elizabeth A. Alexander, "The Painting Grandpa, Childhood," John White Alexander estate, 1974, author's copy.
5 Arthur F. Jones and Bruce Weber, *The Kentucky Painter: From the Frontier Era to the Great War* (University of Kentucky Art Museum, January 25–March 15, 1981), 71.
6 Colonel Edward Jay Allen's parents wed on December 24, 1816, meaning Alexander's album was executed a few years after the anniversary.
7 Contrary to most biographical accounts, including those of his family, there is no record of him finishing high school, according to the Pittsburgh Central High School enrollment book, 1855–1906, Pittsburgh School District Records 1836–1937, AIS 1969.18, Archives Service Center, University Library System, University of Pittsburgh.
8 George Thornton Fleming, *My High School Days, Including a Brief History of Pittsburgh Central High School* (Wm. G. Johnston, & Co., Pittsburgh, 1904), 74.
9 Alexander to the Allen family, December 27, 1874, Correspondence, JWA papers.
10 DeWitt Lockman interview with Elizabeth A. Alexander, January 24, 1928, 8-9, JWA papers.
11 Alexander to the Allen family, December 27, 1874, Correspondence, JWA papers.
12 *Pittsburgh Dispatch*, June 2, 1915, Scrapbooks: 1914-1915. JWA papers.
13 Artwork: Sketchbooks circa 1873-1899, frame 3, JWA papers.
14 Alexander to Colonel Edward J. Allen, March 2, 1875, Correspondence, JWA papers.
15 Alexander to Colonel Allen, March 29, 1875, Correspondence, JWA papers.
16 Alexander to Colonel Allen, April 7, 1875, Correspondence, JWA papers.
17 Alexander to Colonel Allen, April 17, 1875, Correspondence, JWA papers.
18 Alexander to Colonel Allen, May 18, 1875, Correspondence, JWA papers. Once he became an illustrator he was paid $8, raised to $10 in October.
19 Alexander to Colonel Allen, May 26, 1875, Correspondence, JWA papers.
20 Alexander to Colonel Allen, October 24, 1875, Correspondence, JWA papers.
21 Alexander to Colonel Allen, November 28, 1875, Correspondence, JWA papers.
22 Alexander to Colonel Allen, July 2, 1876, Correspondence, JWA papers.
23 Alexander to Colonel Allen, September 12, 1875, Correspondence, JWA papers.
24 According to J. Walker McSpadden, John Wesley Beatty and Alexander as youths traveled to Ligonier at the foot of the Allegheny Mountains to sketch near a trout stream.

25 Alexander to Colonel Allen, January 31, 1876, Correspondence, JWA papers.
26 Alexander to Colonel Allen, July 2, 1876, Correspondence, JWA papers.
27 Alexander to Mrs. Allen, March 4, 1877, Correspondence, JWA papers. He was near-certain of orders from a Mrs. Coleman and a Mr. Park.
28 Maria Louise Johnson Reinhart Devoll (Reinhart's widow), "The Life and Experiences of Albert Grantley Reinhart", unpublished, Reinhart estate, courtesy of Roy Pederson, Lambertville, New Jersey, author's copy.
29 Alexander to Colonel Allen, September 30, 1877, Correspondence, JWA papers. The Indiana's port is Philadelphia, not New York.
30 The unpublished biography of Ab Reinhart (see note 28 above) written by his widow gives an account of the two of them being met by Charles and his family at the boat, most likely at Dieppe, and staying with Charles in Paris for a few days. Charles's presence in Paris at this time cannot be verified by other sources.
31 Alexander to Colonel Allen, September 9, 1877, Correspondence, JWA papers.
32 Edward Brown, "Fine Arts in Europe," *Evening Post* (New York), October 27, 1875.
33 William W. Andrews, *Otto H. Bacher* (Education Industries, Inc., Madison, Wis., 1981), 255.
34 Alexander to William Allen, September 17, 1877, Correspondence, JWA papers.
35 Alexander to William Allen, October 16, 1877, Correspondence, JWA papers.
36 Alexander to Mrs. Allen, November 11, 1877, Correspondence, JWA papers.
37 Artwork: Sketchbooks, undated, Box 3, folder 7, JWA papers. Though the book was manufactured in Pittsburgh, the drawings surely date from Munich.
38 Alexander to William Allen, April 27, 1878, Correspondence, JWA papers and Albert Reinhart to J.W. Beatty, February 7, 1916, Correspondence, Carnegie Institute, Museum of Art papers, Archives of American Art.
39 Alexander to Mrs. Allen, May 5, 1878, Correspondence, JWA papers.
40 Alexander to William Allen, April 27, 1878, Correspondence, JWA papers.
41 Lisa N. Peters, "Youthful Enthusiasm Under a Hospitable Sky: American Artists in Polling, Germany, 1870s–1880s," *The American Art Journal*, vol. xxi, nos. 1 and 2, 2000, 67.
42 Alexander to William Allen, July 7, 1878 and October 13, 1978, Correspondence, JWA papers. In the former letter, Alexander notes his address in Polling, and in the latter, the name of his landlord. Marieanne von Konig of Polling, Bavaria in an email to the author, January 10, 2008, confirmed the spelling of the landlord's surname as Seitz.
43 In an undated letter to Norbert Heermann (c.1930s), Mills lists himself, Ritter and "a" Turner as boarders, but does not list Alexander. Charles Mills papers, William H. Gerdts Library, New York (hereafter C. Mills papers).
44 Andrews, *Otto H. Bacher*, 25.
45 Alexander to Colonel Allen, September 22, 1878, Correspondence, JWA papers.
46 These excursions are described in letters to Mrs. Allen of October 6, 1878 and June 1, 1879, Correspondence, JWA papers.
47 1973/74 Alexander estate, Snapshots of some pages from the album, now unlocated, are in the author's collection.
48 A pencil drawing of the Polling skyline appears in a sketchbook manufactured by Adrian Bruger. American Academy of Arts and Letters, New York.
49 Alexander to Colonel Allen, July 14, 1878, Correspondence, JWA papers.
50 Katharine M. Roof, *The Life and Art of William Merritt Chase* (Hacker Art Books, New York, 1975, reprint of 1917 edition), 53.
51 Charles Mills to Norbert Heermann, November 13 (c.1930s). C. Mills papers.
52 According to Charles Mills in a letter of November 13 (c.1930s), the diploma was signed by John W. Alexander, Charles Corwin, Frederick Freer, Alden Fordham, S. W. Hettes (or Hottes), Charles Lang, Otto Krehbiel, Charles Mills, Louis Moeller, Louis Ritter, Jean Seliger, Francis Strowbridge, Ross Turner, W. E. Turner, and officers, J. Frank Currier, President, Frank Duveneck, Treasurer and M. O. Wooff, Secretary.
53 Alexander to William Allen, July 7, 1878, Correspondence, JWA papers.
54 Roof, *William Merritt Chase*, 44.
55 Charles Mills to Norbert Heermann, undated. C. Mills papers.
56 Alexander estate, 1973/74, unlocated, slide owned by author.
57 *Munich Portrait*, Peter Juley Photograph Archives, Smithsonian Institution.
58 Alexander to Edward Elisha Phelps, August 2, 1879, Correspondence, JWA papers.
59 Michael Quick, *An American Painter Abroad: Frank Duveneck's European Years*, Cincinnati Art Museum,

October 5, 1987–January 3, 1988, 49. Likewise, in the undated Charles Mills letters to Norbert Hermann, Mills corroborates that Alexander and Ritter accompanied Duveneck, C. Mills papers.

60 Charles Mills to Norbert Heermann, October 3 (1930s), C. Mills papers.

61 Alexander to Mrs. Allen, October 19, 1879, Correspondence, JWA papers.

62 Handwritten account of Duveneck's Boys by Charles Mills of unknown date lists members of the Duveneck School in Florence, including those who followed from Munich and others who joined from elsewhere. Frank and Elizabeth Boott Duveneck papers, 1851–1972: Correspondence: Francis B. and Josephine Duveneck, 1879–1971, Archives of American Art, Smithsonian Institution. Mills' list differs slightly from that published by Otto Bacher (Andrews, *Otto H. Bacher*, 260).

63 Ibid.

64 Alexander to Mrs. Allen, December 28, 1879, Correspondence, JWA papers.

65 Ibid. This letter describes the episodes described in this paragraph.

66 Alexander to Edna Allen, c.June 1880, collection of Elizabeth Cahill.

67 Alexander to Mrs. Allen, March 17, 1880, Correspondence, JWA papers.

68 William Dean Howells, *Indian Summer*, introduction and notes by Scott Bennett; text established by Scott Bennett & David J. Nordion (Indiana University Press, Bloomington and London: 1971), 43. Howells kept a diary of his stay in Florence from December 1882 to April 1883 which was serialized in *Harper's Monthly* beginning July 1885 and published as a book in February 1886. Any reference to an Alexander-like character would be by recollection as he had left Florence by the time Howells wrote his book.

69 Andrews, *Otto H. Bacher*, 262.

70 Alexander to Colonel Allen, June 11, 1876, (Correspondence, JWA papers) confirms that Alexander visited the Centennial Exhibition in Philadelphia the first week of June.

71 Alexander to Colonel Allen, March 4, 1880, Correspondence, JWA papers.

72 Andrews, *Otto H. Bacher*, 262.

73 Warren Adelson et al., *Sargent's Venice* (New Haven, Yale University Press, 2006), 188.

74 Andrews, *Otto H. Bacher*, 262.

75 Otto Bacher, *With Whistler in Venice* (New York, Century Co., 1909), 34–5.

76 Alexander to Albert Grantley Reinhart, July 19, 1880, Reinhart/Devoll estate, collection of Mary Anne Goley.

77 "How Whistler Posed for John W. Alexander," *World's Work*, March 1905, 5994.

78 The author is grateful to Eric Denker for identifying the location depicted in the painting.

79 Andrews, *Otto H. Bacher*, 262.

80 Eric Denker, author of *Whistler and His Circle in Venice* (Corcoran Gallery of Art, 2003), brought to my attention Whistler's etching of the same subject.

81 Adelson et al, *Sargent's Venice*.

82 Alexander signed and made a caricature-like drawing in Katherine Bronson's Birthday Book (private collection, Venice) on the page for those born on October 7. This information came to me by way of Richard Ormond who introduced me to Rosella Manoli who confirmed the existence of the entry.

83 "Honors to an Artist," undated news clipping, Scrapbook: c.1877–95, frame 2, JWA papers.

84 E.R. and J. Pennell, *The Life of James McNeill Whistler* (Philadelphia: J. B. Lippincott Co. 1911), 192.

85 Ibid.

86 Alexander to Mrs. Allen, March 17, 1880, JWA papers.

87 I am indebted to David R. Grinnell, Reference and Access Archivist and Zachary Brodt, Records Manager, University of Pittsburgh Library System, for identifying the dispute which would have been the subject of Alexander's assignment. The strike did not take place.

88 Elizabeth Allen (Mrs. Edward J. Allen) to Mary, December 19, 1880 (collection of Elizabeth Cahill).

Chapter 2

1 DeWitt Lockman interview with Elizabeth Alexander, January 24, 1928, 22, JWA papers.

2 Ibid.

3 "The Academy of Design," *New York Times*, March 30, 1882, 31.

4 Linda Merrill et al., *After Whistler, The Artist and His Influence on American Painting* (High Museum of Art, November 22, 2003–February 8, 2004), 134; Merrill made this correlation in her catalogue essay.

5 *New York Times*, March 30, 1882.

6 David Dearinger, *Paintings and Sculpture in the Collection of the National Academy of Design*, ed. Mary Lublin and John Davis (Manchester, Hudson Hills Press, 2004), 13.

7 Alexander to Edward Phelps, December 20, 1881.

8 January 27, 1883.

9 Records of Alexander's appointment as an instructor in the School of Science is based solely on an index card in his faculty file and the article in the *Alumni Princetonian* of April 28, 1898 (email to the author, June 12, 2008 from Lynn Durgin, Seeley G. Mudd Manuscript Library, Princeton University). His appointment could have been as early as the beginning of the school term in September 1881 rather than the second half.

10 Clarke was not listed in the enrollment book for Central High according to David Grinnell, Reference and Access Archivist, Archives Service Center, University of Pittsburgh Library System, in an email to the author of July 31, 2012.

11 Mary Anne Goley, "John White Alexander's Princeton Legacy," *Princeton University Library Chronicle*, Vol. LXXV, No. 2, winter 2014, 270-4.

12 Photographs: Personal, c.1882–1912, frame 1 & 2, JWA papers.

13 *Bric-a-Brac*, Princeton student yearbook, 1882–3, 128. This is the reference for Alexander giving classes for the Sketching Club. My thanks go to Gretchen Oberfranc, former editor of the Princeton University Library Chronicle, for bringing it to my attention.

14 Alexander to Edward Phelps, March 5, 1883, JWA papers.

15 Jefferson is mentioned in a letter of March 22, 1875 to Colonel Allen. JWA papers.

16 Jervis McEntee diary, June 12, 1884, Jervis McEntee papers, 1850–1905, Archives of American Art, Smithsonian Institution.

17 DeWitt Lockman interview with Elizabeth Alexander, January 24, 1928, 28, JWA papers.

18 For an image see Series 10: Photographs, c.1870–1915, not scanned, box 40 OV, no. 12, JWA papers.

19 Sarah J. Moore, "John White Alexander (1856–1915): In Search of the Decorative," Ph.D. thesis, City University of New York, 1982, 105, note 39. Despite the critique, the painting is not recorded as being exhibited at the National Academy.

20 Alexander in three letters to Colonel Allen, May 23, 1884 from Tangier, June 10 from Madrid and July 16 from Dordrecht, describes their adventures and plans. JWA papers.

21 Artwork: Sketchbook 1884, JWA papers.

22 Postcards of these two paintings were mounted in an album that was part of the Alexander estate in 1973/74. The album is currently unlocated but the author took snapshots of the album pages.

23 Artwork: Sketchbook 1884, JWA papers.

24 Arthur Hoeber, "Thomas Shields Clarke," *Brush and Pencil*, August 1900, vol. vi, no. 5, 193-8.

25 There have been various readings of this quote. I believe it reads "a grand slip up" rather than "a grand step up."

26 *A Prize* may be a second aesthetic genre picture exhibited in the Pennsylvania Academy of the Fine Arts annual exhibition for 1882, but otherwise unknown.

27 Alexander to Colonel Allen, July 16, 1884, JWA papers. Which exhibition is unknown.

28 A color reproduction of this portrait exists in the files of the Abbe Museum, Bar Harbor, Maine.

29 Cleveland Abbe and Josephine Genung Nichols, *Abbe-Abbey Genealogy: In Memory of John Abbe and his Descendants* (New Haven, The Tuttle, Morehouse & Taylor Company, 1916), 243.

30 "Opening of the Exhibition at the American Art Galleries," *Brooklyn Daily Record*, November 8, 1885, JWA papers.

31 Alexander's portrait was three-quarter length in a white dress as recorded in Notes and Writings: Registers of Paintings and Exhibitions, circa 1887–1913, Portraits painted before 1887, JWA papers. Since, according to the Report of Record, Town Hall, Bristol, Rhode Island, she was born in 1867 (not 1871), the possibility of this being a portrait to mark her debut is likely. She was married to Arthur Rotch in 1892. Widowed, she married Ralph Curtis in 1897. Sargent's portrait of Colt is in the collection of the Cleveland Museum of Art.

32 *Evening Sun* (New York), February 24, 1905, JWA papers. This same article indicates that Alexander took several blank canvases to the session but no oils survive, only a charcoal sketch.

33 Harrison S. Morris, *Confessions in Art* (New York, Sears Publishing Company, Inc., c.1930), 159.

34 Albert Ludovici, *An Artist's Life in London and Paris, 1870–1925* (New York, Minton, Balch & Co., 1926), 87.

35 Charles de Kay, "John White Alexander," *Smith's Magazine*, vol. viii, no. 6, 918.

36 Charles de Kay, "The Old Poetic Guild in Ireland," *The Century*, April 1890, vol. xxxix, 893-901. Seeing as Alexander's illustrations were of de Kay's stories of Ireland, it is possible de Kay may not have been with Alexander in London and Paris.

37 Unidentified newspaper, c. summer 1887, Series 9: Printed Materials, box 3, folder 30, JWA papers.

38 On January 8, 1887 there appeared "I will Protect the Imported Porker", January 8, 1887, and on January 15 "Cleveland Can't Bury New York, Charles A. Dana's Presidential Cat-e-gory."

39 Alexander to Phelps, February 4, 1887, JWA papers.

40 Alexander to Phelps, September 24, 1887, JWA papers.

41 Alexander to Phelps, January 5, 1887, JWA papers.

42 Alexander to Phelps, April 22, 1887, JWA papers.
43 Alexander to Phelps, May 21, 1887, JWA papers.
44 Alexander to Phelps, May 26, 1887, JWA papers.
45 Alexander to Phelps, January 13, 1887, JWA papers.
46 Randall Gabrielan, former executive director, Monmouth County Historical Society, N. J., speculates in an email of November 2, 2003 to the author that what was once Alexander's studio was lost to fire.
47 *The World* (New York), July 24, 1888, Scrapbooks, JWA papers.
48 Randall Gabrielan, *Rumson: Shaping a Superlative Suburb* (Mount Pleasant, S.C.: Arcadia Publishing, 2002), 62. Henry M. Alexander's property was at 35 Ward Avenue.
49 Randall Gabrielan provided the author with a copy of the Rumson map, 1899 Wolverton Atlas of Monmouth County, Grid J2, with the identity of property owners filed with Monmouth County Historical Commission, Hall of Records.
50 DeWitt Lockman interview with Elizabeth Alexander, January 24, 1928, 26. JWA papers.
51 *The World* (New York), July 24, 1888, Scrapbooks, JWA papers.
52 This characterization of the triple portrait appears in Notes and Writings: Registers of Paintings and Exhibitions circa 1887–1913, Box 2, folder 11, frame 5, JWA papers.
53 Reference to the Manierre children's portrait can be found in Notes and Writings List of Paintings, circa 1893–1943, box 2, folder 12, frame 2, JWA papers.
54 Artwork: Bound Vol. 2, circa 1885–1996, box 3, folder 20, frame 2, JWA papers.
55 Bess's paternal grandmother was a Cabell from Virginia.
56 Alexander to Helena de Kay Gilder, November 17, 1887, Richard Watson Gilder Papers, The Lilly Library. Indiana University.
57 Series 10: Photographs, c.1870–1915; Photographs, Works of Art, Paintings, c.1885–1889: box 5, folder 54; JWA papers.
58 *Central New Jersey Times*, August 16, 1888, Scrapbooks: JWA papers.
59 *The World* (New York), July 24, 1888.
60 *The Epoch*, January 18, 1889, Scrapbooks: JWA papers.
61 *Town Topics*, undated, Scrapbook circa 1877–1895, frame 7, JWA papers.
62 Alfred Trumble, *Representative works of contemporary American artists* (New York: Garland Publishing, c. 1877, reprint, Introduction.
63 David Huntington et al., *The Quest for Unity: American Art between World's Fairs, 1876–1893* (Detroit Institute of Arts, August 22–October 30, 1983), 13.
64 Mariana Griswold Van Rensselaer, *Book of American Figure Painters* (Philadelphia, J. B. Lippincott Co. 1886, no pagination).
65 Huntington et al., *The Quest for Unity*, 17.
66 On the page where Alexander is discussed there appears, in the upper right corner, a caricature by Frances C. Lyons Houston made in the summer of 1885 when they were in East Gloucester. At the bottom of the page is a reproduction of a still life by Alexander.
67 DeWitt Lockman interview with Elizabeth Alexander, January 24, 1928, 25. The portrait was among Burnham's theatrical collection auctioned on December 11 and 12, 1922 at Walpole Galleries, New York.
68 "Town Topics," undated, Scrapbook circa 1877–1895, box 17, folder 1, frame 7, JWA papers.
69 A reproduction of the painting showing a signature and date in the lower right can be found in Photographs: Box 38/45, JWA papers.
70 "The Fellowcraft Election," *New York Times*, February 21, 1890, Scrapbooks, JWA papers.
71 Ruth Bohan, *Looking into Walt Whitman: American Art, 1850–1920* (University Park, Pennsylvania State University Press, 2006), 86.
72 Horace Traubel, *With Walt Whitman in Camden*, vol. ii (New York, D. Appleton), 549.
73 *Walt Whitman in Camden: A Selection of Prose from Specimen Days* with Preface by Christopher Morley and photographs by Arnold Genthe (Camden: The Haddon Craftsmen, 1938), 301.
74 Cahill family papers, Alexander to Harold Allen, February 25, 1886 and Artwork: Sketchbooks, circa 1873–1899, box 2, folder 32, frames 13 and 14, JWA papers.
75 *Walt Whitman in Camden*, 301.
76 Bohan, *Looking into Walt Whitman*, 91.
77 Richard Watson Gilder, *Letters of Richard Watson Gilder*, ed. Rosamond Gilder (Boston & New York, Houghton Mifflin Co., 1916), 186, 406.
78 DeWitt Lockman interview with Elizabeth Alexander, February 1, 1928, 1, JWA papers.
79 Alexander to Stephen Alden Tracy, May 5 (c.1890) and a subsequent letter the Friday before departure, Tracy family letters, Cornish, New Hampshire, author's copy.
80 Ibid.
81 This practice was followed by the Tracy family according to a conversation with the daughter of Stephen P. Tracy on July 7, 2000.
82 Alexander to Tracy, May 5, 1890.
83 *A Circle of Friends: Art Colonies of Cornish and Dublin* (Thorne-Sagendorph Art Gallery, Keene State College, Keene, N.H., March 9–April 26, 1985), 35, Fig. 37.

84 There are at least seven Cornish landscapes. Six are revealed in installation photographs of the 1916 Carnegie Memorial exhibition. A seventh is currently part of the Jean and Graham Devoe Williford Charitable Trust, Fairfield, Texas. This contradicts the listing of four Cornish landscapes in the 1916 memorial catalogue.

85 For a discussion of Alexander and the still life genre see Mary Anne Goley, "Out of the Kitchen into the Parlor, The Art of Still Life by John White Alexander" (Federal Reserve Board, Washington, D. C, June 27–September 8, 1995).

86 Alexander to Tracy, November 18, 1890, Tracy family papers, author's copy.

87 Thomas Nelson Page, *Harper's Monthly Magazine*, December 1890,
111-18, illus. 117.

88 *The Sun* (New York), November 29, 1890, JWA papers.

89 *New York Times*, April 26, 1891. JWA papers.

Chapter 3

1 Biographical Information: Personal Documents and Ephemera, box 1, folder 2, frame 7, JWA papers.

2 Alexander's signature appears in the Fremdenbuch der Klosterwirtschaft on June 18 and 20, 1891. The location of the original book is unknown. Both the Museum Polling and the Archives of American Art, Smithsonian Institution own copies.

3 DeWitt Lockman, interview with Elizabeth Alexander, February 1, 1928, 3, JWA papers.

4 Alexander to Phelps, November 14, 1891, Correspondence, JWA papers.

5 DeWitt Lockman, interview with Elizabeth Alexander, February 1, 1928, 3, JWA papers.

6 Richard Muther, *The History of Modern Painting* (New York: Macmillan, 1896), 700.

7 Ibid., 702.

8 Ibid., 703.

9 Alexander to Colonel Allen, December 26, 1891, JWA papers.

10 Ibid.

11 Elizabeth Alexander essay about Ivan Pranishnikoff, Alexander estate 1973/74, author's copy.

12 DeWitt Lockman, interview with Elizabeth Alexander, February 1, 1928, 3, JWA papers.

13 Biographical Information: Essays by Elizabeth Alexander about Others in Their Circle, undated, JWA papers.

14 Paul Fisher, "'The Dear Little Tobacconized *Salon*': Henrietta Reubell as Queer *Salonnière* in Henry James's Paris," in *Transforming Henry James*, ed. Anna De Biasio, Anna Despotopoulou, and Donatella Izzo (Newcastle upon Tyne, Cambridge Scholars Publishing, 2013), 2.

15 Biographical Information: Essays by Elizabeth Alexander about Others in Their Circle: "Miss Henrietta Reubell," undated, JWA papers.

16 Fisher, "*The Dear Little Tobacconized Salon*," 7.

17 Emily Montgomery (Skinner) formerly Mrs. Paul W. Bartlett to Mrs. Burwell, The Mint Museum, January 15, 1938, Dwelle History Collection, 1937–2007, The Mint Museum Archives, Charlotte, N.C., accession no. AR2013.2.

18 Quoted in Fisher, "The Dear Little Tobacconized Salon," 9.

19 Quoted in Paul Fisher, "'Her Smoking Was the Least of Her Freedoms': Henrietta Reubell, Miss Barrace, and the Queer Milieu of Henry James's Paris," *Henry James Review*, vol. xxxiii, no. 3 (Fall 2012), 247.

20 Biographical Information: Essays by Elizabeth Alexander about Others in Their Circle, *Henrietta Reubell*, undated, JWA papers.

21 Beatrix Whistler to Henrietta Reubell, Library of Congress, Manuscript Division, Pennell-Whistler Collection, PWC 14/1256/1.

22 Essay by Elizabeth A. Alexander, "Whistler as We Knew Him," Alexander estate 1973/74, author's copy.

23 Alexander to Colonel Allen, December 26, 1891, JWA papers.

24 Fisher, "'Her Smoking Was the Least of Her Freedoms,'" 173.

25 Armand Dayot to Alexander, May 1, 1892, JWA papers.

26 Russell T. Clement, Annick Houzé, and Christiane Erbolato-Ramsey, *A Sourcebook of Gauguin's Symbolist Followers: Les Nabis, Pont-Aven, Rose + Croix* (Westport, Conn.: Praeger, 2004), 694.

27 Elizabeth A. Alexander, "Whistler's Garden," Alexander estate, 1973/74, author's copy.

28 In Elizabeth A. Alexander's handwriting, undated, box 1, folder 78, frames 32-35 JWA papers.

29 DeWitt Lockman, interview with Elizabeth Alexander, February 1, 1928, 4. JWA papers.

30 Biographical Information: Essays by Elizabeth A. Alexander about Others in their Circle: "Le Pouldu," undated, JWA papers.

31 Alfred Thornton, *The Diary of an Art Student of the Nineties* (London: Sir Isaac Pitman & Sons, 1938), 91.

32 Biographical Information, Essays by Elizabeth Alexander about Others in Their Circle: "Le Pouldu," JWA papers.

33 Thornton, *The Diary of an Art Student of the Nineties*, 9.

34 Bogomila Welsh-Ovcharov, "Paul Gauguin's Third Visit to Brittany, June 1889–November 1890," in

Gauguin's Nirvana: Painters at Le Pouldu: 1889–90, ed. Eric M. Zafran (New Haven, Conn.: Yale University Press, 2001), 17.

35 Madame Fernande Rivet, wife of the mayor of Pont-Aven, identified the style of coif for the author, October 2000.
36 Biographical Information, Essays by Elizabeth Alexander about Others in Their circle: "Le Pouldu," undated, JWA papers.
37 The canvas was discovered in recent times by Berry-Hill Galleries as a separate canvas under the *Portrait of Mrs. Paul W. Bartlett*.
38 Image in the collection of the author.
39 Madame Fernande Rivet pointed out that a woman wears the coif of her native département no matter where she lives.
40 Photographs, box 6, folder 10, unscanned, JWA papers.
41 DeWitt Lockman, interview with Elizabeth Alexander, February 24, 1928, JWA papers.
42 Ibid.
43 DeWitt Lockman, interview with Elizabeth Alexander, February 1, 1928, JWA papers.
44 Ibid.
45 *The Sun* (New York), July 12, 1895, Scrapbook circa 1877–1895, JWA papers.
46 Ibid.
47 Alexander owned a postcard of both paintings that was mounted in a photograph album found in the artist's estate in 1973 by the author.
48 *The Sun* (New York), July 12, 1893, Scrapbook circa 1877–1895, JWA papers, describes all three salon entries. Other than through this written description *Portrait Jaune* is known only by a black-and-white reproduction.
49 Artwork: Sketchbooks, circa 1896, box 3, folder 4, frame 11, JWA papers.
50 Ibid. frame 28.
51 Louis de Fourcaud, "Les Arts Decoratifs aux Salon. I. Le Champs-de-Mars," *Revue des arts Decoratifs*, 14, no. 11, May 1894, 343.
52 "Le Salon du Champs-de-Mars," *Le Gaulois*, May 9, 1893, Scrapbook, 1877–1895, JWA papers.
53 *The Sun* (New York), July 12, 1894.
54 All three portraits are listed in "Notes and Writings: Registers of Paintings and Exhibitions circa 1887– 1913," box 2, folder 11, frame 5, "Incomplete List / Portraits Painted between 1887 and 1891", JWA papers.

Chapter 4

1 Alexander to Phelps, August 18, 1893, JWA papers.
2 DeWitt Lockman interview with Elizabeth Alexander, February 1, 1928, 6-7. JWA papers.
3 Ibid., 10.
4 "The New Salon in Paris," *New York Times*, April 24, 1894.
5 Emma Zorn to her mother, c. March 27, 1893 (ZAR 1186) and March 31, 1893, (ZAR 1187), Zorn Museum, Archives, Mora Sweden. Additionally Zorn gifted a print of Omnibus inscribed "'Homage' to Mrs. Alexander" (Irina Reed 1973/74).
6 Scrapbook: circa 1877–95, JWA papers.
7 Ibid.
8 Scrapbook, circa 1877–1895, JWA papers.
9 For a discussion of the symbolism of the mirror in *Devant La Glace* see Moore, "John White Alexander", 159-160.
10 In the *Monroe County Appeal*, May 11, 1967, it was stated on the occasion of the gift of the portrait to the Mark Twain Research Foundation, that Clemens is wearing a dress made by the wife of the artist "to please his taste." The source of this information was Phyllis Harrington, secretary to Clara Clemens Gabrilowitsch. Phyllis Harrington Papers, Mark Twain Birthplace SHS, MO DNR/Division of State Park, Florida, Mo.
11 By process of elimination this painting is the same as *Overmantle* noted in Notes and Writings: Lists of Paintings circa 1893–1943, box 2, folder 12, frame 5, JWA papers.
It was painted in Paris for Mrs. James W. Alexander, Sr.
12 See Mary Anne Goley, "John White Alexander's Panel for Music Room," *Bulletin of the Detroit Institute of Arts*, vol. 64, no. 4, 1989, 5-15.
13 *La Lanterne* (Paris), April 26, 1895, Scrapbook circa 1877–1895, JWA papers.
14 When the author first met Irina Reed in the early 1970s she owned a terracotta version of Rodin's Jean d'Aire that was a gift of the sculptor to her grandparents.
15 *La Patrie*, April 25, 1895, Scrapbook circa 1877–1895, JWA papers.
16 *L'Eclair*, April 25, 1895, Scrapbook circa 1877–1895, JWA papers.
17 *Harper's Bazaar*, April 6, 1895, Scrapbook, circa 1877–1895, JWA papers.
18 Robin Spencer, *The Aesthetic Movement: Theory and Practice* (London: Studio Vista/Dutton Pictureback, 1972, 31-32).
19 De la Bretonne, *Le Journal*, June 3, 1898, Scrapbook 1895–1900, JWA papers.

20 Helene Pinet, Musée Rodin, Paris, with a specialty on Rodin's models, brought to my attention an invoice in the museum archives for six days of work, signed "J. Very", and dated November 14, 1912. The assumption is that this was for modeling.

21 Elizabeth A. Alexander to Edna Allen, c. December 31, 1894 (collection of Elizabeth Cahill).

22 Ainsworth Rand Spofford, Annual Report of the Librarian of Congress for 1872, 10.

23 Richard Murray, *Art for Architecture, Washington, D.C., 1895-1925* (Washington D.C.: National Collection of Fine Arts, Smithsonian Institution, 1975), n.p.

24 Alexander to Bernard Green, February 1, 1895, Records of the Library of Congress: Buildings and Grounds, Manuscript Division, container 87.

25 Notes and Writings: notes undated, frames 32-4, JWA papers.

26 Royal Cortissoz, "Painting and Sculpture in the New Congressional Library," a series of articles in *Harper's Weekly*, "The Decorations of Mr. J. W. Alexander," 41, no 2092 (January 23, 1897, 82-5).

27 This is not to the same painting as in the collection of the Virginia Museum of Fine Arts.

28 Elizabeth A. Alexander to Edna Allen, December 31, 1894 (collection of Elizabeth Cahill).

29 Quoted from a Pittsburgh paper of October 10, 1895, scrapbook 1895–1900, frame 12, JWA papers.

30 "Honored An Artist," *Pittsburgh Dispatch*, December 10, 1895, Scrapbooks, JWA papers.

31 *Pittsburgh Bulletin*, November 16, 1895, Scrapbooks, JWA papers.

32 Alexander to John Wesley Beatty, November 15, 1895, Carnegie Institute, Museum of Art records, International, Correspondence, 1883–1962, Archives of American Art, Smithsonian Institution.

33 *Philadelphia Item*, January 1896, Scrapbook 1895-1900, box 17, folder 2, frame 29f, JWA papers.

34 John W. Sears, "The Portrait Work of John W. Alexander, " *Modern Art*, vol 4, no. 2, July 1896, 64-6.

35 Alexander and the Delsarte method was the subject of a lecture by Mary Anne Goley, "The Notion of Modernity in the Dynamics of John White Alexander's Figures," at a Symposium, "Modern Movements Exploring the Body in Modern American Art," Randolph College, March 16, 2013.

36 DeWitt Lockman interview with Elizabeth A. Alexander, February 1, 1928, 3.

37 Ruth Butler, *Rodin: the shape of genius* (New Haven: Yale University Press, 1993, 188).

38 *Auguste Rodin, images of desire: erotic watercolors and cut-outs*, introduction by Anne-Marie Bonnet (Munich: Schmirer/Mosel, 2001, 19).

39 Madeleine O'Donnell to Alexander, January 15, 1898, correspondence 1898–1900, JWA papers.

40 Alexander to John W. Beatty, September 13, 1896, Carnegie Institute, Museum of Art papers.

41 "First Annual Exhibition at the Carnegie Galleries," *Arts for America*, Chicago, December 1896, Scrapbook 1895–1900, box 17, folder 2, frame 48, JWA papers.

42 "Pittsburgh Artist Honored," *The Pittsburgh Dispatch*, November 11, 1896, Scrapbook 1895–1900, box 17, folder 2, frame 55, JWA papers.

43 When I first viewed the Alexander estate in 1973/74, I found fourteen Conté crayon drawings. Another one is in the collection of Berea College, Kentucky.

44 Mary Anne Goley, "Kindred spirits, John White Alexander, and Auguste Rodin," *The Magazine Antiques*, November/December 2011, 152.

45 Alexander to Colonel Allen, April 20, 1897, Correspondence, JWA papers.

46 Frantz Jourdain, *Jour et National*, April 23, 1897, Scrapbooks, JWA papers.

47 Louis de Fourcaud, "Champs de Mars," *Le Gaulois*, 1 supplement, April 23, 1897, Scrapbooks, JWA papers.

48 See Mary Anne Goley, "The Tribute of Isabella," *Apollo Magazine*, January 2012, vol. clxxv, no. 594, 58-64.

49 Ibid., illus. 58.

50 DeWitt Lockman interview with Elizabeth A. Alexander, February 1, 1928.

51 Susan Grant, "American Paintings Acquired by the French Government, 1879–1900", M.A. thesis, George Washington University, 1983, 78.

52 Morris, *Confessions on Art*, 159. Alexander to Colonel Allen, August 9, 1896, JWA papers, regarding nomination for Légion d'honneur.

53 Kenneth Neal, *A Wise Extravagance: The Founding of the Carnegie International Exhibitions, 1895- 1901* (University of Pittsburgh Press, 1996), 242, n. 23.

54 Ibid., 21.

55 Alexander to Beatty, September 17, 1897, Carnegie Institute, Museum of Art papers.

56 Ibid.

57 Alexander to Beatty, October 18, 1897, Carnegie Institute, Museum of Art papers.

58 Alexander to Beatty, July 25, 1896, Carnegie Institute, Museum of Art papers.

59 Giovanni Boldini to Beatty, December 30, 1896, Carnegie Institute, Museum of Art papers.
60 George de Forest Brush to Beatty, November 27, 1896, Carnegie Institute, Museum of Art papers.
61 Alexander to Beatty, September 8, 1898, Carnegie Institute, Museum of Art papers.
62 Alexander to Beatty, September 14, 1896, Carnegie Institute, Museum of Art papers.
63 Alexander to Beatty, October 12, 1896, Carnegie Institute, Museum of Art papers.
64 Alexander to Beatty, September 17, 1897, Carnegie Institute, Museum of Art papers.
65 Alexander to Beatty from Saas-Fee, Switzerland, undated, summer 1897, Carnegie Institute, Museum of Art papers.
66 Alexander to Beatty, September 10, 1897, Carnegie Institute, Museum of Art papers.
67 Garnett McCoy, "The Tenth Annual Carnegie Institute International Exhibition," *Archives of American Art Journal*, July 1, 1967, vol 7, nos. 3/4, 23-9.
68 Alexander to Beatty, September 17, 1897, Carnegie Institute, Museum of Art papers.
69 *Pittsburgh Post*, December 12, 1897, Scrapbooks, JWA papers.
70 *Public Ledger*, January 12, 1898, Scrapbooks, JWA papers.
71 "American Artists' Annual Exhibition," *New York Times*, March 19, 1898, Scrapbooks, JWA papers.
72 "A Fakirs' Exhibition," *New York Times*, May 18, 1916, 10.
73 *New York Tribune*, April 21, 1898, Scrapbooks, JWA papers.
74 Ronald G. Pisano and Bruce Weber, *Parodies of the American Masters: Rediscovering the Society of American Fakirs, 1891–1914* (Art Students League, New York, Berry-Hill Galleries, Inc., New York, and the Museums at Stony Brook, New York, 1993), 15.
75 "Der Kaiser in der Secessions-Ausstellung," *Neue Freie Press* (Vienna), April 5, 1898, Scrapbooks, JWA papers.
76 Alexander to Colonel Allen, June 26, 1898, Correspondence, JWA papers.
77 Scrapbooks, JWA papers.
78 *Le Journal*, June 13, 1898, Scrapbooks, JWA papers.
79 Notes and Writings: Registers of Paintings and Exhibitions, circa 1887–1913, JWA papers.
80 Eleanor Butler Alexander married Theodore Roosevelt, Jr. on June 20, 1910.
81 Alexander to Colonel Allen, June 26, 1898, Correspondence, JWA papers.
82 *Philadelphia Enquirer*, January 15, 1899, Scrapbooks, JWA papers.
83 Edwin A. Abbey to Beatty, February 11, 1898. Carnegie institute, Museum of Art.
84 George Boughton to Beatty February 12, 1898, Carnegie Institute, Museum of Art.
85 Walter Gay to Beatty, March 4, 1898, Carnegie Institute, Museum of Art.
86 Benjamin-Constant to Beatty, January 28, 1898, Carnegie Institute, Museum of Art.
87 Humphreys-Johnston to Beatty, September 3, 1898, Carnegie Institute, Museum of Art.
88 Alexander to Beatty, September 22, 1898, Carnegie Institute, Museum of Art.
89 Invitation, Collection of the American Academy of Arts and Letters, New York.
90 Alexander to Harrison S. Morris, December 21, 1898, Carnegie Institute, Museum of Art.
91 Elizabeth A. Alexander to Harrison S. Morris, December 22, 1898, Carnegie Institute, Museum of Art.
92 Alexander to Morris, January 18 1899, Harrison S. Morris Papers.
93 Harrison S. Morris, "The Portraits of John W. Alexander," *Scribner's Magazine*, vol. xxv, March 1899, 340-48.
94 Ibid., 341.
95 Blair Family papers (C0934), 1843–1961, Manuscripts Division, Department of Rare Books and Special Collections, Princeton University Library, 2003.
96 DeWitt Lockman interview with Elizabeth A. Alexander, February 24, 1928, 7.
97 Scrapbooks, JWA papers.
98 *Pittsburg Bulletin*, April 29, 1899, JWA Papers.
99 Moore, "John White Alexander", 272, no. 82.
100 "Pictures for Paris," *New York Times*, March 4, 1900, 22.
101 John B. Cauldwell to Charles Kurtz, May 22, 1899, Charles M. Kurtz papers, Archives of American Art, Smithsonian Institution.
102 Among the members were, Henry Bisbing, Frederick A. Bridgman, Walter Gay, Humphreys-Johnston, Daniel Ridgway Knight, Walter MacEwen, Gari Melchers, Charles Sprague Pearce, Julius Stewart, Julian Story, Eugene Vail, and Edwin Lord Weeks.
103 *New York Journal & Advertiser*, March 1, 1901.
104 "American Art at the Exposition," *New York Herald*, April 1, 1900, 1.
105 *Pittsburg Bulletin*, November 21, 1897, Scrapbooks, JWA papers.
106 Alexander to Beatty, August 28, 1898, Carnegie Institute, Museum of Art.

107 Diane P. Fischer, ed., *Paris 1900: The "American School" at the Universal Exposition* (The Montclair Art Museum, Montclair, N.J.; New Brunswick, N. J.: Rutgers University Press, 1999), 11.
108 Moore, "John White Alexander", 244.
109 Ibid., 245.
110 Ibid., 246.
111 Ibid.
112 Fischer, ed., *Paris 1900*, 92.
113 Mary Anne Goley, "Kindred spirits, John White Alexander and Auguste Rodin," *The Magazine Antiques*, November/December 2011, vol. clxxviii, no. 6, 150-53.
114 DeWitt Lockman interview with Elizabeth A. Alexander, February 24, 1928, JWA papers.
115 Ibid.
116 The author photographed a page of this mounted image from a photo album in the 1971 Alexander estate. I am indebted to Chantal Beauvalot who has written on Albert Besnard, for confirming the identity of Martin's image and the location of the mural.
117 "Society of American Artists Exhibition," *The Sun* (New York), April 8, 1902, Scrapbooks, JWA papers.
118 France, Ministère du commerce, de l'industrie, des postes et des telégraphes, *Exposition universelle internationale de 1900 à Paris, Rapports du jury international* (Paris: Imprimerie nationale, 1904), 67, includes (Paul?) Lambotte and Ph. Zilcken as members of the jury for "gravure et lithographie".
119 Andrews, *Otto H.Bacher*, 256.
120 Two of about fourteen monotypes bear the date 1900.
121 A letter from Whistler to Alexander dated June 28, 1899 confirms a change of address to 190 Boulevard Malesherbes. Alexander Autograph Collection (C0202), Department of Rare Books and Special Collections, Princeton University Library.
122 "Les Arts et La Curiosité," *Gazette de France*, March 14, 1900, JWA papers.
123 Despite Elizabeth Alexander's notes, only three are identifiable: the Gilder portrait, *A Flower* and *Femme aux Fleurs* (private collection). The others are known by Elizabeth's description: Alice sitting profile, pink; Still Life – three bowls white, green, yellow; Black study kneeling peonies, Bess; and Marine.
124 *Temps*, March 1900, JWA papers.
125 Armand Dayot, "John W. Alexander," *Harper's Monthly*, vol. 99, October 1899, 694-704.
126 "The American School," *Current Literature*, November 1900, JWA papers.
127 Lucien Simon to Alexander, June 1, 1900, Alexander Autograph Collection, Manuscripts Division, Department of Rare Books and Special Collections, Princeton University Library.
128 "An American Painter in Paris: John W. Alexander," *International Studio*, vol. xl, no. 42, August 11, 1900, 71-77.
129 Ruth Butler, *Rodin: The Shape of Genius* (New Haven: Yale University Press, 1993), 188.
130 Seven Cowan portraits are listed in *Catalogue of Paintings, John White Alexander Memorial Exhibition* (Department of Fine Arts, Carnegie Institute, Pittsburgh, March 1916), 45.
131 *New York Journal*, October 7, 1900, JWA papers.
132 Alexander to Colonel Allen, April 20, 1897, Correspondence, JWA papers
133 Elizabeth A. Alexander quoted in E. V. Lucas, "John White Alexander and Frederick Carl Frieseke," *The Ladies' Home Journal*, vol. 43, no. 7 (July 1926) 126.

Chapter 5

1 Léon Bazalgette, *Revue franco-allemande*, Munich, September 1900, Scrapbooks, JWA papers.
2 Fischer, ed., *Paris 1900*, 144.
3 "A National Art Gallery," *Home Journal*, November 2, 1900, Scrapbooks, JWA papers.
4 "John W. Alexander Says: Our Salon Must Not Be Too Exclusive," *New York Journal*, November 21, 1900, Scrapbooks, JWA papers.
5 "Alexander, The Painter, Discusses The Outlook For American Artists. 'We Are Attaining An Enviable Position'", *Philadelphia Press*, December 30, 1900, Scrapbooks, JWA papers.
6 "Spring Publications," R.H. Russell, Publisher, New York, Scrapbooks, JWA papers.
7 Reproduced in *The Critic*, June 1901 as copyrighted in 1901 by Russell. Scrapbooks, JWA papers.
8 Elizabeth A. Alexander wrote, "I first met Maude Adams in 1895," in "Notes on Miss Adams, Biographical Information: Essays by Elizabeth Alexander about Others in their Circle, Undated," JWA papers. This statement can not be assumed to be factual.
9 "Town Topics," January 17, 1901, Scrapbooks, JWA papers.
10 *New York Mail & Express*, February 25, 1901, Notes & Writings, Articles about Alexander 1900–01, undated, box 2, folder 7, JWA papers.
11 "The Split in the American Artists' Colony in Paris," *Boston Transcript*, February 28, 1901, Scrapbooks, JWA papers.
12 "American Artists," *Philadelphia Item*, March 4, 1901, Scrapbooks, JWA papers.

13 "Politics and Aesthetics," *New York Herald*, European edition, Paris, April 24, 1901, Notes & Writings, Articles about Alexander 1900–01, undated, box 2, folder 7, JWA papers.
14 "Letters to The Herald," *Paris Herald*, March 9, 1901, Scrapbooks, JWA papers.
15 "Paris American Artists and the Pan-American Show," *New York Evening Post*, February 26, 1901, Scrapbooks, JWA papers.
16 "Hot Shot From Mr. Alexander," *New York Herald*, April 4, 1901 and "Does New York Neglect Art?," *New York Herald*, April 5, 1901, Scrapbooks, JWA papers.
17 "Another Treasure for Pittsburg Lovers of the Beautiful in Art," *Pittsburg Dispatch*, March 30, 1901, Scrapbooks, JWA papers.
18 Charles McAlpin to Alexander, December 14, 1901, Correspondence, JWA papers.
19 Frank H. Goodyear III, et al., *Zaida Ben-Yusuf, New York Portrait Photographer* (London/New York, Merrell in association with National Portrait Gallery, Smithsonian Institution, 2008), 122.
20 *New York Mail & Express*, June 15, 1901, Scrapbooks, JWA papers.
21 Alexander to Beatty, January 10, 1902, Carnegie Institute, Museum of Art papers.
22 *Art Students' League of New York 1902–1903 School Program*, Art Students' League Archives.
23 Alexander was still teaching at Veltin in 1908. See *International Studio*, October 1908, vol. xxxv, no. 140, in which an advertisement appears on page AD.xviii.
24 Malvina Hoffman papers, 1897–1984, Series VIII.A, Sketchbooks, 1901-1964, box 174. Research Library, The Getty Research Institute. The sketchbook bears the inscription, "Anatomy & Alexander's Class, 1901, 1904–1905." Another sketchbook bears the label "Boar's Head, Southampton/ Alexander's Class, 1903–1904."
25 Ibid.
26 Ibid., sketches dated January 23 and 27, 1905.
27 "Exhibition of Paintings by John W. Alexander," Durand-Ruel Galleries, New York, November 24–December 6, 1902 and "The Pictures of John W. Alexander," *Harper's Weekly*, December 13, 1902 vol. 46, 70-71.
28 "John W. Alexander, Exhibition of His Works in Boston," *Philadelphia Item*, April 3, 1903, Scrapbooks, JWA papers.
29 *The New York Tribune*, November 1, 1902 (Scrapbooks, JWA papers) reported that Patton was sitting for his portrait. It was included in the Durand-Ruel exhibit on November 24.
30 Elizabeth Beasley Alexander, the artist's mother-in-law, switched cottages, purchasing Porcupines from Candace Wheeler on January 4, 1901. The contract is on file in the Onteora Club Library Archives, Tannersville, N.Y.
31 Elizabeth A. Alexander was the purchaser of record of The Bushes on November 1, 1911. Contract is on file in the Onteora Club Library Archives, Tannersville, N.Y.
32 Jane Curley, a resident of Onteora who has made its history her specialty, confirms the year of Charles Russell's purchase of a cottage in Onteora in an email of June 30, 2005.
33 Charles H. Russell lent a portrait to the December 1902 exhibition at Durand-Ruel; this could only be the portrait of his daughter Geraldine by Alexander. This negates the entry by Elizabeth A. Alexander in JWA papers, "Notes and Writings: Lists of Paintings circa 1893–1943," box 2, folder 10, frame 30 in which she notes that the portrait was painted in Onteora 1905.
34 "Portraits by John W. Alexander," *New York Herald*, November 28, 1902, Scrapbooks, JWA papers.
35 "Lovely Tableaux for a Charity," *New York Herald*, February 24, 1901, Scrapbooks, JWA papers.
36 *New York Herald*, November 28, 1902.
37 For a discussion of Alexander's Harrisburg project see Mary Anne Goley, "John White Alexander's Industrial Lunettes for the Pennsylvania State Capitol: The Unfinished Story," *IA, The Journal of the Society for Industrial Archeology*, vol. xxxiv, nos. 1 and 2, 2008, 41-57.
38 Colonel Kimball built Buford Lodge in 1902, according to E. Davis Gaillard, *Onteora Hills of the Sky, 1887–1987* (Tannersville, Onteora Club, 1987), 29.
39 Candace Wheeler, *Yesterdays in a Busy Life* (New York and London, Harper & Brothers Publishers, 1918), 313.
40 The names of the summer residents appeared in "Onteora's Own County Fair," unidentified newspaper, September 5, 1903, Onteora Club Library Archives.
41 Ibid. for a description of the mummy costume.
42 Ibid. for a description of the booths and posters by Alexander and Clara McChesney. Jane Curley identified more posters by Elsie Robert in a July 12, 2005 email.
43 Photograph of the posters mounted in a booth on file in Onteora Club Library Archives.
44 *New York Times*, January 8, 1905, Scrapbooks, JWA papers.
45 Scrapbooks: 1904–1907, frame 172, JWA papers.
46 *A Study* might be one of the paintings Overton Ward had in mind in a letter of November 26, 1967 to Miss Wallman, the registrar at the Pennsylvania Academy of the Fine Arts. She wrote of her half-sister, "Anne posed for several paintings by John Alexander … another is owned by Bok Estate." This could be the Bok picture. In an earlier letter, May 10,

1950, Overton Ward lists five pictures for which Anne posed, *The Ring, Study in Black and Green, The Green Gown, The Favorite Corner*, and *Portrait* (Pennsylvania Academy of the Fine Arts object file for both letters). Elizabeth Alexander was incorrect in listing 1906 as the date for *A Quiet Hour* in the memorial exhibition as it was first exhibited at Durand-Ruel in November 1902. *A Study* most likely followed in 1903. Two paintings titled *A Study* were exhibited at the Art Institute of Chicago in October 1903. This was likely one of them.

47 Alexander to Morris, December 10, 1903, Harrison S. Morris papers.

48 "Chicago's Man's Brush Won Academy Medal," *Philadelphia North American*, March 3, 1904 and "John W. Alexander," *Philadelphia Item*, March 3, 1904, Scrapbooks, JWA papers.

49 Charles H. Caffin, "John W. Alexander, The Painter of Idealized Sentiment Through Portraits of Women in Poses," *World's Work*, vol. ix, January 1905, 569.

50 In an October 26, 2014 email to the author, Jane Curley named these Onteora residents from the summer of 1903.

51 Moore, "John White Alexander", 290.

52 Unidentifeid newspaper, April 24, 1904, Scrapbooks, JWA papers.

53 George T. Fleming, *My High School Days, a Brief History of the Pittsburgh Central High School from 1855 to 1871 and Addenda* (Pittsburgh, William G. Johnston & Co., Press, 1904), 95.

54 Elizabeth A. Alexander to Morris, February 9, 1904, Harrison S. Morris papers.

55 The finished portrait of the boy based on a photograph was illustrated in *The Booklover's Magazine*, April 1904, 474.

56 Alexander to Phelps, April 26, 1904, Correspondence, JWA papers.

57 Alexander to his wife, May 16, 1904, Correspondence, JWA papers

58 Ibid.

59 St. Botolph Club Visitor Registration Book 1898–1907, carton 8, Massachusetts Historical Society. Alexander signed the register on March 22, 1903.

60 Alexander to his wife, May 16, 1904. Correspondence, JWA papers.

61 Elizabeth Alexander to Morris, February 9, 1904, Harrison S. Morris papers.

62 Minutes, February 5, 1904, board meeting, Mount Auburn Historical Collections.

63 Alexander to his wife, May 23, 1904. Correspondence, JWA papers.

64 Alexander to his wife, May 19, 1904, Correspondence, JWA papers.

65 Alexander to his wife, letter between May 17 and 19, Correspondence, JWA papers.

66 Alexander to his wife, May 16, 1904, Correspondence, JWA papers.

67 Charles V. Wheeler, Specimens (Washington, DC, privately printed, December 1926). Mrs. Griswold may have seen Alexander in Boston in May at the time of the von Glehn wedding and weeks before both were in Onteora.

68 DeWitt Lockman interview with Elizabeth A. Alexander, February 1, 1928, 24 and in a letter of September 11, 1904, Bradley thanks Elizabeth Alexander for the wonderful summer, Correspondence, JWA papers.

69 Bradley is listed on a program for *Much Ado About Nothing* presented by Charles Frohman at the Colombia Theater, San Francisco, May 1905, Scrapbook: San Francisco Programs: Drama 1904–07, San Francisco History Center, San Francisco Public Library.

70 *Le Figaro*, May 2, 1900, Scrapbooks, JWA papers.

71 J. C. Cartwright, "'le Mardi 31 Janviere 1905': James Hazen Hyde's Costume Ball," http://halfpuddinghalfsauce.blogspot.co.uk/2014/01/le-mardi-31-janviere-1905-james-hazen.html (accessed March 16, 2017).

72 Patricia Beard, *After the Ball: Gilded Age Secrets, Boardroom Betrayals, and the Party That Ignited the Great Wall Street Scandal of 1905* (New York, HarperCollins, 2003), 173-74.

73 Maury Klein, *The Life and Legend of E. H. Harriman* (Chapel Hill and London: University of North Carolina Press, 2000), 330.

74 Ibid., 329.

75 "Heat Bad for Alexander," *New York Times*, July 21, 1905. An estrangement ensued between James W. Alexander and his wife. She sold Porcupine cottage in Onteora on January 24, 1906 (Onteora Club Library Archives) and he began a 26-year world tour in April without his wife but with a male colleague.

76 Klein, *E. H. Harriman*, 330.

77 *New York Tribune*, March 26, 1905, Scrapbooks, JWA papers.

78 "Artists' Society Passes over to the Philistines," *New York Press*, March 24, 1905, Scrapbooks, JWA papers.

79 *New York Herald*, March 24, 1905, Scrapbooks, JWA papers.

80 "Society of American Artists," *New York Commercial Advertiser*, March 27, 1905, Scrapbooks, JWA papers.

81 *Collector & Art Critic*, April 1905, Scrapbooks, JWA papers.

82 A drawing for the frame is in the collection of the New-York Historical Society.

83 "Art Students Fakes on View," *The Sun* (New York), April 25, 1905, Scrapbooks, JWA papers.
84 *American Art News*, May 6, 1905, Scrapbooks, JWA papers.
85 Printed Materials: Exhibition Catalogs undated 1902–1905, Pratt Institute, frame 23, JWA papers.
86 "Fine Arts. Pictures at Pratt Institute by John W. Alexander and F. W. Stout," *Brooklyn Eagle*, April 12, 1905, Scrapbooks, JWA papers.
87 *Standard Union*, April 16, 1905, Scrapbooks, JWA papers.
88 *American Art News*, March 4 and *New York Journal*, April 8, 1905 (Scrapbooks, JWA papers) repeat the same story but in the recounting of sales it extends further back than six months.
89 "Mural Decoration will Cost $175,000," *Pittsburg Post*, June 10, 1905, Scrapbooks, JWA papers.
90 "Want Murals for Library," *Pittsburg Post*, June 9, 1905, Scrapbooks, JWA papers.
91 *Pittsburg Post*, June 10, 1905.
92 For contract see Series 4, Legal and Financial Records, 1775. 1896–1923, box 1, folder 75, JWA papers.
93 "Mural Decorations will Cost $175,000," *Pittsburg Times*.
94 Alexander to Beatty, September 22, 1898, Carnegie Institute, Museum of Art papers.
95 "Alexander will do Mural Works," *Pittsburgh Leader*, June 10, 1905, Scrapbooks, JWA papers.
96 *Newark Advertiser*, January 23, 1906, Scrapbooks, JWA papers.
97 See Sketchbook, c.1905–08, box 6, folder 6, JWA papers.
98 See Pencil Sketches: 1896–1909, box 3, folder 13, frame 12, JWA papers.
99 The winged figure bearing a statue of victory does not appear in this sketch, implying that it was a later addition.
100 Donald Miller in "The Man in the Iron Suit," *The Carnegie Magazine*, vol. li, no. 10, December 1977, 10-16, argues – primarily based on comparisons of images of Alexander – that the figure is a self-portrait of the artist. But using the same method, the same could be said of Carnegie being the knight.
101 Unknown Pittsburgh newspaper, Scrapbooks, 1907-1909. box 19, folder 1, frame 60, JWA papers.
102 Moore, "John White Alexander", 314.
103 Notes & Writings, undated, box 1, folder 78, frames 32-35, JWA papers. The handwriting looks to date from the early 1890s.
104 Richard Wattenmaker, *Puvis de Chavannes and the Modern Tradition* (Art Gallery of Ontario, October 24–November 30, 1975), 98.
105 Kenyon Cox, "Some Phases of Nineteenth Century Paintings, Part III: Mural Painting in France and America," *The Art World*, vol. ii, no. 1, April 1917, 14.
106 Notes and Writings: Notes, undated, box 1, folder 78, frame 33. JWA papers. The handwriting is typical for the 1890s. Alexander's reference is misleading. He meant Besnard's murals for the École de Pharmacie (1883) in the Faculté de Medicine. My thanks to Chantal Beauvalot for this clarification.
107 Gabriel Mourey, *Albert Besnard* (Paris, H. Davoust, 1906), 73.
108 Margaret Henderson Floyd, *Architecture after Richardson* (Chicago, University of Chicago Press, 1994), 227.
109 Charles H. Caffin, "The New Mural Decorations of John W. Alexander," *Harper's Monthly Magazine*, vol. cxiv, no. 684, May 1907, 848.
110 Alexander to Beatty, September 17, 1897, Carnegie Institute, Museum of Art papers.
111 "Notes on Miss Adams," Biographical Information: Essays by Elizabeth Alexander about Others in their Circle, undated, box 1, folder 6, frame 24, JWA papers.
112 *Evening World*, February 1, 1906, Scrapbooks, JWA papers.
113 The painting should be correctly titled *Study in Green and Black* – and not *Study in Black and Green* as it is catalogued by the Metropolitan Museum – in accordance with how it was titled when first exhibited in Buffalo in 1906 and as it is listed in the 1916 memorial catalogue.
114 "At the Albright Art Gallery," *Buffalo News*, May 26, 1906, Scrapbooks, JWA papers.
115 Charles D. Gibson to Alexander, July 14, 1906, Correspondences, JWA papers.
116 *American Art News*, December 30, 1905 and *Pittsburgh Independent* (?), June 9, 1906, Scrapbooks, JWA papers.
117 *New York Herald*, November 11, 1906, Scrapbooks, JWA papers. It is reasonable conjecture that the site of his first Seabright studio was on his father-in-law's property subsequently sold in 1897. The site of the 1906 Seabright studio is unknown.
118 Mrs. James Waddell Alexander, Sr sold Porcupine Cottage on January 24, 1906 (Onteora Club, Library Archives).
119 *Chicago Post*, November 17, 1906, Scrapbooks, JWA papers.
120 "Famous Artist here to Place Paintings," *Pittsburgh Times*, February 19, 1907, Scrapbooks, JWA papers.
121 Carnegie Museum of Art, *International Encounters: The Carnegie International and Contemporary Art, 1896–1996*, ed. Vicky A. Clark, et al. (Pittsburgh: Carnegie Museum of Art, 1996), 154.

122 "Pittsburg's Honest Men, 28, Extolled at Virtue Banquet," *Philadelphia American*, April 1907, Scrapbooks, JWA papers.
123 "Artist Talks to Students," *Gazette Times*, April 4, 1907, Scrapbooks, JWA papers.
124 "Program, The Carnegie Institute, Dedicatory Exercises, April 11, 12, and 13, 1907, Pittsburgh, – Penna.," Scrapbooks, JWA papers.
125 *Pittsburgh Mail*, April 4, 1907 and "Great Exhibition at an End," Pittsburgh Independent (?), June 15, 1907, Scrapbooks, JWA papers.
126 "An American Salon," *Globe and Commercial Advertiser* (New York), April 15, 1907, Scrapbooks, JWA papers.
127 *Boston Transcript*, April 20, 1907, Scrapbooks, JWA papers.
128 April 10, 1907, Scrapbooks, JWA papers.
129 Edward Slavishak, *Bodies of Work: Civic Display and Labor in Industrial Pittsburgh* (Chapel Hill, Duke University Press, 2008), 1 and 5.
130 April 1907, Scrapbooks, JWA papers.
131 "Evelyn Thaw his Model," *New York Times*, June 17, 1907, Scrapbooks, JWA papers
132 (New York?) *Tribune*, June 21, 1907, Scrapbooks, JWA papers.
133 "Famous 'Study in Black and Green.' For Which Evelyn Nesbit Thaw Posed," *Evening World* (New York), June 19, 1907, Scrapbooks, JWA papers.
134 *Chicago World Today*, December 1907, Scrapbooks, JWA papers.
135 "Angry at Evelyn's Picture," *Evening Sun* (New York), June 19, 1907, Scrapbooks, JWA papers.
136 "Not Mrs. Thaw's Money," *New York Times*, June 23, 1907, Scrapbooks, JWA papers.
137 Series 10: Photographs, box 40-42 oversize (not scanned), JWA papers.
138 Bradley to Mrs. Alexander, April 19, 1905 asks if her husband could use her as a model for the coming summer.
139 Overton Ward to Gentlemen, archives of the Pennsylvania Academy of the Fine Arts. May 10, 1950 and Overton Ward to Louise Wallman, registrar, November 26, 1967, The Pennsylvania Academy of the Fine Arts Archives.
140 The portrait could be the one noted in Overton Ward's letter of November 26, 1967 as owned by Edward Bok, editor of *Ladies' Home Journal*.
141 "Alexander Painting Purchased," *New York Times*, April 15, 1908, Scrapbooks, JWA papers.
142 Pisano and Weber, *Parodies of the American Masters*, 15.
143 *American Art News*, October 26, 1907, Scrapbooks, JWA papers.
144 DeWitt Lockman interview with Elizabeth A. Alexander, February 1, 1928, 21.
145 *Catalogue of the Exhibitions at the Century, 1901–1913* (Century Association Records, Century Association Archives Foundation, November 2, 1907), untitled exhibition.
146 "Jersey Artist's Portrait," *Newark News*, December 23, 1907, Scrapbooks, JWA papers.
147 Minutes, Century Club, Board of Management, March 5, 1908, Century Association Archives Foundation.
148 See Scrapbook 1907–1909 box 19, folder 1, frame 92 JWA papers, for a copy of the program; for a history of the club see *Catalogue of the Exhibitions at the Century, 1901–1913* (Century Association Records, Century Association Archives Foundation, November 2, 1907), 591.
149 Goley, *Princeton University Library Chronicle*, 283-5 for a discussion of the Isabella McCosh portrait.
150 "Art, Fair Women," *Nation*, March 2, 1908, Scrapbooks, JWA papers.
151 The canvas presents a conundrum. Though clearly dated 1911, it was exhibited in Alexander's February 1909 retrospective at the National Arts Club leading to the possibility that Alexander made subsequent changes.
152 A portrait of Mrs. Borden Harriman must have been commissioned about this time. It was unveiled the following year on February 2, 1909 (*New York Herald*, February 3, 1909, Scrapbooks, JWA papers).
153 For the program see Scrapbooks, 1907–1909, JWA papers, frame 135.
154 Robin Vedder, "Tableaux Vivants; Performing Art, Purchasing Status," *The Theater Annual*, 1995, vol. xlviii, 14-29.
155 Mary Anne Goley, "John White Alexander's Industrial Lunettes for the Pennsylvania State Capitol: The Unfinished Story." *IA, The Journal of the Society for Industrial Archeology*, vol. xxxiv, nos. 1 and 2 (2008): 41-57.
156 "Art and Artists," *Pittsburgh Bulletin*, October 10, 1908, Scrapbooks, JWA papers.
157 Mourey, *Albert Besnard*, illus. between 54 and 55.
158 "Portraits and Great Panels," *The Sun* (New York), November 3, 1907, Scrapbooks, JWA papers.
159 William Walton, "Alexander's Decoration," *Scribner's Magazine*, vol. xlv, January 1909, 45-57.
160 Artwork: Sketchbook, c.1905–08, box 3, folder 6, frame 13, JWA papers.
161 Birge Harrison, "The Future of American Art," *North American Review*, vol. 189, no. 638 (January 1909).
162 "Mural Paintings Criticized by High School Youths," *Pittsburgh Press*, October 13, 1908, Scrapbooks, JWA papers.

163 "Plan for Development of City by New York Improvement Commission," *Brooklyn Eagle*, March 2, 1907, Scrapbooks, JWA papers.

164 "New Art Gallery in Park," *The Sun* (New York), February 16, 1909, Scrapbooks, JWA papers.

165 "Favor Park Art Gallery, *The Sun* (New York), February 17, 1909, Scrapbooks, JWA papers.

166 "New Portrait Collections," *Brooklyn Daily Eagle*, February 24, 1909 and *Globe* (New York), February 25, 1909, Scrapbooks, JWA papers.

167 Herman Bloch, "The Alexander Exhibition," *New York Call*, February 26, 1909, Scrapbooks, JWA papers.

168 John N. Laurvik, "John W. Alexander, an Analysis," *Metropolitan Magazine*, 31 (December 1909, 369- 76).

169 "Alexander at Arts Club," *American Art News*, February 27, 1909, Scrapbooks, JWA papers.

170 "Jury Here to Judge Art Show," *Pittsburgh Dispatch*, April 8, 1909, Scrapbooks, JWA papers.

171 Minutes, Ways and Means Committee, National Academy of Design Archives.

172 "Academy Picks Alexander," *The Sun* (New York), May 13, 1909, JWA papers.

173 Alexander to Harrison S. Morris, May 30, 1909, Harrison S. Morris papers.

174 Bailey Van Hook, *The Virgin and the Dynamo: Public Murals in American Architecture, 1893–1917* (Athens: Ohio University Press, 2003), 54.

175 Artwork: Pencil Sketches, c.1896–1909, box 3 folder 15, frame 6, JWA papers; frame 15 shows studies for helmets in the style of Greece and Asia Minor.

176 "Mural Paintings for County Courthouse at Wilkesbarre," *Evening Mail*, June 1, 1909, Scrapbooks, JWA papers.

177 Gibson to Alexander, May 13, 1909, Correspondence 1909, JWA papers.

178 Reid to Alexander, May 13, 1909, Correspondence 1909, JWA papers.

179 Herter to Alexander, May 13, 1909, Correspondence 1909, JWA papers.

180 Postcard, Frohman to Alexander, May 14, 1909, Correspondence 1909, JWA papers.

181 Dabo to Alexander, May 15, 1909, Correspondence 1909, JWA papers.

182 Arthur Hoeber, "John W. Alexander," *International Studio*, vol. xxxiv, no. 135, May, 1908, lxxxvx-cviii.

183 Christian Brinton, "The Art of John W. Alexander," *Munsey's Magazine*, vol. xxxix, no. 6, September 1908, 744-55.

184 Walton, "Alexander's Decoration".

185 Charles de Kay, "John White Alexander, Master of Beauty in Line and Eminent among American Mural Painters," *Smith's Magazine*, vol. viii, no. 6, March 1909, 909-19.

186 Laurvik, "John W. Alexander," 369.

187 "Princeton Gives Degrees," *Evening Post*, June 15, 1909, Scrapbooks, JWA papers.

188 Woodrow Wilson to Alexander, May 29, 1909, Scrapbooks, JWA papers.

189 "250 New Princeton Grads," *The Sun* (New York), June 16, 1909, Scrapbooks, JWA papers.

190 Woodrow Wilson to Alexander, May 29, 1909, Scrapbooks 1909–1911, box 20, folder 1, frame 15, JWA papers.

191 *Boston Herald*, June 10, 1909, JWA papers.

192 "'Joan of Arc' on a Mammoth Scale," *Morning Telegraph*, May 12, 1909, Scrapbooks, JWA papers.

193 *New England Magazine*, June 1909, Scrapbooks, JWA papers.

194 DeWitt Lockman interview with Elizabeth A. Alexander, February 24, 1928, 13-19, JWA papers,

195 "Maude Adams in Schiller's 'Joan of Arc,'" *Theatre Magazine*, July 1909, Scrapbooks, JWA papers.

196 Yvonne Shafer, "Maude Adams as Joan of Arc at the Harvard Stadium," *The Journal of American Drama and Theatre*, Fall 1999, vol. xi, no. 3, 30-45.

197 Nora M. Heinmann and Laura Coyle, *Joan of Arc: Her Image in France and America* (Washington, D.C. and London: Corcoran Gallery of Art, 2006), quotes Twain from 1904, n.p. inside title page.

198 *Theatre Magazine*, July 1909.

199 Alexander to Harrison S. Morris, July 6, 1909, Harrison S. Morris papers.

200 Alexander used a similar title in 1912, *A Summer Day*.

201 See Artwork: pencil sketches: box 3, folder 13, frame 20, JWA papers, for a preparatory sketch that shows a study of *Phyllis* without a hat.

202 The upper left portion of this 1909 painting is known today as *Belle* (collection of Dr. Mary Alexander), having been cut from the larger canvas presumably by the artist.

203 "Gallery and Studio Chat," *Buffalo Evening Express*, December 21, 1909, Scrapbooks, JWA papers.

204 Photographs: Studio: Seabright 1888–1908. box 5, folder 34, frames 1, 3 and 4, JWA papers.

205 Henry M. Alexander to Samuel Clemens, January 9 and 15, 1886, The Mark Twain Papers, University of California, Berkeley, California.

206 *The World* (New York), December 8, 1894, Scrapbooks, JWA papers.

207 Samuel Clemens to John W. Alexander, December 30, 1908, Alexander Autograph Collection, Princeton University Library.

208 James Waddell Alexander penned this soulful sympathy note, "My heart bleeds for you." December 25, 1909, The Mark Twain Papers, University of California, Berkeley, California.

Chapter 6

1 John W. Alexander, "The Need of a National Academy, and its Value to the Growth of Art in America," *The Craftsman*, vol. xvii, no. 6, March 1910, 607-18.

2 Elizabeth A. Alexander to Harrison S. Morris, February 24, 1909, Harrison S. Morris papers.

3 Photographs: Personal Photographs circa 1882–1912, box 5, folder 37, frames 19 and 20, JWA papers.

4 Elizabeth A. Alexander to Harrison S. Morris, May 9, 1910, Harrison S. Morris papers.

5 Elizabeth A. Alexander to Harrison S. Morris, May 17, 1910, Harrison S. Morris papers.

6 Elizabeth A. Alexander to Harrison S. Morris, May 24, 1910, Harrison S. Morris papers.

7 Elizabeth A. Alexander, to Beatty, June 6, 1910, Carnegie Institute, Museum of Art.

8 "Alexander on Stage Art," *The Sun* (New York), July 13, 1910, Scrapbooks, JWA papers.

9 For the invitation see Scrapbooks 1910–13, box 21, folder 1, frame 37, JWA papers.

10 Detroit Publishing Co., *"Thistle Publications", Office Catalogue of Works of Art ... for our Offices and Salesmen Only* (1912).

11 "'Chantecler' Preparations," *Christian Science Monitor*, August 14, 1910, Scrapbooks, JWA papers.

12 "Alexander on Stage Art," *New York Sun*, July 13, 1910, Scrapbooks, JWA papers.

13 "Even Richmond, Ind. Has a Better Art Exhibition Than New York," *New York Times Sunday Magazine*, September 25, 1910, Scrapbooks 1909–1911, box 20 folder 1, frame 131, JWA papers.

14 "Alexander Back," *Philadelphia Item*, September 20, 1910, Scrapbooks, JWA papers.

15 "The Need of a National Academy, and its Value to the Growth of Art in America," *The Craftsman*, 607.

16 DeWitt Lockman interview with Elizabeth A. Alexander, February 24, 1928, 24, JWA papers.

17 "Even Richmond Ind. Has a Better Art Exhibition Than New York," (as n. 12 above).

18 "Mr. John W. Alexander Home from the Old Country," *New York Herald*, September 19, 1910, Scrapbooks, JWA papers.

19 Elizabeth A. Alexander to Mrs. Sheuber, November 20, 1910, Archives of The Modern Art Museum of Forth Worth.

20 "Portrait of Mr. Cleveland," *New York Herald*, January 6, 1910, Scrapbooks, JWA papers.

21 *American Art News*, May 6, 1909, Scrapbooks, JWA papers.

22 Milton W. Brown, *American Painting from the Armory Show to the Depression* (Princeton: Princeton University Press, 1955), 197, Background, note 3.

23 "City May Give Site for Art Academy," *Evening Journal*, December 20, 1910, Scrapbooks, JWA papers.

24 "Arts and Grafts," *Evening World*, January 3, 1911, Scrapbooks, JWA papers.

25 "Town Topics," unidentified newspaper, March 2, 1911, Scrapbooks, JWA papers.

26 *Evening Post*, December 30. 1910, Scrapbooks, JWA papers.

27 *New York Times*, May 23, 1911, Scrapbooks, JWA papers.

28 "No Building in Bryant Park, *New York Tribune*, April, 25, 1911, Scrapbooks, JWA papers.

29 "MacDowell Club Displays", *American Art News*, June 17, 1911, Scrapbooks, JWA papers.

30 Brown, *American Painting*, 5.

31 John Sloan, *John Sloan's New York Scene; from diaries, notes and correspondence,* 1906-1913, ed. Bruce St. John, intro. by Helen Farr Sloan (New York: Harper & Row, 1965, 586.

32 Birge Harrison to Alexander, February 27, 1911, Correspondence, JWA papers.

33 *Evening Post*, Dec 12, 1910, Scrapbooks, JWA papers.

34 "More Paintings for State Capitol," *Pittsburg Press*, June 23, 1911, Scrapbooks, JWA papers.

35 Wisconsin Capitol Building Commission, Minutes, vol. i, ser. 833, August 23, 1911, Wisconsin Historical Society Archives.

36 "'Sunlight' by J.W. Alexander Bought by 'The Friends of American Art'," *Chicago Tribune*, November 13, 1910, Scrapbooks, JWA papers.

37 The Garman, McLean, Mitchell, and Ward portraits were based on photographs according to Elizabeth A. Alexander's Register of Paintings and Exhibitions circa 1887–1913, box 2, folder 11, frame 21, Notes and Writings, JWA papers.

38 Notes and Writings: Registers of Paintings and Exhibitions circa 1887–1913, box 2, folder 11, frame 21; Mr Porter died April 1, 1910 which may be the reason for the commission.

39 Elizabeth A. Alexander to Mrs. Charles Scheuber, October 31, 1911, Archives of the Modern Art Museum of Fort Worth.

40 Elizabeth A. Alexander to Mrs. Charles Scheuber, February 23, 1911, Archives of the Modern Art Museum of Fort Worth.

41 Elizabeth A. Alexander to Mrs. Charles Scheuber, May 25, 1911, Archives of the Modern Art Museum of Fort Worth.
42 Elizabeth A. Alexander to Mrs. Charles Scheuber, July 16, 1911 on Treetops, Onteora stationery, Archives of the Modern Art Museum of Fort Worth.
43 "J.W. Alexander – Maude Adams Scenery Device Saves Enormous Amounts," *New York Star*, February 11, 1911, Scrapbooks, JWA papers.
44 "Scenery of the Future," *Pittsburgh Independent*, March 4. 1911, Scrapbooks, JWA papers.
45 "New Invention Marks Big Scenic Advance, *San Francisco Chronicle*, March 5, 1911, Scrapbooks, JWA papers.
46 Lorenz Eitner, "The Open Window and the Storm-Tossed Boat: An Essay in the Iconography of Romanticism" *The Art Bulletin*, vol. xxxvii, no. 4 (December 1955) 283.
47 *Philadelphia Ledger*, February 4, 1912, Scrapbooks, JWA papers.
48 I am grateful to Jan G. Reeder, Consulting Curator for the Brooklyn Museum Costume Collection at the Metropolitan Museum of Art for this description in an email of March 16, 2015.
49 Moore, "John White Alexander", 346.
50 Ibid., 347, note 143.
51 G. Mortimer Marke, "The National Association of Portrait Painters. A New American Group," *Arts and Decoration*, May 2, 1912, 258-60.
52 "Distinguished Assembly Listen to Addresses by J.W. Alexander, Pres. Hadley and Prof. Weir," *New Haven Palladium*, June 9, 1911, Scrapbooks, JWA papers.
53 Elizabeth A. Alexander notes, Correspondence 1910–1911, frames 16-17.
54 John F. Weir, to Alexander, November 28, 1911, Correspondence, JWA papers.
55 "Academy Again is Made a Bone of Contention," *Evening Sun*, January 8, 1911, Scrapbooks, JWA papers.
56 Ibid.
57 Minutes. January 2, 1912, Walt Kuhn, Kuhn family papers, and Armory Show records Archives of American Art, Smithsonian Institution, https://www.aaa.si.edu/collections/items/detail/association-american-painters-and-sculptors-meetingminutes- 14154 (accessed March 21, 2017).
58 "Mr Weir Declines," *Evening Sun*, January 4, 1912, Scrapbook, JWA papers.
59 Minutes, December 19, 1911, Walt Kuhn, Kuhn family papers, and Armory Show records Archives of American Art, Smithsonian Institution; https://www.aaa.si.edu/collections/items/detail/association-american-painters-and-sculptors-meetingminutes- 14154 (accessed March 21, 2017); *The World* (New York), December 3, 1911, Scrapbooks, JWA papers.
60 Pach, "Art and the Average Man," *Outlook*, January 1912, Scrapbooks, JWA papers.
61 "Honk! Honk! Or How Famous Artists Drew a Picture at Sixty Miles an Hour," *The World* (New York), March 17, 1912, Scrapbooks, JWA papers.
62 "No Less than Thirteen Artist-Cooks Had a Finger in This Broth of a Picture," *New York Tribune*, March 17, 1912, Scrapbooks, JWA papers.
63 "They Were All Stirring at Once, and in Twenty Minutes Completed Their Brobdignagian [sic] Task," *New York Tribune*, March 17, 1912, Scrapbooks, JWA papers.
64 *Harper's Weekly*, April 6, 1912, Scrapbooks, JWA papers.
65 Col. Louis D. Conley to Walt Kuhn, April 19, 1912, Archives of American Art, Smithsonian Institution, https://www.aaa.si.edu/collection-features/1913-armory-show/highlights (accessed March 21, 2017).
66 Alexander to Beatty, January 14, 1912 and February 28, 1912, Carnegie Institute, Museum of Art.
67 "A Portrait of Miss Maude Adams by J.W. Alexander," *Art & Decoration*, June 1912, Scrapbooks, JWA papers.
68 On a scrap of paper Elizabeth Alexander noted "Mrs. F. H Goodyear/Plaza Hotel – May 25," which suggests the commission occurred around this time. Correspondence, 1912, JWA papers.
69 "Pictures of Women a Feature of Exhibition," *New York Herald*, February 10, 1913, Scrapbooks, JWA papers.
70 *Evening Mail*, February 6, 1913, Scrapbooks, JWA papers.
71 Mrs. Goodyear to Alexander, August 4, 1912, Correspondence, JWA papers.
72 *Evening Sun*, November 10, 1913, Scrapbooks, JWA papers.
73 DeWitt Lockman interview with Elizabeth A. Alexander, February 24, 1928, JWA papers.
74 The painting is seen on the artist's easel: see Photographs: Studio; Onteora, New York circa 1913, frame 4, JWA papers. The actual date of the photograph has to be the summer of 1912 because it was taken by the same photographer as the Weir portrait.
75 These two paintings have been variously titled *Onteora* and *A Summer Day*, but the Alexander papers contain photographs annotated *Full Length Study* and the titles appear on a list: Notes and Writings: Lists of Paintings circa 1893–1943, box 2, folder 14, frame 19, JWA papers.
76 There is conflicting evidence about which pictures Edson modeled for. As previously noted, Overton Ward wrote to the Pennsylvania Academy of the Fine Arts on May 10, 1950

that her half-sister Anne Raynor Ward was the model for *The Ring* along with *Study in Green and Black* and others that are not in dispute. Mrs. Alexander wrote to Macbeth Gallery on October 22, 1928 (the Philadelphia Museum of Art object file for *A Quiet Hour*) that Edson modeled for *The Gossip*, *The Ring*, *June*, *The Window* (unidentifiable), *Her Birthday*, and a small panel, *The Rose* (unidentifiable). Based on the dates of execution, I would conclude that Edson was not the model for *The Ring* but did pose for all of the decorative figure paintings during the summers of 1911 to 1914.

77 George Dudley Seymour to Alexander, June 3, July 3 and July 13, Correspondence, JWA papers.

78 Bear and Fox Inn register, Onteora Library Archives.

79 Seymour to Alexander, July 3 and October 14, 1912, Correspondence, JWA papers.

80 In an email of April 15, 2015, Judith Schiff, Chief Research Archivist, Manuscript and Archives, Yale University, identified the colors of the academic gown worn by Weir as appropriate for the School of Fine Arts.

81 "Club Pageant Gay Festival," *The Sun* (New York), December 29, 1912, Scrapbooks, JWA papers.

82 Henry Tyrell, "Mixing up Bohemia and Society at the MacDowell Club Festival," *The World* (New York), December 22, 1912, Scrapbooks, JWA papers.

83 Walt Kuhn to Vera Kuhn, December 14, 1912, Archives of American Art, Smithsonian Institution, https://www.aaa.si.edu/collections/items/detail/walt-kuhn-new-york-ny-letter-to-vera-kuhn-479 (accessed March 21, 2017).

84 "Club Pageant Gay Festival," *New York Sun*, December 29, 1912, JWA papers.

85 Alfred Stieglitz, "Purposes of the Forthcoming Exhibition by the 'Revolutionists.'" *New York American*, January 26, 1913, Scrapbooks, JWA papers.

86 French to Alexander, October 16, 1912, William M. R. French papers. Letter Press Books, Institutional Archives, the Art Institute of Chicago.

87 Alexander annotates an invitation to a dinner to honor Alexander Drake on February 25, 1913 noting, "I am sorry I cannot be at the dinner. – Chicago from Feb. 20 to Mar. 15." Scrapbooks, JWA papers.

88 *The Art Institute of Chicago Thirty-Fourth Annual Report for the Year 1912–13*, "The Scammon Lectures," 93.

89 *Chicago Inter Ocean*, March 23, 1913, Scrapbooks, JWA papers.

90 "Alexander Shows Genius in Art Exhibit contains 28 Pictures," *Chicago Examiner*, March 3, 1913, Scrapbooks, JWA papers.

91 *Chicago Evening Post*, March 14, 1913, Scrapbooks, JWA papers.

92 H.C. Mansfield to Alexander, June 28, 1914, Correspondence, JWA papers.

93 Walt Kuhn to Vera Kuhn, October 28, 1912, Archives of American Art, Smithsonian Institution, https://www.aaa.si.edu/collections/items/detail/walt-kuhn-paris-france-letter-to-vera-kuhn-chevy-chasemd- 14046 (accessed March 21, 2017).

94 *The Sun* (New York), February 9, 1913, Scrapbooks, JWA papers.

95 "New Place for Exhibits," *New York Tribune*, March 11, 1913, Scrapbooks, JWA papers.

96 Hearn to Alexander, Correspondence 1913; "Old Academy Appeals," *American Art News*, March 22, 1913, Scrapbooks, JWA papers.

97 "With the Cubists," *Chicago Record Herald*, March 21, 1913, Scrapbooks, JWA papers.

98 Elizabeth Lunday, *Modern Art Invasion: Picasso, Duchamp and the 1913 Armory Show that Scandalized America* (Guilford, Conn., Lyons Press, 2013), 83.

99 "Caruso Shows Caricature," *New York Times*, March 22, 1913.

100 Vicky A. Clark, et al., *International Encounters: The Carnegie International and Contemporary Art, 1896–1996* (Pittsburgh: Carnegie Museum of Art, 1996), 57.

101 Ibid., 61.

102 Anna Seaton-Schmidt, "Pittsburgh's Show of Sane Art," *Boston Evening Transcript*, April 30, 1913.

103 Clark, et al., *International Encounters*, 58.

104 James B. Townsend, "Ultra Conservatism in the Painting Shown in the Carnegie Institute this Year," *Craftsman*, vol. ix, July 1911, 379.

105 Christian Brinton, "Contemporary Art and the Carnegie Institute," *The International Studio*, vol. xlix, June 1913, lxix-lxx.

106 "Alexander Tells Story of Morgan," *Pittsburgh Dispatch*, April 6, 1913, Scrapbooks, JWA papers.

107 "They're Not Yet Cubists, But They're Some Cueist," *Pittsburgh Dispatch*, April 3, 1913, Scrapbooks, JWA papers.

108 "National Academy Taking Non-Artists," *New York Times*, May 7, 1913, Scrapbooks, JWA papers.

109 Office of the Corporation of Trinity Church to Alexander, February 25, 1913, Correspondence, JWA papers.

110 Leslie Skelton to Alexander, February 15, 1913, Correspondence, JWA papers.

111 "Dr. Humphreys Honored by Graduates," *New York Times*, February 15, 1913, Scrapbooks, JWA papers.

112 "Superb Exhibit of Art Opens," *Pittsburgh Dispatch*, February 21, 1914, Scrapbooks, JWA papers.

113 Belle Edson was the single model for this "large composition – never completed with three figures" according to Elizabeth Alexander's letter of October 22, 1928 to Mr. McIntyre of Macbeth Gallery; Philadelphia Museum of Art, object file for *A Quiet Hour*.

114 "Fine Arts Building Exhibition," *Chicago Record Herald*, December 7, 1913, Scrapbooks, JWA papers.

115 John Trask to Alexander, August 23, 1913, Correspondence, JWA papers.

116 Moore, "John White Alexander", 377, note 169.

117 Ibid., 377, note 162.

118 "Mural Paintings for the Capitol," *Pittsburgh Sun*, September 12, 1913, Scrapbooks, JWA papers.

119 Alexander to Morris, March 16, 1914, Harrison S. Morris papers.

120 "Many Theatre Parties Attend Various Plays," *New York Herald*, January 6, 1914, Scrapbooks, JWA papers.

121 "Unhung Pictures Will Be Shown, *New York Herald*, January 5, 1914, Scrapbooks, JWA papers.

122 "Judging of Paintings Begun by Eight Jurors," *Pittsburgh Sun*, April 9, 1914, Scrapbooks, JWA papers.

123 *The Century Magazine*, April 1914, vol. xxxiii, 825-75.

124 Ibid., 826-36.

125 Ibid., 837-44.

126 Ibid., 845-50.

127 Ibid., 851-68.

128 Ibid., 869-75.

129 March 20, 1914, Scrapbooks, JWA papers.

130 April 1, 1914, Scrapbooks, JWA papers.

131 Bear and Fox Inn register, Onteora Library Archives.

132 Gilbert to Alexander, May 27, 1914, Correspondence, JWA papers.

133 Notes and Writings: Lists of Paintings circa 1893–1943, box 2, folder 12, frame 23, indicates the artist worked from a photograph.

134 Identification of the medals is courtesy of Mariana L. Cook, Curator of Art, West Point Art Museum.

135 "Two Portraits of the President," *Philadelphia Bulletin*, November 11, 1914, Scrapbooks, JWA papers.

136 Wilson to Alexander, October 14, 1914, Correspondence, JWA papers.

137 "Seeks Academy Park Site," *New York Evening Post*, March 14, 1914, Scrapbooks, JWA papers.

138 *The World* (New York), November 22, 1914, Scrapbooks, JWA papers.

139 *San Francisco Chronicle*, January 3, 1915, Scrapbook, JWA papers.

140 Persia C. Campbell, *Mary Williamson Harriman* (New York: Columbia University Press, 1960), 56.

141 Elizabeth A. Alexander to Beatty, February 15, 1915, Carnegie Institute, Museum of Art papers.

142 Beatty to Elizabeth A. Alexander, February 16, 1915, Carnegie Institute, Museum of Art papers.

143 "New York's Place in Art at Stake," *Evening Post* (New York), March 27, 1915, Scrapbooks, JWA papers.

144 Elizabeth Alexander to Colonel and Mrs. Allen, June 6, 1915, Correspondence, JWA papers.

145 Alexander to Mrs. Edward J. Allen, May 22, 1915, Correspondence, JWA papers.

146 Elizabeth A. Alexander to Mrs. Allen, May 23, 1915, Correspondence, JWA papers.

147 Elizabeth A. Alexander to Mrs. Allen, May 29, 1915, Correspondence, JWA papers.

148 Elizabeth A. Alexander to Colonel and Mrs. Allen, June 6, 1915, Correspondence, JWA papers.

Chapter 7

1 Correspondence, box 1, folders 58-62, JWA papers.

2 Correspondence 1915, frame 6, JWA papers.

BIBLIOGRAPHY

Abbe, Cleveland, and Josephine Genung Nichols. *Abbe–Abbey Genealogy: In Memory of John Abbe and His Descendants.* New Haven, Conn.: Tuttle, Morehouse and Taylor, 1916.

"A Circle of Friends: Art Colonies of Cornish and Dublin." March 9–April 26, 1985, Thorne-Sagendorph Art Gallery, Keene State College, Keene, N.H.; June 22–August 18, 1985, Saint-Gaudens National Historic Site, Cornish, N.H.; June 28–August 18, 1985, Hood Museum of Art, Dartmouth College, Hanover, N.H.; September 9–October 30, 1985, University Art Galleries, University of New Hampshire, Durham; University Art Galleries, University of New Hampshire.

Adelson, Warren, et al. *Sargent's Venice.* New Haven, Conn.: Yale University Press, 2006.

Alexander, John W. "The Need of a National Academy, and Its Value to the Growth of Art in America." *Craftsman* 17, no. 6 (March 1910): 607–18.

Alumni Princetonian. Princeton University, Princeton, N.J., April 28, 1898.

Andrews, William W. *Otto H. Bacher.* Madison, Wis.: Education Industries, 1981.

Art Institute of Chicago. *Thirty-Fourth Annual Report for the Year 1912–13.* Chicago: Art Institute of Chicago, 1913.

Bacher, Otto. *With Whistler in Venice.* New York: Century, 1909.

Beard, Patricia. *After the Ball: Gilded Age Secrets, Boardroom Betrayals, and the Party That Ignited the Great Wall Street Scandal of 1905.* New York: Harper Collins, 2003.

Bohan, Ruth. *Looking into Walt Whitman: American Art, 1850–1920.* University Park: Pennsylvania State University Press, 2006.

Bonnet, Anne-Marie. *Auguste Rodin, Images of Desire: Erotic Watercolors and Cut-outs.* Munich: Schirmer/Mosel, 2001.

Bric-a-Brac. Princeton Student Yearbook, Princeton University, 1882–3.

Brinton, Christian. "The Art of John W. Alexander." *Munsey's Magazine* 39, no. 6 (September 1908): 744–55.

—, "Contemporary Art and the Carnegie Institute." *International Studio* 49 (June 1913): lxix–lxx.

Brown, Milton W. *American Painting from the Armory Show to the Depression.* Princeton, N.J.: Princeton University Press, 1955.

Butler, Ruth. *Rodin: The Shape of Genius.* New Haven, Conn.: Yale University Press, 1993.

Caffin, Charles H. "John W. Alexander, The Painter of Idealized Sentiment Through Portraits of Women in Poses." *World's Work* 9 (January 1905): 5682–98.

—, "The New Mural Decorations of John W. Alexander." *Harper's Monthly* 114, no. 684 (May 1907): 845–56.

Campbell, Persia C. *Mary Williamson Harriman.* New York: Columbia University Press, 1960.

Carnegie Institute. *Catalogue of Paintings, John White Alexander Memorial Exhibition.* Pittsburgh: Carnegie Institute, March 1916.

Cartwright, J. C. "'le Mardi 31 Janviere 1905' James Hazen Hyde's Costume Ball." http://halfpuddinghalfsauce.blogspot.co.uk/2014/01/le-mardi-31-janviere-1905-james-hazen.html.

Clark, Vicky A., et al. *International Encounters: The Carnegie International and Contemporary Art, 1896–1996.* Pittsburgh: Carnegie Museum of Art, 1996.

Clement, Russell T., Annick Houzé, and Christiane Erbolato-Ramsey. *A Sourcebook of Gauguin's Symbolist Followers: Les Nabis, Pont-Aven, Rose + Croix.* Westport, Conn.: Praeger, 2004.

Cortissoz, Royal. "Painting and Sculpture in the New Congressional Library." *Harper's Weekly* 41, no. 2092 (January 1897): 82–5.

Cox, Kenyon. "Some Phases of Nineteenth Century Paintings, Part III: Mural Painting in France and America." *Art World* 2, no. 1 (April 1917): 11–15.

Curry, David Park. *James McNeill Whistler, Uneasy Pieces.* Richmond: Virginia Museum of Fine Arts; New York: Quantuck Lane Press, 2004.

Dearinger, David. *Paintings and Sculpture in the Collection of the National Academy of Design*. Manchester, Vt.: Hudson Hills Press, 2004.

De Kay, Charles. "The Old Poetic Guild in Ireland." *Century* 39 (April 1890): 893–901.

—, "John White Alexander, Master of Beauty in Line and Eminent among American Mural Painters." *Smith's Magazine* 8, no. 6 (March 1909): 909–21.

Detroit Publishing Co., *"Thistle Publications", Office Catalogue of Works of Art … for our Offices and Salesmen Only*. 1912.

Devoll, Maria Louise Johnson Reinhart. "The Life and Experiences of Albert Grantley Reinhart." Unpublished, Reinhart estate (courtesy of Roy Pederson, Lambertville, N.J.), no date.

Downey, Fairfax Davis. *Portrait of an Era as Drawn by C. D. Gibson*. New York and London: C. Scribner's Sons, 1936.

Eitner, Lorenz. "The Open Window and the Storm-Tossed Boat: An Essay in the Iconography of Romanticism." *Art Bulletin* 37, no. 4 (December 1955): 218–90.

Fischer, Diane P., ed. *Paris 1900: The "American School" at the Universal Exposition*. Montclair Art Museum, Montclair, N.J. New Brunswick, N.J.: Rutgers University Press, 1999.

Fisher, Paul. "'Her Smoking Was the Least of Her Freedoms:' Henrietta Reubell, Miss Barrace, and the Queer Milieu of Henry James's Paris." *Henry James Review* 33, no. 3 (fall 2012): 247–54.

—, "'The Dear Little Tobacconized *Salon*': Henrietta Reubell as Queer *Salonniere* in Henry James's Paris." In *Transforming Henry James*, edited by Anna de Biasio, Anna Despotopoulou, and Donatella Izzo. Newcastle-on-Tyne, Cambridge: Scholars Press, 2013.

Fleming, George T. *My High School Days, a Brief History of the Pittsburgh Central High School from 1855 to 1871 and Addend*. Pittsburgh: William G. Johnston and Company Press, 1904.

Floyd, Margaret Henderson. *Architecture after Richardson*. Chicago: University of Chicago Press, 1994.

Fourcaud, Louis de. "Les Arts Decoratifs aux Salon. I. Le Champs-de-Mars." *Revue des Arts Decoratifs* 14, no. 11 (May 1894): 343.

Gabrielan, Randall. *Rumson, Shaping a Superlative Suburb*. Mount Pleasant, S.C.: Arcadia Publishing, 2002.

Gaillard, E. Davis. *Onteora Hills of the Sky, 1887–1987*. Tannersville, N.Y.: Onteora Club, 1987.

Gilder, Richard Watson. *Letters of Richard Watson Gilder*. Edited by Rosamond Gilder. Boston and New York: Houghton Mifflin, 1916.

Goley, Mary Anne. "John White Alexander's Panel for Music Room." *Bulletin of the Detroit Institute of Arts* 64, no. 4 (1989): 5–15.

—, "Out of the Kitchen into the Parlor, the Art of Still Life by John White Alexander." Federal Reserve Board, Washington, D.C., June 27–September 8, 1995.

—, "John White Alexander's Industrial Lunettes for the Pennsylvania State Capitol: The Unfinished Story." *IA, The Journal of the Society for Industrial Archeology* 34, nos. 1 and 2 (2008): 41–57.

—, "Kindred Spirits, John White Alexander and Auguste Rodin." *Magazine Antiques* 178, no. 6 (November–December 2011): 150–53.

—, "The Tribute of Isabella." *Apollo Magazine* 175, no. 594 (January 2012): 58–64.

—, "John White Alexander's Princeton Legacy." *Princeton University Library Chronicle* 75, no. 2 (winter 2014): 270–74.

Goodyear, Frank H., III, et al. *Zaida Ben-Yusuf, New York Portrait Photographer*. London and New York: Merrell; Washington, D.C.: in association with National Portrait Gallery, 2008.

Grant, Susan. "American Paintings Acquired by the French Government, 1879–1900." M.A. thesis, George Washington University, 1983.

Harrison, Birge L. "The Future of American Art." *North American Review* 189, no. 638 (January 1909): 24–34.

Heinmann, Nora M., and Laura Coyle. *Joan of Arc: Her Image in France and America*. Washington, D.C., and London: Corcoran Gallery of Art, 2006.

Hoeber, Arthur. "Thomas Shields Clarke." *Brush and Pencil* 6, no. 5 (August 1900): 193–98.

—, "John W. Alexander." *International Studio* 34, no. 135 (May 1908): lxxxv–xcviii.

Howells, William Dean. *Indian Summer*. With introduction and notes by Scott Bennett; text established by Scott Bennett and David J. Nordion. Bloomington and London: Indiana University Press, 1971.

"How Whistler Posed for John W. Alexander." *World's Work* (March 1905): 5994.

Huntington, David, et al. *The Quest for Unity: American Art between World's Fairs, 1876–1893*. Detroit: Detroit Institute of Arts, 1983.

Jones, Arthur F., and Bruce Weber. "The Kentucky Painter: From the Frontier Era to the Great War." University of Kentucky Art Museum, Lexington, January 25–March 15, 1981.

Klein, Maury. *The Life and Legend of E. H. Harriman*. Chapel Hill and London: University of North Carolina Press, 2000.

Laurvik, John N. "John W. Alexander, An Analysis." *Metropolitan Magazine* 31 (December 1909): 369–76.

Lucas, E. V. "John White Alexander and Frederick Carl Frieseke." *Ladies' Home Journal* 43, no. 7 (July 1926): 16–17, 126.

Ludovici, Albert. *An Artist's Life in London and Paris, 1870–1925.* New York: Minton, Balch, 1926.

Lunday, Elizabeth. *Modern Art Invasion: Picasso, Duchamp and the 1913 Armory Show that Scandalized America.* Guilford, Conn.: Lyons Press, 2013.

McCoy, Garnett. "The Tenth Annual Carnegie Institute International Exhibition." *Archives of American Art Journal* 7, no. 3/4 (July 1, 1967): 23–29.

Merrill, Linda, et al. *After Whistler: The Artist and His Influence on American Painting.* New Haven, Conn.: High Museum of Art, 2003.

Miller, Donald. "The Man in the Iron Suit." *Carnegie Magazine.* 51, no. 10 (December 1977): 10–16.

Moore, Sarah J. "John White Alexander (1856–1915): In Search of the Decorative." Ph.D. thesis, City University of New York, 1992.

Morris, Harrison S. "The Portraits of John W. Alexander." *Scribner's Magazine* 25 (March 1899): 340–48.

—, *Confessions in Art.* New York: Sears Publishing, 1930.

Mourey, Gabriel. "An American Painter in Paris: John W. Alexander." *International Studio* 40, no. 42 (August 1900): 71–77.

—, *Albert Besnard.* Paris: H. Davoust, 1906.

Murray, Richard, *Art for Architecture, Washington, D.C., 1895–1825.* Washington, D.C.: National Collection of Fine Arts, Smithsonian Institution, 1975.

Muther, Richard. *The History of Modern Painting.* New York: Macmillan, 1896.

Neal, Kenneth. *A Wise Extravagance: The Founding of the Carnegie International Exhibitions, 1895–1901.* Pittsburgh: University of Pittsburgh Press, 1996.

Page, Thomas Nelson. "P'laski's Tunaments." *Harper's Monthly* (December 1890): 111–18.

Pennell, J. and E. R. *The Life of James McNeill Whistler.* Philadelphia: J. B. Lippincott, 1911.

Peters, Lisa N. "Youthful Enthusiasm under a Hospitable Sky: American Artists in Polling, Germany, 1870s–1880s." *American Art Journal* 21, nos. 1 and 2 (2000): 56–91.

Pisano, Ronald G., and Bruce Weber. *Parodies of the American Masters: Rediscovering the Society of American Fakirs, 1891–1914.* New York: Art Students League, Berry-Hill Galleries, Inc., and Museums at Stony Brook, N.Y., 1993.

Quick, Michael. *An American Painter Abroad: Frank Duveneck's European Years.* Cincinnati: Cincinnati Art Museum, 1988.

Roof, Katharine M. *The Life and Art of William Merritt Chase.* New York: Scribner's, 1917; repr. Hacker Art Books, 1975.

Sears, John W. "The Portrait Work of John W. Alexander." *Modern Art* 4, no. 2 (July 1896): 64–66.

Shafer, Yvonne. "Maude Adams as Joan of Arc at the Harvard Stadium." *Journal of American Drama and Theatre* 11, no. 3 (fall 1999): 30–45.

Slavishak, Edward. *Bodies of Work: Civic Display and Labor in Industrial Pittsburgh.* Durham, N.C.: Duke University Press, 2008.

Sloan, John. *John Sloan's New York Scene: From Diaries, Notes and Correspondence,* 1906–1913. Edited by Bruce St. John, with introduction by Helen Farr Sloan. New York: Harper and Row, 1965.

Spencer, Robin. *The Aesthetic Movement: Theory and Practice.* London: Studio Vista/Dutton Pictureback, 1972.

Spofford, Ainsworth Rand. "Annual Report of the Librarian of Congress for 1872." Library of Congress, Washington, D.C.

Thornton, Alfred. *The Diary of an Art Student of the Nineties.* London: Sir Isaac Pitman and Sons, 1938.

Townsend, James B. "Ultra Conservatism in the Painting Shown in the Carnegie Institute This Year." *Craftsman* 9 (July 1911): 379–85.

Traubel, Horace. *With Walt Whitman in Camden.* Vol. 2. New York: D. Appleton, 1915.

Trumble, Alfred. *Representative Works of Contemporary American Artists.* New York: Scribner's, 1877; repr. Garland Publishing, 1997.

Van Hook, Bailey. *The Virgin and the Dynamo: Public Murals in American Architecture, 1893–1917.* Athens: Ohio University Press, 2003.

Van Rensselaer, Mariana Griswold. *Book of American Figure Painters.* Philadelphia: J. B. Lippincott, 1886.

Vedder, Robin. "Tableaux Vivants; Performing Art, Purchasing Status." *Theater Annual* 48 (1995): 14–29.

Walton, William. "Alexander's Decoration." *Scribner's Magazine* 45 (January 1909): 45–57.

Wattenmaker, Richard. "Puvis de Chavannes and the Modern Tradition." Art Gallery of Ontario, October 24–November 30, 1975.

Wheeler, Candace. *Yesterdays in a Busy Life.* New York and London: Harper and Brothers, 1918.

Wheeler, Charles V. *Specimens.* Privately printed, Washington, D.C., December 1926.

Whitman, Walt. *Walt Whitman in Camden: A Selection of Prose from Specimen Days.* With preface by Christopher Morley and photographs by Arnold Genthe. Camden, N.J.: Haddon Craftsmen, 1938.

Who's Who in New York City and State. New York: L. R. Hammersly, 1909.

Zafran, Eric M. *Gauguin's Nirvana: Painters at Le Pouldu 1889–90*. New Haven, Conn.: Yale University Press, in association with the Wadsworth Athenaeum Museum of Art, Hartford, Conn., 2001

Archives

Archives of American Art, Smithsonian Institution, Washington, D.C.
- Carnegie Institute, Museum of Art papers
- Charles M. Kurtz papers
- Frank and Elizabeth Boott Duveneck papers, 1851–1972
- Francis B. and Josephine Duveneck correspondence, 1879–1971
- Jervis McEntee papers
- John White Alexander papers
- Walt Kuhn, Kuhn family papers, and Armory Show records
- William Macbeth Gallery records

Archives of The Modern Art Museum of Forth Worth, Texas

Art Students' League Archives, N.Y.

Century Association Records, Century Association Archives Foundation, N.Y.

Charles Mills papers, William H. Gerdts Library, N.Y.

Dwelle History Collection, 1932–2007, Mint Museum Archives, Charlotte, N.C.

Malvina Hoffman papers, Getty Research Institute, Los Angeles

Mark Twain Papers, University of California, Berkeley

Mount Auburn Historical Collections, Cambridge, Mass.

Musée Rodin, Paris

National Academy of Design Archives, N.Y.

Onteora Club Library Archives, Tannersville, N.Y.

Peter Juley Photograph Archives, Smithsonian Institution, Washington, D.C.

Phyllis Harrington Papers, Mark Twain Birthplace, SHS, MO DNR/Division of State Park, Florida, Mo.

Princeton University Library, Department of Rare Books and Special Collections
- Alexander Autograph Collection (C0202)
- Blair Family papers (C0934)
- Harrison S. Morris papers (C0003)
- Laurence Hutton papers (C0080)

Records of the Library of Congress: Buildings and Grounds

Report of Record, Town Hall, Bristol, R.I.

Richard Watson Gilder Papers, Lilly Library, Indiana University

San Francisco History Center, San Francisco Public Library

St. Botolph Club Records, Massachusetts Historical Society

University of Pittsburgh, Archives Service Center, University Library System

William M. R. French papers, Letter Press Books, Institutional Archives, Art Institute of Chicago

Wisconsin Capitol Building Commission, Wisconsin Historical Society Archives

Zorn Museum Archives, Mora, Sweden

INDEX